PHILOSOPHY
OF NATURE

MUIRHEAD

HEGEL
In 7 Volumes

PHILOSOPHY
OF NATURE

Volume III

G W F HEGEL

First published in 1970

Reprinted in 2002 by
Routledge
2 Park Square, Milton Park, Abingdon, Oxon, OX14 4RN
or
270 Madison Avenue, New York, NY 10016

First issued in paperback 2010

Routledge is an imprint of the Taylor & Francis Group

© 1970 Routledge

British Library Cataloguing in Publication Data
A CIP catalogue record for this book
is available from the British Library

Philosophy of Nature (Vol III)
ISBN 978-0-415-29581-9 (hbk)
ISBN 978-0-415-60677-6 (pbk)
Hegel: 7 Volumes
ISBN 978-0-415-29530-7
Muirhead Library of Philosophy: 95 Volumes
ISBN 978-0-415-27897-3

HEGEL'S
PHILOSOPHY
OF NATURE

EDITED AND TRANSLATED
WITH AN INTRODUCTION AND EXPLANATORY NOTES BY

M. J. PETRY
M.A., D.Phil.(Oxon.)

VOLUME III

Routledge
Taylor & Francis Group

LONDON AND NEW YORK

CONTENTS

The words in roman are those of Hegel's headings which appeared in the first edition of this work. The words in italics did not appear as headings in the text, but such identification of these passages was made on the contents page of the first edition of the work.

SECTION THREE

Organic Physics
(*Organics*)

§ 337

The real nature of the body's totality **constitutes the infinite process in which individuality determines itself as the** particularity **or finitude which it also negates, and returns into itself by re-establishing itself at the end of the process as the beginning. Con-**
5 **sequently, this totality is an elevation into the** primary ideality of nature. **It is however an** *impregnated* **and negative unity, which by relating itself to itself,** has become essentially *self-centred* and *subjective*. It is in this way that the Idea has reached the initial immediacy of *life*. Primarily, life is
10 *shape,* or the universal type of life constituted by the *geological* organism. Secondly, it is the particular formal subjectivity of the *vegetable* organism. Thirdly, it is the individual and concrete subjectivity of the *animal* organism.

The Idea has truth and actuality only in so far as it has subjec-
15 **tivity implicit within it (§ 215). As the mere immediacy of the Idea, life is thus external to itself, and is not life, but merely the corpse of the living process. It is the organism as the totality of the inanimate existence of mechanical and physical nature.**

Subjective animation begins with the vegetable organism,
20 **which is alive and therefore distinct from this inanimate existence. The parts of the individual plant are themselves individuals however, so that the relations between them are still exterior.**

The animal organism is so developed however, that the differences of its formation only have an essential existence as its mem-
25 **bers, whereby they constitute its subjectivity. In nature, animation certainly disperses into the indeterminate plurality of living beings, but these are intrinsically subjective organisms, and it is only in the Idea that they constitute a single animate and organic system.**

A* 9

Addition. Let us look back at the preceding exposition. In the first section we saw (*a*) matter, as the abstract extrinsicality of space. Matter, as the abstract being-for-self of extrinsicality and as offering resistance, is completely individualized, and in a simple atomistic state. As this atomistic state is uniform, matter is still completely indeterminate, but it is absolutely atomistic only to the understanding, not to the reason. (*b*) We then concerned ourselves with particular masses in a state of mutual determination. (*c*) Finally, we dealt with gravity, which constitutes the basic determination in which all particularity was sublated and of an ideal nature. In the *second* section, this ideality of gravity transformed itself into light and then into shape, and is now re-established. The matter there individualized contains:—(*a*) the free determinations as we saw them in the elements and their process; (*b*) its subsequent unfolding of itself into the realm of appearance, in which the self-subsistence of specific gravity is opposed to the reflection-into-other of cohesion; until (*c*) it forms itself into totality in individual shape. This ideality is now result however, for the particular body sublates the different modes of its existence. Like light, it is a unity which is serene and self-identical, but at the same time, it proceeds from the totality of the compacted particularizations which are taken back, into their primary undifferentiation. In itself, individuality is now weighted and lighted; it is triumphant, and produces and preserves itself as the unifying process of all particularities. It is this individuality which is the subject-matter of the *third* section. The living body is always on the point of passing over into the chemical process. Oxygen, hydrogen, salt etc., are always about to emerge, but they are perpetually being suppressed, and the chemical process can only prevail by means of death or sickness. Living being is perpetually exposed to danger, and always bears something alien within it. Unlike inorganic being, it can sustain this contradiction. Speculation subsists in this resolution, and it is only for the understanding that the contradiction remains unresolved. Consequently, life may only be grasped speculatively, for it is precisely in life that speculation has existence. The continual action of life is therefore absolute idealism, for that which it becomes is another term, and yet is perpetually being sublated. If life were realistic, it would respect that which is external to it, but it is perpetually checking the reality of this other term, and transforming it into its own self.

Life is therefore the primary *truth*; it is superior to the stars, and to the sun, which although it is individualized, is not a subject. As the union of the Notion with exteriorized existence, in which the Notion maintains itself, life constitutes the Idea; this is also the meaning of *Spinoza's* proposition

that life is adequate to the Notion, although this is still a completely
+ abstract expression of course. Life is not merely the resolution of the
opposition between the Notion and reality, but of oppositions in general.
Life has being where inner and outer, cause and effect, end and means,
5 subjectivity and objectivity etc., are one and the same. It is the union of
the Notion with reality which constitutes the true determination of life.
This reality no longer has an immediate and independent mode of being
as a plurality of properties existing apart from each other, for the Notion
is simply the ideality of indifferent subsistence. As the ideality we encoun-
10 tered in the chemical process is posited there, individuality is posited in its
freedom. Subjective and infinite form now also has objectivity. This was
not so in shape, because there the determinations of infinite form still have
fixed determinate being as matters. On the contrary, in the abstract
Notion of the organism, the existence of particularities is compatible with
15 the unity of the Notion, for these particularities are posited as transitory
moments of a single subject. In the system of the heavenly bodies however, all particular moments of the Notion exist freely for themselves as
independent bodies which have not yet returned into the unity of the
Notion. The first organism was the solar system; it was merely implicitly
20 organic however, it was not yet an organic existence. The gigantic
members of which it is composed are independent formations, and it is
only their motion which constitutes the ideality of their independence.
The solar system is merely a mechanical organism. Living existence posits
all particularity as appearance however, and so holds these gigantic mem-
25 bers within a unity. In life therefore, light is the complete master of
gravity. Consequently, living existence is the individuality which has sub-
jugated the further particularizations of gravity within itself, and which is
immanently active. The self-maintaining Notion is first posited as self-
sublating reality. The individuality of the chemical body can fall victim
30 to an alien power; life has its contrary within itself however, and in itself
it is a rounded totality, or its *own object*. Mechanism constituted the first
part of the philosophy of nature, chemistry constituted the apex of the
+ second part, and teleology constitutes this third part (see §194 Add. 2). Life
35 is a means, but for this Notion, not for another; it is perpetually reproducing its infinite form. *Kant* had already determined living existence as con-
+ stituting its own end. There is change here, but it is only present on behalf
of the Notion, for it is merely the otherness of the Notion that changes. It
is only in the absolute negativity of this negation of that which is negative,
that the Notion can remain in communion with itself. The actuality of
40 organic being is already present in its implicitness, and is the movement of its

becoming. However that which is result, is also that which precedes the result, so that the beginning is the same as the end. Hitherto, this was merely known to us, but it now enters into existence.

As Idea, life constitutes its own movement, and so initiates its subjectification. In this way, it makes itself into its other, into its own counter- 5 action; it gives itself objective form in order to return to itself and to have being as returned-into-self. Consequently, life as such is only present in the third moment, for its principal determination is subjectivity. The earlier stages are merely incomplete pathways leading towards it. We have three kingdoms therefore, the *mineral kingdom, the plant kingdom,* and 10 the *animal kingdom.* +

In the first instance, it is geological nature which constitutes the life that presupposes itself as its own other, and which is therefore merely the ground and basis of life. It certainly ought to be life, individuality, and subjectivity, but it is not the true subjectivity which leads its members 15 back into unity. The moments of individuality, and of return or subjectivity, certainly have to be present as they are in life, but because of their immediacy, they are necessarily separate aspects, and so fall outside one another. Individuality is one aspect, and its process is another. Individuality does not yet exist as active and idealizing life, for it is the inert 20 animation opposed to living activity, and has not yet determined itself as singularity. It also contains activity, but this activity is in part simply implicit, and in part external to it. The process of subjectivity is divorced from the universal subject itself, for at this stage we still lack an individual which would be implicitly active within itself. Consequently, life in its 25 immediacy is self-alienated, and is therefore the inorganic nature of subjective life. All exteriority is inorganic; to the individual for example, the sciences of his inorganic nature are inorganic in so far as he is not yet aware of them, and they simply function within him and constitute his implicit rationality, which he merely has to make his own. The *Earth* is 30 a whole, and is the system of life, but as a crystal it resembles a skeleton, which may be regarded as being dead, for its members still seem to have a formally separate subsistence, and its process falls outside it. +

In the second stage, which is that of reflection, animation begins to be more specialized, so that the individual constitutes its activity within 35 itself as the living process, although only as a subject of reflection. This formal subjectivity is not yet the subjectivity identical with the objectivity which is divided into a system of members. It is a subjectivity which is still abstract, because it merely derives from the alienation which constitutes the terrestrial organism; it is unpliant, punctiform, and merely 40

individual. The subject certainly particularizes itself, maintains itself as subjectivity in its external relation, and forms and pervades its members. Its formal aspect consists in its not yet truly maintaining itself in this relation however, so that it is still torn out of itself. Consequently, the
5 plant is not yet true subjectivity, because although the subject differentiates itself from itself and constitutes its own object, it cannot yet sustain the true differentiation of its members. True self-conservation requires that it should return into itself from this state of differentiation. Consequently, the main determination of the plant consists in its differentiating itself
10 from itself in a merely formal manner, and only in this way maintaining its self-identity. It unfolds its parts, but as these parts, which are its members, are essentially the whole of the subject, it is not differentiated any further. Its leaves, roots, and stalk are also merely individuals. The real being which the plant produces in order to maintain itself is merely
15 the complete equivalent of itself, so it also forms no proper members. Consequently, each plant is merely an infinite number of subjects, and the connection whereby these subjects appear as a single subject, is merely superficial. The plant is unable to maintain its power over its members, for they detach themselves from it and become independent. The inno-
20 cence of the plant is also an expression of the impotence which results from its relating itself to inorganic being, where at the same time its
+ members become other individuals. This second kingdom is the *realm of water* and of neutrality.

The third kingdom is that of *fire*, in which individual subjectivity
25 constitutes a complete animation, and the plant and differences are united. This subjectivity is shape, like the primary system of forms; but at the same time the members are not parts, as they still were in the plant. Animal existence maintains itself in its otherness, but this is an actual difference, and at the same time there is a positing of the ideal nature of
30 the animal's system of members. This constitutes the initiation of the
+ living subject, soul, etheriality, the essential process of articulation into members and expansion. This formation is posited immediately in time however, and the difference is timelessly retracted into its unity. Fire releases itself into members, and is ceaselessly passing over into its product,
35 which is ceaselessly led back to the unity of subjectivity, so that there is an immediate absorption of its independence. Animal life is therefore the Notion displaying itself in space and time. Each member has the entire soul within it, and is only independent through its being connected with the whole. Sensation, which is the faculty of finding oneself within one-
40 self, is the highest determination of this sphere, and first occurs here;

it is the persistence of self-identity within determinateness, a free self-communion within determinateness. The plant is not aware of itself within itself, because its members are independent and opposed individualities. Animal nature constitutes the explicated Notion of life; prior to this there is no true animation present. These three forms constitute life. 5

Chapter One
Geological nature
(*The terrestrial organism*)

§ 338

The primary organism, in so far as it is initially determined as immediate or implicit, is not a living existence, for as subject and process, life is essentially a self-mediating activity. Regarded from the standpoint of subjective life, the first moment of par-
5 ticularization is that the organism converts itself into its own presupposition, and so assumes the mode of immediacy, in which it confronts itself with its condition and outer subsistence. The inward recollection of the Idea of nature as subjective life, and still more as spiritual life, is basically divided
10 between itself and this unprocessive immediacy. This immediate totality presupposed by *subjective* totality, is simply the *shape* of the organism; as the universal system of individual bodies, it is the terrestrial body.

Addition. In the chemical process, the Earth is already present as this
15 totality; the universal elements enter into the particular corporealities of the Earth, and are partly causes and partly effects of the process (§ 328 Add. II. 185,34). This is simply abstract motion however, for the corporealities are merely particular. The Earth is now certainly a totality, but as it is only the implicit process of these bodies, the process falls outside its
20 perenniating product. The content of this totality cannot lack any determination belonging to life, but as extrinsicality constitutes the mode of these determinations, this content lacks the infinite form of subjectivity. Consequently, as it is presupposed by life as its foundation, the Earth is posited as being unposited, for the positing is concealed by
25 the immediacy. The other moment is then the self-dissolution of this presupposition.

A.

History of the Earth

§ 339

As this organism **has being merely as an implicitness,** its members do not contain **the living** process within themselves **but constitute an external** *system.* The forms of this system exhibit the unfolding of an underlying Idea, **but** its *process of formation* belongs to the *past.* The powers of this process, 5 which nature leaves behind as independent and extra-terrestrial, are the connection and position of the Earth within the solar system, its solar, lunar, and cometary life, and the inclination of its axis to the orbit, and the magnetic axis. Standing in closer relationship to these axes 10 and their polarization are the distribution of sea and land, the connected diffusion of land in the northern hemisphere, the division and tapering off of the land masses towards the south, the additional separation into an old and a new world, and the further division of the old world into the 15 various continents. These continents are distinguished from one another by the physical, organic, and anthropological characteristics which distinguish them once again from the younger and less mature characteristics of the new world. Mountain ranges etc., may also be considered here. +

Addition. 1. The powers of this process appear independently of their product, while the animal, which is a process in itself, contains its powers, for its members are the potences of its process. The Earth on the contrary is as it is merely because it has this place in the solar system, and occu-pies this position in the planetary series. In animal existence however, 25 each member contains the whole, so that the extrinsicality of space is sublated within the soul, which is omnipresent within its body. If we speak in this way however, we are positing a spatial relationship again and this is not the soul's true relationship. The soul is certainly omnipresent, but undivided, not as an extrinsicality. The members of the geological 30 organism are in fact external to one another however, and they are there-fore without a soul. The Earth is the most eminent of all the planets. It is the middling planet, and exhibits individuality, and it owes this kind +

of existence solely to the permanence of its relations. If any one of these relations lapsed, the Earth would cease to be what it is. The Earth appears as the dead product of these relations; but it is maintained by these conditions, which form a single chain or whole. As the Earth is the universal individual, moments such as magnetism, electricity and chemism come forth freely by themselves within the meteorological process. The animal is no longer magnetism however, and electricity is something which is subordinate to it.

2. It is precisely because the Earth itself is not a living subject, that the process of formation does not reside within it. Consequently, the Earth is not born out of this process, as living being is; it endures, it does not produce itself. It is for this reason that the persistence of the Earth's members is not a mark of the Earth's superiority. Living being on the contrary has the virtue of being born and passing away. In its singularity, living being is the manifestation of the genus, but it is also in conflict with the genus, which exhibits itself through the destruction of the singular. In so far as the process of the Earth has being for itself as a universal individual, it is simply an inner necessity, for it is merely implicit, and does not exist in the members of the organism. In the animal however, each member is both product and productive. *Considered* within the limits of the Earth's individuality, this process is to be *seen* as a past event, which leaves its moments behind it as independencies extraneous to the Earth.[1] *Geognosy* attempts to expound this process as a conflict between the elements of differentiation, i.e. fire and water. According to the *vulcanists*, the Earth's shape, stratifications, and rock species etc. are of igneous origin. The theory put forward by the *neptunists* is equally one-sided, for they assert that everything is the result of an aqueous process. Forty years ago[2], in Werner's time, these two theories were the cause of much controversy. Both their principles have to be recognized as essential, but by themselves they are onesided and formal. In the crystalline form of the Earth, in volcanoes, springs and in the meteorological process in general, fire is just as operative as water.

Three aspects of the terrestrial process have to be distinguished. (a) The

---

[1] This does not mean that the three most primary moments, which are moons and comets, as well as the immature and declining planets, are the empirical residua of the terrestrial process, discarded by the Earth. Nor does it mean that this last moment, that of the declining planets, is an anticipatory pattern of the condition the Earth will attain at some time or another. As I understand Hegel and the subject matter, it means that the Earth has to be represented as having run through, and as still having to run through, the individual stages of the process, and that these stages have their stereotyped original in these more abstract terrestrial bodies.

Note by Michelet.

[2] From the lectures given in the summer term of 1830.

universal and absolute process is the process of the Idea, it is the process which is in and for itself, and by which the Earth is created and maintained. The creation is eternal however; it has not only taken place once, but is eternally producing itself, for the infinite creative power of the Idea is a perenniating activity. Consequently, we do not see the universal emerge in nature, which means that the universality of nature has no history. Science and government etc. have a history however, for they are the universal within spirit. (b) The process also exists on the Earth, but only in a general way, for it does not produce itself as subject. It is the general vitalization and fructification of the Earth i.e. the possibility which the living subject draws from this vitalized being. It is the meteorological process which makes the Earth the animated ground and basis of living being. (c) In the Scriptures it is said that, 'Heaven and Earth shall pass away,' and in this sense the Earth must certainly be *regarded* as having had an origin and as passing away. The Earth and the whole of nature are to be regarded as produced; the *Notion* makes this *necessary*.[1] One's second task is then to *point out* this determination in the constitution of the Earth in an *empirical* manner; this is the principal subject-matter of geognosy. It is immediately apparent from the constitution of the Earth, that it has had a *history*, and that its condition is a result of successive changes. It bears the marks of a series of prodigious revolutions, which belong to a remote past, and which probably also have a cosmic connection, for the position of the Earth with regard to the angle which its axis makes with its orbit could have been *changed*. The surface of the Earth bears evidence of its having supported a vegetation and an animal world which are now extinct (a) at great depth, (b) in immense stratifications, and (c) in regions where these species of animals and plants do not thrive.

This state of the Earth, according to *Ebel's* description in particular, ('On the structure of the Earth' vol. II p. 188 et seq.), is roughly as follows:— Petrified wood, even whole trees, and dendrolites etc. may be found in fletz-formations, and to an even greater extent in alluvial terrains.

[1] There appears to be a contradiction here between the assertion that the Earth has an origin and is passing away, and the former assertion (a) that its creation has no beginning, but is being eternally engendered. It may be resolved easily enough if we call to mind what was said in the introduction (§247 Add. I. 206–208) about the eternity of the world. It was pointed out there, that as nature is the manifestation of the Idea, its having flowed from the creative activity of the Idea is certainly eternal, but that because of its positedness and dependence upon the Idea, the finite and individual being within it must also have been engendered. Consequently, the necessity of the Earth's being regarded as an engendered being also lies in the Notion of nature, or the being of the Idea in the form of otherness. Nevertheless, the empirical indications of this engendering can do no more than prove that the present constitution of the Earth is the result of a great revolution, they cannot demonstrate that it has been engendered as this general and universal individual.

Note by Michelet.

Immense forests, which have been flattened, lie buried below beds of deposit at depths of 40–100 feet, and sometimes even of 600–900 feet. The vegetable state of many of these forests is preserved intact; the barks, roots, and branches are filled with resin, and make an excellent fuel, while
5 other vegetable material is petrified into siliceous agate. For the most part, the different species of wood are still identifiable. Palm-trees are often found for example; one might mention a fossilized forest of palm-tree trunks in the Neckar valley not far from Kannstadt, etc. In the fossilized forests of Holland and the Bremen area, the trees that are found
10 are usually intact, and lying flat, firmly joined to their root stocks. Elsewhere the trunks are broken off cleanly, and separated somewhat from their root-stocks, which are still firmly fixed in the ground. In East Friesland, Holland, and the Bremen area, the crowns of these trees all lie
+ pointing south-east or north-east. These forests have grown in these
15 areas, but on the banks of the Arno in Tuscany, fossilized oaks may be found, lying incidentally beneath palm-trees, and flung together with fossilized sea-shells and huge bones. These immense forests occur in all the alluvial terrains of Europe, the Americas and northern Asia. Sea-shells, snails, and zoophytes have pride of place in the animal kingdom
20 with regard to numbers. In Europe, they occur wherever there are fletz-formations, and consequently they may be found throughout the continent. They are just as common throughout Asia, in Anatolia, Syria, Siberia, Bengal, and China etc., in Egypt, Senegal, and at the Cape of Good Hope, and in America. They are to be found at great depths in the
25 strata immediately overlaying the primitive rocks, and to an equal extent at the greatest heights. They occur on Mont Perdu for example, which is in the highest part of the Pyrenees, and rises to an altitude of
+ 10,968 feet. The explanation *Voltaire* gave of this was that fish and
+ oysters etc., had been taken up there by travellers as provisions. They
30 also occur in the Jungfrau, which is the highest peak of the limestone Alps, and rises to 13,872 feet, and on the Andes in South America, at
+ heights ranging from 12,000 to 13,242 feet above sea-level. Remains of this kind are not dispersed throughout the whole of the massif, but only in certain strata, where they occur in families in the strictest order, and are
35 so well preserved, that they seem to have settled there peacefully. In the most ancient of the stratified formations, which are the immediate overlayers of the primitive rocks, the shells of sea-animals are on the whole much less in evidence, and only certain species occur. They increase in number and variety in the later fletz-formations however, and it is
40 there also that fossil fish are to be found, although only very rarely. Fossil

plants first occur in the more recent stratified formations however, and the bones of amphibia, mammals, and birds, are only to be found in the most recent of these rocks. The most remarkable bones are those of quadrupeds such as elephants, tigers, lions, bears, whose species are now extinct. All these huge animals merely lie near the surface under sand, 5 marl, or loam, in Germany, Hungary, Poland, Russia, and particularly in Asiatic Russia, where the tusks are excavated, and give rise to a considerable trade. *Humboldt* found mammoth bones in the vales of Mexico, Quito, and Peru, always at the height of between 7,086 and 8,934 feet above sea level. In the River Plate he found the skeleton of a huge animal 10 12 feet long and 6 feet high. Traces of violent revolution and exterior + generation are not only to be found in these remains of the organic world, but are equally apparent in the geognostic structure of the Earth, and in general, in the whole formation of alluvial terrain. Within mountain ranges, which are themselves configurations giving rise to individual 15 peaks and further chains, there are whole formations consisting entirely of boulders or debris which have been fused together. The nagelflue found in Switzerland is a species of rock consisting of smoothed stones cemented together by sandstone and limestone. The stratifications of its beds are extremely regular; one stratum for example will consist of large 20 stones almost all of which are six inches thick, the next of smaller stones, and the third of still smaller stones, and this will then be followed by a bed consisting of larger boulders. This breccia is composed of the most varied kinds of debris; granites, gneisses, porphyries, amygdaloids, serpentines, siliceous schists, hornstones, flints, saline and compact lime- 25 stones, argillaceous and ferruginous stones, and alpine sandstones, are all to be found in it. One nagelflue contains more of one kind of debris, another contains more of another kind. One of these nagelflues forms a chain of mountains, the breadth of which varies from 1 to 3 leagues; it reaches heights of between 5,000 and 6,000 feet above sea-level (Rigikulm 30 is 5,723 feet high), and therefore rises above the Swiss tree-line. With the exception of the Alps and the Pyrenees, this chain is not exceeded in height by any other mountains in France and England. Even the highest peak of the Giant's Mountains in Silesia is only 4,949 feet + high, and the Brocken only reaches 3,528 feet. Finally, there are the 35 frightful signs of tremendous laceration and demolition apparent in all primitive massifs, and granite ranges and rocks. These formations are cleft longitudinally and transversally by innumerable joints and valleys etc., which have been superimposed upon one another by stages. 40

All this is a matter of history, and has to be accepted as a fact; it is not the concern of philosophy. If we want to explain this fact, we have to acquaint ourselves with the way in which it has to be dealt with and considered. The history of the Earth took place in former times and has now
5 reached a state of quiescence. It is a life which once fermented within itself and embodied time; it is the spirit of the Earth, which has not yet reached opposition. It is the movement and dreams of a being that sleeps, until it awakes and acquires its consciousness in man, and so stands over against itself as im-
+ mobile formation. The main interest of the empirical aspect of this former
10 state of the Earth is taken to be the determination of time by the science of geognosy i.e. in designating the oldest stratum of rocks etc. The geological organism is usually grasped mainly by determining the order of succession of its various formations, but this is only an external explanation. The granitic primitive rocks which constitute the deepest
15 strata, and which were formed one after the other, are said to be the first, and to be followed by regenerated granite, which has disintegrated and been deposited. The upper strata, such as fletz-formations, are supposed to have been deposited at a later date; solution is said to have run into the
+ fissures etc. These are mere occurrences however, and display nothing but
20 a temporal difference. Nothing whatever is made comprehensible by the succession of stratifications, which is in fact completely devoid of the necessity which characterizes comprehension. Dissolutions in water or fire are quite
+ simple aspects of organic fermentation, and cannot express it fully. They are as inadequate to the comprehension of it as is the process of oxidation and dis-
25 oxidation, or the completely superficial reduction of it to the opposition of the carbon and nitrogen series. This whole style of explanation is nothing but a transformation of collaterality into temporal succession. I make use of it when I see a house with a ground-floor, first-floor, second-floor, and roof, and after reflecting, conclude very wisely that the ground-floor was
30 built before the second-floor etc. Why is the limestone more recent? Because in this instance limestone overlays sandstone. This is not difficult to grasp. Intrinsically, this interpretation is of no rational interest. The process has no other content than the product. It is nothing but a vain curiosity, which attempts to see that which is juxtaposed in the further
35 form of succession. Interesting conjectures may be made about the wide intervals separating revolutions of this kind, about the profounder revolutions caused by alterations of the Earth's axis, and about revolutions due to the sea. In the historical field these are hypotheses however, and this explanation of events by mere succession has nothing whatever to
40 contribute to philosophic consideration.

There is something profounder in this sequence however. The significance and spirit of the process is the intrinsic connection or necessary relation of these formations, and here succession in time plays no part. The
universal law of this sequence of formations may be understood without
reference to its historical form, and this law is the essence of the sequence. 5
It is only rationality which is of interest to the Notion, and at this juncture
this consists of understanding the dispositions of the Notion within the
law. The great merit of *Werner* is that he has drawn attention to this
sequence, and on the whole assessed it correctly. The intrinsic connection +
exists at present as a juxtaposition, and must depend upon the constitution 10
or content of these formations themselves. The history of the Earth is
therefore partly empirical, and partly a conclusive ratiocination from
empirical data. The point of interest is not to determine the conditions +
prevailing millions of years ago (and there is no need to stint on the years),
but to concentrate upon that which is present in the system of these vari- 15
ous formations. As an empirical science it is extremely diffuse. One is
unable to grasp everything in this corpse by means of the Notion, for it is
riddled with accidence. Philosophy has a similarily minimal interest in
acquainting itself with rational and systematic legislation in the dismal
condition of chaos, or in getting to know the temporal sequence and 20
external causes by which this legislation has come into being. +

The production of living being is generally envisaged as a revolution
out of chaos, in which vegetable and animal life, organic and inorganic
being, were together in a single unity. The alternative postulate is that
there was once a general living existence which has dispersed into various 25
species of plants and animals, and into the races of mankind. Such prodi-
gies are the postulates of the sensuous intuition of an empty imagination
however, for it is not permissible to assume the sensuous appearance of
this fission in time, or the temporal existence of such a general man.
Natural and living being is not mixed, it is not a general medley of forms, 30
it does not resemble an arabesque. There is essentially *understanding* in
nature. The formations of nature are determinate and bounded, and it is +
as such that they enter into existence. Consequently, even *if* the Earth was
once devoid of living being, and limited to the chemical process etc., as
soon as the flash of living being strikes into matter, a determinate and 35
complete formation is present, and emerges fully armed, like Minerva
from the brow of Jupiter. The account of the creation given in Genesis +
is still the best, in so far as it says quite simply that the plants, the animals,
and man were brought forth on separate days. Man has not formed
himself out of the animal, nor the animal out of the plant, for each is 40

instantly the whole of what it is. Such an individual certainly evolves in various ways, but although it is not yet complete at birth, it is already the real possibility of everything it will become. Living being is the point at which the soul is present; it is subjectivity and infinite form, and is
5 therefore immediately determined in and for itself. The crystal already exhibits complete shape or totality of form as point, so that the point's ability to grow is merely a quantitative change. This is even more the
+ case with living being.

3. The particular formations of the Earth are the subject-matter of
10 *physical geography*. The unity of the Earth, as the diversity of its formation, is an inert deployment of the independence of all its parts. It is the firm structure of the Earth, which has life as universal animation, and not yet as soul. It is the inorganic Earth, which deploys its members as the inanimate shape of a rigid body. Its filiation into water and land, which first unite and interpermeate in
15 subjective being, into firm land and islands, and into the figuration and crystallization of the same into valleys and mountains, all this belongs to its purely mechanical formation. It may certainly be said in this connection, that the Earth is more contracted in one place, and more expanded in another, but the bare statement has no meaning. The concentration in the north gives
20 rise to common products, vegetation, and animals, while in the southern extremities of the continents, animal forms are particularized and individualized into various genera and species which are peculiar to those parts. This appears at first to be accidental, but the activity of the Notion consists in grasping the necessary determinations of that which appears
25 to sensuous consciousness as a contingency. Contingency also has its sphere of course, but only in the inessential. The line of lands and mountains might also be traced back to magnetic axes passing from the north-west to the south-east. As a linear direction however, magnetism in general is a completely formal moment, for its power is already suppressed in the globe, and is even
30 more subordinate to the subject. In order to grasp the entire configuration of the globe, its firm stratification would have to be considered, and compared not only with the sea but with its currents, for they express the free and implicit movement of the Earth. In general, a formation which has a propension towards a determination opposed to that of the sphere, tends to be pyramidal. Conse-
35 quently, it forms a broadness or base within the sphere, which tapers off
+ towards the other side. This is why the land falls away towards the south. This structure is scoured everywhere in a west-easterly direction by the incessant circular movements of the currents however. The movement might be said to push and press this solid mass eastwards, so that the structure bulges on the
40 eastern side like a bent bow, while on the western side it is convex and rounded.

Nevertheless, the land in general is split into two parts i.e. the old world, which is shaped like a horseshoe, and the new world, the main extent of which is north-south. The existence of the new world became actual through the connection created when it was discovered, and so brought into the general system of peoples. This discovery was fortuitous how- 5 ever, and its recency is not the only factor in the newness of the conti- nent, for everything within it is new. As civilization has developed there with neither the horse nor iron, it has lacked the powerful instruments of positive difference. No continent of the old world has been coerced by another, while America is merely a part of Europe's booty. Its fauna 10 is weaker than that of the old world, although it possesses an exuberant flora. The mountain ranges of the old world generally run from west to + east, or from south-west to north-east, while in America, which is the butment of the old world, they run from south to north. American rivers flow eastwards however, particularly in South America. In general, the 15 new world exhibits an incomplete division like that of the magnet, sepa- rated as it is into a northern and a southern part. The old world exhibits a complete tripartite division however. Its primary part is Africa, which cor- responds to compact metal or the lunar principle, and is stunned by the heat. Its humanity is sunk in torpor, it is the dull spirit which does not 20 enter into consciousness. Its second part is Asia, which is the bacchantic + eccentricity of the comet, the wild middle, which brings forth only from it- self, engenders without form, and is unable to master its centre. Its third + part is Europe, which constitutes the rational region of the Earth, or conscious- ness, and forms an equilibrium of rivers, valleys, and mountains, the 25 centre of which is Germany. Consequently, the continents are not con- tingent, for as divisions they are not a matter of convenience, but embody essential differences. +

B

The Earth's structural composition
(*Geology and Oryctognosy*)

§ 340

The immediacy of physical organization **does not begin with the simple enveloped form of the germ, but with an egression** 30 **which has fallen apart into a duality. The principles of this duality**

are the concrete **graniticity which constitutes the** core of mountains, **and already** exhibits the developed triad **of moments within itself, and calcareousness, which is a difference reduced to neutrality.** The moments of the first principle progress into
5 formations through a series of stages, the further configurations of which are *partly* transitions, **of which the granitic principle** remains the basis only as being internally more unequal and unformed, and *partly* a dispersion of its moments into more determinate differentiation, and into the more ab-
10 stract mineralogical moments of the metals and orycto-
+ logical objects in general. **This development finally loses itself** in mechanical stratifications, and in alluviums devoid of immanent formation. **The development of the second or neutral principle proceeds side by side with this, partly as a weaker**
15 **transformation, and so partly as the external mixing of the two principles, which results from their entering into concrescent formations.**

Addition. *Werner's* mineralogy distinguishes between *rock-types* and
+ *types of vein*: *geology* treats of the former, and *oryctognosy* of the latter.
20 Scientific mineralogy has now abandoned this terminology however, and it is only miners who retain the distinction. Rock-types are now considered in their concrete mass, and geology concerns itself with the further formation of a form basic to them and their modifications, in which they remain concrete configurations. The types of vein constitute the secondary
25 and more abstract aspect which develops out of this, and as these veins also form mountains, this aspect may not be sharply divided from the first. Abstract formations of this kind are crystals, ores, and metals, where differentiation has been reached. They have constituted themselves as neutralities, and can form concrete shapes, for it is precisely in these ab-
30 stractions that shape becomes free. The types of vein are seams consisting of some determinate gangue, a certain sort of stone and earth. They have a definite grain or inclination, so that they form an angle with the horizon. These strata are now traversed at various angles by veins, and it is these that are so important in mining. *Werner* thought of them as fissures filled by a
+ mineral quite different from that of which the rock-mass is composed.

The physical formation of the Earth is so constituted that its surface erupts into organic centres or points of totality, which unite the whole within themselves, and then allow it to fall apart, exhibiting it as a particular production. This self-disclosing contraction passes over into the diffusion of its moments. In a way these centres are *cores*, which represent the whole in their *shells* and crusts, by means of which they disperse into the general foundation, as into their element. +

The core and root of these formations is not a simple unity, but the developed totality of formation, which contains within itself the already separated moments. This is the existence of the organic unity as it is able to produce itself 5 in the universal individuality of the Earth. This core is granite, which is so compact, hard, and firm, that its individual parts are not easily obtained in a pure state. It consists throughout of an incipient *crystallization*. Granite is the innermost substance, the middle and foundation of the whole; other formations attach themselves initially to both sides of its ranges. Although 10 it is the primary rock, it has three constituents. These constitute a single and extremely hard mass however. Granite is known to consist of (*a*) the brittle punctiformity of *silica* or *quartz* which is the absolute earth; (*b*) *mica*, the surface which develops itself into opposition, the self-disclosing punctiformity, the moment of combustibility which contains the germ of all abstractions; and (*c*) 15 *felspar*, the suggested but still undeveloped neutrality and crystallization of lime in silicates, for it will be found to have a two to three per cent potash content. It is this simple earthy triad which now develops *in accordance* + *with its different aspects*, and in a more determinate manner into the two directions of the process. In the one case, this whole contains the differences as its 20 form, and remains the same, while only its content is variously modified. In the other, the differences permeate the substance, and become simple abstractions. The first is the formation of the Earth as it appears at this juncture; the second is difference, but it has lost all chemical significance, and is simply the formation of simple physical bodies. More exactly, we have (*a*) the exterior forming of 25 the primitive rock; (*b*) the effacing of the existent moment of the totality, and the pure segregation of this as an abstraction, or fletz-formation; to which (*c*) the crumbling into indifferent existence of alluvial terrain attaches itself.

1. In *primitive rocks*, and throughout all further formations, the anti- 30 theses of (*a*) *siliceousness*, (*b*) *argillaceousness* and that connected with it, and (*c*) *calcareousness*, are always evident. Primitive limestone stands opposed to granite, so that the *siliceous* and *calcareous series* constitute an essential antithesis. *Steffens* has drawn attention to this in his early writings, and it is one of his most valuable observations. Most of his views are the crude and 35 undisciplined utterances of a wild and hazy imagination however. The + different character of the two sides is clearly apparent in primitive rocks, and is a determining principle. The calcareous aspect constitutes total neutrality, and its modifications have more effect upon exterior formation than upon the diversity which specifies itself internally. On the contrary, 40

there is a more determinate difference present in siliceous formations where granite constitutes the basis.

(a) The granite masses constitute the primary formation, and are the highest. The other rocks rest on the granite in such a way that the highest always occupy the lowest position, and the others in their turn rest upon these. The rock-structures closest to granite are modifications of it, for they are the further eductions of one of its aspects, in which the preponderance of the two aspects varies from place to place. Granite rocks are surrounded by beds of *gneiss, syenite, mica-schist* etc., which are clearly lighter transmutations of it. *Ebel* says that, 'A species of rock constituting one flag shades into that of another by a gradual change in composition. It is in this way that compact granite passes into veined granite and gneiss. Similarly, it is by a series of relationships between its constituents that the hardest gneiss shades off into the softest kind of mica-schist, which passes in its turn into *primitive argillaceous schist.*' etc. These latter rocks occur very close together, so that it is easy to see the transition. Consequently, the primary object of geological studies is to grasp the lay-out of the general masses, and the Notion of the moments. The thoughtless enumeration which proclaims a new genus or species as soon as any small difference is discovered, is to be avoided. It is most important to follow the nature of the transitions from one stratification to another. Although nature only keeps to this order in a general way, and produces numerous diversifications of it, its basic features are persistent. Although nature deposits these features in indifferent juxtaposition as parts of the whole, it indicates necessity through the transition of the various stratifications into one another. It does not do this merely by means of a gradual diminution however, for even for the intuition, the variety of the species occurs in precise accordance with Notional distinction. Nature specifies these transitions as a mixture of the qualitative and quantitative, demonstrating in this way that it is by both that species are differentiated from one another. As the orbicules, nests, and centres of one rock begin to form another, they are partly intermingled, and also partly dissevered externally. *Heim* in particular has shown a truly philosophical attitude while drawing attention to this transition, in which one rock breaks out in another. Syenite stands in close relation to granite, for instead of mica, it contains only *hornblend*, which is more argillaceous than mica, but resembles it. Mica-schist initiates determinate *flattening out.* Quartz almost dwindles into imperceptibility, and the prevalence of clay increases until in argillaceous schist, which is the general *slate-formation and* the next change of form, foliation and clay predominate completely, and the specific nature of quartz, felspar, mica and hornblend formations dissolves and disintegrates. This dissolution allows formlessness to predominate, for it initiates the progressive transformation of granite. There is much besides that belongs here, but only as a dwindling of the determinations of granite. Mica-schist is changed into *porphyry*, which consists mainly of clay, and of other masses such as hornstone, and which still contains *grains of felspar and quartz*. Primordial porphyry still belongs to the 5 primitive rocks. Schist has various aspects; it becomes harder and more quartz-like in its *siliceous* form, while in *greywack-slate* and *greywack* it becomes sandier, so that clay is no longer predominant. In the Harz for example, greywack is an inferior reproduction of granite, looks like sandstone, and is a mixture of quartz, argillaceous schist, and felspar. This is + even more the case with *greenstone*, which consists of hornblend, felspar, + and quartz, hornblend being its main constituent. The whole of the further development of the *trappean formation*, which is however more + mixed, and which is the limit of these absolute rocks, is directly related to these formations. +

As we said therefore, the development here is from granite to the disappearance of its particular constituents. Although this is a basically triadic development, these moments fall apart, and there is an emergence of one or the other. In *basalt*, which is the centre, the elements are once more completely compenetrative. Basalt contains 40 parts silica, 16 parts clay, 20 9 parts potash, 2 parts talc, and 2 parts natron. The rest of it consists of manganese oxide and water. The truth in the assertion of its volcanic origin is that it belongs to the igneous principle, but it is no more formed by fire than it is by water. An inner deformation appears in basalt, and is even + more apparent in *amygdaloid, olivine, and augite* etc., which are abstract 25 formations, and have reached a complete internal particularization. Subsequent to this there is nothing but the formal mixture or formal segregation of these elements. The further details have to be classified in accordance with the following principle. (*a*) One line of transformation is merely a modification of granite, in which traces of this basic triad are still 30 constantly present. These traces are found in gneiss, mica-schist and porphyry, and right down the scale through greenstone, greywack, basalt, and amygdaloid, as far as ordinary sands. (b) The other line is the splitting up of the concretion into abstract forms. It is here in particular that the antithesis of the siliceous and calcareous series occurs: (*i*) in ranges of 35 rock, and (*ii*) within these ranges, in what were once said to be types of vein.

(*b*) So far we have mainly considered siliceous formations; but the whole passes over in its other aspect into the *talcous form* of saline earth. This is the igneous element, which occurs irregularly here and there as *serpentine* and similar rocks, and which has the property of bitterness. +

28

(c) This igneous form is then generally opposed to the neutrality of calcareousness, but as it is permeated by metallicism, this neutrality has qualitative unity, and is therefore completely permeated by organic formation. *Primitive limestone* is already associated with granite, and is just as compact as the granitic
5 rocks. Consequently, the primitive rocks have ranges of limestone about them. This primitive limestone, which stands opposed to granite, passes into the less compact form of chalk by means of *transition-limestone*. One also finds formations in which granite and limestone are very intermixed. Primitive limestone permeates mica for example, 'Primitive limestone
10 accompanies schist rocks, and mingles with them. Within these rocks it alternates in shallow layers, strata, and huge beds, and sometimes forms
+ chunks of rock in which the schist is almost entirely effaced.'[1]

2. These main formations pass over into the so-called *fletz* and alluvial *rocks*, where these moments, segregated as almost pure earths, represent the com-
15 pletely decomposed totality. They pass in fact into *sandstone beds, argillaceous and loamy stratifications, coal*-seams, peat-bogs, bituminous schists, rock-salt stratifications, and finally into chalk beds which also mix with the rock-salt beds, *gypsum beds,* and *marl.* As graniticity becomes more of an indeterminate mixture, the particular parts of the different formations emerge in greater
20 abstraction; differences are therefore obliterated as in trap and greywack, which belongs to the transitional and fletz species. Yet as granite, and that which belongs to it, draws itself together into abstraction, so that its solidity, compactness, and self-tenacious totality is lost and foliated, it has affinity with a counter-sequence, in which there is a separation of various ores, and of
25 the crystals which accompany them; iron separates out particularly early. These ores occur everywhere, interspersed throughout whole rock-masses and stratifications, and even more extensively in seams and layers. The interior is opened so that abstract formations may emerge. These various seams are the productions of particular elements from the more concrete principle
30 of the various species of rock, and as they are a less entrammeled production, they yield these multifarious crystalline formations and pure figurations. In granite, they are still all but completely absent, although granite does contain tin. No metals are present in primitive limestone, so it is only when there is a further unfolding of the primitive rock as secondary lime-
35 stone, that metal occurs. Initially, it is rocks which for themselves are more abstract or mixed, that allow these abstractions to appear. Cavities open, in which rock-crystal formations have attained their special shape, and detached themselves from their connection with the rock.

The lodes are regarded as nests and pockets of these species of stone, and as

[1] von Raumer 'Geognostical Researches' p. 13.

something diffused throughout the rock in a merely mechanical manner. According to the neptunists, the rock is supposed to have fissured and split while drying out, and the metallic magma and other solutions are supposed then to have oozed into the cracks. This can explain very neatly how + these wounds were healed, but as an interpretation it lacks thought, and 5 the relationship is not as mechanical as this. This is in fact a physical relationship, in which developed determinate being is sublated by the parts of the totality which simplify themselves. It is precisely for this reason that the determinate being is now forced out in an abstract form. The lodes usually run counter to the grain of the rock; they form as it were, fault-planes, not merely 10 of the spatial shape, but in a physical sense. According to *Trebra's* observations lodes fall in gentle slopes.   +

These lodes ought not to be regarded as contingent features of rock-types, for although contingency also plays a necessarily large part here, we have to recognize the essential connection between the two formations. 15 Miners encounter many of the characteristics of this relationship, and one of the most important aspects of their experience consists in determining the series of metals and other formations which occur together. Gold is + always found together with quartz for example, and either occurs with quartz alone, or with copper and lead, silver and zinc etc. It does not occur 20 with quicksilver, tin, cobalt, molybdenum, or wolfram. Silver associates + more freely, and is much more frequently found with other metals, most commonly with galena, and accompanied by zinc ores. Quicksilver occurs with quartz, calcareous spar, iron, and therefore also with sparry iron-ore, but rarely with copper. The various kinds of quicksilver are 25 usually found together, and all of them occur principally in argillaceous formations. Copper and its various ores usually occur alone. Tin does not occur with silver, lead, cobalt, calcareous spar, or gypsum etc. There are metals such as iron, which occur in all rock-formations. Other metals such as molybdenum, titanium, tantalum, wolfram, uranium, and tin, are more 30 confined to the primitive rocks. Molybdenum and wolfram for instance, disappear with the primitive formations. Gold occurs most abundantly about the equator. Some lodes yield precious metals, others base metals, and here there are significant relations which are indicative of a higher connection. The Riegelsdorf and Saalfeld cobalt formations of the 35 Thuringian Mountains only become rich where the lodes have sunk into the primordial and *moribund sandstone* formation. At Andreasberg in the + Harz, schist and greywack constitute the rock-type, and the lodes yield base metals when they pass into the beds of siliceous schist; in Klaustal, this happens where they fill tapering crevices in the clay, and in the 40

Freiberg mining district, the same phenomenon occurs in porphyry. Metals are also met at determinate depths. Horn silver and white antimony-ore only occur at shallow depths. In the Tyrol, there is a bed of sparry iron-ore, argillaceous iron-stone, and brown spar, in which they occur
5 where the copperpyrites peters out. At La Gardette in Dauphiné, pure gold lies near the surface, particularly where there is a break-through of crevices containing ferric ochre. The size of the fissure also influences the formations it contains. At Sayn-Altenkirchen, iron-glance occurs where the lode narrows, and iron stone of the brown, black, and spar varieties,
+ where it broadens. 'Topazes occur in a greasy mica, which is modified into lithomarge, and in a friable lithomarge which is sometimes pure, and sometimes mixed with a good deal of ferric-ochre; this lithomarge also owes its formation to the mica, and is accompanied by quartz and china-clay. On topazes as well as euclase crystals, very clear imprints of ex-
15 tremely fine flakelets of lithomarge may be seen. This ought to be sufficient proof of the simultaneous formation of these minerals. It is the same with the emeralds of the Salzburg area. In gneiss, mica detaches itself, and forms broad seams up to several feet in thickness. Emeralds are seldom found in gneiss; they may always be found in mica however, where
20 the crystals never occur in a compact mass, but are spread about and embedded in an irregular manner. Emerald-crystals also bear the imprints of
+ the flakes of mica which surround them.'[1]

3. The final moment, which is the transition from fletz-formation to *alluvial terrain*, is a mixture, and consequently complete formlessness, an
25 abstract stratification of *clay, sand, lime, and marl*. These are the general outlines of the progression, at the basis of which lies the determining Notion. The primitive rock develops until it loses its mineralogical constitution, and joins up with a vegetable being. Argillaceousness and coal formations are clearly degenerate forms of *peat*, in which there is no dis-
30 tinction between mineral and vegetable, for although peat is formed in a vegetable manner, it still belongs to an equal extent to the mineral kingdom. On its other side, it is the calcareousness which in its ultimate formations develops into the osseous substance of the animal. Limestone is initially granular; it is marble, and its composition is thoroughly min-
35 eral. The further productions of limestone, which occur partly in fletz-formations, and partly in alluvial terrains, pass over into *shell formations* however, and it is difficult to say whether these are mineral or animal. These petrified animal formations are to be found in abundance in

---

[1] *Spix* and *Martius* 'Travels' vol. I, p. 332. Cf. Frischholz, in Moll's 'New Annals' vol. 4, no. 3.

limestone quarries, but although they occur in the form of shells, they are not to be regarded as the residua of an extinct animal world. There are also limestone formations which are not the residua, but merely the rudiments of the animal forms in which limestone formation terminates. This is therefore an intermediate stage falling between limestone and true petri- 5 fications. It has to be regarded merely as a further development of conchyliaceousness, and as something purely mineral, for formations of this kind have not yet reached the consummate form of the animal. It is in this way that the antithesis of the siliceous and the calcareous series gives faint indication of a superior organic difference, for the limits of these series 10 link up on one side with vegetable nature, and on the other with animal nature. *Steffens* has also brought out this aspect of the matter, but he has gone too far in his interpretation of it by asserting (*a*) that these formations have sprung out of a vegetable and animal terrestrial process, and (*b*) that the first series is carbonaceous, the second nitrogenous. +

The organic formations which begin in the geological organism belong mainly to argillaceous schists and limestone stratifications. They are dispersed partly as the forms of individual animals and plants, but mainly in huge integral masses, thoroughly formed organically. They may also be found in coalmeasures, where a distinct arborescence is often recognizable. Consequently, 20 if *breccias* are also taken into account, there is as much organic formation in the geological organism, as there is in inorganic. This certainly disposes one to admit that there was once an organic world there which has since been destroyed by water. But where did this world come from? It has arisen out of the Earth. This is not an historical event however, for it is perpetually doing so. It is in the Earth 25 that it has its substance. These organic forms, particularly where they occur singly and do not constitute the whole rock-mass, are present where beds pass over into each other. It is on this *boundary* that the moments which are allowed to fall apart by processless nature, are posited in a unity. The dividing line is the principal site of organic formations such as petrifications, and of such formations 30 as are neither animal nor vegetable, but pass beyond the form of the crystal as essays and experiments in organic formation. It is as schists and limestones that inorganic being opens itself most readily to these formations, for as schist partly transforms its terrestrial elements into sulphureousness, and partly maintains the principle of metallicism within itself, it sublates the fixedness of its subjectivity. 35 Its punctiformity, unfolded by bitumen, and containing a general differentiation, receives from metallicism the continuity of an absolute subject and predicate. It is infinite, and falls into vacillation between organic and inorganic nature. Similarly, as calcareousness is the neutral principle, it contains in its aspects the moment of reality and subsistence, and simple metallicism occurs 40

here by reason of the simplicity of its continuity, as the qualitative unity which annuls the indifference of these aspects. Calcareousness therefore has a unity which includes aspects of the neutral substance, and a neutral substance which has unity. It is in this way that calcareousness expresses the transition to
5 organic being, for it restrains the relapse into dead neutrality on one side, and into moribund abstraction and simplicity on the other. These organic forms are still-born, and should not be regarded as having actually lived and then died. Some of them undoubtedly have lived, but it is not these that are being considered. Bonefibres have not existed as veins or nerves and then hardened, and
10 neither have these forms. It is nature in its organic-plasticity which engenders organic being in the element of immediate being, and therefore as a moribund
+ shape, and thoroughly crystallizes it. At this juncture nature therefore resembles the artist, who uses stone or a flat canvas in order to represent human and other shapes. The artist does not strike people dead, dry them out, pump them with
15 petrifaction, or press them into stone (although he can also do this, for he casts models into moulds); in accordance with his idea, and by means of his tools, he produces forms which are not living, but which represent life. Nature also produces forms, but it does so directly, without needing this mediation. That is to say that the Notion is not present as something represented, and the
20 thing as something confronting the imaginative subject which works upon it. The Notion does not have the form of consciousness, but is immediately within the element of being, and is not detached from it. It has to work upon the material in which the moments of organic being are present in their totality. This is not a question of a universal life of nature, in which the animation of
25 nature is ubiquitous, it is a question of the essence of life. It is this essence which has to be comprehended and exhibited in the moments of its actuality or totality, and these moments have to be demonstrated.

C

The Earth's life

§ 341

This crystal of life, this inanimate organism of the Earth, which has its *Notion* in the sidereal connection outside it,
30 but has its **own peculiar** process pre-supposed as its past, is the *immediate subject* of the meteorological process. **As the implicit being of the totality of life, this inanimate organism is**

no longer fertilized by this process into individual formation (see
§287), but into **animation**. The land, and to a greater extent the
sea, are therefore the real possibility of life, and at every point they
are perpetually breaking out into **punctiform** and **ephemeral**
animation. The land breeds lichens and infusoria, the sea immeas- 5
urable multitudes of phosphorescent points of life. It is precisely
because the generatio aequivoca has this objective organism exter- +
nal to it however, that it is confined to the organization of these
points; it does not develop within itself into determinate members,
nor does it reproduce itself (ex ovo). 10

Addition. Initially, the geological organism of the Earth was the product
of the process in which its shape developed. As it is the productive individuality underlying that process, it now overcomes its rigidity, and unfolds into subjective animation. Nevertheless, it excludes this animation
from itself, and surrenders it to other individuals. In other words, as the 15
geological organism is only implicit animation, it is not identical with true
living existence. Yet as it is implicitly the negativity of that which belongs
to it, and the sublation of its own immediacy, it posits the inwardness of
that which belongs to it, while retaining this other as its own. It is precisely as the ground and basis of the individual animation which it bears, 20
that the Earth is fertile therefore. It is merely an indeterminate mode of
animation however, for although life certainly breaks out on it everywhere, it only does so meagrely. This universal life of the Earth has living
parts which are the elements constituting its universal and inorganic nature. Yet
as the Earth is also a particular body vis-à-vis its satellites, the sun and the +
comets, this perenniating production, which is the conservation of this
system of differentiations, is the absolute and universal chemical process.
As the gigantic members of this diremption are free and independent
individualities however, their relation exists in its purity as the free process of motion, while the comets are themselves a perpetually new produc- 30
tion of this process. The reality of the process is reached as real individual
unity comes into the plenitude of its being through the absorption of
apparently independent shapes. This occurs first in the individual chemical
process, and it is precisely for this reason that this process is profounder
and more basic than the universal process. As the universal process of the 35
elements is the universal process of diverse matters however, the individual
process cannot dispense with it. In their truth, the sun, comet and moon,
which are the free independent members of the universal process, are now
the elements; air exists as atmosphere, and water as sea, while fire exists

as a terrestriality contained by the fertilized and dissolved Earth, and separated as the fructifying power of the sun. The life of the Earth is the process of the atmosphere and of the sea. Within this process the Earth engenders these elements, each of which is by itself its own life, and all of which merely
5 constitute this process. Here the chemical principle has lost its absolute significance and is no more than a moment; it is reflected into independent being, and brought under the subject, by which it is quelled and held fast. As a free subject, each element is related to the others through its substance; and the formation of the organic Earth contains the modal existence of its organic life.
10   1. The *atmosphere* is the first determinate moment of the life of the Earth. The meteorological process vitalizes the Earth, but it is not its life-process, for its vitalization is simply the real possibility of subjectivity issuing forth on the Earth as living existence. As pure movement, and as substance which is of an ideal nature, the atmosphere certainly contains the life of the celestial spheres,
15 for its changes are connected with the motion of the heavens. At the same time, it materializes this motion in its element however. It is the rarefaction and pure tension of the Earth, the relationship between gravity and heat. It runs through the periodic movement of the year, as well as that of the month and the day, and expresses it as changes of heat and gravity. These periodic fluctuations fall into
20 a further difference: where axial rotation preponderates, the diurnal period is prevalent, so that at the equator, while there is a consistent daily pattern in the *rise* and *fall* of the barometer, there is no annual variation within this relationship. In our part of the world however, this daily rise and fall is less noticeable, and pattern of variation is more constantly related to the moon.
25   Gravity here is interior gravity or elasticity as pressure, but in its essence, it is variation of specific gravity. It is a movement or atmospheric fluctuation which is related to *temperature* variation. It is so related however, that these variations unite the opposed determinations of ordinary temperature and the temperature of light, the first of which is given out, and the second of which is introduced
30 through light. The latter is generally air in its clarity and pure elasticity, and gives rise to a high barometer reading, while the former belongs to the moment of formation, and is present when elasticity passes over into rain or snow.[1] It is precisely in the air that these abstract moments return into themselves.
   Just as heavenly motion materializes in the air, so on the other side sea and
35 earth invade it, and evaporate into it by a processless and immediate transition. The air individualizes both of them within itself, partly into the universal atmospheric process, in which it attains its supreme independence by dissolving water

---

[1] This is why rain sometimes cools, and is sometimes followed by an increase in temperature.
Note by Michelet.

and earth into odours, and by discharging and changing itself into water; partly by individualizing itself into meteors, as transient comets, that is to say, into the earths which it generates, or aerolites; partly as noxious emanations, + *miasmata*, which are harmful to animals; and partly as *honey-dews* and *mildews*, animal and vegetable blights. +

2. The composition of the neutral Earth or the *sea*, owes just as much to the motion of *ebb* and *flow*, which is determined by the changing position of the sun and the moon, as it does to the shape of the Earth. The sea draws its + neutrality from the Earth, just as the air, which is the universal element, draws its tension. As sea opposed to the air, the Earth evaporates; but as opposed to the 10 sea, it is the crystal which expels the superfluous water from itself in springs, which flow together to form rivers. As fresh water however, this is merely abstract neutrality. On the contrary, the crystal of the Earth passes over into the physical neutrality of the sea. Consequently, the origin of inexhaustible springs ought not to be explained in a mechanical and completely superficial 15 way by means of percolation; volcanoes and thermal springs form another aspect, which is equally unamenable to this interpretation. Just as springs are the lungs and secretory glands by which the Earth transpires, so volcanoes are its *liver*, in that they represent the spontaneous generation of heat within it. Vicinities which are perpetually giving off dampness are to be found everywhere, 20 particularly in beds of sandstone. Consequently, I do not regard the hills as collectors of rain-water, which infiltrates into them. Like Naiads, the genuine springs which engender rivers such as the Ganges, the Rhône and the Rhine, have an inner life, endeavour, and activity. The Earth excretes + the abstractness of its fresh water, and in these outpourings this water 25 hurries towards its concrete animation, which is the sea. +

The sea itself is an animation which is superior to that of the air. It is the subject of bitterness, and of neutrality and dissolution. It is a living process which is always on the point of breaking out into life, but as water contains all the moments of the process, this life is always falling back into it. These 30 moments are the point of subjectivity and neutrality, and the dissolution of the subject into this neutrality. The sea has the same fertility as the firm earth, and to an even higher degree. The generatio aequivoca is the general mode of vitalization manifested by sea and land, while in animation proper, the existence of an individual presupposes another of its kind 35 (generatio univoca). 'Omne vivum ex ovo' used to be accepted as a + proposition, and if the origin of certain animalcula was not known, + recourse was had to fabrications. There are organisms that produce themselves immediately however, and procreate no further; infusorial animacula agglomerate and become another formation, so that they serve only 40 as a transition. This universal animation is an organic life which is self-kindling, and which acts upon itself as a stimulant. The sea is not the same as spring and salt water, it contains not merely kitchen-salt, but also bitter-salt, and as an organic being which displays its procreativeness at 5 every point, constitutes concrete salinity. Like water in general, it has a constant tendency to pass away and transform itself, for its aqueous form is only maintained by atmospheric pressure. The bad smell which is a feature of the sea, is a life which is as it were perpetually dissolving into putrefaction. Sailors speak of the *blooming* of the sea in summer. In July, 10 August and September, the sea becomes polluted, turbid and slimy; further west in the Atlantic Ocean, this takes place a month earlier than it does in the Baltic. The sea is full of an infinite multitude of vegetable points, threads and surfaces; it constitutes a tendency to break out into + vast expanses of phosphorescent light. This phosphorescence is a superficial 15 life which concentrates itself into a simple unity. The unity is also fully intro-reflected however, for this luminescence often occurs in fish, and in other animals which already belong to living subjectivity. The whole surface of the sea is also partly an infinite sheen however, and partly a vast and immeasurable expanse of light, consisting entirely of living points which 20 enter into no further organization. If one takes this water from the sea, the animation perishes immediately, leaving a *gelatinous slime* which is the beginning of the vegetable life with which the sea is filled from its surface + to its depths. In each fermentation there is already an immediate appearance of animalcula. Finally however, the sea also progresses into deter-25 minate formations, into infusorial animalcula, and other tiny transparent mollusca, which live longer, but which are still completely rudimentary + organisms. While studying various *Salpae*, *A. von Chamisso* made the fine discovery of a Salpa which was so fertile, that its very numerous embryos, like the free petals of a plant clustered about its stem, were arranged in 30 tiers, and formed a garland or circle. Here many have a single life, like the + polyps, and then come together again in a single individual. This lower animal world includes a multitude of luminous species, but as it attains to nothing more than a momentary and gelatinous existence, the subjectivity of animal being can scarcely coach it into luminescence, into the external 35 appearance of self-identity. This animal world is unable to hold its light within it as inner selfhood, so that it is transient, and merely breaks out of itself as a physical light; the millions of living beings deliquesce rapidly into their element again. It is in this way that the sea displays a host of stars, densely crowded into galaxies; they are not inferior to the stars of 40 heaven, for they have their origin in organic formations, while their celestial counterparts are only abstract points of light. The heavens exhibit light in the rawness of its primary crudity; here it breaks out of animal being as an animality, like the phosphorescence of rotten wood; it is a flicker of animation, and of the emergence of the soul. It has been rumoured around the town that I have compared the stars to a rash on an organic body, where the skin breaks out into an infinite multitude of red spots, or to an ant-heap (see above § 268 Add. I. 258,33), objects which also exhibit intelligence and necessity. In fact I make more of a concrete than I do of an abstract being, more of an animality, though it present nothing but jelly, than of the host of stars. And discounting fish, the further content of the marine world includes polyps, corals, lithophytes, crustacea, zoophytes etc., each drop is a living globe of infusorial-animalcula etc. The sea contains animation within itself in a more immanent manner than the land, in so far as its fluid nature does not facilitate the punctualization of animation into a living being which breaks loose from the sea and preserves itself against it. The neutrality of the sea draws this incipient subjectivity back into the insensibility of its womb, and so causes its vital power, which this subjectivity had taken as its own, to dissolve again into the universal. The earliest doctrines certainly treated the sea as that from which all living existence emerges. But this very *emergence* entails the repulsion of the sea, and the living creature only exists by tearing itself away from the sea, and maintaining itself in the face of this neutrality. Consequently, the sea in its fluidity makes no advance upon elementary life, and the subjective life which is cast and drawn back into it again, is also imbued with this persistent and undeveloped torpidity. This is so even in more developed organisms such as whales, which are still mammals.

3. As the gigantic corpse of a vanished life that was formerly immanent, the *land* is this individual concretion which disengages itself from neutrality, it is the compact crystal of the lunar element, while the sea is the cometary element. These two moments penetrate each other in subjective living existence however, so that gelatination or slime becomes the vessel of internally durable light. Like water, the earth exhibits infinite and universal fertility, but while it is mainly animal existence which breaks out in water, the land tends to bring forth vegetable life. The sea favours animality, because neutrality is in itself a propagation; the earth maintains itself in punctualization, and is therefore more congenial to vegetable life. The earth covers itself everywhere with green vegetation, with indeterminate formations which can equally well be classed as animal life. Individual vegetation must of course be engendered from seeds of the

same genus, but universal vegetation lacks this degree of individuality. It
++ consists of the lichens and *moss* which break out on any stone. Vegetable
being will always occur where there is earth, air and moisture. *Mildew* is
a vegetable formation, and appears immediately wherever anything
+ decomposes. *Fungi* also spring up everywhere. This vegetation, as not yet
formed individually, consists of formations such as lichens and fungi,
which are both inorganic and organic, and which it is difficult to classify
with any certainty, for they are made up of peculiar compact substances
of an embryonically animal nature. *Rudolphi* writes ('Plant Anatomy' §14
10 and §17), 'Lichens exhibit nothing that may be considered as characteristic
of plant structure. All writers agree that they have no true parenchyma,
and that they are quite devoid of tubes or vascularity. I have found no
proof that what are called their reproductive parts really are such, and it is
perhaps more likely that they are germination-buds, by which the lichens
15 propagate themselves in a way similar to that of many true plants. Their
propagation proves nothing therefore. The vegetable nature of many of
them is apparent in their pigment, their gummy and resinous constituents,
and their sugary mucilage and tannin. The structure of fungi differs considerably from that of plants. I have examined a good number of them,
20 and find that their substance is of a kind that may well be called animal.
In the softer fungi one finds a fibrous mucous tissue which closely resembles that found in animals, but which differs completely from the firm
cellular structure of plants. The Boletus cetatophorus exhibits a lanuginous
tissue which is in no way plant-like, but clearly constitutes a transition
25 from soft fungi to the ligneous variety, the substance of which might be
compared with the trunk of the gorgonia.' 'If one considers the animal
composition of fungi, and its response to galvanization,' says baron
Alexander von Humboldt,[1] 'one will more readily discard the opinion that
fungi belong to the vegetable kingdom and are true plants. This is most
30 apparent from the way in which they are engendered, for it is precisely
when animal or vegetable matter decays or decomposes, that new formations are brought forth out of this putrefaction. The Clavaria militaris is
only engendered out of dead caterpillars for example.' This infinite
multitude of formations does not establish the point of a germ or seed,
35 which has being only where subjectivity is reached. One cannot say that
+ fungi grow, for they deploy themselves suddenly, as crystals do. We
should not regard vegetation of this kind as being produced from spores,
any more than are the multitudes of rudimentary animal formations such

---

[1] 'Experiments on stimulated muscle and nerve fibres' (Berlin 1797), vol. I, sect. vi, pp. 171–180.

as infusoria, *intestinal worms*, and swine-*gargets* etc. This universal anima- 4
tion is not only found in the sea and on land therefore, but also occurs on
independent living subjectivity. The determinations of vegetable and
animal being, such as cellular tissues, seeds, eggs, growth and so on, are
attributed to these formations by means of induction. Determinateness of 5
this kind cannot be confirmed however, and in reality there is none.
Fungi, lichens and similar formations belong in general to the vegetable
kingdom, but because nature does not hold firmly to the Notion in its
manifestations, they lack this determinateness. Indeterminateness and
freakishness give rise to the rich variety of their forms. The Notion is not 10
to be drawn from them, they are to be measured by the Notion. Corrupt
anomalisms of this kind, which are neither fish nor flesh, are moments of a
total form, but they are isolated moments.

§ 342

**This division of the universal and self-external organism, and
this merely punctiform transitory subjectivity, raises itself by 15
virtue of the implicit identity of its Notion, to the existence of
this identity, which is the vitalized organism, the subjectivity
which constructs its members within itself. This subjectivity
excludes from itself the purely implicit organism of physical
nature in its universal and individual forms, and confronts it. 20
But at the same time, it has these powers as the condition of its
existence, and the stimulus as the material of its process.**

Addition. The deficiency in this display of organic being, and in immediate
organic being in general, consists in the Notion's still being immediate. Here
the Notion is merely internal fulfillment within the element of indifference, 25
but its moments are physical realities which are not intro-reflected, and which
do not form a unity in the face of this indifference. As the universal fulfillment
pervades these moments however, it returns into self; their indifference is the
one-sided moment which draws itself together into negativity as an individual.
Substance divides itself into absolute opposites, not only into differences. Each 30
of these is a totality, for it is intro-reflected, indifferent to the other, and essentially a unit. This unity is not only essential however, for the reality of these
opposites is itself this oneness or negativity i.e. their existence in itself constitutes the process.
  Consequently, life is essentially this completely fluid pervasion of all 35
the *parts* of the whole, i.e. of the parts which are indifferent to the whole.

These parts are not chemical abstractions, but have a complete and substantial life of their own. Although it is a life of parts, it is ceaselessly dissolving itself within itself, and brings forth nothing but the whole. The whole is the universal substance, so that it is the ground as well as the
5 resulting totality, and it is this as actuality. It is the unit which holds the free parts bound within it; it sunders itself into these parts, communicates its universal life to them, and holds them within itself as their power or negative principle. This is so posited that their independent circulation takes place within this principle, which is however the sublation of their
10 particularity, and the becoming of the universal. This is the universal sphere of movement within the individuality of actual being. More closely considered, this sphere is the three sphere totality which constitutes the unity of universality and actuality. This unity contains the two spheres of its opposition, and the sphere of its reflection into itself.

15 *Firstly.* Organic being is actual being which is self-maintaining, and which runs through the process in its own self. It is its own universal, and sunders itself into its parts. These parts sublate themselves by bringing forth the whole. The genus and organic being stand side by side. The consequence is that the genus immediately becomes unified with inorganic being. Consequently,
20 organic being sunders itself into the two universal extremes of inorganic nature and genus, and constitutes their *middle* (U-S-P). With each of these it still forms an immediate unity, being itself both genus and inorganic nature. Consequently the individual still has its inorganic nature within itself, and nourishes itself from itself in that it consumes itself as its own in-
25 organity. By this however, *it divides itself within itself* into its members, i.e. dirempts its universality into its differences. This is the course of the process within it as the non-excluding diremption and self-relatedness of organic being. The universal has to actualize itself within itself, and it is precisely through this movement, by which it becomes for itself, that it assumes sentience.
30 As this organic genus, organic being is turned against itself as this immediate universal. This is its process of individualization; it enters into an opposition to itself which corresponds to its subsequent opposition to that external to it. This other term is still enveloped within the Notion. Nevertheless, in so far as the singular is already presupposed here, it links its own universality, which
35 is the genus, to particularized universality. This latter is one extreme, and becomes absolute particularity and singularity by being taken up into the absolute genus. Here we have the particular parturition of the moment of individuality. This is the becoming of the individuality which enters into the process as already in being. Nothing emerges from the process but what is already there. It is the
40 process of self-digestion, the division of its members, and the *formation* of its

moments. The members are destroyed as well as engendered, and the soul is the simple being which persists within this general activity. In this process the individual is able to break away from the soul by means of the genus. It is precisely the process within the genus which makes it into a unified being which has negativity within it, and which is therefore opposed to the genus as the 5 universal.

Secondly. The universal is existent, and the organic unit is the power which controls and consumes this negation of itself, this external being. Consequently, this only exists as sublated. Organic being is an immediate unity of individuality and universality. It is therefore organic genus, the exclusive unity, which 10 excludes the universal from itself. It is the genus devoid of the power of negativity or life, and is therefore organic being positing for itself its inorganity. The genus is the absolute universal, which posits itself in the face of the abstract universal; but through this, it has also released the moment of singularity, which constitutes the negative relation opposed to this inorganic being. Previously, 15 the individual constituted the middle, and the sides the universal extremes, now the genus is the common element. Consequently, organic being is here united with inorganic being by means of the genus (P-U-S), and has power over it because it is the absolute universal. This is the *process of nutrition*. Inorganic being is universality as genus devoid of actuality; here pre- 20 dominance falls partly to the Earth or individuality in general, and partly to the singularity which frees itself from this. This universality is mere passivity. However, the universality as it is in itself i.e. in its actuality, is the emergence of its inorganic nature, together with organic nature, into a state of juxtaposition. The first has the form of singularity, the second that of universality. Both of 25 them are abstractions, for the substance is identical with the modes in which it has determined itself.

(*a*) The determinateness remains a universality that belongs within the element and principle; *that which is for organic being cannot be alien to it.* The reflection of organic being takes back the implicitness of its inorganic world; 30 this world exists only as a sublation, of which organic being is the positor and bearer. It would be equally onesided to seize upon this activity alone however. It is rather the Earth, as this universal organic being, which makes the sun and its elements, as well as each organic being. Implicitly however, it is both. This positedness of inorganic being is its sublatedness; it is not implicit. Organic 35 being is independent being; but for organic being, inorganic being as implicitness is predominantly the indifferent existence of both. This subsequently passes over into tensioned existence however, into the form of being-for-self proper to organic being.

(*b*) This immediate being of organic existence as genus is to an equal extent 40

42

a simple mediation by inorganic being. Its being depends upon this otherness which is the abstract universality of this opposition to itself. It is the genus freed from individuality. This genus itself also contains life however. In the generatio aequivoca therefore, it passes over by means of itself into organic
5 being. In general, the existence of organic being is the act in which the whole Earth individualizes and contracts itself; it is the intro-reflecting of the universal. As the result of this, it is an intro-reflectedness that has become quiescent however. This stabilized intro-reflectedness is expressed in higher plants and animals, which do not shoot up out of the earth like fungi, and are not devoid of
10 individuality like gelatinous beings or lichens, which are merely the rudimentary expressions of organic life in general. The Earth in its existence only attains to general reflection however, and breaks here into the immediacy of its becoming. Intro-reflected being is now established for itself, and proceeds in its own sphere. It has its own existence, which persists in opposition to that
15 of the Earth, holds firm to its negative essence, disowns its origin, and exhibits its becoming by itself.
Thirdly. The genus is the actual being brought forth here. It is the power which dominates the individual and constitutes its process. It sublates this singular, and brings forth another being which constitutes the actuality of the
20 genus, and which precisely because of this, is also divided vis-à-vis the inorganic nature into which the genus sinks. Organic being, mediated in this way with the genus by means of inorganic being (S-P-U) constitutes the *sexual relationship.* The conclusion of the syllogism is the relation of the two terms which constitute the organic whole, or the diremption of this whole into two opposed
25 and independent sexes. It is the sublation of the singular, and the becoming of the genus, but of the genus as a singular and actual being which recommences the process. The result is therefore that the singular has separated itself from the genus. Consequently, this independent being is related to being which is indifferent to it as genus. The genus has sundered itself into two independent
30 beings, each of which is to itself the whole of this object, and yet external to it. In the first process we have being-for-self, in the second representation and cognition of another, and in the third the unity of both, i.e. of the other and itself. This is the true actualization of the Notion, for it is the complete independence of both, in which each simultaneously recognizes itself as itself in the
35 other. It is the relation which has reached the purity of its ideal nature, in which each term is itself of an ideal nature as an implicit universal, and the complete integration of subject and object is established within the self as such.
Organic being begins with singularity, and raises itself to genus. This progress holds the immediate implication of its opposition however. The pure
40 genus descends to singularity, for the consummation of individuals in the genus

43

by means of their being sublated is also the becoming of the immediate singularity of the child. Consequently, the other moment of the universal life of the Earth is the actual organic living being, which projects itself into its genus. Initially, this is vegetable nature, which is the first stage of being-for-self, or intro-reflectedness. It is merely immediate and formal being-for-self however, it is not yet true infinity. The plant puts forth its members from itself as free moments, and is merely the subjective point of life. Consequently, vegetable being begins where animation gathers itself into a point which maintains and produces itself, and engenders itself anew by self-repulsion.

Chapter Two

The vegetable organism
(The plant)

§ 343

The subjectivity by which organic being has singularity develops into an objective organism in the shape of a body, which articulates itself into mutually distinct parts. In the plant, which is merely subjective animation in its primary
5 **immediacy, the objective organism and its subjectivity[1] are still** immediately identical. **Consequently, the** process whereby vegetable subjectivity articulates and sustains itself, is one in which it comes forth from itself, and falls apart into several individuals. The singleness of the whole individual
10 is simply the basis of these, **rather than a subjective unity of members; the part—bud, branch, and so on, is also the whole plant.** A further consequence is that the *differentiation of the organic parts* is merely a superficial *metamorphosis,* and that one part can easily assume the function of the
15 other.

Addition. The geological organism is devoid of *ideality,* for it is the bare system of shape. The subjectivity of plant-life now exhibits this ideality however. As the ideality which is present in all its members, life is essentially living being however, and this living being is merely stimulated
20 from without. Consequently, the causal relationship falls away here, for in life in general, all the determinations of the understanding cease to be
+ valid. The nature of these categories has to be perverted if they are still to be employed here. Then it can be said that living being is its own cause. To assert the sublime proposition that, 'Everything lives in
+ nature,' is supposed to be speculative. The Notion of life, or life *in itself,* is of course everywhere; it is to be clearly distinguished from real life

---

[1] First edition, 'The universality of life and its singularity.'

however, which is the subjectivity of living being, in which each part has a vitalized *existence*. It is only as a whole that the geological organism is alive therefore, not in its singularity. Its animation is merely implicit, and does not have the presence of existence. Living being also differentiates itself into subjective and inanimate being however. On the one hand it constitutes the prerequisite of its being framed within the individual, by expressing itself in lignification and bones, as is the case with the geological organism as a whole. On the other hand, living being is also the shape which has substantial form dwelling within it. This form is not only determinative on account of the spatial relationships of the separate parts, but is also the productive restlessness which determines the process of physical properties in order to bring forth shape.

The plant is the primary subject which is for itself, and yet still has its origin in immediacy. It is however the feeble and infantine life which *is not yet intrinsically differentiated*. As with every living being, it lies in the nature of a plant to be particularized. The particularity of the animal is at the same time so constituted however, that the subjectivity which is opposed to it as soul is also universal, while the particular being of the plant is identical with its general animation in an entirely immediate manner. This particular being is not a state which might be distinguished from the internal life of the plant, for the quality of the plant completely pervades its general vegetative nature, and is not distinct from it, as it is in the animal. The members of the plant are only particular in relation to one another therefore, not in relation to the whole. These members are wholes in their own right, as they are in the inanimate organism, where they are also still external to one another in stratifications. As the plant now posits itself as its other, and so perpetually idealizes this contradiction, this is merely a formal separation however. That which it posits as the other is not truly another, for it is the same individual as the subject.[1]

The *growth* which predominates in vegetable being is therefore self-*augmentation* as a *change of form*. Animal growth is merely a change in size however, in which at the same time there is a persistent unity of shape, for the totality of the members is taken up into the subjectivity.

[1] *Goethe* 'On Morphology' (1817), vol. I, pp. X–XI. 'The more imperfect the creature, the more similarity there is between its parts, and the more they resemble the whole. The more perfect the creature, the more dissimilar its parts become. In the first case the whole is more or less the equivalent of the parts, while in the second case the whole is not the equivalent of the parts. The more the parts resemble one another, the less they are subordinate to one another. The subordination of the parts is indication of a more perfect creature.'

Note by Michelet.

The plant assimilates the other being into itself as it grows, but as self-multiplication, this assimilation is also a self-emergence. It is not the individual coming to itself, it is a *multiplication of individuality*, in which the single individuality is merely the superficial unity of the many. The
5 singularities remain a mutually indifferent and separated plurality; the substance from which they proceed is not a common essence. This is why *Schultz*, in his 'The nature of the living plant' vol. I p. 617, says that 'the growth of plants is an incessant *formation* of new and *additional*
+ parts which were not previously present.' Consequently, as the parts
10 of the plant do not relate themselves to one another as inner qualitative differentiations, their *homogeneity* entails their *falling asunder*. In other words, this organism is not systematized into *viscera*. Although it produces itself in externality, it still grows entirely out of itself, and is not a sort of external crystalline accretion.

§ 344

15 It is in this way that the process of formation, and of the reproduction of the *single* individual, coincides with the process of the genus, **and is a perennial production of new individuals.** The individualized universality of the subjective unit of individuality does not separate itself from the real
20 nature of particularization, but is merely submerged within it. **As the plant is not yet a self-subsistent subjectivity distinct from its** *implicit* **organism** (§ 342), **it is unable to determine its place freely and** so move from its site. **What is more, it is not self-subsistent in the face of the physical particularization and**
25 **individualization of its implicit organism, so that** its nutrition is a continuous flow, not an intermittent intussusception, **and** it relates itself to the universal elements, not to individualized inorganic being. It is **even less** capable of animal warmth and sensibility, **for its members are themselves**
30 **individuals, and tend to be mere parts, and it is not the process which leads them back into a simple negative unity.**

Addition. All organic being differentiates itself within itself, and maintains the unity of multiplicity. Animal life is the truth of organic being however, and as such advances to a higher determinate difference, of
35 which the difference pervaded by substantial form is merely one aspect, the other being the self-subsistent substantial form, which is distinguished

from this submergence. Consequently, the animal feels. The plant has
not yet advanced to this internal difference however; if it had, the unifying point of selfhood and the organic crystal would already constitute
the two aspects of its life. The vital principle of the animal is its soul, but
the vital principle of the plant is still submerged in a process of mutual 5
externality. In the animal on the contrary, there is one animation, and it +
is present in a dual manner (a) as an indwelling vitalization, and (b) as the
incomposite existence of the unity of selfhood. It is true that both moments, as well as their relation, also have to be present in the plant; one
part of this difference falls outside its existence however, while animal 10
being has *sentience*, which is the absolute return of living being into
itself. A plant existence on the contrary, is merely the one bodily organism, within which the pure unity of self-identity is still not of a real
nature, but because it has not yet become objective, is only present in
the Notion. Consequently, the articulated body of the plant is not yet 15
the objectivity of the soul; the plant is *not yet objective to itself*. The unity
here is therefore external to the plant, and resembles the process of the
terrestrial organism, which falls outside the Earth. Light is the external
physical self of the plant, towards which it strives in the same way as the
lonely person seeks company. The plant has an essential and infinite re- +
lationship with light, but like weighted matter, it is primarily searching
for its self. This simple selfhood, which is external to the plant, has
supreme power over it, and *Schelling* says therefore, that if the plant were
conscious, it would venerate light as its god. The process of self-preserva- +
tion is the winning of self, self-satisfaction, the attainment of sentience. 25
The plant's self is external to it however, so that it tends rather to be
drawn out of itself as it strives towards it. Consequently, its return into
itself is a perpetual egression, and vice versa. The plant multiplies itself
in order to preserve itself (§ 343). The externality of the subjective
and identified unity of the plant is objective in its relationship to light, 30
as is the external appearance of light in gelatinous marine formations
(see § 341 Add. III. 36,27), and in the colours of tropical birds (see Add. to
§ 303 II. 83,23). The power of light is even apparent in animal being therefore. The formation of man's self is more internal than this, although
southern man also fails to guarantee his individuality or freedom objec- 35
tively. It is primarily their sap, and in general a vigorous individualiza- +
tion, that plants receive from light. Without light plants certainly become larger, but they remain tasteless, colourless, and odourless. That
is why they turn towards the light. Potato plants which sprout in the
darker parts of a cellar will creep several yards across the floor towards 40

a chink of light on the other side of it, and in order to reach the opening
where they can enjoy the light, they will climb up the wall as if they knew
+ the way. Sunflowers and a host of other flowers face the sun, and turn as
it moves across the sky. If we approach a field full of flowers in the evening
5 and come upon it from the east, we shall see few or none of the flowers,
for they will all be facing the sun. If we come upon the field from the
west however, we shall see a fine display. We shall also fail to see the
flowers if we approach the field from the east early in the morning, for
it is only through the action of the sun that they face the east. 'Some
+ flowers,' says *Willdenow*[1], 'like the Portulaca oleracea and the Drosera
rotundifolia, do not open to the sun until noon. Others only open at
night . . .' such as the magnificent Torch-thistle (Cactus grandiflorus),
+ which only blooms for a few hours.

(*a*) We have noticed that the subjective unit of the plant now coincides
15 completely with its quality and particularization, so that the plant's
negative selfhood is not yet self-relating. Consequently, this self also
continues to fall short of the existence of the purely non-sensuous being
we call soul; it is still sensuous, no longer as a sensuous material plurality
it is true, but as a sensuous unity of material beings. The sensuous element
20 now remaining for this unity is space. Consequently, as the plant cannot
yet completely nullify that which is sensuous, in itself it is not yet pure
+ time. It therefore occupies a determinate place, which it is unable to
annul, although it unfolds itself within it. It is as process however that the
animal relates itself to place and nullifies it, although it then also posits it
25 anew. This is precisely the way in which the ego wills a change of place,
by moving itself as a point, and so changing its immediate sensuous
subsistence as point. Here the ego, as the ideality of the unit, wills its
distinctness from its sensuous unity. The motion of the heavenly bodies
constitutes a single system, but although the bodies also have an un-
30 doubtedly free motion, this is not contingent. The bodies do not posit
their place as particulars, for this place is posited by the time of the system,
which is rooted in the sun through law. In magnetism also, it is the opposed
qualities which constitute the determining principle. In the subjective
living being which is its own time however, there is a positing of the
35 negation of place in an absolutely indifferent manner, or as inner indifference. The plant has not yet mastered the indifferent and mutually
external subsistence of space however, so that its space is still abstract.
The movement of pistils and anthers towards each other, and the

---

[1] 'Outlines of Botany' ed. *Link* (6th edition 1821), p. 473.

oscillations of Conferva etc., have to be regarded merely as a simple growth, and as lacking any arbitrary determination of place. Plant movement is determined by light, heat, and air. *Treviranus*[1] illustrates this from the Hedysarum girans, 'At the end of each stem this plant has a larger leaf, + the shape of which is elliptical and lanceolate, and on either side of it, 5 attached to the same main stem, are two smaller petiolate stipules. The movement of the main stems and leaves consists of their rising in the light and drooping in the dark. This movement takes place in the joints, by means of which the leaf is joined to the stem, and the stem to the branch. Even the reflection of the sun from a wall twenty paces away brought 10 about a distinct erection of the leaves, while the screening of the sunlight by an opaque body or by a passing cloud, caused them to droop. *Hufeland* + noticed that a full noontide sun, as well as the concentration of sunlight through a burning glass, gave rise to a quivering movement in the main leaves, and in the plant as a whole. Moonlight and artificial light had no 15 influence on this movement. The second movement, which is confined to the tiny lateral leaves, consists of the alternate erection and drooping of each of these pairs of leaflets ranged on either side of the same twig. This movement only ceases with the death of the plant; there are no immediate external causes of it, although it is most marked at the time of fertiliza- 20 tion.' Nevertheless, *Treviranus* attributes a spontaneous movement to the zoospores of Conferva, even after they have escaped from these plants.[2] + The movement of Conferva is said to be partly oscillatory, 'The separate cilia lashed their unattached ends from right to left and from left to right; they often rotated, so that these ends seemed to describe a circle.' Move- 25 ment of this kind is still not a voluntary movement however.

(*b*) If the plant broke off its relation to that external to it, it would exist as a subjective being, and so establish its self-relatedness. Consequently, the precise reason for the plant's intussusception being continuous, is that the plant does not have the nature of true subjectivity; its individuality is 30 perpetually falling apart into its particularity, and is therefore unable to hold on to itself as an infinite being-for-self. Only the self as self excludes externality, and it is precisely as a self-relatedness that it constitutes the soul of this relation. In the self-relatedness, the self forms both sides of this relationship, which is therefore an internal circuit of the soul, keeping 35 itself aloof from inorganic nature. As the plant has not yet attained to this selfhood however, it lacks the inwardness which would be free of external

---

[1] 'Biology, or Philosophy of Living Nature' vol. V, pp. 202–203.
[2] *Treviranus*, loc. cit. vol. II, pp. 381 et seq., 507; vol. III, p. 281 et seq.

relatedness. Thus air and water are perpetually acting upon the plant; the plant does not sip water. At night, or during the winter, the action of light is of course interrupted or weakened externally, but this is a difference which is external to the plant, and is not part of the plant itself. Conse-
5 quently, it is possible gradually to change the plant's activities by placing it in a lighted room at night, and in a darkened room during the day. It was in this way that *de Candolle* changed the dormant periods of Mimosas
+ and various other plants in a matter of a few nights. He did it by keeping lamps burning. The rest of plant behaviour depends upon the seasons and
10 the climate; northern plants, which are dormant during the winter, gradually change this characteristic in southern regions. Similarly, the plant does not yet relate itself to individual being, and this is also because it is not the self-relatedness of a self. Its other is not an individual therefore, but elemental inorganic being.

15 (c) Many investigations have been made into the thermic qualities of plants and a great deal of controversy has developed. *Hermbstädt* in par-
+ ticular has devoted much attention to this subject.[1] It has indeed been claimed, that a slightly higher specific temperature has been detected in plants than in their environment, but this is not conclusive. Heat is a
20 conflict of altered cohesion; plants do not exhibit this change in cohesion however, and are devoid of the ignition of internal fire which constitutes animal life. It is certainly true that a thermometer placed in a hole bored through a tree has indicated a significant difference between the tempera-
+ ture outside and that inside. Temperatures of $-5°R$. outside and $+2°$ in-
25 side, and $-10°$ outside and $+1°$ inside etc., have been recorded. These differences are however the result of wood being a bad conductor of heat, and of the trunk receiving heat from the ground. *Treviranus* says more-over (loc. cit. vol. V, p. 16), that there are, 'more than 4,600 experiments by *Fontana*, which show that plant temperature is entirely dependent
+ upon the temperature of the medium in which the plants are situated.' *Treviranus* continues (p. 19), 'There certainly are plant genera capable of bringing forth heat and cold in certain circumstances, and therefore of *withstanding* the influence of the outside temperature. It has often been observed that there was an increase in heat on the surface of the
35 spike (spadix) of the Arum maculatum, and other species, over a period of four to five hours, during the time at which it was beginning to
+ break out of its spathe. In the case of the Arum maculatum, this took place between three and four o'clock in the afternoon, and the heat

---

[1] Cf. *Treviranus*, loc. cit. vol. V, p. 4 et seq. *Willdenow*, loc. cit. pp. 422–428.

decreased again over the same period of time. The maximum temperature of the Arum maculatum exceeded that of the air outside by 15–16°F., and that of the Arum cordifolium by 60–70°F.[1] The *Ice* +
plant (Mesembryanthemum crystallinum) develops cold, undoubtedly from its saltpetre content. In the first instance, the heat probably has as 5
little to do with protecting the plant from cold during its period of fertilization, as the cold has to do with protecting the plant from heat in the second instance.' The plant is none the less devoid of this internal process +
therefore, for as it sprouts forth, it merely rigidifies. The animal is the fluid magnet however, and its different parts pass over into one another and 10
so develop heat, the precise principle of which resides solely in the blood. +

(*d*) The plant's lack of sensibility may also be attributed to the coincidence between its subjective unity and its quality and particularization; unlike that of the animal, its being-within-self is not yet a nervous system which is independent of external being. Only that which has the faculty 15
of sense can endure itself as other, assimilate this opposition by the resilience of its individuality, and venture into conflict with other individualities. The plant is the immediate organic individuality, in which the genus preponderates, and reflection is not individual. The individual plant does not return into itself as such, it is an other, and it therefore lacks *sentience*. The 20
sensitivity of certain plants is merely a mechanical elasticity. It is not an example of sentience, and resembles the dormant state of plants, in which the relationship to light is the active principle. *Treviranus* touches upon this point (loc. cit. vol. V, pp. 206–208), 'There has been a tendency to regard stimulation by external and purely local agents, and the move- 25
ments which this brings about, as feeling; and of course, the resemblance of these movements to the contractions of muscle-fibres is unmistakeable,'
—but this can also take place without the faculty of sense. 'This kind of stimulation is particularly evident in the organs of fertilization: the pollen is scattered from the anthers when the stamens are touched, and mechani- 30
cal stimuli give rise to movements of pistils and stamens, particularly that of the filaments towards the pistil when the former are touched.' *Treviranus* (ibidem p. 210) cites the observation of *Medicus* as particular proof that the cause of this stimulation is external, 'A number of plants in the colder +
regions give absolutely no evidence of stimulation in the afternoon, and 35
when the weather is hot and dry, while in the morning, after a heavy dew,

---

[1] *Link* 'Principles of the Anatomy and Physiology of plants' (Göttingen, 1807) p. 229 observes that, 'The flower has a very offensive smell; in my opinion, the sole cause of the generation of heat is the release and decomposition in the air of the oil or carburetted hydrogen which produces the stench.'

and for the whole of the day if there is gentle rain, they are very susceptible to it. In warmer climates, the stimulation of plants is only evident
when the sky is bright. The precise state in which all plants are most susceptible to it, is when the pollen ripens and the pistil covers itself with a
5 lustrous oil. 'Various species of Mimosa, and other plants also belonging to
the leguminous family, provide the best known examples of leaf-stimula-
tion.' The Dionea muscipula has a large number of leaves arranged in a
circle around the stem, and the leaves of the Oxalis sensitiva consist of
twelve pairs of oval-shaped leaflets. When these plants are touched, they
10 close up their leaves. The leaves of the Averrhoa Carambola are pinnate,
+ and droop when one touches their stalk.'[1] The anatomical observations
+ of *Rudolphi* and *Link* confirm this. *Rudolphi* ('Anatomy of Plants' p. 239)
says, 'In these plants there is a peculiar articulation of the petiole and of the
partial petioles. The leaves are contracted at the base, while other pinnate
15 leaves are wider at the base, or at least not narrower. In these plants moreover, the petiole is much thicker immediately above the joint than it is
elsewhere, so that the contracted joint is even more evident. Incidentally,
this thickening consists solely of cellular tissue, which usually lignifies at
an early stage. When *Cassia* and *Lupins* etc. are cut, everything soon closes
20 up, as it does when the plants are dormant, and the parts do not open
again. Fresh Mimosa will droop at the slightest touch. If it is picked up
quickly again when it is diseased or exhausted, it cannot be stimulated for
a long time, and it will also take some time before it raises its drooping
parts. *Mirbel* tells us of the Mimosa which *Desfontaines* took with him on a
25 journey. At the first jolt of the carriage it closed all its leaves, but later on
they gradually opened again, and stayed open for the rest of the journey,
+ almost as if they had got used to the swaying of the vehicle.' *Link* says
(loc. cit. p. 258), 'In the wind, the leaves close, but they open up again in
spite of it, and finally become so used to it, that it ceases to have any effect
30 upon them.' In the 'Supplements to the Principles' (I p. 26) he says that,
'The stimulation is confined solely to the area of shock. A leaflet can be
subjected to very violent actions without the leaves nearby being affected.
Each stimulus seems to be confined to, and to affect, only the place where
it is produced.' Here, then we undoubtedly have nothing but the simple
35 phenomenon of contraction and dilation. It displays itself here more
rapidly and more suddenly than in the slower operation of the change in
activities mentioned above (*b*).

---

[1] *Treviranus*, loc. cit. vol. V, pp. 217–219.

§ 345

As the plant is organic being however, its articulation is also essentially differentiated into abstract formations such as cells, fibres and the like, and into more concrete formations, which however retain their original homogeneity. As the shape of the plant is not a subjectivity liberated from individuality, it is still closely 5 related to geometrical forms and crystalline regularity, and the products of its process are even more closely related to those of the chemical process.

Remark

Goethe's 'Metamorphosis of Plants' marks the beginning + of a rational conception of the nature of the plant, for it has 10 forced attention away from a concern with mere details, to a recognition of the unity of a plant-life. In the category of metamorphosis, it is the identity of the organs which predominates. The other necessary aspect of this substantial unity is however the determinate differentiation and the special function of the mem- 15 bers, by which the life-process is posited. The physiology of the plant is necessarily more obscure than that of the animal body, because it is simpler, its assimilation passes through fewer intermediaries, and change occurs as immediate infection. As in every natural and spiritual life-process, the crux of the matter in 20 both assimilation and secretion, is the substantial change, i.e. the general immediate transformation of one external or particular material into another. A point occurs at which the tracing of this mediation as either a chemical or mechanical series of gradations breaks down and becomes impossible. This point is + omnipresent and pervasive, and it is ignorance of this simple identification and of this simple diremption, or rather the failure to acknowledge them, which makes a physiology of living being an impossibility. Interesting particulars concerning the physiology of the plant are given in the work of my colleague Prof. C. H. 30 Schultz ('The Nature of the Living Plant, or Plants and the Vegetable Kingdom' 2 vols.). I mention this work in particular, because some of the special characteristics of the life-process of the plant mentioned in the following paragraphs are taken from it.

Addition. The plant's objectivization is entirely formal, it is not true objectivity. The plant not only develops outwards generally, but the preservation of its self as an individual is only accomplished through the perennial positing of a fresh individual.

5 (*a*) It is simply the presence of a *point* (utricle), a germ, grain, node, or whatever one may call it, which constitutes the *type* of the whole plant. This point puts out threads, forms itself into a *line* (you can call this
+ magnetism if you like, but it lacks polar opposition); and this linear extension checks itself once more, to constitute a fresh grain, a fresh node.
10 These nodes are continually developing further through self-repulsion, for the plant splits up within a thread into a multitude of germs, each of which is a whole plant. It is in this way that members are produced, each of which is the whole. It makes no great difference whether these nodulations keep together within a single individual, or whether they fall apart into
15 several individuals. This reproduction is not mediated by opposition therefore, it is not a unified emergence, although the plant can also rise to this. The emergence of true separation in the opposition of the sex-relationship belongs to the power of the animal however. We shall speak later of the merely superficial form of it found in the plant. *Conferva*
20 provide the simplest and most immediate example of this plant type, for they consist of nothing but these green threads, and are devoid of all further formation. They constitute the primary rudiments of aquatic vegetation. *Treviranus* describes them thus (loc. cit. vol. III, pp. 278–283), 'The fresh water Conferva (Conferva fontinalis L.) propagate themselves
25 by means of an oval plumule. The apicula of the delicate thread of which this plant consists, swells into a plumule, which after some time separates itself from the thread and establishes itself nearby. It soon puts forth an apicule, which elongates itself into a complete water-thread. The propaga-
+ tion of all the species classified by *Roth* under the genus Ceramium, takes
30 place in approximately the same simple way. At various times, but mainly in the spring, they form bacciform bodies on the surface of their stem or branches. These bodies usually contain one or two smaller grains, and when they are fully ripe they either fall off or open, and discharge their seed. In Conferva proper (Conferva R.), in the Water-net (Hydrodictyon
35 R.) 'in Rivularia and many Tremella, the reproductive organs,' (?), 'of which there are two kinds, are situated in the substance of the plant. They consist either of small grains, which are arranged regularly in rows, and which are already present in the initial formation of the plant, or they occur as larger ovular bodies, which have the same diameter as the inner
40 tube of the Conferva, and only form at a certain period in the life of these

Phytozoa. In some Conferva the grains are arranged in a zig-zag or a spiral, in others they occur in star-shaped figurations, right-angled parallelograms, etc. They may also be arranged in the shape of a branch, the branches forming a whorl about a common stem. They flow out and are the beginnings of new Conferva. Very different from these smaller ₅ grains is a larger variety of round '(ovular and bacciform)' body which forms in some articulated Conferva (Conferva setiformis, spiralis, and bipunctata R.), and only at a certain period of their life (in May, June, and July). At this time the smaller primordial grains leave their regular position, and unite to form larger oval or spherical bodies. As these bodies are formed, ₁₀ the Conferva loses its green colour, and all that remains is a transparent, colourless skin, which contains a brownish fruit in each of its articulations. When this membrane has finally disintegrated, these fruits fall to the ground, and remain there until the following spring, when a Conferva of the same kind as before develops from each of them in a way which ₁₅ seems to bear more resemblance to an animal coming out of its shell, than to germination in grains of seed.' In the same work (p. 314 et seq.), *Treviranus* credits Conferva with a kind of *copulation* and coupling.   +

(*b*) In higher plant-forms, and particularly in shrubs, immediate growth occurs at once as a division into *twigs* and *branches*. In the plant we dis- ₂₀ tinguish between roots, stem, branches and leaves. Nothing is more generally realized however, than that each branch and each twig constitutes a complete plant, which has its root in the plant as it does in the soil, and that when a branch or twig is broken off and layered, it puts forth roots and constitutes a whole plant. This also happens when individualized ₂₅ parts of a plant are accidentally severed from it. *Treviranus* says (loc. cit. vol. III p. 365), 'The propagation of plants by division never occurs spontaneously in the parts, but always artificially, or by chance. The ability to propagate itself in this way is possessed to a remarkable degree by the Tillandsia usneoides, a parasitic plant of the Bromeliaceae family. If any + part of this plant is torn off by the wind and caught up in the branches of a tree, it takes root at once, and grows just as well as if it had sprung from seed.' It is well known that strawberries and a number of other plants put out *stolons*, i.e. runners, which grow from the root. These filaments or petioles form nodes (why not 'spontaneously in the parts?'). If these ₃₅ points touch the earth, they also strike root, and bring forth other plants. *Willdenow* (loc. cit., p. 397) mentions that, 'The *Mangrove* (Rhizophora mangle) bends its branches down to the earth perpendicularly, and turns them into trunks. In the tropical parts of Asia, Africa, and America therefore, the watersides are often covered for a mile or more ₄₀ with the multitudinous trunks of a single tree, the top of which forms a dense coverage, closely resembling clipped foliage.'

(c) The branches grow from *buds* (gemmulae). *Willdenow* (loc. cit., p. 393) quotes *Aubert du Petit Thouars*, 'Vessels elongate themselves from each bud, and pass down through the plant; strictly speaking, the wood is therefore a product of the root fibres of all the buds, and the ligneous plant is an aggregate of a number of growths.' *Willdenow* then continues, 'If a grafted tree is opened up at the side of the graft, it will also be quite apparent, that fibres from a graft run for a short distance into the main stem. *Link* has noticed this, as I have.' On pages 486–487 he has more to say about this *bud grafting*. 'We know that a bud from a shrub or a tree will grow when it is grafted on to another stem, and that it is to be regarded as a distinct plant. There is no change at all in its nature, as it continues to grow as if it were situated in the earth. *Agricola* and *Barnes* were even more fortunate with this kind of propagation; they simply set the buds straight in the earth, and raised perfect plants from them. A noteworthy feature of this kind of artificial propagation is that if the branches or eyes (gemmae) are made into fresh plants by setting, grafting or bud grafting, or in any other way, the plant from which they were taken reproduces itself not (only), as a species, but also as a subvariety. The seed only reproduces the species, which can grow forth from it as a subvariety in sundry variants. Consequently, while grafting and bud grafting will produce no modification in the Borsdorfer apple, quite distinct subvarieties are to be obtained from its seed.' These buds retain their individuality to such a degree when they form the branch of another tree, that a dozen varieties of pear may be grown on a single tree for example.

The *bulbs* of monocotyledons are also buds of this kind, and propagate themselves by division. *Treviranus* says (loc. cit., vol. III, pp. 363–334), 'Bulbs are peculiar to monocotyledons. In some plants they grow on the upper part of the root, in others, such as the Lilium bulbiferum and the Fritillaria regia, in the axil between the stem and the petiole. They also grow in the flowers, as in several species of Allium. Those plants whose roots bear bulbs' (i.e. simply divide themselves), 'usually produce infertile seeds. These seeds may become fertile however if the brood bulb is destroyed as soon as it appears. Each leaf of the Fritillaria regia is capable of producing bulbs, even when detached from the stem. When a leaf is cut from this plant close to the bulb in autumn, gently pressed between blotting paper, and kept in a warm place, it sprouts fresh bulbs at its lowest extremity, where it was joined to the root. The extent to which this development takes place is directly related to the gradual withering away of the leaf. In many of the plants whose bulbs occur in the axils of the leaves or on the stems, the bulbs occasionally detach themselves of their own accord from the parent stem, and once they are separated from it, put forth roots and leaves. It is this in particular which deserves to be called viviparous germination. In the Lilium bulbiferum, Poa bulbosa, and several species of Allium, this phenomenon occurs without artificial aid. In the Tulipa gesneriana, Eucomis punctata, and a number of other succulent monocotyledons, it can be brought about artificially if the flowers are removed from these plants before fertilization, and the stem with the leaves on it is set in a shady spot.' *Willdenow* (loc. cit. p. 487) actually says that, 'Pothos and Plumiera may even be propagated from leaves;' to which *Link* adds, 'This property is particularly remarkable in the Bryophyllum calycinum.' If a leaf from this plant is placed horizontally on the ground, it puts out fibres and rootlets all round its margin. *Link* says ('Principles' p. 181), 'We therefore have examples of rooting gemmae which grew from the petiole. *Mandirola* was the first to propagate trees artificially from leaves. It is possible for a gemma to grow from any part, so long as it contains spiral elements and cellular tissue.' In short any part of the plant can exist immediately as the complete individual; this is never the case with animals, apart from polyps and other completely rudimentary animal species. Strictly speaking therefore, a plant is an aggregate of a number of individuals constituting a single individual, the parts of which are however completely independent. It is this independence of its parts which constitutes the *impotence* of the plant. The animal on the contrary has viscera, dependent members, the whole existence of which is dependent solely upon the unity of the whole. If the viscera are injured (that is, the vital internal parts), then the life of the individual is destroyed. The animal organism can also have members removed of course, but the plant consists of nothing but these removable members.

Goethe's great sense of nature has therefore led him to define the growth of plants as a metamorphosis of one and the same formation. He published his 'Metamorphosis of Plants' in 1790, but botanists have treated it with indifference, and precisely because it presents a whole, have not known what to make of it.[1] Although the plant disembodies into several individuals, it is at the same time a complete shape; it is an organic totality, the completeness of which includes its root, stem, branches, leaves, blossom, fruit. The totality also posits differentiation within itself of course, and we shall develop this presently. *Goethe* sets out to show however, that in all these different parts of the plant there is a

[1] *Goethe* 'On Morphology' vol. I (1817): 'The Metamorphosis of Plants' pp. 66, 70, 126.

simple basic life which is self-contained and enduring, and that all its forms are nothing more than the exterior transformations of the identity of one and the same primary essence; also that this is not only so in the Idea, but in existence too, so that each member can pass over very easily into the
5 other. This is spiritual, a fleeting breath of forms, which does not attain to qualitative and fundamental difference, but is merely a metamorphosis of an ideal nature within the material being of the plant. In their existence, the parts are intrinsically the same, and Goethe[1] grasps the difference
+ between them merely as an *expansion* or *contraction*. Cases are on record
10 for example, in which trees have been planted upside down, their roots in the air and their branches and twigs in the ground, with the result that the former have sprouted into leaves, buds and blossoms etc., while the latter have become roots. In double flowers, in roses for example, extra nutrition has merely transformed the filaments (dust-fibres), anthers
15 (dust-pouches), and in the Wild Rose the pistil (style) too, into petals, which are either changed completely, or still show traces of their original form. Many of these petals still retain the nature of the filament, so that they are petal on one side and filament on the other, for filaments are simply nothing but contracted leaves. There are Tulips which are called
20 monstrosities, for they have petals and cauline leaves. Petals themselves are nothing but the attenuated leaves of the plant. The pistil too is merely a contracted leaf. Pollen (seed-dust), which on Rose-bushes is a yellow powder for example, also partakes of the nature of the leaf. The capsule and the fruit also participate fully in the nature of the leaf, and sometimes
25 leaves can still be seen on the back of the fruit. The stone of the fruit also exhibits the nature of the leaf. The *thorn* of wild plants becomes a leaf in their improved counterparts; in poor soils, Apple, Pear, and Lemon trees have thorns, which disappear and change into leaves when the trees are
+ cultivated.[2]
30   It is in this way that the whole production of the plant displays the same uniformity and simple development, and this *unity of form* is the *leaf*.[3] Consequently, one form can easily be acquired by another. Even the seed has the implicit character of a kind of leaf, for its *cotyledons* or *seed-lobelets* are merely unelaborated leaves consisting of a cruder material. The tran-
35 sition here is to the *stem*, from which leaves sprout forth. These leaves are often pinnate, and so approximate to flowers. When this has continued as a prolongation for some time (as it has in Conferva), the cauline-leaves

---

[1] 'On Morphology' p. 58.
[2] Cf. *Willdenow*, loc. cit. p. 293.
[3] *Goethe* 'On Morphology' pp. 59, 83–85.

develop nodes. Leaves develop from these *nodes*; lower down a stem they have a simple form, higher up they are incised, distinct, and divided. In those lower down the stem, the periphery or margin is still unformed.[1] In this description which he gives of an *annual plant*, Goethe therefore continues as follows, 'Yet the further formation of the plant spreads continuously from node to node by means of the leaf. In appearance, the leaves are now more jagged, deeply incised, composed of several leaflets; in the latter instance they present us with complete branches in miniature. The Date-palm provides us with a striking example of such a successive and extreme diversification of the most simple leaf-shape. The midrib moves forward in a series of several leaves; the simple flabelliform leaf is torn and divided, and a highly compound leaf is developed which closely resembles a branch.' (*Goethe* loc. cit. p. 11). The leaves are now more finely elaborated than the cotyledons, for they draw their sap from the stem, which already has an organization (ibidem p. 12).

With regard to the difference between the species, I should like to draw attention to the important fact that the course of leaf-development which displays itself in one species, is also the principal determinant in the different species themselves. Consequently, the leaves of all the species taken together exhibit the complete development of a leaf. This can be seen in a series of *Pelargoniums* for example, in which the leaves which are at first very different, subsequently pass into one another by transitions. 'It is well known that botanists find a great deal of the specific difference between plants in the formation of their leaves. On examining the leaves of the Sorbus hybrida, one discovers that some of them are still almost completely anastomosed; it is only the somewhat deeper incisions of the dentate margin, between the lateral costae, which indicate that nature is here striving towards a more marked separation. In other leaves, these incisions become deeper, mainly at the base and on the lower half of the leaf. It is quite evident that each lateral costa is meant to become the midrib of a separate leaflet. In other leaves, the lowest lateral costae are already separated into distinct leaflets. The lateral costae which follow have already developed the deepest incisions; it is clear that a freer impulse towards ramification would have overcome the *anastomosis*. This is accomplished in other leaves, in which two, three, or four pairs of lateral costae are detached from below upwards, and the original midrib pushes the leaflets apart by growing more rapidly. Consequently, this leaf is half pinnate, and still semi-anastomosed. The predominance of breaking apart

[1] Cf. *Goethe* loc. cit. pp. 7–10.

into ramification, or of anastomosis, changes in accordance with the age of the tree and its condition, and even in accordance with the nature of the year. I have in my possession leaves which are almost entirely pinnate. If we now consider the Sorbus aucuparia, it becomes evident that this species
5 is only a continuation of the evolutionary history of the Sorbus hybrida, and that these two species are only distinguished from one another by the
+ fact that the Sorbus hybrida has a disposition towards a greater compactness of tissue, while the Sorbus aucuparia attempts to reproduce itself
+ more easily.'[1]

+ Goethe then passes from the leaves to the calyx (loc. cit. pp. 15-20), 'Sometimes we see the transition to inflorescence take place more slowly, and sometimes more rapidly. In the latter case, we usually observe that the cauline leaves begin to contract again from their periphery, and in particular, to lose their various peripheral divisions, while in their lower parts,
15 where these leaves are joined to the stem, there is a varying measure of expansion. At the same time, if we look at the stem, we shall see that even where the distances between the nodes are not perceptibly increased, the stem does at least assume a finer and slenderer shape than before. From this it has been concluded that excessive nutrition hinders the inflorescence of
20 a plant. We often see this transformation occur rapidly, and in this case the stem above the node of the last-formed leaf is suddenly lengthened and tapered as it shoots up. The calyx occurs at its extremity as a number of leaves grouped about an axis. The leaves of the calyx are the same organs as the cauline leaves, but they are now grouped about a common centre.
25 What is more, in many flowers we see unaltered cauline leaves drawn together, immediately under the corolla, into a kind of calyx. As they still retain their complete leaf-form, we have only to appeal to the evidence of our eyes, and to that of botanic terminology which designates them by
+ the name of "floral leaves" (folia floralia). The cauline leaves transform
30 themselves where they gradually contract, and so grade imperceptibly into the calyx as it were. These leaves are made even more unrecognizable by their joining up, and by their growing together at the sides. The leaves which are thus pushed and crowded together so closely, present us with the bell-shaped or so-called monophyllous calyces, which are more or less
35 incised from the top inwards. Nature forms the calyx therefore, by joining a number of leaves around a single centre, and consequently a number of nodes also, which she would otherwise have produced at separate times, and at some distance from one another. In the calyx therefore, nature does

[1] Schelver's 'Critique of the doctrine of sex in plants.' First continuation (1814), pp. 38-40.

not produce a new organ.' The calyx is merely a point, and that which was formerly disposed throughout the whole stem is gathered around it.

The *flower* itself is merely a duplication of the calyx, for the petals and sepals are very similar. Here too, in the 'transition of the calyx to the crown' (corolla), *Goethe* does not indicate any antithesis. 'Although the colour of the calyx usually remains green, and similar to the colour of the cauline leaves, it frequently changes in one or the other of its parts, at the apices, the margins, on the dorsal, or even on its inner side, while its outer side still remains green. We shall always find that this colouring is associated with a refinement of form. Consequently, ambigenous calyces occur, and may with equal correctness be regarded as corollas. The corolla is frequently produced by an *expansion*. The petals of a plant are usually larger than its sepals, and it is noticeable that the organs which were contracted in the calyx, now expand again as petals into a higher degree of refinement. Their delicate texture, their colour and their smell, would quite disguise their origin from us, if we could not watch nature at work in a number of unusual instances. In the calyx of a Carnation for example, there is often a second calyx, which is partly quite green, and displays the primordium of a monophyllous and incised calyx; it is partly lacinated, and transformed at its apices and on its margins into the actual beginnings of petals, which are delicate, expanded, and coloured. In a number of plants the cauline leaves are more or less coloured long before inflorescence, while others become completely coloured as inflorescence approaches. An almost completely developed and coloured petal also appears frequently on tulip-stems; there is an even more remarkable phenomenon, in which one half of a leaf of this kind is green because it belongs to the stem and remains firmly attached to it, while the other half is coloured and taken up into the corolla, so that the leaf is torn into two parts.[1] The conjecture that the colour and smell of the petals derive from the presence of the male seed is probably correct. It is probably present in them in an insufficiently isolated form, mixed and diluted rather with other saps. We are of the opinion, that the matter which fills the petals does not possess the highest degree of purity, although it is certainly very pure, for the highest purity would appear to be white and colourless, and not exhibit the beautiful phenomenon of colours.' (*Goethe* loc. cit. pp. 21–23).

Fructification is the highest development of light within the plant; here also *Goethe* points out, 'the close affinity between the petals and the *organs of pollination*.' 'This transition often occurs regularly, as for example

---

[1] This is the case with the monstrosities previously referred to.

in the *Canna*. A true petal, slightly modified, contracts its upper margin;
an *anther* appears, for which the rest of the petal functions as a *filament*. In
flowers which are often double, we are able to observe this transition in
all its stages. There are several varieties of Roses within whose fully formed
5 and coloured petals, other petals can be seen, which are sometimes contracted in the middle, and sometimes at the side. This contraction is
brought about by a tiny callosity which shows itself as a more or less
complete anther. In some double Poppies, fully-formed anthers are borne
on slightly modified petals of heavily doubled corollas. The organs which
10 are called *nectaries*,' (paracorolla is a better term), 'are petals approximating
to stamens. Various petals have small pits or *glands* which secrete a honey-
like sap, which is a still unelaborated fertilizing fluid. At this juncture
there is a complete absence of all the factors which have caused the broad-
ening out of the cauline leaves, sepals, and petals, and a feeble and ex-
15 tremely simple filament develops. It is precisely those vessels which
otherwise elongated and broadened themselves, and sought for one
another, that are now present in an extremely contracted condition.' Thus
the pollen acts all the more powerfully exteriorly, on the pistil. *Goethe*
also traces the pistil back to the same type, 'In many cases the *style* closely
20 resembles a filament without anthers. If this examination has made it
clearly evident that there is a close affinity between the female and male
parts, we are quite prepared to say that the coupling is a spiritual anastomosis, and at least to flatter ourselves for a moment, that we have brought
the concepts of growth and generation closer together. We often find that
25 the style has grown together out of several separate pistils. In the pistil of
the *Iris*, together with its *stigma*, we can see the complete form of a petal.
It is certainly not so strikingly obvious that the umbelliform stigma of the
Sarracenia is composed of several leaves, although its greenness is evidence
+ of this' (*Goethe*, loc. cit. pp. 23–26; 30–34). A physiologist says of the
30 anthers, 'The margins of the sepalulii curled inwards as the anthers
formed, so that at first a hollow cylinder developed, at the tip of which
there was a fascicle of tiny hairs. Later, when the anthers became fuller
and more perfect, these hairs fell away. A similar transformation was
apparent in the style (stilus), where one, and often several sepals curled in-
35 wards from the margin to form an incurvation (arcuarentur). A simple cavity
developed first from this, and then the ovary. The fascicle of hairs situated
at the summit of the cavity did not wither as did those on the anthers,
+ but on the contrary, assumed the nature of a perfect hilum (stigma).'[1]

---

[1] Herm. Frider. Autenrieth, 'De Discrimine sexuali' etc. (Tübing. 1821 pp. 29–30).

The *fruit* and the *capsule* can also be shown to be transformations of the leaf, 'Here we are speaking specifically of those capsules which contain the so-called angiosperms. In Carnations, the *seed-capsules* have often changed back into calyx-like leaves, and there are in fact Carnations in which the conceptacle has changed into a genuine and perfected calyx. In ₅ these instances, the apical incisions of the calyx still bear faint traces of the styles and stigmas, and instead of seeds, a more or less complete corolla develops from the interior of this second calyx. What is more, nature has herself revealed the leaf's hidden fertility to us in extremely diverse ways, by means of regular and constantly recurrent forms. Thus, the unmis- ₁₀ takably modified, but still recognizable leaf of a Lime-tree, will produce from its midrib a petiolule bearing a perfect blossom and fruit. The immediate fertility of the cauline leaves is even more strikingly, and one may say curiously, apparent in Ferns, where it gives rise to the scattering of countless seeds which are capable of growth. We cannot fail to recognize ₁₅ the shape of the leaf in seed-vessels. The *legume* for example is a simple folded leaf; *siliquas* are formed from the superpositing of several leaves. It is most difficult to trace this resemblance to the leaf in seed-vessels which are either succulent and soft, or ligneous and firm. The relationship of the seed-capsules to the anterior parts is also apparent in the stigma, which in ₂₀ many cases is sessile, and inseparably bound up with the capsule. We have already indicated the relationship of the stigma to the shape of the leaf. It can be confirmed by observation that various seeds transform leaves into their immediate integuments. The traces of such leaf-forms, which are imperfectly adapted to the seed, may be seen on many alated seeds, such ₂₅ as those of the Maple. We have managed to keep to the line of enquiry we selected, by confining our consideration consistently and exclusively to the plant as an *annual*. However, in order to give requisite completeness to this investigation, it is now necessary to pass on to a consideration of buds. The buds needs no cotyledons. . . .' etc. (*Goethe*, loc. cit. pp. 36–40, ₃₀ 42–43). Later, we shall also have occasion to speak of the powers and functions of *perennial* plants.

These are the principal concepts of the Goethean metamorphosis of plants. *Goethe* has ingeniously represented the unity of the plant as a spiritual gradation. Metamorphosis only constitutes one side however, it ₊ does not account for the whole; the difference of formations also has to be considered, and it is here that the special process of life first makes its appearance. Two aspects of the plant have to be distinguished therefore, (*a*) this unity of its entire nature, the indifference of its members and formations to its change of form, and (*b*) the diversity of its development, the ₄₀

course of its actual life. The sexual difference which this organization has developed is merely indifferent and superfluous however, The plant's vital process is a distinct process of the whole within each of its parts; branches, twigs, and leaf all have an entire and distinct process of their own, because
5 each is also the whole individual. The *vital process* of the *plant* is therefore complete within each part, for the plant is particularized throughout, without there being as yet any primary diremption of its process into the various functions. Consequently, the process of the plant, as an immanent differentiation, appears in its beginning, as in its final product, merely
10 as formation. In this respect the plant occupies a position midway between the mineralogical crystal and the freer shape of the animal; for animal being exhibits oval and elliptical form, while crystalline being, in its straight lines, constitutes the form of the understanding. The shape of the plant is simple. The understanding is still dominant in
15 the straight line of the stem, and in the plant in general, the preponderance of the straight line is still very marked. The shape of the cells in the interior of the plant is partly alveoliform and partly elongated. Then there are the fibres, which although they certainly intertwine in spirals, subsequently straighten out again of their own accord, and do not
20 resume their rounded form. In the leaf, the surface is predominant. The various leaf-forms exhibited by plants as well as flowers are still extremely regular, and a mechanical uniformity is noticeable in their determinate incisions and acuminations. Leaves are dentate, jagged, acuminate, lanceolate, peltate, cordate, but yet their regularity is no longer abstract.
25 One side of the leaf is not the same as the other, for it is more contracted underneath, while on top it is more expanded and rounded. Globularity is finally dominant in the fruit. This is a commensurable roundness however, it is not yet the higher form of roundness exhibited by the animal.
　　Numerical determinations such as three or six, which are a characteristic
30 of the understanding, are also still dominant in plants. Six predominates in bulbs for example, and in the calyx of flowers the numbers six, three and four are dominant. Yet the number five also occurs, and in such a way that if the flower has five filaments and anthers, there are also five or ten petals present, and the calyx then also has five or ten sepals etc. *Link* says
35 ('Principles' p. 212), 'Actually, only five leaves seem to constitute the complete *whorl*. If there are six or more, it is certain that two or more concentric whorls are present. If there are four leaves in a whorl, there will be a gap for the fifth. Those leaves are indication of a less perfect form, and likewise, if there are two or only one, there will be gaps for two or a third.'
40 　　Like its shape, the plant's *saps* also vacillate between chemical and organ-

ic matter, and the plant-process itself is still intermediate between that of chemicals and that of animals. Plant products consist of acids such as citric acid, and are certainly not wholly chemical substances any longer, for although they are not yet as undifferentiated as animal being, they are already too undifferentiated to be chemical, and cannot be accounted for 5 simply by oxygenation and hydrogenation. This is even truer of animal being, of respiration for example. Chemistry is unable to deal with organic water permeated with life and individualized, for this water is a spiritual band. +

§ 346

Animation is a process, and to the same extent as it is singleness, this process has to explicate itself into the triad of processes (§ 217– 10 220).

Addition. The process of the plant falls into three syllogisms. As has already been indicated (§ 342 Add.), the *first* of these is the universal process, the process of the vegetable organism within itself, the relation of the individual to itself. In this process, which is that of formation, the 15 individual destroys itself, converts itself into its inorganic nature, and by means of this destruction, brings itself forth from itself. In the *second process*, living being does not contain its other, but faces it as an external independence; it does not constitute its own inorganic nature, but meets it as an object, which it encounters through an apparent contingency. 20 This is the process which is specified in the face of an external nature. The *third* process is that of the genus, and unites the first two. This is the process of the individuals with themselves as genus, or the production and preservation of the genus. In it, the genus is preserved by the destruction of individuals, as the production of another individual. Inorganic nature 25 consists here of the individual itself, while the nature of the individual is its genus. This genus is also distinct from the individual however, and constitutes its objective nature. In the plant, these processes coincide, and are not so distinct as they are in the animal. It is precisely this which constitutes the difficulty one encounters in expounding the nature of the 30 vegetable organism.

A

The process of formation

§ 346a

As it accords with the simple nature of vegetativeness itself, the *inner* process of the plant's relation to itself is at the same time a relation to externality, and an externalization. One side of this process is its substantiality, it is an immediate transformation,
5 partly of the nutritive influxions into the specific nature of the plant species, and partly of the internally transformed fluidity of the vital sap into formations. The other side of the process is its self-mediation. This begins (*a*) with the simultaneously *outward* direction of the diremption into root and leaf, and with the inner
10 abstract diremption of the general cellular tissue into wood-fibre and life-vessels. The wood-fibre also relates itself externally, and the life-vessels contain the internal circulation. The self-mediating preservation which occurs here is (*b*) growth as a production of the new formations. It is diremption into abstract
15 self-relation, into the induration of wood (which reaches petri-faction in tabashir and suchlike formations) and of other parts, and into the permanent foliaceousness of the bark. (*c*) The gathering of self-preservation into unity is not unification of the individual with itself, but the production of a new plant-individual, the bud.

20 *Addition.* In the process of formation we begin with an immediacy consisting of the germ of living being. This is merely a posited immediacy however, for the germ is also a product, and is in fact a determination which first occurs in the third process. The process of formation ought to be confined to the process of inwardness constituting the production of
25 the plant from within itself. The self-production of vegetable being is a self-emergence however, so that what is brought forth is another, the bud. This is also directly involved in the process outwards, so that the first process cannot be grasped without the second and third. The developed form of the process of formation would be the visceral process of the
30 individual. Consequently, it is precisely because the plant has no viscera, but only members which have a relationship with externality, that it lacks this process. It is however an essential aspect of the organic process in

general, that it should destroy, infect, and assimilate that which comes to it from without. As water is absorbed, it is immediately affected by the force of animation, so that it is posited at once as pervaded by organic life. Does this occur immediately, or in a succession of transformations? The main point about the plant is that this transformation occurs without mediation. In more highly organized plants however, as in animal being, one is able to trace the numerous intermediate stages through which this process passes. Yet the immediate infection into lymph also occurs here without being mediated by the members of the activity. In plants, and especially in the lower forms, there is no mediation by means of opposition; opposition gives rise to no conjunction, nutrition is a transformation which is devoid of process. Consequently, the inner physiological construction of the plant is also extremely simple. *Link* and *Rudolphi* have shown that it merely consists of simple cells, together with spiral-vessels and tubes.

1. The *germ* is that from which the whole Notion of the plant unfolds; it is the nature of the plant, but as it still lacks reality, it is not yet Idea. The plant occurs in the *grain of seed* as a simple and immediate union of the self and the genus. On account of the immediacy of its individuality therefore, the grain of seed is an indifferent entity. It falls into the earth, which constitutes its universal power. When we say that a soil is good, we simply mean that it has this open organic power or possibility; just like a good head, it has potential. The essential power of the seed, which comes of its being in the earth, sublates its terrestriality, and actualizes itself. However, this is not the opposite of indifferent existence, as it is of its inorganic nature. The placing of the seed in the earth means that the seed constitutes power. This fostering of the grain of seed in the earth is therefore a mystical, magical action. It shows that the seed contains secret powers which are still dormant, and that in reality it is something other than what it is as it lies there. It resembles the child, which is not merely a helpless human shape giving no indication of reason, but which is the implicitness of the power of reason, and something quite distinct from this being which can neither speak nor perform any rational action. Baptism moreover is precisely the solemn recognition of the child's admission into the realm of spirits. The magician who infuses an entirely distinct significance into this grain which I crush in my hand, and for whom a rusty lamp is a mighty spirit, is the Notion of nature. The grain is the force which conjures the earth and masters its power.

(a) The initial development of the germ is mere growth or increase; implicitly it is already the whole plant, the whole tree etc., in miniature. The parts are already fully formed, and are merely enlarged, formally duplicated, and indurated etc. For that which is to be already is, so that its becoming is this simply superficial movement. This becoming is to an equal extent a qualitative structuring and shaping however, and it is therefore an essential process. 'The germination of the seed first takes place through the agency of moisture. In perfect plants the future *caudex* can be seen distinctly in the future plant or embryo, and forms the *conical part*, which is usually called the *radicle* (radicula, rostillum). The *apical part* from which the future root sprouts is lower down. A marked elongation of the upper part is not common; this elongation is generally called a *scape* (scapus). Sometimes, this part also gives indication of a gemma or *plumule* (plumula). The two seed-lobes or *nuclear organs* (cotyledons) which develop later, and represent the *seed-leaves*, often grow from the sides of the embryo. It is incorrect to regard the radicle as the future root, for it is merely the *caudex* growing downwards. If one watches the larger plant-seeds carefully during germination, for example, those of Wheat, Pumpkins, and Beans (the first of which is divided into three parts), one will see how much thinner and more delicate are the true roots which emerge from these bodies.'[1] The apical part germinates if it is pointed upwards, but it grows into an arc, and turns its apex downwards. 'The germ consists of the *radicle* (rostellum) and the *plumule* (plumula). The root grows from the former, and the part of the plant above ground from the latter. If the seed is placed wrongly in the ground, so that the radicle points towards the surface, it will never grow upwards. It grows longer, but still passes into the earth, and turns the seed over in order to reach its proper position.'[2] In this connection, *Willdenow* has made the following discovery, 'The Water-nut (Trapa natans) has no radicle. These nuts put out a long plumule, which grows in a perpendicular direction towards the surface of the water, and puts out piliform, branching leaves at wide intervals along its sides. Some of these leaves turn downwards and take firm root in the bottom. It is evident from this that some seeds can dispense with the radicle, although a fertile seed devoid of plumule and cotyledon is quite unthinkable. So far, no one has ever presumed to deny that any seed had a plumule. It is worth noting that in bulbaceous plants the radicle is transformed into the bulb, while in some which like Cyclamens have a *middle* caudex, it constitutes the axis.' (The middle caudex, 'belongs neither to the descending nor to the ascending caudex. Sometimes it has the appearance of a root, and sometimes of a stem. In the first case it is tuberous, and in the second either beet-like or

[1] *Link*, 'Principles' pp. 235–236 (236 to § 6).
[2] *Willdenow*, loc. cit. pp. 367–369.

bulbous, as for example in the Ranunculus bulbosus etc.') 'Finally there +
are plants in which the radicle disappears soon after the seed has germi-
nated, and the true root develops at the side.'[1] The diremption of the unit
into two aspects, one having affinity with the earth, the ground, the concrete universal, the universal individual, and the other with the pure, 5
abstract, ideal nature of light, can be called polarization.

The *stem* comes between leaf and root as the *first* diremption, for here
we are considering plants with a developed determinate being, and this
does not include fungi and the like. The stem is not strictly essential
however, the leaf can grow directly from the root, and many plants are 10
restricted to the two main moments of leaf and root. This constitutes the
great difference between *monocotyledons* and *dicotyledons*. The first order
includes bulbaceous plants, Grasses, and Palms. These constitute the
Hexandria and Triandria of *Linnaeus*, who had not yet drawn attention
to this difference (*Jussieu* was the first to do so), and who still failed to +
make any distinction here. The question is in fact, whether the leaflet
(χοτυληδών) put out by the seed is double or simple. In monocotyledons,
the root and leaf constitute the initial antithesis, and so exhibit the primary
composite nature of the plant. However, this composition does not
advance to the opposition in which a distinct stem occurs between root or 20
bulb, and leaf. Palms certainly have a stem, but it is merely formed by the
attachment of the leaves to one another at their base, as is quite evident
from the outside. 'Palms only have branches at the top of the trunk, and
their twigs are merely floriferous. It looks as though the branches have
been absorbed by the excessive size of the leaves. Ferns are precisely the 25
same in this respect. Even in our indigenous grasses and many bulbaceous
plants, one rarely sees branches which are not floriferous.'[2] The antithesis
of cells and wood-fibres occurs within the substance of these plants, but
they have no medullary rays. The leaf-veins are either not curved, or only
slightly so, and in grasses they run in straight lines. Monocotyledons are 30
as devoid of a true stem as they are of a completed flat-leaf; they are nothing
more than this enveloped bud, which opens, but never completely develops. +
Consequently, they never produce fertile seed; pith is the constituent of their
root, and of the whole of their stem. The stem is a continuation of the root, it
has neither buds nor branches, but is continually renewing its roots, which die 35
off and are bound together by wood-fibres. The overwhelming power of light
prevents the internalization of the plant into wood; the leaf does not die off, but

[1] *Willdenow*, ibidem. pp. 370–371, 380 (p. 31).
[2] *Link*, 'Principles' p. 185.

puts forth fresh leaves. In the Palm, the trunk and branches seem to consist of leaves however, and conversely there are also varieties of stem in which the stem remains one with the leaf. This is the case with the Cactus for example, where stem grows out of stem. 'The joints, which are commonly regarded as leaves, are parts of the stem. The leaves of this plant are awl-shaped fleshy apices, which are often surrounded at the base with small prickles. They fall off directly after the development of the member' (i.e. the joint of course); 'and a scar or fascicle of prickles indicates their former position.'[1] These plants remain a succulent leaf which withstands the light; instead of wood, they merely produce prickles.

(b) The *cellular tissue* of the plant constitutes its general texture, and as in animal being, consists of small cells; it is the universal animal and vegetable product, the moment of fibriformity. 'Each cell is separate from the others, and has nothing in common with them. In the bast, the cells assume an oval form which is either a simple, apiculate, or an attenuated form.' In this fundamental determination of the plant, there is an immediate distinction between the utricle and the elongated cells. (a) 'The *regular tissue* consists of (*i*) the *parenchyma*, the lax or spongy cellular tissue which is composed of large cells; it is very easily recognized, and occurs mainly in the bark and the pith of the trunks. (*ii*) The *bast*, which is fibrous and compact, and is the real cellular tissue, occurring mainly in the filaments, the support which carries the pistil, and similar parts. Its cells are very long and narrow, but are still distinguishable. It is only in the inner bark, the wood, and the nerves of the leaves, that there is any great difficulty in recognizing the structure of the bast or fibrous tissue. It consists of extremely thin and narrow cells, which assume an attenuated and apiculate form. (b) *Irregular* cellular tissue occurs in the species of vegetable life in which only a seed-vessel (sporangia), and the rest of the supporting body (thallus) are distinguished externally. In *Lichens* the thallus is either crustaceous or leaflike. The crust consists entirely of irregular *coacervations* of sphericle vesicles or cells, *which vary greatly in size*. *Algae* are markedly different from lichens. If one dissects their thallus at its thickest part, one sees very distinct but apparently gelatinous linins, which are skeined in various ways. The fundament of some Algae is a membrane, which is often mucilaginous, frequently gelatinous, but never soluble in water. *Fungaceous* tissue consists of fibres, which are readily recognizable as cells. Grains are scattered everywhere between the fibrous tissue, just as they are in Lichens, where they might be regarded as gemmae.

---

[1] *Willdenow*, loc. cit. p. 398.

So much for the outward form of cellular tissue. How then does the cellular tissue develop and alter? It is evident that new cellular tissue forms between the old cells. The grains in the cells may well be the *farina* of the plants.'[1]

The first diremption related itself immediately to the process outwards, for the root stands in reciprocal relation to the earth, as does the leaf to the air and light. The *second* diremption is more intimate, and is the plant's own division of itself into the wood-fibre or the active *spiral-vessel*, and into the organs which Professor *Schultz* has called life-vessels. Professor Schultz is as thorough in his empiricism as he is in his philosophic confirmation of the subject, although in certain details, the latter is open to some reassessment. This division of the plant in its interior formations, the generation of spiral elements etc., is an immediate production, and in general a mere multiplication. The medullary cells multiply, as do the spiral-vessels, wood-fibres etc. *Link* makes this particularly clear, 'The spiral-vessels are raphes which are rolled spirally to form a tube, and they develop their *scalariformity* as their torsions grow together in pairs. It is a scalariformity which cannot unroll. The spiral-vessels become taut or compressed through the accretion of neighbouring parts. This produces the undulate curvatures of the *transversal bands*, and the apparent cleavages of the transversal striae when two torsions have been pushed on to one another. Perhaps there are also true *cleavages*. The vessels which have such bands or points are the *punctate* and *pitted* vessels which I consider to be similar in kind to the scalariform vessels.' At first only the transversal lines remain; torsions which have grown very closely together in spiral-vessels merely exhibit small pits instead of lines, incisions, and transversal striae. 'The *annular vessels* arise from the rapid growth of the adjacent parts, which causes the torsions of the spiral-vessels to be torn apart, and to be left standing separately. It is not surprising that there are more old and modified vessels to be found in rapidly growing roots, and in other parts where numbers of these spiral vessels have to fulfill their functions, than in those parts where the growth proceeds at a gentler pace. The spiral-vessels spread into almost every part of the plant, and constitute its skeleton. The reticulated fascicles of spiral-vessels distributed throughout the leaves, after they have been stripped of all the intervening cellular tissues, are actually called the skeleton of the leaf. *It is only in the anthers and the pollen that I have never found spiral-vessels.* They are always accompanied by bast, and it is the

[1] *Link*, 'Principles' pp. 12 ('Supplements' I, p. 7), 15-18, 20-26; 29-30, 32.

fascicles of the vessels which are mixed with the bast that we call *wood*. Cellular tissue which surrounds the wood is called *bark*, and that which is completely surrounded by wood, *pith*.'[1]

'In many plants, all these vessels are missing; they have never been
5 found in plants which have anomalous cellular tissue, such as Lichens, Algae, and Fungi. Genuine plants with regular cellular tissue either have spiricles or do not. Mosses and Liverworts, and few aquatic plants such as Chara, are devoid of this feature. I do not know how spiral-vessels
+ originate. *Sprengel* thinks it certain that as they are present in the form of
10 cellular tissue, they must develop out of it. I cannot see why this should be so. It seems likely to me, that they develop between the cells of the bast, from the sap which is discharged there. Be that as it may, the spiral-vessels do grow, and new ones grow between them. Apart from these vessels, to which one may give the general name of spiral-vessels (I call
15 them *true vessels*, in contrast to scalariform and pitted vessels), I have discovered no other vessels in plants.'[2] Where then are the life-vessels?

It might be concluded from what *Link* says in the 'Supplements' (II p. 14), that it is the linear form of the wood-fibres which gives rise to the spiral-vessels. 'I find that I am compelled to reaccept the old view that
20 simple elongated *fibres* are present in plants. It is difficult to decide whether they are solid or hollow. The simple fibre, without a trace of branches, by no means extends throughout the whole plant. It is easy to see that where the twigs join the stem, the twig-fibres *adhere* to those of the stem, *and appear to form a wedge within it*. Even within the same stem and bran-
25 ches, they do not appear to proceed uninterruptedly. The *fibre-vessels* always lie in fascicles, which in the oldest stems form annular coacerva-tions together with the bast. They usually surround a fascicle of spiral-vessels, although in some plants there are also simple fibre-vessels which exhibit no trace of spiral elements. These vessels lie in straight lines, and
30 in the fascicles they are approximately parallel. In tree-trunks and roots they are found to be more divergent, and interwoven as it were. They occur in most plants, and are general in Phanerogams. In many Lichen and Algae one finds only convoluted threads, which are easily distinguish-able in Fungi. Yet there are Fungi, Lichens, and Algae which show *no
35 trace of them, and which merely exhibit vesicles and cells*.' Thus the original antithesis of grain or node and simple length, is seen again in the anti-thesis of utricle and fibre, while spiral-vessels tend towards rotundity.

---

[1] *Link*, 'Principles', pp. 46–49; 51–58; 64–65.
[2] *Link*, 'Principles', pp. 65–68.

Oken's treatment of this passing of cellular tissue into spiral-vessels certainly conforms to the principles presented above (§ 344 Add. III. 48, 12), but he embellishes it with the schematism of a philosophy of nature which is now dated. To quote him: 'The spiral-vessels are the system of light within the plant. I am fully aware of the extent to which this doctrine stands in opposition to the hitherto accepted tenets. I have made exhaustive investigations however, and have assessed opinions and experiments. I can say quite confidently that there is nothing which might cast doubt upon the validity of this result, and it is a result which has been reached constructively by the philosophy of nature.' This construction is merely an assertion however. 'If they are the system of light, then they perform the *spiritual* function within the plant, or the function of simple polarization. The spiricle arises from the opposition between light and the cellular tissue, or from the opposition between the Sun and the planet. A light-ray traverses the utricle or the germ. The utricles, cells, or mucilaginous points (in its seed-form the plant consists of nothing more), gradually arrange themselves side by side along this polar line. In the conflict between the sphere, and the line introduced into it by light, the mucilaginous globules, although they range themselves together linearly, are perpetually being pulled down to the level of chemism by the planetary process of the cellular tissue. It is from this conflict that the spiral form arises. Here, I have merely touched upon the significance of the course of the Sun; the lighted part of the plant, and that part of it in the shadow, change from moment to moment, so that the different parts are successively stem and root.'[1]

(c) *Finally*, the other side of this is the process itself, the activity within the first determination of the plant, universal life. This is the formal process of simply immediate transformation, it is the infinite living power constituted by this infection. Living being is stable and determined in and for itself. By coming into conflict with it, external chemical influence is immediately transformed. Consequently, any undue encroachment by chemical action is immediately mastered by living being, which preserves itself through its contact with an other. It poisons and transforms this other in an immediate manner. It therefore resembles spirit, which transforms and appropriates that which it sees; for what it sees becomes *its* perception. In the plant, this process is also to be grasped in its two aspects, (a) as the absorbing action of the wood-fibres, and (b) as the action whereby the sap in the life-vessels acquires a vegetable

---

[1] *Oken*, 'Text-book of the Philosophy of Nature' (1st edition), vol. II, pp. 52–54.

74

nature. The absorption and the circulation of the vegetable and organically constituted sap, are the essential moments of the Notion, although there may also be variations in particular instances. The action of the vital sap has its principal seat in the leaf. In the plant, each member does not
5 have special functions, as it does in the animal however, and the leaf is just as absorbent as the root and the bark, since it already stands in a reciprocal relation to the air. As *Link* says ('Supplements' I p. 44), 'One of the most important functions of leaves is to prepare the sap for the other parts.' The foliage is the pure process of the plant, and
10 that is why *Linnaeus* suggests that the leaves might be referred to as its
+ lungs.

Link comments on the *functions* of the vessels, and of cellular tissue in general. 'Undamaged roots do not absorb coloured liquids, and these liquids are also unable to penetrate the coloured cuticle. The nutritive
15 sap first passes through *imperceptible* apertures in the cuticle, and fills the cells at the tip of the roots, before being absorbed by the vessels. The saps pass through the various vessels, and in particular through those ducts in the cellular tissue which are not enveloped in any special integument. They also exude through spiral-vessels etc. There is air in the spiral
20 vessels, and in all vessels associated with them. The sap in the fibre-vessels exudes from them in the cells, and spreads out in all directions. The air-vessels are always accompanied by fibre-vessels. It still seems to me that the *stomates* on the cuticle function as excretory glands.' ('Supplements' II pp. 18, 35). For '. . . oils, resin, and acids are the secretions and
25 waste products of plants.'[1] In their 'Journey to Brazil' (vol. I p. 299), *Spix* and *Martius* also speak of the gum which forms between the bark and the wood of the Hymenaea Courbaril L., a tree which is called the Jatoba or Jatai by the natives. 'By far the greatest part of the resin occurs under the tap-roots of the tree, when the earth has been cleared away from them.
30 Usually, this clearing away can only be carried out once the tree has been felled. Round cakes of resin, pale yellow in colour, and weighing from six to eight pounds, are sometimes found under old trees. They are formed by the liquid resin having trickled together gradually. This formation of resinous masses between the roots seems to throw some
35 light on the origin of *amber*, which had been accumulated in the same way before it was picked up by the sea. Insects, and particularly ants, are
+ found in pieces of jatai-resin, just as they are in amber.'
The spiral-vessels perform the primary function of absorbing the

[1] *Schultz*, 'The Nature of the Living Plant', vol. I, p. 530.

moisture which is *presented* to the plant as an *immediacy*. The secondary
function is therefore the organization of this moisture into sap. In accordance with the nature of the plant, this organogenesis takes place in an
immediate manner. The plant has no stomach etc., as the animal has.
The sap circulates throughout the whole plant. It is because the plant is ₅
alive, that this tremulation of vitality within itself, this restlessness of
time, is one of its features. It corresponds to the circulation of the blood in
animals. As early as 1774, Abbé *Corti*[1] had observed a kind of circulation +
of the sap in a Conferva (in the Water-horsetail, Chara Lin.). *Amici*[2] made +
a fresh examination of this in 1818, and with the aid of the microscope, ₁₀
made the following discoveries, 'In every part of this plant, in the most
delicate of its root fibrilla, as well as the finest green threadlets of its
stem and branch, the sap which these plants contain may be seen to
circulate regularly. There is an uninterrupted circulation, in which white
transparent globules of various sizes move constantly and regularly at a ₁₅
rate which increases gradually from the centre to the lateral partitions.
They stream in two alternating and opposed directions, one up and the
other down, and through both halves of a single cylindrical canal or
vessel, which is devoid of any partition. This canal runs lengthwise through
the plant-fibre, but is interrupted here and there by nodes, and is sealed ₂₀
by a partition which bounds the cyclosis. The circulation is frequently
spiral also. The circulation moves throughout the whole plant therefore,
and in all its fibres. It moves from one node to another, and in each
sector bounded by these nodes, there is a separate circulation, which is
independent of the rest. Only one such simple circulation takes place in ₂₅
the root-fibres, for there is only one such central vessel there. The vessel
in the green filaments of the plant is multiple however, for the large central
vessel is surrounded by several small vessels, which are similar to it, and
divided from it by their own partitions. If such a vessel is loosely bound,
or bent at a sharp angle, the circulation is interrupted as if by a natural ₃₀
node, and then continues to circulate above and below the ligature or
bend, as it did formerly throughout the whole sector. If the vessel is
restored to its former state, the original movement also reasserts itself.
When such a vessel is cut transversally, all the sap which it contains does
not flow out immediately. It is only the sap from that half in which the ₃₅
movement was towards the cut which flows out, the rest continues

[1] 'Osservazioni microscopiche sulla Tremella e sulla circolazione del fluido in una pianta aquajuola
dell' Abate *Corti*' Lucca 1774. 8.
[2] 'Osservazioni sulla circolazione del succhio nella Chara. Memoria del Signor Prof. G. *Amici*.'
Modena 1818. 4; with an engraving.

+ around the gyrus'[1] Professor *Schultz* has observed this flow in some more
developed plants such as the Chelidonium majus (Greater Celandine),
+ which has a yellow sap, and also in Euphorbia. The description which
Schultz gives of this is simply the activity of the Notion; an intuition of
5 thought presents itself externally. The flow is a movement from the
centre to the parietes, and from the parietes back again. Together with
this horizontal flow there is a flow upwards and downwards. With regard
to the parietes, the process is of such a kind, that they are also unfixed;
everything produces itself from them. The flow may be observed as a
10 tendency towards the formation of a globule which is perpetually being
redissolved. If the plant is cut in two, and the sap is allowed to run into
+ water, globules which resemble the blood globules of animal being are
to be seen. The flow is so slight, that it cannot be perceived in every
species. In the plants examined by Professor *Schultz*, the flow is not
15 through a single tube as it is in the Chara, for they have two vessels, for
the ascending and descending movements. Investigations will have to be
made to find out whether or not this circulation is interrupted in grafted
trees. Now it is by circulation, which moves throughout the whole, that
the many individuals which form a plant are combined into a single
+ individual.

i. *Schultz* (loc. cit. vol. I pp. 488, 500) now describes this double process (see above III. 75, 38) as follows. *Firstly*, 'The *wood-sap* is the nutriment
of the plant, which is still imperfectly assimilated' (barely particularized).
'It is only later that it is made more fully organic, and is transported into
25 the circulatory system. Wood is the *means* by which air and water are
assimilated, and this assimilation is a living activity.' Wood consists of
cellular tissues and spiral-vessels; it absorbs water by means of the wood-
fibres of the roots, and air from above.' It is the function of the *papillae*,
which are clearly visible at the tips of many roots, to absorb the nutritive
30 sap, which the spiral vessels then take from them for further distribution.'[2]
Capillary tubes, and the law of capillary action, are irrelevant to the explanation of plants, when the plant is thirsty, it wants water, and so absorbs it.

ii. The *second* aspect is the quite original and extremely important
35 discovery made by *Schultz*, that a sap moves once it is assimilated. This

---

[1] 'Vienna Yearbooks' 1819, vol. V, p. 203. (*Martius*' paper on, 'The Structure and Nature of
Chara' in the 'Nova acta physio-medica' of the Leopold. Carolin. Academy of Naturalists; vol. I,
Erlangen 1818. 4. L.C. *Treviranus* of Bremen; 'Observations on the Chara' in *Weber's* 'Contributions
to Natural Science', vol. II, Kiel 1810. 8).

[2] *Link*, 'Principles', p. 76.

is a movement which is difficult to observe however, so that it is not possible to point it out in all plants. The wood-sap is still almost tasteless and merely has a faint sweetness, it has not yet been elaborated into the peculiar disposition of the plant, which has a particular taste and smell etc. *Schultz* now says of this *vital sap* (loc. cit. pp. 507, 576, 564), 'The circulation which goes on in plants throughout the whole winter is the movement of a fully organized sap which extends into all the external parts of a closed system. It extends into the root, the stem, the flowers, leaves and fruits. All these parts also have their assimilative function, but this is always in *polar* opposition to the circulation, and the movement of the wood-sap within it is quite *different* from the movement of the *circulatory system*. What is more, wood-sap only passes into vital sap in the extremities of the external parts of the plant, that is to say in the leaves, where leaves are present, as well as in the flowers and in parts of the fruit. On the contrary, wood-sap does not pass from any bundle of wood-fibres into the life vessels. Wood-sap passes into the bark by means of the leaves.' That is why bark dies if it has no correlation with buds or leaves. In this connection, *Link* cites the following experiment, '*Meyer* isolated sections of bark by cutting round them, and removing strips. He discovered that the sections which survived were those carrying a bud and leaves, while those which were devoid of these features soon withered. I have repeated these experiments on Apricot trees and confirmed them. A section of bark without gemmae and leaves, when it was isolated in this way, soon wasted and dried up, as well as allowing no gum to flow. Another section, from which three gemmae and leaves were removed, took longer to dry out when it was isolated, but also allowed no gum to flow. Yet another section, with three undamaged buds and leaves, did not waste away once it was isolated, but remained green all over, and allowed gum to flow at its base. The first formation on a piece of detached bark was a layer of parenchyma, a fresh pith as it were. This was followed by a layer of bast, with individual spiral-vessels and scalariform tissues. The fresh bark from the parenchyma covered all this. This parenchyma is the first formation therefore, and also constitutes the fundament of the young stem and the embryo. To some extent there was a formation of new pith, wood, and bark.'[1]

iii. *Thirdly*, the plant's vital sap passes over into product. 'When a plant is breaking into leaf, it is easy to separate the bark from the wood in every part of it. This is because of the delicate soft substance called

---

[1] *Link*, 'Supplements' I, pp. 49–51.

cambium, which forms *between* the bark and the wood during foliation. The vital sap is in the bark however, not immediately beneath it.' This third sap is a neutral substance, 'The cambium does not move, and has a periodic existence in the plant. Cambium is the residuum of the entire
5 individual life of the plant, just as fruiting is of its generic life. It is not a fluid, as are the other vegetable saps, but is the delicate embryonic shape of the whole formed totality of the plant. It is the undisclosed totality, as is a non-ligneous plant or the lymph of animal being. The cambium is formed by the circulation from the vital sap of the bark, and this
10 formation gives rise simultaneously to the wood and to the layer of bark. The uniformity of the cambium also gives rise to the cellular tissue. In cellular tissue therefore, the antithesis between the cells and the fluid content of this tissue is the counterpart of the antithesis between the life-vessels and the vital-sap in the vascular system of the circulation,
15 and between the spiral-vessels and the wood-sap in the assimilative system.[1] As the roots and branches become longer, the new embryonic formations arrange themselves at their tips; those formations originating in the homogeneous substance go to the top, those originating in the cambium go to the side, but there is no essential difference between them. In Ferns,
20 Grasses, and Palms, one node forms on top of another. In bulbaceous plants, the nodes grow side by side, the roots emerge on one side of them, and the buds on the other. In the higher plants this external nodulation is no longer so evident, and one sees instead a ligneous and corticose body, which forms at the tips of the nodes.'[2]
25 In summarizing the preceding exposition, we have first of all to distinguish the following three moments in the interior formative process of the plant: (*i*) the diremption into root and leaf, as itself an exterior relation, constituting the interior nutritive process or wood-sap; (*ii*) the interior relation of the pure process in itself, consisting of the vital sap; and

---

[1] If *Link's* scalariform, punctate, pitted, and annular vessels (see above p. 72), are identical with the life-vessels, then the trichotomies of saps and vessels are present in their completeness. What is more, the description of these vessels given there, touching as it does upon their cleavages, apertures, and annulars, accords very well with the location of the circulation. The exposition of the plant's complete process of formation which is given in the text, thus finally rounds itself off into a self-contained sphere with great clarity. For if the cells of the cellular tissue, as the original element of the plant, and in conjunction with the cambium which constitutes their neutral content, develop through the action of light into the bast, the fibre, and the spiral-vessels which make up the differentiated exterior through which the plant draws the wood-sap from its surroundings: then this sap transforms itself, by the return of the process into itself, into the vital-sap, which constitutes the culminating point of the plant's activity; and as it engenders the cambium, this culminating point also initiates the process once again, turning that which was formerly present as an immediacy, into something posited.   Note by Michelet.

[2] *Schultz*, 'The Nature of the Living Plant' vol. I, pp. 632, 636, 653, 659.

(*iii*) the general product, which is (*a*) the cambium of the botanists, (*b*) the inorganic secretion of the etheric oils and salts, and (*c*) the internal diremption of the plant into wood and cortical substance. Secondly, we have the formation of the nodes as a generic multiplication, and finally the bud, which shows traces of the process of sexual differentiation.   5

2. The sap which has been endowed with a vegetable nature, and its product, which is the division of that which was formerly undifferentiated, into *bark* and *wood*, may be compared to the diremption of the individual which occurs in the universal life-process of the Earth, i.e. the diremption into vital activity as such, which took place in the past, 10 and is external to the individual, and into the system of organic formations constituting the material substratum and residuum of the process. The plant resembles the animal in that it is perpetually destroying itself by positing itself in opposition to being. The plant does this by lignification, the animal by the formation of its osseous system. The latter supports the 15 animal organism, but as abstract immobile being, it is the moment of calcareous excretion. The plant also posits its inorganic basis or skeleton within itself. The unreleased power, the pure self which sinks back into inorganic nature precisely because of its immediate simplicity, is the wood-fibre. If this is regarded chemically, it is carbon, or the abstract subject as exhibited 20 by the root, which remains in the earth, and is pure wood, devoid of bark and pith. Wood itself is not heat but it has an igneous potential as combustibility, and so frequently passes on to sulphureousness. In some roots, fully-formed sulphur is produced. The root is such a contortion and extirpation of ┼ surfaces and lines, such a tangle, that the surface is obliterated into a solid con- 25 tinuity, which comes very near to being quite inorganic, and is devoid of any distinction of shape. *Oken* regards the wood-fibres as nervethreads, 'The spiral-vessels are for the plant, what nerves are for the animal'[1]. The ┼ wood-fibres are not nerves however, they are bones. The plant only attains to this simplification as abstract self-relatedness; this reflection- 30 into-self is a dead substance, for it is merely abstract universality.

The process of *wood-formation* in its further details is very simple. *Link* describes it in his 'Principles' (pp. 142–146) as follows, 'There is a considerable difference between the inner structure of the stem in monocotyledons, and in dicotyledons. In the former, the *rings of wood* which sep- 35 arate the pith from the bark are absent; the wood fascicles are scattered throughout the cellular tissue, sparsely in the middle, and more densely near the bark. In the dicotyledons, the disposition of all the wood-fascicles

[1] *Oken*, 'Text-book of the Philosophy of Nature', vol. II, p. 112.

is circular. Nature never draws precise boundaries however, and such scattered fascicles are found in *Cucurbitaceae*, and a few other plants. It is generally the case that the cellular tissue is accompanied by bast, yet in some cases there are fascicles of very narrow, elongated cellular tissue or
5 bast, which occur in the stem at some distance from the vascular bundles. For example, some Labiatae have such bundles of bast in the four corners of the stem, and many *umbelliferous* plants have them in their protruding edges. In monocotyledons, the *growth of the stem* and the *formation of the layers of wood* occurs in a simple and ordinary manner. Not only do the
10 parts become longer and more extended, but new parts form between the old; cells form between cells, vessels between vessels. The cross section of an older stem resembles that of a younger stem in every respect. In dendriform Grasses, the parts harden in an extraordinary manner.' *Willdenow* notes (loc. cit. p. 336) that, 'Silica has been found in many
15 grasses, such as Bamboo-cane (Bambusa arundinacea) etc., and in Hemp and Flax for example, is also a constituent of the plant-fibre. It also appears to be present in the wood of the Alnus glutinosa and the Betula alba, for when their wood is turned on the lathe, it often emits sparks.'

Link continues, 'The dicotyledons are quite different in this respect.
20 *During the first year*, the wood-fascicles form a circle, and are separated from each other and surrounded by parenchyma. In this initial stage they simply consist of bast, with a bundle of spiral-vessels inside. It is mainly the bast which adnates, and inserts itself between the parenchyma'—thus giving rise to alternate layers of fibres and parenchyma. 'The wood-
25 fascicles spread laterally, compress the parenchyma, and finally form a continuous ring, which encloses the pith. The bast in this wood-fascicle is alternately compact and lax, and it is probable therefore, that new bast has inserted itself between the old. Inside the ligneous ring, and adjacent to the pith, there are still some wood-fascicles, which are disposed in a
30 circle. The so-called *medullary rays* originate in the alternate layers of bast, as well as the compressed parenchyma.' They are extensions of the pith therefore, proceed outwards towards the bark,[1] occur between the longitudinal fibres, and are not present in monocotyledons. 'It is the ligneous ring which first separates the pith from the bark. The wood-fascicles
35 subsequently spread inwards and the ligneous ring becomes broader. Rows of scalariform vessels are seen radiating towards the pith' (undoubtedly in a vertical direction however). 'On the inner side of the ring,

---

[1] Would this not make them the fibres of the life-vessels?
Note by Michelet.

around the pith, there are separated fascicles of spiral vessels which are arranged in a circle. However, the medullary cells have become larger, not smaller, although in relation to the thickness of the stem, the amount of pith has diminished. The pith is reduced therefore as its outer part diminishes, and is pressed laterally into rays. However, this reduction is not the result of its being compressed into a smaller space at the centre. Consequently, the first (innermost) fascicles of spiral-vessels are not pushed inwards by the adnate wood; on the contrary, new fascicles are perpetually being formed in the pith, and those formed earlier spread laterally, and compress the parenchyma. The scalariform tissues were formed from the spiral-vessels; and as the spiral-vessels are in the first instance somewhat separated from each other, the scalariform vessels also form rows leading inwards. It is evident from all this, that the layer of wood forms because scattered fascicles of spiral-vessels and bast meet and join laterally, and also because new fascicles of spiral-vessels are constantly growing in a circle on the inside, and joining up laterally.'[1]

'In each of the following years a new ligneous layer inserts itself between the bark and the wood. As in the first year, there are strata which grow on to the wood-fascicles, and so enlarge them. It is very likely therefore, that in the following years a new ligneous strata of this kind will form about the wood. It is in this way that fresh parenchymatous strata are established in the outer bark, and new strata of bast in the inner bark. There is a distinct and precise transition from one strata to another however, which shows that the adnascent growth also takes place in the interstices of the vessels and of the cellular tissue of the older stratum; it also takes place in the pith, until it has filled out. Fresh parts are inserted everywhere, but it is only on the outside that the increase takes place on a very noticeable scale. In the adnascent growth itself, there is no difference between the strata, for the woods grows uniformly and uninterruptedly throughout. Difference occurs only in the compactness and looseness of the strata. The older layers do not retain their thickness however; they become progressively thinner, and finally so thin, that it is scarcely possible to distinguish and count them any longer. Thus a genuine contraction occurs, which narrows the bast cells. Adnascent growth finally ceases in the interior of the wood when there is no more pith to be assimilated. From May until July I examined year-old twigs almost daily, and for a long time I found no trace of a second-year ring. When the ring appeared at last, it did so *quite suddenly*, and what is more, it was already of a consider-

[1] *Link*, 'Principles', pp. 146–151 ('Supplements' I, pp. 45–46).

able size. I am inclined to think therefore, that the annual ring was formed by a sudden contraction of the wood. This contraction must take place *about St. John's Day or soon after it,* and it can have no connection with the annual growth of wood. If what takes place is merely the accretion of a
5 fresh ring around the outermost layer, then during the spring and summer, one could not fail to notice the annual ring of the previous year.'[1] The forming of the annual ring is also a perpetually new production therefore, it is not the simple conservation found in animal being.

3. This production is simultaneously bound up with the internal re-
10 sumption of individuality, and this constitutes the engendering of the *bud.* The bud is a new plant on the old one, or at any rate the simple resumption implicit in the primordium of a new plant. 'Each bud puts forth a foliate twig, and at the base of each petiole there is another bud. This is the way in which growth in general takes place. Yet the development from bud to
15 bud would continue indefinitely were it not that each bud withers as soon as it has produced blossom, and the blossom and fruit have matured. The opening of the flower, and of the fruit which follows it, constitutes the necessary limit to the growth of the twigs.'[2] The blossom is thus an annual plant.[3] With this, the process of the plant preserves itself by re-
20 producing itself, and at the same time producing another plant. The process is therefore mediated by the moments indicated; with regard to production, it is still the formal process in which there is a simple bursting
+ forth of that which was involved as the main germination began.

B

Process of assimilation
(*The process of assimilation*)

§ 347

The process of formation is linked directly to the second process,
25 **which is that of self-specification in accordance with**
externality. The seed only germinates when it is stimulated from
without. What is more, the diremption of the plant-form into root

---

[1] *Link,* 'Supplements' I, pp. 46–48; II, 41–42 ('Principles', pp. 151–153).
[2] *Willdenow,* loc. cit., pp. 402–403.
[3] *Goethe,* 'On Morphology', p. 54.

and leaf, is itself a diremption[1] directed towards the earth and water, and towards the light and air. In the first instance it is concerned with the absorption of water, in the second, with the assimilation of this water, as well as light and air, by means of leaf and bark. The result of the return-into-self in which assimilation terminates, is not sentience, or the inner subjective universality of the self opposed to externality. It is rather, that light draws the plant out of itself by constituting its external self, so that the plant strives towards it, and branches out into a plurality of individuals. The plant in itself draws from light the specific animation and invigoration which constitute its aromatic properties, the volatility of its scent and savour, the lustre and depth of its colour, and the compactness and vigour of its structure.

Addition. The process in accordance with externality coincides with the first process in such a way, that in its living existence, the process of root and leaf has being merely as a process towards externality. Consequently, the sole difference between the two processes consists partly of the outward aspect having to be considered more determinately. Principally however, it depends here upon the extent to which the return-into-self of the becoming of self (which is sentience, or the satisfaction of the self in overcoming inorganic nature), has the *peculiar* formation of also being a development outwards, and cannot therefore be taken into the process of formation. The self which is present in the shape enters into the process outwards in order to accomplish its self-mediation by means of this mediation, and so bring the self forth for the self. The self does not maintain itself however; in the plant, this self-satisfaction does not give rise to unified self-relatedness, but to a formulation in accordance with light. This takes the place of the senses. The self is intro-reflected in its determinate being of shape; this means here that its determinate being or shape is a complete individual in all its parts, and has its own being. It is not itself a universal individual in its determinate being however, so that it is not the union of itself and the universal. The other singularity to which it relates itself is merely a part of the whole, and is itself a plant. The self does not become object of the self, it does not become its own self; the second self to which the plant, in accordance with the Notion, has to relate itself, is external to it. The self does not become for the plant, it is only in light that the plant becomes a self to itself. In its being lighted or becoming light, the plant does not turn

---

[1] In the second edition 'outwards' was added.

into light, but is merely produced with the help of it, and within it. In the plant therefore, the selfhood of light, as an objective presence, does not become vision. Within the plant, the sense of sight remains mere light and colour, and is not the light which has been reborn in the midnight of sleep, in the darkness
+ of the pure ego, it is not the *existent* negativity of *spiritualized* light.

This *closed sphere of relations with externality is annual*, even though in other respects the plant, as a tree, is perennial. It is not only the opening of the flower-bud which is annual, for so also are the roots and leaves, or all the parts and organs involved in the rest of the external relationship.
10 *Willdenow*, (loc. cit. pp. 450–451) says that the leaves fall, 'in the autumn in northern climates, but last for several years in other climates.' Whereas *Willdenow* accounts for defoliation by the stoppage of the sap however (p. 452), *Link's* explanation of this phenomenon is diametrically opposed to this ('Supplements' I. 55), 'The shedding of the leaves seems to be pre-
15 ceded by a superabundance of sap rather than a lack of it. Defoliation was accelerated by making incisions in the bark which completely ringed it. The precise result of this was a cessation in the bark of the return flow of the sap. It now seems to me that the prime cause of leaf-shedding lies in a weakening of the bark partly by the growth of the trunk, and partly by
20 cold.' The roots also die off and reproduce themselves: 'The root of the plant is constantly changing. Fibres and branches are perpetually dying and being replaced by others. The multitudes of fibres and hairs which grow out of the root, are drawn forth by moisture, and spread in all directions. It is in this way that the root is drawn away into moist sur-
25 roundings. Roots also exude moist substances, and this probably accounts for the sand which clings to them. As the older roots soon appear to become useless, perhaps because of the excessive displacement of the spiral-vessels, they manure and putrefy the earth. The main root seldom lasts more than a few years, and it dies after it has put out branches, and
30 stems with new roots. In trees the trunk grows into the earth, and finally replaces the root. It is not only the root which tends to grow downwards, for this tendency is by no means absent in the stem; a few days after germination it can already be found to have penetrated well into the ground.'[1]
35 The *external nature* to which the plant relates itself is not individualized, but consists of the elements. The plant relates itself to (*a*) light, (*b*) air, and (*c*) water.

1. While the process between the plant and the elements of air and water

---

[1] *Link*, 'Principles', pp. 137 ('Supplements' I, pp. 39, 43), 140.

is general, the plant's *relationship to light* displays itself particularly, in the opening of the *flower-bud*. As a production of a new shape, this also belongs to the first process however, while as an indication of sexual difference, it belongs to an equal extent to the third process. It is therefore evidence of the interpenetration of the various processes of the plant, and 5 the mere superficiality of their distinctness. It is in light that the various aspects of the plant acquire their vigour, aroma, and colour. Light is the ground of these qualities, and also keeps the plant upright. 'It is in light that the leaves become green; yet there are also green parts of the plant which are completely hidden from the light, e.g. the inner bark. Fresh 10 leaves, grown in the dark, are white; yet if they are excluded from the light until they have grown and are more vigorous, they take on a greenish tinge. In the light, flowers become more beautifully coloured however, and there is an increase of aromatic oils and resins. In the dark, everything becomes paler, less scented, less vigorous. In hot houses, plants put out 15 long shoots, but they are feeble, and as long as they are deprived of light, they lack both colour and scent.'[2] The bark and the leaf constitute the self of +
the process, and it is precisely because they are unseparative that they are green. This colour, which is the synthesis of blue and yellow, is preserved with the neutrality of water, and sundered into its chromatic constituents, the yellow 20 subsequently passing over into red. It is the cultivation of a range of flowers in all these colours and their combinations, which constitutes the art of horticulture. +
In its relationship to its external self, the plant does not at the same time comport itself chemically. As is the case with vision, it appropriates this self, and possesses it inwardly. In light, and in relationship to light, the 25 plant is for itself; in the face of the absolute power and most intimate ideality of light, it consolidates its own individuality. In this it resembles an individual human being, who precisely in his relationship to the state which constitutes his essence, his absolute power, and his ethical substantiality, becomes an essential, mature, and independent individual. 30 Similarly, it is through its relationship to light, that the plant assumes its integrated particularity, and its specific and determinate vigour. These aromatic plants occur mainly in southern latitudes; a spice-island will spread its scent many miles out to sea, and exhibit a magnificent display of flowers.
35

2. It is evident that *the plant determines the air within itself by means of the aerial process*, for by appropriating and so differentiating the element of air, it subsequently expels it from itself as a determinate gas. This process

[2] *Link*, 'Principles' pp. 290-291.

comes very near to being chemical in nature. Plants exhale; they convert air into water, and water into air. This process is a *respiration*. During the day the plant breathes out oxygen, and during the night, carbon dioxide.[1] The obscurity of this process is due to the closed constringency of the plant. If
5 intussusception is taken to be the appropriation of ready-formed parts, from which only the heterogeneous element is separated out, this is tantamount to saying that the plant draws in carbon dioxide from the air, while leaving the rest of the air (oxygen etc.) outside. This supposedly philosophical way of regarding the matter is based upon experiments in which plants give
10 off oxygen when under water, and when exposed to light. This is just as much a process in conjunction with water however, and plants also decompose the air and take in oxygen. The process by no means reduces itself to this determinate chemical state however, for if it did, organic life would be destroyed. From a chemical point of view, both nitrogen and hydrogen are untransformable
15 substances; consequently, any chemical explanation of the passage from nitrogen to hydrogen, which occurs in the transformation of air into water, is useless. It is however oxygen, or the negative self, which mediates here. The process is not confined to this mediation however, for it returns into the firmness of carbon; conversely the plant follows the opposite and corresponding course,
20 and dissolves this punctiform substance into air and water. The plant contributes towards the humidity of the atmosphere, and also absorbs water from it; everything negative is to the same extent positive. In the plant itself however, this process constitutes its formation, and contains three moments, in which the plant becomes (a) a firm ligneous self, (b) an aquiferous and neutral being, (c) an
25 aerial process of a purely ideal nature (cf. § 346a, Add. p. 79 and note).

Link gives the following account of this process of the plant with the air, 'I found that oxygen is indispensable to the life of the plant, but that the plant does not grow in it at all. However, I found that when carbondioxide is mixed with oxygen in the ratio of about 1:12, it enables the
30 plant to grow excellently in light; carbon dioxide is then decomposed, and oxygen developed. In the dark, carbon dioxide is harmful to the plant. *Saussure's* experiments showed that plants absorb oxygen, change it into *carbon dioxide* which they then decompose, and exhale oxygen. Parts which are not green do not absorb oxygen, but *convert it immediately into carbon*
35 *dioxide*. That which is extracted from the fertile soil constitutes the nutrition of plants. Oxygen draws carbon from it in order to form carbon dioxide. Soil from deep below the surface is not suitable for plant nutrition, although it becomes so after long exposure to the air.' A shower will

---

[1] *Link*, 'Principles' p. 283.

then put everything right. '*Saussure* noticed that bare roots, which withered when they were exposed to irrespirable gases and their apicals were dipped in water, survived in oxygen. *They transformed this oxygen into carbon dioxide*. If they were still attached to the stem however, they absorbed the carbon dioxide, and developed oxygen from the leaves.'[1] +
It is therefore completely erroneous to regard the process with the air as an appropriation by the plant of something already formed, which it augments in a merely mechanical manner. Such a mechanical interpretation has to be rejected completely, for a complete transformation takes place. This is an accomplishment due to the majesty of living being, for 10 organic life is precisely the power by which inorganic being is mastered and transformed. And besides, where else is the potash supposed to come from which is found so frequently, particularly in immature plants, in unripe grapes for example?[2]

Willdenow (loc. cit. pp. 344–355) describes the *organs* of this process of 15 the plant with the air as follows, 'The stomates (pori, stomata) are to be seen on the cuticle of the plants; they are extraordinarily delicate oblong fissions, which open and close. As a rule, they are open in the morning and closed in the hot midday sun. They may be seen on all parts of the plant which are exposed to the air, and which are green in colour. They 20 are more abundant on the lower than on the upper side of leaves. They do not occur on aquatiline leaves, or on the surface of leaves which float on the water. They are missing in Water algae, Mosses, Lichens, Fungi, and similar plants. No canal runs inwards from this cuticular opening however, and there were therefore no connected tubes to be found. The 25 opening terminates, without any further functional accessory, in the closed cell.'

3. Next to the aerial-process, the *aqueous-process* is of most importance, for it is moisture which first makes the plant fertile. Moisture has no impulse for itself, but without water the germ remains inanimate. 'The 30 grain of seed may lie there for countless years, lacking any vital impulse, inert, and locked up within itself. Its animation is a happy accident, without which it would either continue to persist in its state of indifference, or finally perish. The impulse of the sprouting consists of freeing this growth from terrestrial influence, and growing forth from its (own) elaborated 35 nutrition. In the life of the leaf, the growth from the elaborated nutrition (of the root) is freed from the accidents of what has already been elabor-

---

[1] *Link*, 'Supplements' I, 62–63; 'Principles' pp. 284–285.
[2] Cf. *Link*, 'Supplements', I. 64.

ated, and achieves the natural dimensions of its circumscribed form as opposed to the exuberance of its terrestrial influences.'[1]

Most plants do not require soil for nourishment; they may be planted in powdered glass or in pebbles, which remain unaffected by them, i.e.
5 from which they are unable to draw any nutrition. The plant gets on just as well with water, although if possible the water should have some
+ oleaginous content. 'Helmont was the first to discover that if a tree is planted in a pot filled with earth, its increase in weight is much greater than the decrease in the weight of the earth. He concluded from this, that
+ water is the plant's proper means of subsistence. Duhamel grew an Oak tree in nothing but water, and it continued to grow for eight years. Schrader in particular has made accurate investigations into plant growth
+ in sublimated sulphur sprinkled with pure water. Plants grown in this way do not bear ripe seeds however. It is not surprising that plants which
15 are not raised in their proper soil, but in either water alone, sand, or sulphur, should fail to reach their full perfection. A plant from a chalky soil will never thrive in sand alone, and on the other hand, when psammophytes are planted in a rich soil, they generally fail to bear ripe seeds. It may be that salts act as manure and not merely as stimulants, but they
20 are harmful in excessive amounts. The insoluble constituents of a soil are not a matter of indifference to plant-growth, and are not only of significance in so far as they percolate or retain water. When sulphur is exposed to the air, it will accelerate the germination of seeds, as will lead oxide, and without any trace of disoxidation.'[2] 'When moisture begins to fail,
25 plants often feed on themselves, as is shown by bulbs which are laid out to dry, and which grow leaves and flowers, but consume the whole bulb in doing so.'[3]

One aspect of the process in accordance with externality is brought about by the root, and the other by the leaf. This process is the digestion
30 of the plant drawn outwards, and in the Chelidonium and other plants, it is a circulation extending from the root to the leaf. The formation of nodes within the plant itself is the product of this process. This developing and forming out of itself, which gives rise to this product, may be regarded as an internal ripening of the plant. By this ripening, the plant also
35 arrests these developments however, and so gives rise to the multiplication of itself in buds. The first impulse is mere buddage, or the purely formal increase of that which is already present; it is often the case for example,

[1] Schelver, loc. cit. Continuation I, p. 23; loc. cit., p. 78.
[2] Link, 'Principles', pp. 272–274; 278–279.
[3] Willdenow, loc. cit., pp. 434–435.

that the bud also gives rise to leaves, which also bud, and so on indefinitely. However, as soon as inflorescence takes place, the flower-bud is at one and the same time an *arrest* and retraction of the outward forming which constitutes *growth* in general. 'All the shrubs and trees of our regions have two periods of sap-pressure every year. The main period occurs in the ₅ spring, and is the result of the quantity of saps which the root has absorbed during the winter. If we tap trees in our part of the world, we shall find no sap until about St. Fabian and St. Sebastian's Day, on January 20th. If there is a mild spell after that, the sap will not flow unless the cold weather returns. From the late autumn until the middle of January, the sap does ₁₀ not flow at all.' Later on, it also ceases to flow once the leaves have opened. It only flows twice therefore, once when the root begins to be active in January, and then for as long as the leaves are still actively feeding the bark. 'In the second period, the sap-pressure is not so great, and de- velops when the days are longest. As this development usually takes place ₁₅ about St. John's Day, it is also called St. John's sap. It is brought about by the moistures absorbed during the spring. In warm latitudes, the two pressures are equally strong, so that the plants there grow with greater luxuriance.'[1] Thus, in those regions also, there are two separate periods of sap pressure. In such tropical plants however, growth and the suspension ₂₀ of growth occur simultaneously, while in our part of the world, the one is present only when the other is absent. As the reproduction of living being exhibits itself as the repetition of the whole, the production of fresh buds is also accompanied by the production of a fresh annual ring, or a fresh diremption of the plant; for just as the buds of the following year ₂₅ form about St. John's Day, so too does the new wood, as we have already seen above (§ 346a. Add. 2 p. 82).

In general the fruitfulness of trees is increased by checking their growth outwards, but this may also be brought about in a particular way, i.e. by grafting. The precise reason for this is that the alien branch is not in full ₃₀ communion with the outward growth constituting the life of the entire plant. The graft therefore (*a*) bears more fruit, because its independence relieves it of simple sprouting, and its particular life enables it to under- take more fructification; and (*b*) better and finer fruit, because, 'the root of the parent stock which serves the cultivated growth is always pre- ₃₅ supposed, and the organ which is grafted is also already presupposed by the cultivated growth.'[2] Ringing the bark, as is done with Olive trees, also

---

[1] *Willdenow*, loc. cit., pp. 448–449 (pp. 419–421).
[2] *Schelver*, loc. cit., p. 46.

checks growth, and makes the tree more fruitful. Incisions also promote root-growth.

The general *character* of this process is not that of an endless growth outwards however; it is rather, that the plant consolidates itself, or with-
5 draws inwards. The blossom is precisely this moment of return, of being-for-self, although the plant can never really reach selfhood. The flower is this node, and this is not merely the growing bud; as a nodulation which checks growth, it is the assemblage of more delicately developed leaves (petala). From the punctiform cellular basis of the cellular tissue or
10 primary germ, and through the linearity of the wood-fibre and the surface of the leaf, the plant has reached rotundity of shape in the flower and the fruit. The concentration of the plurality of leaves exhibits the point once again. It is primarily the flower, the shape which is raised into light and self-hood, which displays colour. The mere neutrality of green is already
15 coloured in the calyx, and this is still more the case with the flower. What is more, the flower differs from the leaves of trees by giving out scent, it does not smell only when it is bruised. The differentiation into organs finally occurs in the blossom. The organs have been compared with the sexual parts of the animal; they are an image of self-relating
20 individuality engendered on the plant itself. The flower is the self-enveloping vegetable life, which now develops a corolla about the germ as an inner product, whereas the sole direction of its previous activity was outwards.

C

Generic process
(*The generic process*)

§ 348

Consequently, the plant now brings forth its light from itself,
25 as its own self. It does this in the blossom, in which the chromatic neutrality of green is specifically determined for the first time. The generic process is the relationship of the individual self to the self, and as a return into itself, it checks the growth of sprouting from bud to bud, which is for itself unlimited. The plant
30 does not attain to a relationship between individuals as such how-ever; it merely attains to a difference, the sides of which do not in

themselves, and at the same time, constitute the complete individuals, and are not determinative of the whole individuality. Consequently, this difference is also no more than a beginning and intimation of the generic process. The germ is to be regarded here as one and the same individual, the vitality of which runs through 5 this process, and which, by returning into itself, has not only advanced to the maturity of a seed, but has likewise preserved itself. This progression is on the whole superfluous however, for in its producing of fresh individuals, the process of formation and assimilation is itself already a reproduction. +

Addition. The final act of the plant is the opening of the blossom. By this the plant makes itself objective, assimilates light, and produces this externality as its own. That is why *Oken* says ('Text-book of the Philosophy of Nature', vol. II, p. 112) that the blossom is the brain of the plant.[1] However, others of the same school were of the opinion that the + plant has its brain, the root, in the ground, while its sexual organs face the sky. The blossom is the culmination of the plant's subjectivity, it is the resumption of the whole as an individual, having its opposition within itself, and with itself. This opposition also faces itself as an externality however, for this unfolding of inflorescence is itself a further succession. 20 'The stem blossoms earlier than the branches, the branch earlier than the collateral branches, and so on. On one and the same branch the lower blossoms break out before those above.'[2] Yet as the plant preserves itself at the same time as it produces other individuals, the significance of this productiveness is not merely that the plant transcends itself by constant 25 nodulation, but rather that the condition of this productiveness is the cessation of growth, and the arrest of this sprouting. If this negation of the plant's coming out of itself is now to attain *existence*, this means no more than that the independent individuality of the plant, which for itself is substantial form, which constitutes the Notion of the plant, and which for 30 itself is present in the whole of it,—that this idea matrix of the plant becomes *isolated*. It is true that this isolation merely brings forth another fresh individual, but it is precisely because this individual checks multiplication, that it merely constitutes a differentiation within itself. It is this that one finds taking place in the plant if one considers the fate of its 35

---

[1] *Schelling* says the same: 'Journal for Speculative Physics', vol. II, pt. 2, p. 124.
Note by Michelet.
[2] *Link*, 'Supplements', I, p. 52.

sexual parts. As with generation in general, there is no point here in investigating the content of the unfertilized seed, and what is added to it by fertilization.
+ Crude chemical interpretations will miss the point here, because they kill living being, and are only able to grasp that which is dead, not that which has
5 life. The fertilization of the plant consists solely of its ranging its moments in this abstraction of separated determinate being, and of positing their unity once again by means of contiguity. This movement, as a movement between abstract, differentiated, activated, but existent moments, and because these moments are abstract, constitutes the plant's actualization, which it displays upon itself.
+ 1. Since *Linnaeus*, this display has generally been regarded as a sexual process. It could only be this however, if its moments consisted of whole plants, and not merely of their parts. Whether or not the sexual difference and the impregnation which are found in animals are also present in plants, is therefore a well-known point of controversy among botanists.
15 (a) With regard to *sexual difference*, it has to be pointed out that the differentiation reached by the plant, in which there are two vegetative selves, each of which has the impulse to identify itself with the other, is only present as a determination analogous to that of the sexual relationship. For that which enters into relationship does not consist of two in-
20 dividuals. There are only a few plant-forms in which this difference of sex occurs in such a manner, that the two sexes are the distinctive features of two separate plants. These are the *Dioecia*, which include some of the most important plants such as Palms, Hemp, Hops etc. Consequently, these dioecious plants constitute an important indication of impregnation. In
25 *Monoecia* such as Melons, Pumpkins, Hazels, Firs, and Oaks however, the male and female plants are found on the same plant, so that such plants are hermaphroditic. The *Polygamia*, some of whose flowers have a distinct sex, and some of which are hermaphroditic, also belong here.[1] These differences often vary very considerably during the growth of the plants
30 however. For example, in dioecious plants such as Hemp and Mercurialis etc., a plant will show an early disposition towards being female, and yet subsequently become male. Thus the difference here is only quite partial, and the different individuals cannot therefore be regarded as having distinct sexes, for they have not yet been completely imbued with the principle con-
35 stituting their opposition. This is because they are not completely pervaded by this *principle*, which is not a universal moment of the entire individual, but a separated part of it, and because it is in accordance with this alone that both individuals relate themselves to one another. The opposed moments of the

[1] *Willdenow*, loc. cit., pp. 235–236.

sexual relationship proper must consist of whole individuals, the completely intro-reflected determinatenesses of which are diffused throughout their entirety. + The entire disposition of the individual must be bound up with its sex. It is only when the inner generative forces have completely penetrated and saturated individuality that the impulse is present in the individual, and 5 the sexual relationship is established. The original sexuality of the animal merely develops into a force and an impulse, but this is not the external production which in the plant constitutes the formative principle of its organs.

As the *sexual parts* of the plant are not an integral part of its individual- 10 ity, but form a distinct and closed sphere, the plant is sexless. This is true even of Dioecia. On the one side we have the *filaments* and *anthers*, which constitute the male sexual parts, and on the other the *ovary* and *pistil*, which constitute the female sexual parts. *Link* describes them as follows ('Principles' pp. 215–218, 220), 'I have never found vessels in the anther, 15 which consists for the most part of large, round, and angular cells. These cells are only longer and narrower where nerves' (?) 'are to be found. It is in the anther that the pollen occurs. This is usually loose, and consists of tiny globes, which are very occasionally attached to minute threadlets; in some plants it is resinous substance, in others an animal substance con- 20 sisting of phosphate of lime and phosphate of magnesia. In their exterior form, and in the regular arrangement of leaves around them, the anthers of Bryophates bear a close resemblance to stamens. The vascular fascicles never run from the pedicel or the middle of the ovary straight into the pistil, but inosculate into it from the outer opercula of the fruit, or the 25 surrounding fruits. That is why the base of the pistil sometimes appears to be hollow, and a strong and delicate strip of cellular tissue runs through the middle of the pistillary cord. There is no other canal running from the stigma by means of which the seeds are fertilized.' (Does this mean that this cellular tissue does not actually reach the seeds?) 'These vessels often 30 stop short of the stigma, or run from the stigma, past the seed, to the fruit outside, and from there to the pedicel.'

(b) The controversy concerning the presence of true sexual organs in the plant, leads on to the question of the occurrence of *copulation* as such. The following account, which is well known in Berlin, proves that actual 35 fructification does occur: 'In the Berlin botanical garden, there is a female Chaemerops humilis, which had borne flowers for thirty years prior to + 1749, but never any ripe fruit. In that year *Gleditsch* fertilized it with the pollen of the male plant, which had been sent to him from the *Bosian* + garden at Leipzig, and obtained ripe seeds. In the spring of 1767, *Kölreuter* 40

94

sent some of the pollen of the Chaemerops humilis gathered in the Karlsruhe botanical garden to *Gleditsch* at Berlin, and the rest to *Eckleben*, + the head gardener at St. Petersburg. In both cases, the pollination of the female palm was successful. The palm at St. Petersburg was already a + hundred years old, and its blossoming had been consistently sterile.'[1]

(c) Although this compels us to admit that an actual fertilization takes place, *the third question*, that of its *necessity*, still remains open. As buds are complete individuals, plants propagate themselves by stolons, and leaves and twigs merely have to come into contact with the earth in order to
10 possess a distinct fertility as independent individuals (§ 345. Add. III. 57, 12), the plant's production of a new individual by means of procreation, or the synthesis of the sexes, is a game and a luxury, and is not essential to propagation. The conservation of the plant is itself merely a self-multiplication. Impregnation by means of sexual union is not necessary, for the
15 form of the plant is its entire individuality, and this for itself is already fertilized, even when it is untouched by another individual. Thus many plants have fertilizing organs, while their seeds are sterile, 'Many Mosses can have stamens without needing them for reproduction, as they have sufficient means of propagation in gemmation. If plants remain un-
20 fertilized however, at least for several generations, should they not also be able to bear germinating seeds, as do Aphides? *Spallanzani's* experiments + seem to prove that they are able to.[2]

If we now ask whether a plant can bear ripe seeds without the pistil receiving pollen from the filaments and anthers, the answer is that
25 although in many cases the plant does not bear ripe seeds, there are most certainly cases in which it does. It is generally true therefore, that the condition of the fertilization of most plants is the *contiguity* of the pistil and the anther-dust, although there are many plants in which this is not the case. The reason for this is in fact, that although the feeble life of the plant
30 certainly makes the attempt to assume sexual difference, it fails to accomplish this fully. In general, the nature of the plant is indifferent to this difference, so that certain plants mature and develop of their own accord even when their anthers and stigma have been nipped off and their life has therefore been damaged. These plants fulfil themselves of their own
35 accord therefore, so that their seed is in no way superior to their buds. In hermaphrodites such as Melons and Pumpkins, the two parts mature at different times, or at such a distance and in such a position, that they are

---

[1] *Willdenow*, loc. cit., p. 483; *Schelver*, loc. cit., pp. 12–13.
[2] *Link*, 'Principles' p. 228.

unable to become contiguous. In many flowers therefore, and especially in the *Asclepias*, there seems to be no possibility of the pollen reaching the pistil.[1] In some plants this must be effected by insects or wind etc.

2. Where sexual differentiation and the generic process are present, the further question of how this process is to be regarded now presents itself, for it is not necessary for the ripening of the seed. Should it be regarded as completely analogous to the generic process in animal being?

(*a*) In plants, the generic process is *formal*, and it is only in the animal organism that it assumes its true significance. In the generic process of animal being, the genus is the negative power of the individual, and as such realizes itself by sacrificing the individual, and setting another in its place. In the plant however, this positive side of the process is already present in the first two processes, for relatedness to the outer world is already a reproduction of the plant itself, and so coincides with the generic process. Strictly speaking therefore, the relationship of the sexes should be regarded as being to an equal extent, or even predominantly a *digestive process*. At this juncture, digestion and procreation are the same. In the animal, digestion fashions and develops the individual itself; in the plant however, it is another individual which comes into being here, the precise equivalent of this in the immediate digestion of growth being nodulation. All that is necessary for the production and maturing of buds, is the checking of the rampant growth. It is by means of this checking that the whole plant recapitulates itself in buds and fruit, and disperses into a multitude of grains, all of which are capable of existing by themselves. Consequently, the generic process is of no importance to the nature of the plant. It shows that the reproduction of the individual takes place in a *mediated* manner, and is even an entire process. In the plant however, the whole of this sexual differentiation and production of seeds is also an immediate generation of individuals.

(*b*) What happens when actual contiguity occurs however? The anther opens, and the pollen escapes and touches the pistillary stigma. After this *release* the pistil *withers*, and the receptacle, the seed and its integument, swell up. All that is necessary for the generation of individuals is however that the growth should be negated; even the *fate of the sexual parts* is merely a checking, a negation, a pulverization, a withering away. Checking or negation is also necessary in animal life. Each sex negates its being-for-self, and posits its identity with the other. It is not through this negation alone that this living unity is posited in the animal however, for the

---

[1] Cf. *Link*, 'Principles', p. 219.

affirmative positing of the identity of both individuals, which is mediated by this negation, also belongs here. This is accomplished impregnation, the germ, that which is engendered. Only negation is necessary in the plant however, for as each part of the plant is immediately an individual, so that the plant constitutes the original element of identity, the affirmative identity of individuality, which is the germ or idea matrix, is itself already immediately and implicitly present throughout it. In the animal however, the negation of the independence of the individuals also becomes an affirmation as a feeling of unity. It is merely the negative side which is present in the plant, and its precise occurrence is in the pulverization of the pollen, which involves the withering of the pistil.

(c) Schelver has even regarded this negative aspect as a *poisoning* of the pistil. He says, 'If one removes the anthers from Tulips, they produce neither capsule nor seeds, and remain infertile. However, it still does not follow, from the fact that the anthers are necessary to the perfection of the plant's fruit, and ought not to be removed,' (this in itself is certainly not always so, as we have seen, III. 95, 31) 'that they constitute the fertilizing sex. Even if they did not serve the purpose of fertilization, this would not make them a superfluous part which might be removed or damaged without harming the life of the plant. The removal of the petals and other parts can also harm the development of the fruit, but we do not say on this account that their removal entails the eradication of the fertilizing sex of the fruit. May not the excretion of the pollen also be a necessary prerequisite of the ripe germ? On the other hand, anyone who examines the matter impartially, will probably discover that although in general the removal of the stamina from plants will have a harmful effect upon their fertilization, in some climates there are also plants whose fertilization benefits from this operation. What is more, sterile plants can often be made fertile if their roots and branches are pruned, incisions are made in their bark, or they are tapped of nutritive material etc. However, Spallanzani has also removed the male flowers from monoecious plants such as the clypeiform Musk-Melon and Water Melon, without any detrimental effect, for from the non-pollinated fruits he obtained ripe seeds which generated again.'[1] The same result was obtained with dioecious plants whose female flowers were enclosed in glass vessels. When trees and roots etc. are pruned in this way in order to improve fruiting, their excess nutrition is tapped. This may be looked upon as arboreal bloodletting. A number of experiments and counter-experiments were then

[1] *Schelver*, loc. cit., pp. 4–7 (14–15).

made; some people have been successful with them, and some have not. 'The fruit will not *ripen* until the *plant's growth and sprouting are over*, for if vegetation is in possession of its youthful vigour, and is continually making fresh efforts to grow outwards, it is impossible that it should at the same time be checked, or that the maturation in which its fruit is formed, should reach completion. That is why young plants in general, like all those rich in sap or heavily nourished, seldom bear ripe fruit. In the so-called perfoliate flowers and fruits for example, after the partial formation of the fruit has already taken place, its very apophyses are often repulsed again, or changed into shoots. *The pollen checks growth therefore, and works upon the stigma like a lethal poison.* In fact, the style always withers as soon as the germ begins to swell and ripen. Now if this defunction is not the result of the involution of the vegetative process, the germ will not ripen without external help. This help can be provided by the pollen however, for the pollen itself is the breaking-out and appearance of the culminating impulse of rankness or disrupted growth. It is mainly the *oil* in the pollen which constitutes its power to kill growth.' The reason being that the plant engenders for itself a combustible being-for-self. 'In every part of the plant, oil, wax, or resin constitute the final outer gloss of its covering. After all, is not oil in itself the limit of vegetable matter, its highest and final product? Oil comes near to surpassing the nature of the plant, and is similar to the fatty material of animal being. The essence of the plant perishes in the transition to oil. That is why oil has the power to check the further sprouting of the germ. The so-called hybrids show that the pollen can also fertilize other plants.'[1] Consequently, the fertilization brought about by the contiguity of the stigma and the oily substance, is merely the negation which overcomes the separateness of the sexual parts. It is not a positive unity. In a recent number of his periodical,[2] *Schelver* deals with the incompetence of the experiments relating to this subject.

3. The result of this destructive process is the formation of the *fruit*. The fruit is a bud which is not immediate, but is posited by the developed process, while the bud in general is merely the formal repetition of the whole. However, the fruit is expressly the production of a seed, and that is why it is also in the fruit that the plant reaches its consummation.

(*a*) The *seed* which is engendered within in the fruit is a superfluity. In so far as that which is to be engendered is merely something new, the seed

[1] Schelver, loc. cit., pp. 15-17.
[2] 'Critique of the doctrine of sex in plants', Second continuation (1823).
Note by Michelet.

as such is not superior to the bud. The seed is the undigested plant however, and in the fruit the plant shows that it has brought forth its own organic nature
+ from itself, and by means of itself. Nevertheless, in many plants which have no seeds, the preservation of the genus is not effected in this way,
5 the generic process having already coincided with the process of individuality.

(b) The seed is seed as such, and the pericarp is its *integument*, which consists of either a *husk* or *fruit*, or of a more ligneous *casing*. Within this, the entire nature of the plant is finally concentrated into what is
10 generally a rotundity. The leaf, which has spread out into a line and surface from the simple Notion of the individual exhibited by the seed, has drawn itself together as a strong and aromatic covering for this seed. In the seed and the fruit, the plant has brought forth two organic essences; they are mutually indifferent however, and fall apart. It is the earth which becomes
15 the power giving birth to the seed, it is not the fruit which constitutes its womb.

(c) As it *ripens*, the fruit also rots; for if it is damaged, it will ripen more easily. It is certainly said that no fruits will form where the pollen is carried to the female parts by insects. *Schelver* has shown however, that in the case of Figs, it is precisely their being damaged which causes them
20 to ripen. He quotes (loc. cit. pp. 20–21) Julius *Pontedera* ('Anthologia,'
+ Patavii 1720. c. XXXII.) on *caprification*, 'In our part of the world, the fruits of most plants soon ripen and fall off if they suffer external injury, and that is why the Apple, and other fruit-bearing trees whose fruits fall off before maturing, have been helped by covering (induntur) them with
25 stones, and fixing their roots, (fixe radice). This procedure often prevents the loss of the fruit. Country people often obtain the same result with almond trees, by driving an oaken wedge into them. In other cases, plugs (caulices) are bored into the trees as far as the pith, or incisions are made in the bark. It is this which makes me think that there is a certain
30 kind of midge (culicum), which breeds on the blossom of the barren (i.e. male) palms, and throngs about the embryos of the fertile trees. It bores into these embryos, and affects them with a salutary nibble (medico morsu) as it were, with the result that all the fruits stay on the tree and ripen.'
35 *Schelver* continues (pp. 21–24), 'It seems that fertilization by means of insects first became widely known on account of the Cynips Psenes, which is thought to fertilize the Fig tree. As this caprification is only necessitated by the climate, there is even less reason to think that the transported pollen is the fertilizing agency.' Caprification owes its name
40 to the fact that the insect which has to puncture the good Fig tree in order

that it may bear ripe fruit, is found only on another inferior species of Fig tree (Caprificus), which is planted in the vicinity on this account.' Johann *Bauhin* says, 'The midges engendered in the rotting fruit of the wild Fig tree fly on to the fruit of the cultivated tree (urbanae). They then *draw off its superfluous moisture* by puncturing and opening it, and so promote and hasten its maturation. *Pliny* (XV. 19) says that a dry soil, which causes the figs to dry and burst at an early stage, has the same effect upon fertilization as do the insects; also, that in districts where a lot of dry dust from the roads gets on to the trees, and the superfluous sap is absorbed, caprification is unnecessary. In our regions, where the male tree and the insect are missing, Fig seeds do not mature, because the figs do not get fully ripe. There is no evidence however that the figs which matured in hot countries without caprification, were merely a ripe receptacle, and were devoid of any ripe seeds.' Consequently, a lot depends upon the warmth of the climate and the nature of the soil. The nature of the fruit is checked by caprification; this alien and lethal influence fashions and completes the reproduction of the plants themselves. The insect effects the maturation of the fruit by puncturing it, not by bringing pollen from elsewhere. It is generally the case that fruits fall and ripen earlier once they have been punctured.

'So long as the lower life is in control however, the flower, the pollination and the fruit remain dormant. Yet when the flower finally opens, the hidden nature of the plant dominates throughout to its fullest extent; growth and germination are suspended, and the colouring and the scent of the flower are often developed in every part. When pollination is dominant however, that which has unfolded into maturity dies away; all parts of the plant begin to wither, the leaves soon fall, the outer bark dries and becomes loose, and the wood hardens. In the final stage the fruit is dominant, and the same vitality enters into every part, so that the root puts out scions, and gemmaceous eyes well up in the bark; new leaves begin to bud in the axils of the old. Pollination is a self-contained purpose of vegetation, it is a moment of the entire vegetative life which passes through every part of the plant, and which, merely by attaining to a distinct manifestation in the anthers, finally breaks through to a form of its own.'[1]

---

[1] *Schelver*, loc. cit., pp. 56–57, 69.

§ 349

That which has been posited in the Notion however, **is that
the process displays the individuality which** returns into itself,
**and shows that the parts, which in the first instance are individuals,
also belong to the mediation, and are transient moments within it.**
5 **Consequently, it also exhibits the sublation of the** *immediate
singularity* **and extrinsicality of vegetable life.** **This moment
of negative determination** is the basis of the transition **to the
true** organism, **the exterior formation of which accords with the
Notion in such a way, that the parts have an essential existence as**
10 **members, and subjectivity exists as the one which pervades the
whole.**

Addition. The plant is a subordinate organism, destined to tender itself to
+ its organic superior and be consumed by it. The light in the plant's colour is a
being-for-other, and the aerial form of the plant itself constitutes odour-for-
15 other. Similarly, the etheric oil of the fruit concentrates itself into the combustible granularity of sugar, and becomes a fermented liquid. At this juncture
the plant reveals itself as the Notion, which has materialized the principle of
light, and converted the aqueous element into the essence of fire. The plant
itself is the movement of the igneous element within itself, and passes over
+ into fermentation. The heat which it gives out is not its blood however, but
its destruction. This animal process is higher than the nature of the plant, and
constitutes its destruction. As the stage of flower-life is merely that of an
external relationship, while life consists of a self-related distinctness, the
contiguity within the flower, whereby the plant posits its individuality,
25 constitutes its death, for it violates the principle of the plant. This contiguity is a positing of individual being; it posits the singular as being
identical with the universal. In this way the singular is degraded however,
no longer immediately, but merely through the negation of its proper
immediacy. It is thus that it is raised into the genus, which now comes
30 into existence within it. With this however, we have reached the higher
+ Notion of the animal organism.

Chapter Three

The animal organism
(*The animal*)

§ 350

Organic individuality **exists as** *subjectivity* in so far as[1] **the externality proper to shape is idealized into members, and in its process outwards, the organism preserves within itself the unity of selfhood.**[2] This constitutes the nature of the *animal*, in which the actuality and externality **of immediate** singularity 5 is countered by the *intro-reflected* **self of singularity** or the *subjective* universality which is *within itself* (§ 163).

Addition. In the animal, light has found itself, for the animal checks its relationship with an other. The animal is the self which is for the self, it is the existent unity of differences, and pervades their distinctness. The 10 plant's tendency towards being-for-self gives rise to the plant and the bud, which are two independent individuals, and are not of an ideal nature. Animal being consists of these two posited in unity. The animal organism is therefore this duplication of subjectivity, in which difference no longer exists as it does in the plant, but in which only the unity of 15 this duplication attains existence. True subjective unity exists in the animal therefore; it is an incomposite soul, which contains infinity of form, and is deployed into the externality of the body; what is more, it has a further relation with an inorganic nature, an external world. Nevertheless, animal subjectivity consists of bodily self-preservation in the face of 20 contact with an external world, and of remaining with itself as the universal. As this supreme point of nature, animal life is therefore absolute idealism. This implies that it contains the determinateness of its corporeality in a completely fluid manner, and that it has incorporated this immediacy into subjective being, and continues to do so. 25

---

[1] Addition to the first and second editions, 'its singularity has being as the concrete moment of universality'.

[2] The first and second editions, 'inwardly contains its individual sun'.

It is here therefore that gravity is first truly overcome, for the centre has been filled, has itself as object, and has therefore initiated its true being-for-self. The Sun and the members of the solar system are independent, and present us with a spatial and temporal interrelatedness, not one which accords with the physical nature of these bodies. If animal being is now also a sun, then the stars are after all interrelated within it in accordance with their physical nature; they are taken back into the sun, which holds them within itself in a single individuality. In so far as the animal's members are simply moments of its form, and are perpetually negating their independence, and withdrawing into a unity which is the reality of the Notion, and is for the Notion, the animal is the existent Idea. If a finger is cut off, a process of chemical decomposition sets in, and it is no longer a finger. The unity which is produced has being for the implicit unity of the animal. This implicit unity is the soul or Notion, which is present in the body in so far as the body constitutes the process of idealization. The subsistence of the mutual externality of spatiality has no significance for the soul. The soul is incomposite and finer than any point, but incongruously enough, attempts have been made to locate it. There are millions of points in which the soul is omnipresent, yet it is precisely because the extrinsicality of space has no significance for it, that the soul is not present in any of them. This point of subjectivity is to be firmly adhered to; the other points are merely predicates of life. This is not yet the pure and universal subjectivity which is for itself however, for it is only aware of itself through feeling and intuition, not through thought. This means that it is only in that singularity which is posited as of an ideal nature when it is reduced to simple determinateness, that this subjectivity is conjointly reflected into itself. It is only objective to itself in a determinate and particular manner, and is the negation of any such determinateness, without transcending it. It therefore resembles sensual man, who can indulge in every appetite without rising above this indulgence and grasping the thought of his universality.

§ 351

The animal is able to *move itself* to a certain extent, because like light,[1] which is ideality severed from gravity, its subjectivity is a liberated time, which as it is removed

[1] Addition to the first and second editions, 'and fire'.

from the real nature of externality, **spontaneously** *determines its place*. The animal's *vocal faculty* is bound up with this, for as **the actual ideality of soul,** animal *subjectivity* dominates the abstract ideality of time and space, and displays its autonomous movement as a free vibration *within itself*. **It** **has** animal *heat* as a permanent process of the dissolution of cohesion, **and of the independent subsistence of parts** in the permanent preservation of its shape. **What is more, it has** *interrupted intussusception,* **as a self-individualizing relation with an individual and inorganic nature.** Above all it has *feeling* however, **for** as **the existent ideality of determinate being, it is the** individuality which is immediately *universal* in determinateness, **and abides by itself and preserves itself in its simplicity.**

Addition. In the animal the self is for the self, and the immediate consequence of this is that the differentia specifica or absolute distinguishing feature of the animal, is the completely universal element of its subjectivity, the determination of *sensation*. The animal's self is of an ideal nature, it is not effused and immersed in materiality, but is merely active and present within it. At the same time however, it finds itself within itself. This ideality, which constitutes sensation, also constitutes the supreme bounty of nature's existence, for everything is included within it. It is true that joy and pain etc. also form themselves corporally, but the whole of their bodily existence is still distinct from the simple being-for-self of the existence into which they are taken back as feeling. When I see and hear, I am simply communing with myself, and this is merely a form of the pure perspecuity and clarity that is within me. Although this awareness is punctiform, it is infinitely determinable, and as it has itself as its object, the subject of which is the ego=ego of sentience, it maintains the lucidity of its simplicity. The animal is related theoretically to another by means of sensation. The plant's relation with externality is either practical or a matter of indifference however, and in the first instance it does not allow the object to subsist, but assimilates it. It is certainly true that the animal, like the plant, treats externality as something which is of an ideal nature. At the same time however, this other is left alone as a persistent subsistence, although in this way is still related to the subject, and does not remain indifferent to it. It is a relatedness which makes no demands. Because of its sensation, the animal is inwardly satisfied, for it is modified by an other, and it is precisely this inner satisfaction which establishes the theoretical relationship. That which enters into a practical

relationship is not satisfied inwardly, for an other is posited within it. It has to react to this modification posited within it, sublate it, and make it identical with itself, for it was a disturbance. In its relationship with the other, the animal is still satisfied inwardly however, because it can
5 bear the modification brought about by externality, by simultaneously positing the ideality of its nature. The other merely consists of the consequences of sensation.

(a) The sensuous aspect of the animal is certainly weighted, and remains bound to the centre. The animal's singularity of place is exempt from
10 gravity however, for gravity is not rigidly binding upon the animal. Gravity is the universal determination of matter, although it also determines singularity of place. The precise mechanical relationship of gravity consists of something being determined in space, and having this determination only in something outside it. However, as a self-relating
15 singularity, the animal does not have singularity of place as something determined from without. As a singularity which is in communion with itself, the animal is indifferent to inorganic nature, and in its free movement is only related to it by means of space and time in general. Consequently, the singularization of place lies within the power of the animal
20 itself, and is not posited by means of another. It is the animal itself which posits this place. In all things apart from animals, this singularization is fixed, for it is only in the animal that the self has being-for-self. Of course, the animal is not exempt from the universal determination of singularity of place, but it posits its own place. It is for this very reason that the
25 subjectivity of the animal is not merely distinguished from external nature, but also distinguishes itself from it. This positing of itself as the pure and proper negativity of *various specific* places etc., is an extremely important distinguishing faculty. The whole of physics is the form which develops in contradistinction to gravity. In physics however, form does
30 not attain to this freedom from the torpor of gravity, and it is in the subjectivity of the animal that the positing of this being-for-self in the face of gravity is initiated. Physical individuality is also subject to gravity for even its process exhibits determinations of place and gravity.

(b) The animal's vocal faculty is a high prerogative, and we may well
35 marvel at it. It is the expression of sensation and of sentience. It is through its voice that the animal displays its internal being-for-self. It is only the sentient creature which can show that it is sentient however. Birds of the air and other animals emit cries when they feel pain, need, hunger, satiety, pleasure, joyfulness, or are ruttish. The horse neighs when it goes
40 into battle, insects hum, cats purr when they are pleased. The theoretical

emanation of the singing bird is a higher kind of vocal faculty however, and is so advanced that it has already to be distinguished from the general vocal power possessed by animals. The fish live in water and are mute, but the element of the birds is the air, and they soar freely through it; separated from the objective gravity of the earth, they emanate into the air, 5 and express their sentience in their own element. Metals have a ring, but this is not yet vocal; a voice is the spiritualized mechanism expressing itself in this particular way. Inorganic being first exhibits its specific determinateness when it is stimulated into doing so, when it is struck. The resonance of animal being is autonomous however. Subjective being 10 reveals its psychic nature by vibrating inwardly, and by merely making the air vibrate. By itself, this subjectivity in its completely abstract state is the pure temporal process which as the self-realizing time of the concrete body, is vibration and tone. It is because its own activity consists of making the bodily organism vibrate, that the animal is able to produce a 15 sound. This production gives rise to no exterior change however, merely to movement, and the movement which it produces is merely abstract and pure vibration. This brings forth nothing but a change of place followed by the precise cancellation of the same, and is therefore a negation of specific gravity and cohesion, as well as precise reinstatement 20 of the same. The vocal faculty comes closest to thought, for in the voice pure subjectivity becomes objective, not as the particular actuality of a condition or sensation, but in the abstract element of space and time.

(c) Animal warmth is related to the vocal faculty. The heat yielded by the chemical process can also rise to the intensity of fire, but it is transitory. 25 The animal is the lasting process of autonomous movement however, a process which consumes and produces itself. As such, animal being is perpetually negating and reproducing material being, and is therefore constantly generating heat. This is particularly so in the case of warm-blooded animals, in which the opposition between sensibility and irrit- 30 ability is more highly developed (see below § 370 Add.), and whose blood exhibits a distinct irritability, which may be regarded as a fluid magnet.

(d) As the animal is a true self, which is for itself and has attained to individu-ality, it establishes its separateness and particularity. It detaches itself from the 35 universal substance of the Earth, which has an external determinate being for it. For the animal, the externality which has not come under the domination of its self, is a negative and indifferent being. The immediate implication of this for the animal is that its inorganic nature has individualized itself, for it does not withdraw from its element. This relationship with inorganic nature constitutes 40

the general Notion of the animal. The animal is an individual subject, which
relates itself to individual being as such. It does not, like the plant, relate
itself only to elementary being, and it only relates itself to subjective
being in the generic process. In that it has a relationship to light, air,
5 and water, the animal also has a vegetable nature. It has the further
characteristic of sensation however, and this, in man, is accompanied by
+ thought. *Aristotle* consequently enumerates three souls as the three determinations of the development of the Notion, the vegetable, the animal,
and the human. As an intro-reflected unity of various singularities, the
+ animal exists as a spontaneously self-producing end, and is a movement which
returns into its *particular* individuality. The process of individuality is a closed
circulation, which in organic being in general constitutes the sphere of being-
for-self. As this being-for-self is the Notion of organic being, the *essence* or
inorganic nature of organic being is particularized for it. As a self which is for
15 itself, organic being is to an equal extent self-relating however, so that
in the relationship of its being-for-self with inorganic nature, it posits
the distinctness of this being-for-self. It interrupts this exterior relationship because it is satisfied and sated, because it has sensation, and is a self
which is for itself. When it is asleep, the animal sinks into identity with
20 universal nature; when it is awake, it enters into a relationship with individual organic being, although it also interrupts this relationship. The life
of the animal is the successive fluctuation between these two determinations.

§ 352

As living universality, the animal organism is the Notion,
25 which passes **syllogistically** through its three determinations.
Each **syllogism** is **implicitly** the same **totality** of substantial unity, and **in keeping with the** determination of its form,
is at the same time the *transition* into the others. The
existent totality **of the animal is therefore the** *result* **of this**
30 **process.** Living existence has *being*, **and preserves itself** only
as this reproductiveness, not as mere being. **It has being only**
because it turns itself into what it is. It is a pre-existent end, and
is itself merely result. The organism is therefore to be considered
(*a*) **as the individual Idea, which is simply self-related in its process,**
35 **and which inwardly coalesces with itself, i.e. shape;** (*b*) **as Idea**
which relates itself to its other, its inorganic nature, and posits the
ideal nature of this other within itself, i.e. assimilation; (*c*) **as the**

Idea relating to an other which is itself a living individual, and thereby relating itself to itself in the other, i.e. the generic process.

Addition. The animal organism is the microcosm, the centre of nature which has become for itself. Within it, the whole of inorganic nature has 5 recapitulated itself, and is idealized, and it is this that has to be demonstrated by the more detailed exposition of it. As the animal organism is the process of subjectivity which is self-relating in the midst of externality, the rest of nature is present here, for the first time, as something external, for animal being preserves itself in this relationship with that which is 10 external to it. For the plant however, which is drawn outwards without really preserving itself in this relation with an other, the rest of nature is not yet present as something external. As animal life is its own product and purpose, it is simultaneously both end and means. The end is a determination which is of an ideal nature, and which is already present as 15 an antecedent. As the realizing activity which then occurs has therefore to conform to the determination which is present, it brings forth nothing new, so that the realization is to an equal extent a return-into-self. The accomplished end has the same content as that which is already present in the activation, so that living existence with all its activities fails to 20 extend this content. The organization itself is to an equal extent both end and means, for it consists of nothing which is subsistent. As the viscera and the members in general are in a state of reciprocal activity, they are always posited as being of an ideal nature, and as each member is a centre which produces itself at the expense of all the others, it has existence 25 only by means of the process. In other words, that which is sublated and reduced to means, is itself end and product. As that which develops the Notion, the animal organism is the Idea which merely manifests the Notion's differences. It is in this way that each moment of the Notion contains the others, and is itself a system and a whole. Each system is im- 30 plicitly the whole, and the unity and subjectivity of the whole is brought forth in the transition of these determinate totalities.

The first process is that of the self-relating, self-embodying organism, which contains its other. The second process is directed against inorganic nature however, against the otherness of its implicit being, and is the 35 basic division and active Notion of living existence. The third process is + higher, for it is the process of singularity and individuality, or of the individual opposed to itself as the genus with which it is implicitly identical. These processes are developed in the fullest and clearest way in the human organism, which is the perfect animal. In general therefore, a universal type is present in this supreme organism, and it is in and from this type that the significance of the undeveloped organism may first be ascertained and assessed.[1]

A

Shape
(*Formation*)

§ 353

1. The functions of the organism

5   **Shape is the animal subject, as a whole which is related only to itself. The developed determinations of the Notion exist in the subject, and are displayed there by this whole. Within subjectivity these determinations in themselves are concrete, although they constitute (a) the simple elements of this subjecti-**
10 **vity. Consequently, the animal subject is :** (*i*) the externality of its *simple and universal being-in-self,* by which actual determinateness, as particularity, is *immediately* taken up into the *universal,* and through which the universality of this particularity constitutes the subject's undivided identity
15 with itself, i.e. *sensibility:* (*ii*) *particularity,* as susceptibility to external stimulation, and the receiving subject's subsequent outward reaction to the stimulation, i.e. *irritability:* (*iii*) the unity of these moments, the animal subject's *negative* return to itself **from external relationship,** and the
20 consequent *singularity* of its engendering and positing itself, i.e. *reproduction,* which is the reality and basis of the first two moments.

Addition. The plant allows its wood and bark to die, and its leaves to fall, whereas the animal constitutes this negativity itself. The plant is only able to
25 maintain itself in the face of its mutation by leaving what changes in a state of

---

[1] Anatomy and physiology deal with the Notion of this type, zoology with its reality, and medicine with the contest between these two aspects.

Note by Michelet.

indifference. The animal is its own negativity however, it transcends its shape, and does not interrupt its growth in its digestive and sexual process. Its own inner process, as the negativity of itself, fashions itself into viscera. By shaping itself as an individual in this way, the animal is a unity of shape and individuality. Sensibility is the sentient being, and in the spirit it is the ego; it is the universal subjectivity of the Notion with itself, and if it is touched by something else, it immediately transforms it into itself. The particularity which is first posited as of an ideal nature, comes into its own in irritability, the activity of the subject consisting of its repelling the other to which it relates itself. Although irritability is also sensation, subjectivity, it is so in the form of relationship. However, while sensation is merely irritability as negated relation to an other, a reproduction is the infinite negativity which makes externality mine, and makes something external out of me. This is developed sensibility, which is the primarily real universality, and is not abstract. Reproduction passes through sensibility and irritability, and absorbs them; it is therefore derivative or posited universality, and although it is self-producing, it is at the same time concrete singularity. Reproduction is the initiation of the whole, the immediate unity-with-self in which the whole has at the same time entered into relationship. The animal organism is essentially reproductive, reproduction constitutes its actuality. In living existence, the higher natures are those in which the abstract moments of sensibility and irritability have a distinct existence; lower living existence is no more than reproduction, but in its higher natures it contains profounder differences and preserves itself in this more cutting diremption. Thus there are animals which are nothing but reproduction; they are an amorphous jelly, an active and intro-reflected slime, and in them there is as yet no distinction between sensibility and irritability. These are the general moments of animal being, but they are not to be regarded as properties, each of which acts in a particular way, as colour has a particular effect upon sight, and taste upon the tongue etc. It is true that nature also deploys the moments separately and in a state of reciprocal indifference, but it does this quite exclusively in the shape, i.e. in the dead being of the organism. Nothing in nature is as distinct in itself as is the animal, but as its nature is the speculative Notion, nothing is so difficult to grasp. Despite the animal's having the nature of a sensuous existence, it still has to be grasped in the Notion. In sensation, living existence exhibits supreme simplicity, for everything else is a mutual externality of qualities. Yet at the same time, living existence is fully concrete, for it allows the moments of the Notion, which have reality in a single subject, to assume a determinate being. Lifeless existence is abstract however. In the solar system, the Sun corresponds to sensibility, comet and Moon constitute the moments of difference, and the planet is reproduction. In the system each body is an independent member however, while in the case of the animal, the members are contained in a single subject. This idealism, which recognizes the Idea throughout the whole of nature, is at the same time realism, for the Notion of living existence is the Idea as reality, even though in other respects the individuals only correspond to one moment of the Notion. In real, sensuous being, philosophy recognizes the Notion in general. One must start from the Notion, and even if it should as yet be unable to exhaust what is called the 'abundant variety' of nature, and there is still a great deal of particularity to be explained, it must be trusted nevertheless. The demand that there should be an explanation for this particularity is generally vague, and it is no reflection on the Notion that it is not fulfilled. With the theories of the empirical physicists the position is quite the reverse however, for as their validity depends solely upon singular instances, they are obliged to explain everything. The Notion holds good of its own accord however, and singularity will therefore yield itself in due course (see § 270 Add. I. 281, 27).

§ 354

2. The systems of shape

These three moments of the *Notion* **are (b) not merely implicitly concrete elements, for** they have their reality in three systems, i.e. the *nervous system*, the *system of the blood*, and the *digestive system*. **As totality, each of these systems differentiates itself internally in accordance with the same Notional determinations.**

(*i*) **Thus the system of sensibility determines itself into:** (*a*) **The extreme of abstract self-relation, which is at the same time a transition into immediacy, into inorganic being and absence of sensation. This remains an incomplete transition however, and it constitutes the osseous system, which encloses the entrails. Outwardly this system is the firmness protecting the entrails from without. (*b*) The moment of irritability, i.e. the cerebral system and its further diffusion in the nerves, which also have an inner and outer reference as nerves of sensation and motion. (*c*) The system pertaining to reproduction, which contains the sympathetic** nerves together with the ganglia, and in which there is merely a subdued, indeterminate and involuntary sentience.

(*ii*) **Irritability** is stimulation by an other, and the reaction of self-preservation in the face of this; conversely and to an equal extent, it is active self-preservation, and in this it submits itself to another. Its system consists of: (*a*) **Muscle** in general, which is **abstract (sensible) irritability**, and the **simple conversion** of receptivity into reaction. As a division of immediate self-relatedness, the muscle finds an outer hold on the skeleton, differentiating itself initially into extensor and flexor, and subsequently into the further special systems of the extremities. (*b*) **Pulsation,** which is inward activity, or irritability differentiated for itself in the face of another, and concretely self-related and contained. Pulsation is living self-movement, the material of which can only be a **fluid,** or **living blood.** This movement can only be circulatory, and initially specified into **particularity** in accordance with origin, it is in itself a circulation which is duplicated and at the same time orientated **outwards.** As such, it constitutes the pulmonary and portal systems, in the first of which the blood animates itself within itself, and in the second of which it **kindles** itself against another. (*c*) The **irritable self-coalescing totality,** by which[1] pulsation constitutes the circulation which returns into itself from its centre in **the heart,** through the differentiation of arteries and veins. It is precisely as such that this circulation is an **immanent** process, in which there is a general supply of blood for the **reproduction** of the other members, and from which these members draw their nourishment.

(*iii*) As a system of glands, together with skin and cellular tissue, the digestive system is **immediate** and **vegetative reproduction.** In the intestinal system proper however, it is a **mediating reproduction.**

Addition. Sensibility, irritability, and reproduction also have existences of their own; the first as the nervous system, the second as the system of the blood, and the third as the digestive system. Consequently, 'all animal bodies may be analysed into the three different constituents of which all their organs are composed, i.e. cellular tissue, muscular fibres, and nerve pulp'.[2] These are the simple abstract elements of the three systems. How-

---

[1] Addition to the second edition, 'universal'.

[2] *Treviranus,* 'Biology', vol. I, p. 166.

ever, as these systems are equally undivided, so that each point contains all three in an immediate unity, they do not constitute universality, particularity and singularity, which are the abstract moments of the Notion. On the contrary, each of these moments exhibits the totality of the Notion
5 in its determinateness, the other systems being present as existences in each of them. Blood and nerves are present everywhere, as is also the lymphatic and glandular element which constitutes reproduction. The unity of these abstract moments is the animal lymph, from which the internal members of the organism develop. Along with its internal self-
10 differentiation, this unity also envelopes itself in skin, which constitutes its surface, or the general relation of the vegetable organism with inorganic nature. Now although each system is the developed whole, and as such contains the moments of the other systems, the single form of the Notion remains predominant in each of them. The immediate shape is the dead and quiescent
15 organism which constitutes the inorganic nature of organic individuality. As the organism is this quiescent being, the self or Notion is not yet actual, and its production is not yet posited; one might say that it is merely an inner self, and that it is we who have to grasp it. In its determination, this exterior organism constitutes a relation with equally indifferent shapes; it is the
20 mechanism of the whole, a whole which is articulated into its distinct parts.

As self-identity of sensation, sensibility reduced to abstract identity is insensibility; it is motionless and moribund, and it deadens itself, but it is never separated from the sphere of animation. It is in fact the production of bone, whereby the organism first establishes its basis. Consequently,
25 even the osseous system still participates in the life of the organism. 'In old age the bones become smaller, and the cranium and cylindrical bones get thinner; their medullary cavity seems,' as it were 'to get larger, at the expense of the osseous substance. As a whole, the dry skeleton of an old person becomes comparatively lighter; that is why, quite apart from the
30 bending of their backs, old people become smaller.' (In comparison with cartilages) 'bones in general possess more vitality, simply on account of their having a larger number of blood vessels. Further evidence of this vitality is to be found in their being more susceptible to inflammation and forms of disease, in their reproduction, in the ready absorption of their
35 extremities, in *the greater ease with which their sensibility* may be stimulated,
+ and even in their composite structure.'[1] Bone is the sensibility belonging to shape as such, and like the wood of the plant, it is a simple and consequently moribund force, which is not yet process, but abstract reflection-into-self.

[1] *Autenrieth (Jh. Heinr. Ferd.)*: 'Manual of Physiology', Pt II, § 767; § 772.

It is at the same time moribund reflection-into-self however, and it therefore corresponds to the vegetable bud, which in the production of itself, also brings forth something else.

(a) In the *first instance* it has the shape of an *osseous nucleus*, for it is with this that all bones begin. Like the vegetable node which becomes a ligneous fibre, 5 the osseous nuclei multiply and become elongated. They are to be found at the extremities of the limbs, and contain the marrow as that which is not yet expressly developed into their nerves. Bone-marrow is fat; that is why the bodies of thin people contain fluid marrow or little at all, while fat people have plenty of it. The life peculiar to the bone consists of the *periosteum*, which dies 10 internally, and only lives on the surface of the bone, for the whole of its production proceeds outwards. It is a subdued and self-enveloped force, and + through it, the osseous system together with the system of the skin, falls within the existence of reproduction. As it develops towards totality from nucleus and line, the bone bursts open, and the nerve appears in the place of the 15 marrow. The nerve is a nucleus which allows its filaments to sprout from its centre. However, in this totality of connection, the bone ceases to belong to shape as such, its marrow becomes a point of animated sensibility, which diffuses itself in lines, dimensions proceeding from it as moments of the totality. As nucleus, the bone is the immediately sensible moment of shape. As skeleton 20 however, its primary and more precise determination consists of its relating itself to external being as something stable, hard, and simply firm. By this it attains mechanical objectivity, and a support against the general firmness of the earth.

(b) The prolongation of the bone is the *middle term* of transition, in which 25 shape degenerates into an externality which has another being as its internality. The bone is the inner moment or immediate firmness of the limbs, but at their extremities it ceases to be internal. In the plant, wood constitutes the inside and bark the outside, although in its seed the wood is overcome, and only constitutes the outer husk. Similarly, bone becomes the outer covering of the viscera. This 30 covering no longer has a centre of its own, but is still discontinuous at first, and has its own articulation held together by its own line, i.e. the sternum. However, it finally becomes a pure surface again, and so lacks internality of its own. This is a reversion to the point or line, from which lines radiate to form a flatness which is merely an enveloping surface. This is the totality which has not yet 35 rounded itself off, and so still has the tendency to turn outwards. The *second* aspect of the determination of the bone is therefore that it is subservient to another, having another within itself as subject, and extending outwards into firm terminations such as horns and claws etc. The skin extends into nails and heels etc., it is the most indestructible element of the organism, 40 for after everything else in a corpse has turned to dust, it is not uncommon for the skin to be still visible on some parts of it.

(c) As the bone, which is interrupted in the central vertebration of the *spinal column*, is now at the same time returning into itself, its third formation is the
5 hollow *cranium*. The form of the spinal column constitutes the basis of the skull-bones, and it is possible to trace their derivation from it. The sphenoidal bone has the tendency to dominate the centre entirely however, and to completely
+ reduce the skull-bones to a surface which lacks a centre of its own. At the same time however, this complete abolition of nuclear form passes over into its re-
10 instatement, the *teeth* now constituting this return of the nuclei into themselves. The teeth pass through the process, for they are negative, active and effective, and therefore cease to be merely passively distinct. Immediate sensibility has here become irritability. In the teeth, the periosteum is no longer external, but
+ is merely internal membrane. The bones, like the periosteum, are without sen-
+ sation, although they acquire it in syphilitic lymphatic diseases.

The spinal column is the basic organism of the bone, and all else is merely a metamorphosis of it, i.e. inwardly a tube, with its continuations outwards. It was *Goethe* in particular who realized that this is the funda-
+ mental form of bone formation. Guided by a fine organic feeling for
20 nature, he followed out the full details of the transitions in a treatise which he wrote as early as 1785, and which he published in his 'Morphology.'[1]
Goethe communicated the treatise to *Oken*, who immediately paraded its ideas as his own in a programme which he wrote on the subject, and so
+ gained the credit for them. *Goethe* showed (and it is one of the finest in-
25 tuitions he has had), that the cranial bones, i.e. the sphenoidal bone, the zygomatic or cheek bone, up to the bregmatic or frontal bone, which is the iliac bone of the head, are developed wholly and exclusively out of
+ this form. Here however, as also in vegetable being, identity of form is not a sufficient explanation of this transformation. How is it that these bones
30 now become an enveloping structure instead of an internal centre? How is it that they now have the determination of becoming external fulcrums for extremities such as arms and legs etc., of combining with each other and at the same time being movable? It was *Oken*, not *Goethe*, who in-vestigated this second aspect, i.e. the introjection of the spinal column into
35 the separate bones. The spinal column is the centre of the osseous system, which dirempts itself into the extremes of the cranial bone and the ex-tremities, and at the same time joins them together. The former is the cavity which forms an outwardly closed and rounded structure through

[1] Cf. 'On Morphology', pp. 162, 248, 250-251, 339.

the unification of the surfaces, the latter is the longitudinally extended development, which enters into the centre, and fastens itself along the muscles, mainly by cohesion.

In sensibility, the moment of differentiation is the nervous system, which is directed outwards, and involves connection with an externality. It is now either feeling, immediately posited from outside, or a self-determination. It is mainly the motor nerves which proceed from the spinal cord, and it is above all the sensory nerves which proceed from the brain. The former constitute the practical aspect of the nervous system, and the latter its susceptibility to determination, to which the sense organs belong. In general the nerves are concentrated upon the brain however, and also branch out from it again by ramifying into every part of the body. The nerve is the condition under which sensation is present wherever a body is touched; it is also the condition of the will, and in general of any self-determining end. Apart from this, we still know very little about the organization of the brain. 'We know from experience that there is a partial or total cessation of the function of the particular organs which bring about voluntary actions and of their capacity for sensation, if there is any damage or destruction of the nerves leading from these parts, or of the spinal column, the cerebellum, or the cerebram with which these nerves are connected. The individual nerve-fibres and their sheaths are united into fascicles by cellular tissue, and these fascicles are more or less tightly combined into a larger tactile cord. Even the medullary fibres of the nerves are ubiquitously and variously interconnected by small lateral canals filled with marrow, which seem to form very fine nodules at their points of contact. In this respect a nerve fascicle resembles a tightly stretched net, the threads of which are almost parallel as the result of its having been pulled lengthwise into a cord.'[1] When the brain *communicates* with another part of the body, and the nerves of this particular part have been affected, we should not conclude that the affection was borne solely by this particular nerve-fibre. Nor should it be thought that the brain has exerted an influence upon a particular nerve-fibre through the external association of the nerves. The communication is made through the common nerve-trunk, and yet on account of the general presence of will and consciousness, it is still determined. A nerve-fibre is connected with many others, and when it is affected, they all are. This does not produce a plurality of sensations however, nor, conversely, does the general nerve-trunk proceeding from the brain set all the nerves in motion.

---

[1] *Autenrieth*, loc. cit., pt. III, § 824; § 866; § 868.

Knots are formed on the nerves by the sensibility which has withdrawn into itself. This sensibility is the extremity of internality, by which sensible being is no longer abstract; it consists of the general system of ganglia, and in particular of what are called the sympathetic nerves, and
5 is a system which is not yet separated out or developed into determinate forms of sensation. These nerve-knots may be regarded as the cerebella of the abdomen, but they are not absolutely independent and self-contained, for they communicate with these nerves, which have an immediate connection with the brain and the spinal sinews. They are at the same
10 time independent however, for they are distinguished from these nerves
+ by their function and structure.[1] This division into the cephatic and abdominal cerebram is the reason why headaches originate in the ab-
+ domen. 'It is remarkable that the extension of the eighth nerve stemming directly from the brain should terminate in the stomach, for one could
15 almost say that it stops at its upper orifice, leaving the rest of the stomach to the sympathetic nerve. It is here therefore that *a more distinct feeling* seems to find its *limit*. This upper orifice plays a marked and significant role in many diseases, and autopsies show that inflammations are more common in its vicinity than they are in any other part of the stomach. To
20 a great extent, nature left the selection of food, masticating, swallowing, and the final evacuation of the useless matter to choice, while she withdrew the proper business of digestion from voluntary control.'[2] In the somnambulistic state, where the external senses are cataleptically rigid, and self-consciousness is internal, it is the inner vitality that incites the ganglia and
+ brain of this dim and estranged self-consciousness. Consequently, to quote *Richerand*,[3] 'The internal organs are withdrawn from the control of
+ the will through the sympathetic nerves.' These nerve-knots have an
+ irregular system.[4] *Bichat* says that, 'The ganglionic system may be divided into ganglia of the head, the throat, the thorax, the abdomen, and the
30 pelvis.'[5] Ganglia occur throughout the whole of the body therefore, though principally in the parts belonging to the internal structure, and especially in the abdomen. 'A series of these nerve-knots occurs on either side, in the openings between the vertebrae, where they are formed by the posterior roots of the spinal sinews.'[6] Through their interconnections

---

[1] Cf. *Autenrieth*, loc. cit., pt. III, § 869.
[2] *Autenrieth*, loc. cit. pt. II, § 587.
[3] 'Nouveaux éléments de Physiologie', vol. I, Prolegom. CIII.
[4] *Autenrieth*, loc. cit., pt. III, § 871.
[5] 'Recherches physiologiques sur la vie et la mort' (4th ed. Paris, 1822). p. 91.
[6] *Autenrieth*, loc. cit., pt. III, § 870.

they form the so-called sympathetic nerves, and then the plexus semi-lunaris, solaris, splanchnicus, and finally the communication of the semi-lunar ganglion, by means of its ramifications, with the thoracic ganglia. 'In many cases, what are called the sympathetic nerves are found to be interrupted, the part in the thorax being separated from that in the stomach (pars lumbaris) by an interstice. After having furnished the neck with a number of threads, it often becomes thicker. The nerve threads of this system are very different from those of the actual cerebro-spinal system. The latter are thicker, less numerous, whiter, denser in tissue, and exhibit little variety in structure. On the other hand, the ganglia are distinguished by their extreme thinness (ténuité), the very large numbers of their threads, particularly near the plexus, their greyish colour, the marked softness of their tissue, and the great variety in which they usually occur in the various specimens.'[1] There is a controversy as to whether these ganglia are independent, or whether they originate in the brain and spinal marrow. The relationship of the nerves to the brain and the spinal marrow is often thought of as an origination, but this conception has no definite meaning. It is taken to be an undeniable truth that the nerves originate in the brain. But although on the one hand the nerves are identical with the brain, they are also separate from it; separation of this kind does not imply that the brain is antecedent to the nerves however, any more than that the fingers originate in the palm of the hand, or the nerves in the heart. Individual nerves can be removed without impairing the vitality of the brain, just as parts of the brain can be removed without destroying the nerves.

As the sensibility of the outer organism passes over into the differentiation of irritability, its simplicity is overcome, and passes over into the opposition of the muscular system. The gemmation of the bone is taken back into the simple differentiation of the muscle, the activity of which constitutes the real material relation with inorganic nature, the mechanism's process with that outside it. Organic elasticity is the softness which withdraws into itself when it is stimulated, just as it overcomes its having given way, and resists itself by reasserting itself as line. The muscle is the unity of these two moments, both of which also exist as kinds of movement. Treviranus[2] puts forward the proposition, 'that contraction is accompanied by an actual increase in cohesion.' The following experiment is a good illustration of this. 'Erman (Gilbert's 'Annals of Physics' 1812 art. I, p. 1) took a glass cylinder open at both ends,

---

[1] Bichat, loc. cit., pp. 90, 92.
[2] Treviranus loc. cit., vol. V, p. 238.

sealed the bottom of it by means of cork with a platinum wire passing through it, and filled the cylinder with water. He placed part of the tail of a live Eel in the water, and then sealed the upper opening of the cylinder in the same way. A platinum wire also passed through this upper cork,
5 and in addition to this, a narrow glass tube open at both ends. When the upper cork was pressed, a certain amount of water entered the tube, and its level was carefully marked. *Erman* noticed that when he connected the spinal cord with one wire and the muscles with the other, and brought both wires into contact with a voltaic pile, the water in the small tube
10 fell each time the muscles contracted. It fell to the extent of four or five
+ lines, and what is more, it did so jerkily.'[1] Moreover, muscles such as those of the heart may be stimulated without this having any effect on their corresponding nerves. Similarly, the muscles set in motion in the galvanic battery also leave the nerves untouched.[2] *Treviranus* also main-
15 tains (vol. V, p. 346) that his 'Hypothesis that the transmission of stimu- lated volition to the muscles, and the convergence of external impressions on the brain, are effects of various of the nerves' component parts, the former being due to the nerve-sheaths, and the latter to the nerve-pulp,'
+ has not yet been refuted.
20 Muscular movement is the elastic irritability which, as moment of the whole, posits a self-dividing movement of its own. This movement checks the circu- latory influx, but as a self-contained movement, this irritability posits out of itself the igneous process by which this subsistent circulatory inertia is overcome. This dissolution of subsistence constitutes the pulmonary system, which as
25 the external process with inorganic nature in the element of air, is of a truly ideal nature. This process constitutes the spontaneous movement which is peculiar to the organism, and which draws in and expels as an elasticity. The blood is the result of this, and is the external organism which returns to itself, doing this within itself and by means of itself. It is the living individuality which
30 engenders the members into viscera. As rotatory and self-pursuing movement,
+ and absolute quivering within itself, the blood constitutes the individual life of the whole, in which nothing is distinguished. This is animal time. This rotatory movement then divides itself into the cometary or atmospheric process, and into
+ the volcanic process. The animal's *lungs* correspond to the leaf, which relates
35 itself to the atmosphere, and constitutes this recurrent and self-interrupting process of respiration. The *liver* on the other hand is the return from the come- tary process into the being-for-self of the lunar process; it is the being-for-self

[1] *Treviranus*, loc. cit., vol. V, p. 243.
[2] ibid., vol. V, p. 291.

which seeks its centre, it is the heat of being-for-self, hostility to being other than itself, and the burning up of this otherness. The pulmonary and hepatic processes are intimately inter-connected. The volatile and winnowing pulmonary process moderates the heat of the liver, and is invigorated by it. The lung is in danger of turning into liver, of nodulating itself, and consequently of destroying itself by 5 taking the heat of the being-for-self into itself. The blood divides itself into these two processes: its own, that of the lung, and that of the liver. Each of these contains its own circulation, for what appears as an artery in pulmonary circulation, appears as a vein in the portal system, and conversely, the veins entering the portal system appear as arteries. The system of living movement is the system 10 opposed to the external organism; it is the *power* of digestion, which is the power of overcoming the external organism. At this juncture, this inorganic nature is necessarily threefold. Firstly, it is the universal exterior lung. Secondly, it is the particularized element, or the universal relegated into the organic moment as the lymph, and into the entire being of the organism. Thirdly, it is 15 the individualized moment. The blood elaborates itself from the air, the lymph and the digestion, and is the transformation of these three moments. From the air it takes oxygen, which is the pure dissolvent and the light of the air. From the lymph it takes the neutral fluid, and from the digestion the substantial moment of singularity. It is in this way that the entire individuality opposes itself again, 20 and engenders shape.

(*a*) As the blood in the pulmonary circulation has its own movement, it constitutes this purely negative immaterial life, which here has nature as air in pure subjection to itself. The child's first breath is its own individual life; + previous to this it swam in lymph, and functioned in a vegetative and imbibing 25 manner. In emerging from the egg or womb the child breathes, and so relates itself to nature as to something which has become air, something which is not the former continuous flow, but rather the interruption of it. This interrupted-ness is the simple organic irritability whereby the blood produces and realizes itself as pure fire. 30

(*b*) It is the blood which sublates the neutrality of swimming in the lymph. It overcomes this neutrality by stimulating and moving the whole exterior organism, and so disposing it towards its return into itself. This movement too is a digestive system, a cycle of differing moments. The lymphatic vessels form their own glands or filters everywhere. The lymph digests itself in these glands, + and finally conducts itself into the thoracic duct. It is in this way that the blood acquires its general fluidity, for it must not coagulate. From its watery neutrality, the lymph changes into fat such as bone-marrow. It does not attain a higher animalization therefore, but becomes vegetable oil, and serves as nutriment. Consequently, hibernating animals become very fat in summer, and feed 40

on themselves during the winter, so that they are quite thin in the spring.
(c) Lastly, the blood is the main digestive process of the individual, which is
the *peristaltic movement* in general. As this process of singularity, it divides itself
into three moments. (*i*) It is the dull interior moment of being-for-self, the
hypochondro-melancholic generation of its sleep. This is the venous blood in
general, which becomes this nocturnal force in the *spleen*. This blood is said to
be carbonized, but it is precisely in this carbonization that it becomes earth or
absolute subject. (*ii*) Its subsequent centre is the portal system, where its subjectivity is movement, and becomes an activity, a consuming volcano. Activated
in this way in the liver, the blood operates upon the chyme, which is prepared
in the stomach. Digestion begins in the stomach, after the food has been masti-
cated and saturated with the salivary lymph. The gastric and pancreatic juices
are, as it were, the acids which break down the food in fermentation. This is
the chemico-organic moment of lymphatic activity and heat. (*iii*) In the
duodenum, the fire of the bile, which is produced by the venous blood of
the portal vein, gains true and complete mastery over the food. The outward-
orientated process which is still active in the lymph, is changed into being-for-
self, and now constitutes the self of the animal. The chyle which the blood has
produced returns into it; the blood has engendered itself.

This is the great interior circulation of individuality; the blood itself is its
middle, for the blood itself is the individual life. As the substance which is
common to all the parts, the blood is the irritable principle uniting them
all in an inner unity. Although the blood is the alteration of cohesion and
specific gravity in that it constitutes the heat, it is not merely the dissolution of heat, for it is the real animal dissolution of all the parts. Just as all
victuals change into blood, so the blood in its turn is the common source
of all nutriment. This constitutes the completely real aspect of pulsation.
It has been said that the juices are inorganic because they are secretitious, and
that it is only the solid parts of the body which are alive. In themselves, distinctions such as this are somewhat meaningless however, and what is more, the
blood is not life, but is the living subject as such, which is opposed to the genus
or universal. The seedy vegetarians of India will eat no flesh, and refuse to take
an animal's life; the law-giver of the Jews merely forbad the consumption of
blood, the blood being regarded as the life of the animal. The blood is this
infinite and continuous agitation, this welling forth from itself; the nerve
is at rest however, and remains where it is. The infinite distribution, and
this dissolution of the division, accompanied by redivision, is the immediate expression of the Notion. The Notion might be said to appear here
before the eyes; it occurs in an immediately sensuous way in the description given of it by Professor Schultz, according to whom globules have a

tendency to form in the blood, although they do not actually do so. The blood will conglobe into globules if it is allowed to run into water, but the living blood itself will not do so. Thus, it is only when the blood is dying and it is exposed to the atmosphere, that its conglobulation becomes evident. The concrete existence of these globules, like atomism, is a fig- 5 ment of the imagination, and is based upon false evidence obtained when the blood is drawn forcibly from the organism. The primary determina- + tion of the blood is pulsation; the circulation is the vital point, and the mechanical explanations of it given by the understanding are of no value, for it eludes the finest anatomical and microscopical investigations. It is 10 said that the internal firing of the blood from the air entails the inhalation of the atmosphere, and the exhalation of nitrogen and carbon dioxide. Nothing can be grasped by means of this chemistry however, for it is life, and not a chemical process which constitutes the continuity of respiration.

The concentration of this internal differentiation into a single system, 15 is the heart, which is the vital muscular principle. This system is connected throughout with reproduction. There are no nerves to be found in the heart, for it is the pure vitality of centralized irritability, the pulsating muscle. As absolute movement, and the natural living unity of the process + itself, the blood is movement, it is not moved. Physiologists search for all kinds 20 of forces to explain its movement. 'The cardiac muscle first thrusts the blood outwards, and then the walls of the arteries and veins and the pressure of the firm parts help to drive it. It is true that the impulse in the heart no longer operates in the veins, so that the effect there must be produced solely by pressure from the walls of the veins.' All these mechanical explanations offered by physi- + ologists are inadequate however, for they cannot explain the origin of this elastic pressure of the walls and the heart. They tell us that it comes, 'From the irritation of the blood,' which implies that the heart moves the blood, and that the motion of the blood in its turn motivates the heart. This is a circle, a perpetuum mobile however, and because of the equilibrium between its forces, 30 it must at the same time remain immobile. This is precisely why it is rather the blood itself which constitutes the principle of movement. The blood is the leaping point through which the contraction of the arteries coincides with + the relaxation of the ventricle of the heart. There is nothing incompre- hensible or unknown about the *autonomy* of this movement, unless 'com- 35 prehension' is taken to mean that some extraneous cause is to be shown as working upon it. This 'extraneous cause' is only an external necessity however, and is therefore not a necessity at all. The cause itself is something distinct, and the cause of this same thing still has to be looked for, so that there is a perpetual progression to something else. This leads to the spurious infinity, the 40

inability to think and conceive of the universal as the ground and simplicity which is the unity of opposites, and which is therefore immovable and yet moved. The blood is this unity, it is the subject which is just as much the initiation of a movement as the will is. In that it constitutes the whole movement, the
5 blood is the ground as well as the movement itself. It is precisely as such, that it separates from itself into a single moment however, for it distinguishes itself from itself. The movement here is precisely this self-separation, by which it constitutes the subject or thing, and the sublation of this separation as the inclusion of itself with that opposed to it. However, it is precisely because the
10 opposite constitutes the implicit sublation of itself, and brings about the return from its own side, that the movement appears as a part and result. It is in this way that the living and animating force of the blood proceeds from shape, but its interior movement also requires the outer movement, which is strictly mechanical. It moves, and holds the parts in their negative qualitative difference, but
15 it cannot dispense with the simple negative principle of external movement. Thus, an invalid who has been inactive for a long time, on account of amputations for example, develops anchylosis; there is a diminution in the amount of
+ synovia, his cartilages ossify, and his muscles become flabby through lack of external movement.
20   In one respect the blood-circulation itself is to be regarded as this general circulation by which each part participates in this circular movement; inwardly however, it is to an equal extent completely elastic, and not merely this circular movement. The movement even varies somewhat throughout the various parts of the body. It is slower in the portal system and inside the cranium than it is
+ elsewhere, while in the lungs it is more accelerated. In a whitlow, the artery (radialis) has a hundred pulse-beats to the minute, while the artery on the healthy side of the finger has only seventy, and synchronizes with the pulsation of the heart. What is more, the arteries and veins pass into each other by means of the finest canals (capillary vessels), some of which are so fine that they are devoid of
+ red blood-globules, and merely contain a yellowish serum. 'In the case of the
+ eye,' says *Sömmerring*, 'it seems that the arteries are continued in finer branches, which no longer contain red blood. These branches pass initially into a similar vein, but finally into veinlets carrying red blood.' Here therefore, there is no transition of that which is properly called blood; a movement is posited in which
35 the blood vanishes and appears again, and this is an elastic vibration, not a progression. The transition is not immediately perceptible therefore, or is only rarely so. There is also an abundant anastomosis of the veins, and particularly of the arteries; this gives rise partly to the larger arteries, and partly to quite large plexa, and here therefore it is quite inconceivable that there should be any
40 ordinary *circulation*. The blood is driven into the anastomising branch from both

sides, giving rise to an equilibrium which is not a flow in one direction, but merely an interior quivering. One direction might perhaps be thought to preponderate in a single branch, but with several complete coronas, or plexa of anastomoses, one direction cancels out the other, and converts the movement into a general interior pulsation. If one of the *arteries* is opened, the blood will spurt much further when the heart is contracted, than it will when it is relaxed. In the arteries, the period of contraction lasts a little longer than the period of distension, while the opposite is true of the heart. However, it must not be thought that the blood moves round the animated *arterial* system in a series of waves, or that if the whole length of an artery were uncovered, it would resemble a rosary thread. Throughout the whole of its length, and in all its branches, the arterial system has a uniformly cylindrical appearance; it oscillates faintly with every beat of the heart, and exhibits a uniform lateral expansion which is scarcely perceptible in any but the larger trunks, while during the contraction of the heart, it shrinks as it were.'[1] Circulation certainly occurs therefore, but it is *oscillatory.*

It is in the lung and the liver that the distinction between arterial and venous blood becomes a reality. There one has the opposition between the extensor and flexor muscles. The arterial blood is the diffusive, dissolving activity, and the venous blood is the movement into itself; the pulmonary and hepatic systems constitute their special life. The chemical explanation of the difference here is that the arterial blood has a higher oxygen content, and is therefore a brighter red, while the venous blood contains more carbon, and when shaken in oxygen, also becomes a brighter red. This explanation of the difference merely states the fact however, it does not express the nature of these two kinds of blood, and their relatedness within the whole system of circulation.

The general process is this return of the self from its cometary, lunar, and terrestrial course, to itself; this return from its viscera to its unity. The return is therefore its general digestion, in which its quiescence is its determinate being. It therefore returns into shape in general, and this constitutes its result. It is precisely by dividing itself into viscera that this shape-sublating process shapes itself, and so forms the alimentary process, which also has shape as its product. Now this nutrition does not consist of the arterial blood's ridding itself of its oxygenated fibrin. The exhalatory vessels of the arteries are more of an elaborated vapour, an entirely general aliment, from which each individual part of the body takes what it needs to form its contribution to the whole. This lymph originates in the blood therefore, and constitutes the animating aliment. To a

[1] *Autenrieth,* loc. cit., pt. I, § 367–369.

greater extent it is the general animation however, the being-for-self of each member, by virtue of which it transforms inorganic nature or the universal organism into itself. The blood is the animation of each member, it does not supply it with matter. The blood does not supply matter, but is the animation
5 of each member, the form of which is the main thing. This is not merely the function of the artery, but of the blood in its dual capacity as vein and artery. The heart is ubiquitous therefore, and each part of the organism is merely the specified force of the heart itself.

Strictly speaking, the reproductive or digestive system is not present as
10 a perfected system of members, for whereas the systems of sensibility and irritability belong to the distinct moments of development, reproduction does not give rise to form. What is more, it is only the whole shape in a formal manner, so that it reaches no distinct division into determinations of form. At this juncture, the reproductive system may only be said to be
15 abstract, since its function appertains to assimilation.

(a) *Reproduction* in its subdued and *immediate form* is the cellular tissue and glandular structure, the skin, simple animal *gelatine*, and tubes. In animals which consist of nothing else, there are as yet no developed differences. The skin constitutes the organic activity of shape; the *lymph* is con-
20 nected with this, and its contact with externality is the whole process of nutrition. The skin is the immediate return of the exterior organism into itself, and through it the organism becomes self-related. At first, the skin is still only the Notion of the internal organism, and consequently the externality of shape. The skin can be and become anything, including nerves and blood-vessels etc.;
25 in its *absorbent* capacity it is the general digestive organ of the vegetative system.

(b) The skin has assumed a differentiated relationship through the claws, bones and muscles, but it now interrupts its absorption, and relates itself to air and water as a singularity. To the organism, the externality to which it relates itself
30 is not merely a universal element, but something individualized, even if it is only an individual mouthful of water. The skin works inwards therefore; in addition to being a general recipient, it now forms the individual orifice of the *mouth*, so that inorganic being is seized upon and taken in as individuality. The individual takes possession of it, obliterates it as a purely external shape, and transforms it
35 into itself. It does not do this by immediate infection, but by an intermediary motion, which causes it to pass through|various moments. This is *reproduction in opposition*. In the higher species of animals, immediate and simple digestion explicates itself into a system of viscera, including the bile, the hepatic system, the *pancreas* or *abdominal gland*, and the *pancreatic* juice.
40 The positing of animal heat derives on the whole from the individual nature of

the shapes it overcomes. The heat is the absolute mediating movement of the intro-reflected organism. This organism has the elements within itself, and so maintains itself in a state of activity by bringing their concerted motion to bear upon the individual piece of food. It infects the food (*i*) with the organic lymph or saliva; (*ii*) with the neutrality of the alkaline and acid principles, the animal 5 gastric and pancreatic juices; and (*iii*) with the bile, submitting the ingested food to the onslaught of the igneous element.

(*c*) The *stomach* and the *intestinal canal* are the inward-turned or visceral *reproduction*. In its immediate function, the stomach is this digestive heat as such, and the intestinal canal separates the digested food (*i*) into the entirely inorganic 10 substance which is to be excreted; and (*ii*) into the completely animalized substance of the blood, which is just as much the unity of the subsequent shape, as it is the heat of dissolution. The simplest animals consist of nothing but an intestinal canal.

§ 355

3. The total shape

However, the differences of the elements and their systems also 15 unite in a general concrete interpenetration in shape. In this unity, each formation of shape contains these elements linked together within it. Shape correspondingly divides or incises itself, (*i*) into the *centres of the three systems* of the head, the thorax and the abdomen. The extremities of these systems function 20 as a mechanical movement and grasping, and constitute the moment of singularity positing itself as distinct from *externality*. (*ii*) In accordance with abstract differentiation, shape[1] distinguishes itself in two directions, outwards and inwards. Every shape shares in both the inwardly and the outwardly ori- 25 entated aspects of each[2] system. The outwardly orientated aspect is in itself differentiated, and as such exhibits this differentiation through the symmetrical duality of its organs and limbs (Bichat's vie organique et animale).[3] (*iii*) In this self-relating

---

[1] Addition to the second edition, 'in its wholeness'.
[2] Addition to the second edition, 'previously determined'.
[3] Addition. *Bichat* ch. I, pp. 7–8: 'Les fonctions de l'animal forment deux classes très distinctes. +
Les unes se composent d'une succession habituelle d'assimilation et d'excrétion. Il ne vit qu'*en lui*, par cette classe de fonctions; par l'autre, il existe *hors de lui*. Il sent et apperçoit ce qui l'entoure,

individuality, the whole as a shape perfected into an independent individual, is at the same time particularized into the sex-relationship, which is an outward relationship with another individual. As shape is self-enclosed, it indicates its two outward
5 directions upon itself.

Addition. Brought together concretely in the whole shape, sensibility, irritability and reproduction form the outer figuration of the organism,
+ the crystal of animation.

(*a*) In the *first instance* these determinations are merely forms, and are
10 sharply separated from one another, as they are in insects. As this determinateness, or in this single form, each moment constitutes a total system. Thus, the head is the centre of sensibility, the thorax of irritability, and the abdomen of reproduction. These centres contain the organism's most important viscera, its inner functions, while the extremities such as
15 hands, feet, wings, fins etc., marks its relation with the outer world.

(*b*) In the *second instance*, these centres are also developed totalities, so that the other determinations are not merely determined as forms, but are displayed and contained in each of these totalities. As each abstract system permeates them all, and is connected with them, and each exhibits
20 the whole shape, the systems of nerves, veins, blood, bones, muscles, skin, glands etc. each constitute a whole skeleton. This establishes the contexture of the organism, for at the same time as each system is interlaced into the domain of the other, it maintains the connection within itself. In the head and brain there are organs of sensibility, bones, and
25 nerves; but all the parts of the other systems, blood, veins, glands, skin, also belong there. It is the same with the thorax, which has nerves, glands, skin, etc.

(*c*) In addition to the two distinct forms of these totalities, there is a *third form*, which belongs to sensation as such, and whose main feature is
+ the link up with the soul. These higher unities assemble the organs of all the totalities about themselves, and have their point of unity in the sentient subject. They present considerable difficulties of a new kind. They constitute connections linking the particular parts of one system with

réfléchit ses sensations, se meut volontairement d'après leur influence, et le plus souvent peut communiquer par la voix ses désirs et ses craintes, ses plaisirs ou ses peines. J'appelle *vie organique* l'ensemble des fonctions de la première classe, parceque tous les êtres organisés, végétaux ou animaux, en jouissent. Les fonctions réunies de la seconde classe forment la *vie animale*, ainsi nommée parcequ'elle est l'attribut exclusif du règne animale.' Bichat's fine perception of nature has here given him profound insight, in enabling him to draw attention to this difference in the organism.

those of this or that other system. The connections are made on account of their functions however, partly by their forming a concrete centre, and partly by their having the implicitness of their associations, or rather, their more basic determination, in the sentient creature. They are soul-like nodes so to speak. As a self-determining entity, the soul is present in the body in a general way, it does not merely conform to the specific connectedness of the corporality.

(i) Thus the mouth belongs to the particular system of sensibility for example, to the extent that it contains the tongue, which is the organ of taste, as a moment of the theoretical process. The mouth also has teeth, which are its extremities, their function being to seize upon what is outside, and to grind it. The mouth is also the organ of the voice and of speech, and other related sensations such as that of thirst are also located there. Laughter, and kissing too, are also matters for the mouth. The mouth therefore unifies the expressions of many sensations. The eye provides another example of this. It is the organ of sight, but in animals as well as man, it also gives rise to tears. Seeing and crying may seem to be remote from one another, but they occur in a single organ, and have the inner ground of their connection in the nature of sentience. They therefore find a superior connection, which cannot be said to lie in the process of the living organism.

(ii) There are also connections of another kind, in which phenomena emerge in widely separated parts of the organic being, their connection being merely implicit, not physical. There is therefore said to be a sympathy between these parts, which is supposed to be due to the nerves. All parts of the organic being have this connection however, so that this cannot be a sufficient explanation of it. The connection is grounded in the determinateness of sensation, and in man, in his spirituality. The development of the voice together with the coming of puberty lies in the interior aspect of sentient nature, and is an example of such a connection. The swelling of the breasts during pregnancy is another example of it.

(iii) Here, the sentient being brings forth relationships which are not physical, but it also isolates the physically connected parts once again. For example, one can will a certain part of the body to be active, and this activity is then brought about by means of the nerves. These nerves are themselves branches of other nerves however, so that they are connected with many other nerves, and unite with them in a single trunk, which is in communication with the brain. The sentient being certainly works throughout the whole of this therefore, but sensation isolates this point of activity, so that it is brought about or mediated by these nerves, without the rest of the body's connectedness being involved. *Autenrieth* (loc. cit. pt. III, § 937) cites the following example of this, 'It is more difficult to explain crying by internal causes, for the nerves which reach the lachrymal glands are from the fifth pair, and this pair also serves many other parts, in which feelings of sadness do not bring about changes, as they do in the lachrymal glands. The soul is able to act outwards in certain directions however, without the particular direction being determined by the anatomical communication of the nerves. By using particular muscles which are also in communication with many other muscles through their common nerve-trunks, we are therefore able to move particular parts of the body in a certain direction, without all these other muscles also taking part in the action. Yet it is also quite clear in a case such as this, that the will only acts through the nerve-trunk common to all these muscles. The separate fibres of this nerve-trunk intercommunicate so multifariously, that if the nerve is cut or ligatured, the soul no longer has any influence upon the muscles it serves, even when all its other means of communicating with these muscles, such as vessels and cellular tissue etc., remain undamaged.' The implicit being of the sentient creature holds supreme sway over the efficacy of the systems therefore. It establishes relationships which are not there physically, or conversely, interrupts those which are.

Symmetry is also present in this shape, although only in its outward aspect;[1] for in relationship with another, self-identity only manifests itself as equality. The different moments of shape which proceed inwards not only lack symmetrical duplication, for anatomists also come across, 'numerous diversities in the form, size, position and direction of the internal organs such as the spleen, the liver, the stomach, the kidneys, and the salivary glands. This is particularly so in the case of the lymphatic vessels, which seldom occur in the same number and volume in any two specimens.'[2] Bichat (loc. cit. pp. 15–17) is quite right when he says that in the system of sensibility, the sensory and motor nerves are symmetrical, for there are two similar pairs on each side. The same is true of the sense organs, for we have two eyes and two ears, and the nose is also symmetrical etc. The osseous system is also extremely symmetrical. In the system of irritability the muscles, and the female breasts etc. are symmetrical. The same is true of the ligaments of the extremities, which facilitate locomotion, and the voice; also of mechanical grasping, for arms, hands and

---

[1] *Bichat*, loc. cit., p. 14.
[2] *Bichat*, loc. cit., p. 22.

legs occur in pairs. *Bichat* (loc. cit. p. 41) regards the lack of symmetry in the larynx, which is a common occurrence, as an exception, 'Most physiologists, and Haller in particular, have attributed lack of harmony + in the voice to the discordance of the two symmetrical sides of the larynx, and to the difference in the strength of its muscles and nerves' etc. On the + other hand, the brain and the heart, as well as the lung, the ganglia, the internal venous system of reproduction, the abdominal muscles, the liver, and the stomach are all asymmetrical. The arrangement of the ganglia in particular is utterly irregular, in that they are entirely lacking in a division into two sides, 'The sympathetic nerve, whose sole purpose is to serve the 10 inner life, displays an irregular distribution in most of its branches. The plexus solaris, mesentericus, hypogastricus, splenicus, stomachicus etc. are examples of this.'[1] +

Uniform duplication is not a complete duplication however. Occupation, habit, activity and intelligence generally, will modify this equality 15 of shape into inequality again, especially in human beings. As a spiritual being, man tends to concentrate his activity upon a single point, and to screw himself up to speak. Unlike the animal, he does not only do this with his mouth in order to take in animal nourishment however, but shapes his form by orientating his individuality outwards, and in a special 20 way concentrating his bodily power into a single point of his body, deploying it in a certain direction, and for particular purposes. He will disturb the equilibrium of this power in order to write for example. In human beings therefore, the right arm and hand are used more than the left. This is of course due to their connection with the whole, for as 25 the heart is on the left, this side of the body is always held back and defended by the right. Similarly, people rarely hear equally well with both ears, and one eye is often sharper than the other. In human beings, the cheeks of the face are seldom quite similar in shape. This symmetry remains much more definite in animals. Thus, there is equality in the 30 strength and form of the limbs, but variation in their agility. However, exercises in which intelligence only plays a small part preserve symmetry in their movements. 'Animals leap with the greatest skill from crag to crag, where the very slightest slip would send them toppling into the abyss, and move with astonishing precision on surfaces scarcely as wide 35 as the extremities of their limbs. Even the ungainliest of animals do not stumble so often as man. In them, the equilibrium in the motor organs

---

[1] *Bichat,* loc. cit. pp. 17–18.

of both sides' is even more rigidly maintained than it is in man, who voluntarily introduces inequality. When people acquire spiritual and other kinds of aptitudes, and develop a fluent style, ability in music and the fine arts, technical skills, the art of fencing etc., the equilibrium is lost.[1] On the other hand, cruder and purely bodily exercises such as drill, gymnastics, running, climbing, tight-rope walking, jumping and vaulting, preserve this equilibrium. Activities such as these are not conducive to aptitudes of the first kind however, and as they tend to be devoid of thought, they are generally obstacles to mental composure.

In the course of this paragraph, shape is considered *firstly* as quiescent, and *secondly* in its relation to an other outside it. The *third* moment of shape is therefore also its relation to another, but to an other which at the same time belongs to the same genus, and in which the individual reaches awareness of itself in sensation, by having a sensation of itself in another. A determination of the whole shape emerges in the male and female. Here there is a difference in habitude, which in man also extends into spirituality, and becomes a distinct natural disposition.

§356[2]

4. The process of formation

In that it is alive, the shape is essentially a process. As such it is indeed abstract,[3] and is the *process of formation within itself,* **in which the organism converts its own members into its inorganic nature, or into means, consuming itself, and producing itself as precisely this totality of members. In**

---

[1] Cf. *Bichat,* loc. cit. pp. 35–40.

[2] In the first edition, this paragraph was preceded by the following passage: 'The Idea of living being is the demonstrated *unity* of the Notion and its reality. However, as an *opposition to this subjectivity* and *objectivity,* it is only essential as *process,* the movement of the abstract self-relation of living being. This movement develops itself within particularity, and as return into self, constitutes the negative unity of subjectivity, as well as totality. As a concrete moment of animation however, each of these moments is itself process, and the whole is the *unity of three processes.*' In the first edition therefore, the three anatomical moments were presented under numbers 1–3, and were separated from the three physiological moments, which then followed as the three processes of shape, assimilation and the genus. This was improved upon in the second and third edition, where there is a fuller interpenetration of the anatomical and physiological aspects. There is a further difference in these editions however, for while four moments of shape are distinguished in the third edition, in the second edition there are only three, numbers 1 and 2 of the third edition being included under one heading.

Note by Michelet.

[3] Addition to the first and second editions, 'animated singularity'.

this process each member is interchangeably both end and means, and maintains itself by virtue of the other members, and in opposition to them. The result of this process is simple **and immediate** sentience.

Addition. As the first process, the process of formation is the Notion of the process. It is the restlessness of formation, but it is this only as a general activity, as general animal process. Indeed, as this abstract process, and in so far as the force of living being is the immediate transformation of externality into animal being, it is to be grasped in conjunction with the external world, as the vegetable process. Organic being in its developed state expresses itself in its particular structure however, the parts of which are not independent members, but merely moments within living subjectivity. Consequently, these parts are sublated, negated and posited by the vitality of the organism. The contradiction here between their being and not being, and between their having come forth from subjectivity while being contained within it, manifests itself as this perpetual process. The organism is the unity of the inner and outer, so that (a) as inner, it is the process of shaping, and the shape is a sublated moment which remains enclosed within the self; or so that this outer, this other, this product, has returned into that which brought it forth. Unlike the plant, the organic unit brings itself forth without becoming another individual; it is a circulation which returns into itself. (b) The otherness or externality of the organism is the untrammelled being of shape, the quiescence opposed to the process. (c) The organism itself is the higher quiescence of both moments, which is the restless self-equality of the Notion. In shaping in general, the blood in its exhalation allows itself to be reduced to lymph, while the sluggish and indeterminate fluidity of the lymph becomes consolidated and ramate, on the one side separating into the opposition of the muscles, which is a movement immanent in shape, and on the other withdrawing into the immobility of bone. The fat or marrow of the bone is this vegetability, which progresses as far as oil, and which excretes a neutrality from itself, not as water, but as the neutral earthy substance of lime, just as the plant progresses as far as the production of silica. Bone is this dead neutrality between the lymph and the marrow.

The individual not only objectifies itself in this way however, but likewise idealizes this reality. Each part is hostile to the others, and maintains itself at their expense, but to an equal extent it also surrenders itself. There is no permanence about the organism; everything is reproduced, even the bones. *Richerand* therefore says of bone-formation (loc. cit. pt. II p.

256), 'If the inner periosteum is destroyed with a stylet, the outer covering separates from the bone, appropriates the phosphate of lime brought to it by the vessels spread throughout its tissue, and forms new bone around the other.' In itself an organ is only determinate in that it conforms to the general purpose, and forms the whole living being. Each member draws on the others for its own needs, for each secerns animal lymph, which is distributed to the vessels and led back to the blood, and each draws its nourishment from this secretion. The process of shaping is therefore conditioned by the consumption of its formations. If the organism is restricted to this process, as it is when the outward activity is interrupted in the case of disease for example, the patient constitutes his own food, and draws sustenance from himself. The organism becomes thinner in an illness because it no longer has the power to assimilate inorganic matter, and is only able to live on itself. Thus, in *Blumauer's* version of the '*Aeneid*', Aeneas' companions consume their stomachs; and in starving dogs, it has actually been discovered that the stomach has been eaten into and partly absorbed by the lymphatic vessels. This process of self-emission and of self-collection inwards, is a perpetual operation. The organism is said to contain nothing of its former self after five, ten or twenty years, for in that time everything material has been consumed away, and only the substantial form persists.

The higher unity is in general that in which the activity of a single system is conditioned by the activity of another system. For example, many experiments and investigations have been made in order to determine the extent to which the digestion, and the circulation of the blood etc. are independent of nervous activity, or the extent to which respiration is independent of the brain etc., and conversely therefore, whether life can still subsist if one or the other of them is stopped. Enquiry has also been made into the influence of respiration upon the circulation of the blood etc. In this connection *Treviranus* cites the case (loc. cit. vol. IV, p. 264), 'of a child born without heart and lungs, and yet possessing arteries and veins.' With these defects it could certainly have lived within the womb of course, but it could not have survived birth. From this example it was concluded that *Haller's* proposition, 'that the heart alone is the driving force behind the circulation of the blood,' was false, and that a fundamental question had been decided. But the question is whether the blood will continue to circulate after the heart has been removed. *Treviranus* (loc. cit. vol. IV, p. 645 et seq.) has conducted various experiments, especially with frog's hearts, but apart from showing how he tortured these animals, they have proved nothing. Nevertheless, he

opposed *Haller's* opinion that it is merely the beating of the heart which produces the circulation of the blood, and maintained, 'that the blood has a motive power of its own, which is dependent upon the nervous system and which has the uninterrupted influence of this system, and especially of the spinal cord, as a necessary condition of its continuance. For if the 5 nerve-trunk and spinal cord of a member are severed, the circulation of the blood in this part stops. From this it follows that, 'each part of the spinal cord, and each nerve-trunk coming from it, sustains the circulation of the blood in those organs which it provides with nerve-branches.' +
Legallois, who, 'does not seem to have dreamt of the possibility of any 10 theory of the circulation of the blood apart from *Haller's*,' opposes *Treviranus* with the hypothesis that, 'the circulation of the blood simply depends upon the contractions of the heart, and it is only through their influence upon this organ, that partial destructions of the nervous system enfeeble or stop the circulation.' In general, *Legallois* is of the opinion 15 that the heart draws its power from the whole of the spinal cord.[1] +
Legallois experimented with rabbits, and also with cold-blooded animals, and reached the following conclusion:—There is certainly a very close connection between any given part of the spinal cord, such as that of the neck, the chest, or the loins, and the circulation of the corresponding 20 part of the body which receives the motor-nerves from that part. When such a part of the spinal cord is destroyed, this has a double effect upon the circulation of the blood. (*a*) As the heart is deprived of the contingent of forces it received from the destroyed part of the cord, the general circulation is weakened. (*b*) The circulation in the corresponding part 25 is weakened first, so that the heart still has to do the same amount of work in the whole range of the circulation, although it no longer has the power of the whole cord. However, if the cord is destroyed in the loins for example, and a ligature is applied to the arteries in that part, circulation is no longer necessary there; as there is spinal cord in the rest of the 30 body, the equilibrium between the heart and the circulation is preserved. What is more, *Legallois* even discovered that this part lived longer, and that when he destroyed the brain and the cervical spinal cord, the circulation continued through the jugular arteries. For example, a rabbit survived for more than three quarters of an hour after its head had been 35 completely removed, for bleeding was prevented, and an equilibrium was therefore established. He made these experiments on rabbits which were between three and ten, or at the most fourteen days old, and found that

[1] *Treviranus*, loc. cit. vol. IV, pp. 653, 272, 266-267, 269-270, 273, 644.

older rabbits died more quickly.[1] The reason for this is that the life of the older animals has a more intensive unity, whereas in the young it is more akin to the life of the polyp. The main evidence cited by *Treviranus* in contesting *Legallois'* conclusions, is that the heart will still continue to beat for a time, even when the destruction of the spinal cord has already arrested the circulation of the blood. At the end of this investigation he uses this evidence to counter *Legallois* with the conclusion that, '*Haller* maintains that the nervous system has no immediate influence upon the beating of the heart, and this view therefore remains unrefuted.'[2] Whatever importance one may attach to determinations and conclusions such as these, one cannot infer more from them than certain differences, e.g. that digestion will still continue after the removal of the heart etc. This continuation is so limited in duration however, that neither function can be regarded as at all independent of the other. The functions of the organization are dependent upon one another to the precise extent of the organization's perfection, i.e. the extent to which its functions are distinct and determinate. In less perfect animals therefore, these functions are more tenacious of life. *Treviranus* (loc. cit. vol. V, p. 267) cites amphibia as examples of this, and mentions, 'toads and lizards which were found alive in stones, in completely sealed cavities,' and which therefore may well have been present at the creation of the world! 'In England recently, observations were made of two lizards which were discovered fifteen feet below the surface of the chalk at *Eldon* in *Suffolk*. At first they seemed to be completely lifeless; little by little they began to show signs of life, particularly after they were placed in the sun. In both creatures the mouth was sealed with a sticky substance which prevented their breathing. One of the lizards was put in water, and the other kept dry. The former succeeded in ridding itself of the sticky substance, and lived for several weeks before it finally died. The other died the following night.' Molluscs, insects, and worms furnish us with much more remarkable facts. They can go without food for months and years. Snails can live for more than a year without a head. The life of many insects is not harmed by their being frozen for a considerable period of time. Some animals can do without atmospheric air for lengthy periods, and others can live in very hot water. Rotifers have been resuscitated after four years etc.[3]

---

[1] 'Moniteur universel' 1811 no. 312. (Cf. *Treviranus*, loc. cit. vol. IV, pp. 273–275).

[2] *Treviranus*, loc. cit. vol. IV, pp. 651–653.

[3] *Treviranus*, loc. cit. vol. V, pp. 269–273 (vol. II, p. 16).

B

Assimilation

§ 357

[1]The sentience of *individuality* is **to the same extent** immediately *exclusive* **however,** and maintains a state of tension with an inorganic nature to which it is opposed **as to its external condition and material.**

Addition. The process outwards is the *real* process, in which the animal no longer converts its own nature into inorganic being, as it does when it is diseased. In this process, the animal must also release the other, which is a moment within the organism, into the abstraction of an immediately present outer world, with which it enters into relationship. This basic division, or expulsion of the Sun and everything else, constitutes the precise standpoint of animation. The *Idea* of life is in itself this unconscious creativeness, it is an expansion of nature, which in animation has returned into its truth. For the individual however, inorganic nature is a presupposition with which it is confronted, and it is this which gives rise to the finitude of living being. The individual is for itself, but as the organic being has this negativity within itself, the connection here is absolute, indivisible, internal, and essential. Externality is determined only as having being for organic being; organic being is that which maintains itself in opposition to it. Organic being is orientated towards externality to the same extent that it is internally strung in opposition to it, and this consequently gives rise to the contradiction of this relationship, in which two independent beings come forth in opposition to each other, while at the same time externality has to be sublated. The organism must therefore posit the subjectivity of externality, appropriate it, and identify it with its own self; this constitutes *assimilation*. The forms of this process are threefold; *firstly* the theoretical process, *secondly* the real, practical process, and *thirdly* the unity of both, the process which is of an ideal and real nature—the adaptation of inorganic being to the end of living being, that is to say instinct, and the nisus formativus.

---

[1] Addition to the first and second edition, 'In its negative return into itself.'

1. The theoretical process

§ 357a

In this external relation, the animal organism is *immediately* intro-reflected, and consequently the ideal nature of this relatedness is the *theoretical* process, **sensibility as outward process,** and indeed **as** *determinate feeling,* which differentiates itself into its *multifarious perceptions* of inorganic
5 nature.

Addition. The self of the organism is the unity of its blood or of the pure process, and its shape; and as such, and because its shape is completely sublated in this fluidity, it contains being as a sublation. It is through this that the organism is raised into pure ideality, which is perfectly transparent universality; it is
10 space and time, and at the same time neither spatial nor temporal. As it perceives something which is distinguished from it by being spatial and temporal, this distinction undergoes an immediate nullification. This movement of intuition is the universal element of *sense*. Sensibility was precisely this vanishing of determinateness into the pure ideality of the soul or ego, which re-
15 mains with itself. Through its sensation, an animal determines itself in a particular way however, and is not merely aware of itself, but of a particular moment of itself. A sentient creature is distinguished from a non-sentient by its becoming a particular moment of itself. In sentient being there is therefore a relation to an other which is immediately posited as
20 the ego's. That which is hard and warm etc. is independent and external, but it is to an equal extent immediately transformed, and given an ideal nature as a determinateness of my feeling; what I contain is the same as that outside me, it is merely its form which is different. Thus, spirit only has consciousness as self-consciousness; in other words, in being related
25 to an external object, I am at the same time for myself. The theoretical process is the free disinterested process of sensation, which also allows for the subsistence of the external being. The different determinations we have seen in inorganic nature are also modifications of sensation, and as such they constitute a diversified relation between inorganic nature and
30 organic being. This is the precise reason for their being called senses.

§ 358

The senses and the theoretical processes are therefore:
(1) *feeling* as such, which is the sense of the mechanical
sphere—of *gravity*, of cohesion and its alteration and of
heat; (2) *smell* and *taste*, which are the senses of *opposition*,
of the particularized *principle of air*, and of the equally 5
realized *neutrality* consisting of **concrete** water and the
opposed moments **of the** dissolution **of concrete neutrality.**
(3) The sense of **ideality, which is also duplicated, in so far as
the particularization which ideality must contain as abstract self-
reference falls apart into two indifferent determinations. It is** 10
duplicated (a) into the sense of **sight, of ideality as manifestation
of external being for external being; this is the sense of** *light*
in general, and more precisely of *colour*, **or of light which has
become determined within concrete externality; and** (b) **into
the** sense of *hearing*, **of sound, of the manifestations of internal** 15
being, which reveals itself as such in its expression.

Remark

We see here how the triad of the Notion's moments passes
over numerically into a quintuplicity. **The more general
ground for the occurrence of the transition at this juncture, is that**[1]
the animal organism is the reduction of the separated moments of 20
**inorganic nature to the infinite unity of subjectivity, although in
this unity, the animal organism is at the same time inorganic
nature's developed totality, the moments of which still exist
separately, because the totality is still a natural subjectivity.**[2]

Addition. Sense is the immediate unity of being and of that belonging to it. 25

[1] First edition, 'The *triad* of the Notion's moments passes over numerically into a *quintuplicity*
at this juncture, because in its totality, the moment of particularity or of opposition is itself a triad.'
[2] Addition to the first edition, '*Universality* therefore, as that which is still inwardly concrete,
and as gravity with its individualizing determinations, has *touch* as its particular sense. This sense
is basic to all the others, and it is therefore better to call it *feeling* in general. *Particularity* constitutes
the opposition, which is the indentity as well as the opposition itself. This particularity is therefore
related to the sense of *light*, as identity which is abstract, but yet precisely for this reason self-
determined, and the constituent of one side of the opposition. It is also related to the two senses of
the essential opposition as such, which are the senses of *air* and of *water*, both of which, like the
other moments, have embodied specification and individualization. *Sound*, as the subjectivity which
reveals itself as a pure being-in-self of subjectivity, belongs to the sense of *singularity*.'

Initially it is feeling, which is the non-objective union with the object, in which however the object is also withdrawn to an equal extent into being-for-self. This unity has two aspects therefore: it is the sense of shape as shape, and the sense of heat. It is only a subdued differentiation which occurs here, be-
5 cause the other is only a generality, and is devoid of any intrinsic difference. The moment of difference—positive and negative—consequently falls apart as figure and heat. Feeling is therefore the sense of the earthy element, of matter, of that which offers resistance, of that in accordance with which I have immediate existence as an individual. The other also communi-
10 cates with me as an individual material being, the being-for-self of which also corresponds to my awareness of it. Matter aspires towards a centre, and the primary satisfaction of this aspiration is the animal, which has its centre within itself. What I am sensible of is precisely this impulsion of matter which is devoid of self, towards an other. The particular ways
15 of offering resistance, such as softness, hardness, elasticity, and smooth- ness or roughness of surface, also belong here. Figure and shape are also nothing more than the manner in which this resistance is limited spatially. These determinations, which we dealt with in various spheres, are bound together in feeling as in a bouquet; for as we saw above (Addition to
20 § 355 III. 128, 8), it is precisely sentient nature which has the power of bind- ing together many widely separated spheres.

Even with regard to their organs, smell and taste are closely related, for the nose and the mouth are very intimately connected. Whereas feeling is the sense of the indifferent existence of things, smell and taste
25 are the practical senses, their object being the real being-for-other of things, whereby things are exhausted.

In light something only manifests itself immediately, as immediate determinate being. Sound however, which is the manifestation of inward- ness, is the posited and produced manifestation of inwardness as inward-
30 ness. In sight, the physical self manifests itself spatially, in hearing it does so temporally. In hearing, the object ceases to be a thing. We see the same thing with both eyes, because they see the same thing, making a single perception of their sight of the object, just as many arrows hit only one point. It is precisely the unity of the direction which cancels the diversity
35 of the sensation. Yet I am also just as able to see a single object in dupli- cate, if while it is in my field of vision, my eyes are concentrating upon something else. For example, if I fix my eyes on a distant object, and at the same time concentrate upon my finger, I am aware of my finger without changing the direction of my eyes, and see both objects at once.
40 This becoming aware of the whole field of vision, is dispersed vision.

There is an interesting article on it by Government Minister *Schultz,* in *Schweigger's* Journal (1816).

As the developed totality of the Notion in nature, the tetrad also goes on to quintuplicity, in so far as the differentiation is not merely duplicated, but itself appears as a triad. We could also have begun with the sense of ideality, which appears as a duality because it is abstract, and yet at the same time ought to constitute the totality here. In nature in general, we began with the ideal nature of extrinsicality, which was space and time. Space and time constitute a duality, because the Notion is concrete (its moments are completely present, and yet appear as thrown apart in abstraction, because the content was not yet posited in its concreteness). Similarly, we now have on the one hand the sense of physically determined space, and on the other hand that of physical time. Space is here determined in conformity with the physical abstraction of light and darkness; time is internal quivering, the negativity of being-in-self. The second member in the division of the totality of sense consists of smell and taste, and retains its place; feeling is then the third member. The arrangement is more or less a matter of indifference, the main point being that the senses in their rationality constitute a totality. As the range of the theoretical relation is determined by the Notion, it is certain that there cannot be any more senses, although some of them can be missing in lower animals.

As feeling, the *sense organs* are the general sensitivity of the skin. Taste is the muscle of the *tongue,* the neutrality which connects itself with the mouth i.e. with the skin which is beginning to become internal, or with the retraction of the vegetative universality of the whole surface. As the sense-organ of smell, the nose is connected with the principle of air, and with breathing. Whereas feeling is the sense of shape in general, taste is the sense of digestion, the passage inwards of that which is external. Smell belongs to the inner organism as the principle of air. Sight is not the sense of an earlier function, but is the sense of the brain, as is hearing. Sense relates itself to itself in the *eye* and the *ear;* in the case of the eye, the objective actuality is an indifferent self however, while in the case of the ear, it is self-sublating. As active hearing, the *voice* is the pure self which posits itself as universal, expressing pain, desire, joy, contentment. When suffering a violent death, every animal has a cry in which it expresses the annulment of its individuality. The senses are space which is saturated and filled, but in the voice, sense returns into its inner being, and constitutes a negative self or desire, which is an awareness of its own insubstantial nature as mere space.

2. The practical relationship
(*The practical process*)

§ 359

The *process which is of a real nature,* **or the practical re-lationship with** inorganic nature, begins with **the self's internal diremption,** the awareness of externality **as** the *negation* of the subject. The subject is, at the same time, positive
5 self-relatedness, the *self-certainty* of which is opposed to this negation of itself. In other words, the process begins with the awareness *of deficiency,* and the *drive* to over-come it. The condition **which occurs here is that of** an external *stimulation,* **in which the negation of the subject which is strung**
10 **in opposition, is posited in the form of an object.**

Remark

Only a living existence is aware of *deficiency,* for it alone in nature is the *Notion,* which is the unity *of itself* and *its specific antithesis.* Where there is a *limit,* it is a negation, but only *for a third term,* an **external comparative.** However,
15 the *limit* constitutes deficiency only in so far as the *contra-diction* which is present in *one term* to the same extent as it is in the *being beyond it,* **is as such immanent, and is** posited **within this term.** The *subject* is a term such as this, which is able to contain and *support* its own contradiction; it is this
20 which constitutes its *infinitude.* **Similarly,** when reference is made to *finite* reason, reason shows **that it is infinite,** and pre-cisely by thus determining itself as *finite*; for negation is finitude, and is only a deficiency for that which constitutes the *sublated being* of this finitude, i.e. for *infinite* self-
25 reference (cf. § 60 Rem.). Through lack of thought, no advance is made beyond the abstraction of the *limit,* so that even where the *Notion* itself enters into *existence* as it does in life, there is a failure to grasp it. This thoughtlessness keeps to the determinations of ordinary thought, such as
30 *impulse, instinct, need* etc., **and does not ask what they are in**

themselves. An analysis of the way in which these determinations are regarded would show that they are negations posited as contained within the affirmation of the subject itself.

An important advance in the true conception of the organism has been made by changing determinations, and replacing the *action of external causes* by *stimulation* through *external potencies*. This is the seed of idealism, which realizes that nothing whatever could have a positive relation to living being, if living being in and for itself did not constitute the possibility of this relation, that is to say, if the relation were not determined by the Notion, and therefore not simply immanent in the subject. For a long time now, certain formal and material relationships in the *theory of stimulation* have been regarded as philosophical, although their introduction is as unphilosophical as any other scientific hotch-potch of reflection-determinations. An example of this is the wholly abstract antithesis in which the faculties of *receptivity* and *action* are supposed to be related to each other as factors in an inverse ratio of magnitude.[1] As the result of this, the difference in the organism, which is to be grasped, has fallen into the *formalism* of a merely *quantitative* variety of *increase* and *decrease, strengthening* and *weakening*, i.e. into the uttermost *violation of the Notion*. A theory of medicine based on these arid determinations is completed in half a dozen propositions, so it is not surprising that it should have spread rapidly and found plenty of adherents. The cause of this aberration lay in the fundamental error of first defining the Absolute as the absolute undifferentiation of subjective and objective being, and then supposing that all determination is merely *quantitative* difference. The truth is rather, that the soul of absolute form, which is the *Notion* and animation, is solely qualitative self- **sublating** differentiation, **the dialectic of absolute antithesis. One may think, in so far** as one is not aware of this genuinely infinite negativity, that one is unable to hold fast to the absolute identity of life, without converting the moment of difference into a simply external moment of reflection. This is of course the

---

[1] *Schelling*, 'First sketch of a systematic philosophy of nature', p. 88. Note by Michelet.

case with *Spinoza*, whose attributes and modes occur in an
+ *external* understanding; life must then completely lack the
+ *leaping point* of selfhood, the principle of autonomous
movement, of internal self-diremption.[1]

5   We must also recognize the crudeness and the completely
unphilosophical nature of the procedure which, **without any
consideration whatever,**[2] replaced the determinations of the
Notion by *carbon* and *nitrogen*, oxygen and hydrogen, and
then **went on to** define the previously intensive difference as
10 the *varying preponderance* of one matter or the other, while
regarding the active and positive relation of the external
stimulus as an *addition* of a deficient matter. In an *asthenic*
+ disease such as nervous fever for example, the *nitrogen* in
the organism is supposed to preponderate, because the
15 brain and the nerves in general are supposed to be *potenti-
ated* nitrogen, *chemical* analysis having shown this to be the
principal constituent of these organic formations. In this case
this is supposed to imply that *carbon* should be added to the
organism in order to re-establish the equilibrium of these
20 *matters*, and so restore it to health. For no other reason
than this, the remedies for nervous fever which have been
discovered empirically are regarded as subjacent to *carbon*.
Superficial collocation and opinion of this kind has been
purveyed as *construction* and *proof*. The crudity of this
25 procedure derives from its regarding the external caput
+ mortuum of a dead matter made doubly dead by chemical
analysis, not only as the *essence* of a living organ, but even
as its *Notion*.

In general, it is ignorance of the Notion and contempt for it,
30 **which** perpetrates this facile formalism by making use of
sensuous materials, such as the matters of chemistry, and of
relationships belonging to the sphere of inorganic nature,
such as the north and south of magnetic polarity, **or even
the difference between magnetism itself and electricity.** Instead
35 of making use of the determinations of the Notion, an
attempt is made to grasp and develop the natural universe
by externally fixing upon its spheres and differences **a**

---

[1] Addition to the first edition, 'as singularity'.
[2] Addition to the first and second edition, 'wanted to give significance of a real nature to the formal determinations, and'

schema prepared **from material of this kind.**[1] A great number +
of different forms is available for this, for selection remains a matter of choice. One may for example, take as
one's schema determinations as they appear in the *chemical*
sphere, and then transfer oxygen and hydrogen etc. to 5
magnetism, mechanism, electricity, male and female,
contraction and expansion etc., in general, to draw opposites from any one sphere, and to **apply** them to the others.

Addition. It is true that the practical process is an alteration and sub- 10
lation of the independent material subsistence of external inorganic nature,
but it is none the less a process which lacks freedom, because in animal
appetite the organism is orientated outwards. People believe that their freedom resides in the will, but it is precisely through their wills that they
enter into a relationship with a reality which is external to them. Man's 15
initial freedom derives from his rational will, which is theoretical, and
resembles the theoretical process of the senses. Consequently, it is the
subject's feeling of dependence which is primary here; the subject
feels that it is not self-contained, and that another negative being is
necessary to it, not contingent. This is the unpleasant feeling of need. 20
The deficiency in a stool which has three legs is in us. In life, the deficiency is in life itself however, although to an equal extent it is also
sublated, for life is aware of the limit as a deficiency. Thus it is a privilege of higher natures to feel pain, and the higher the nature, the more
unhappiness it feels. A great man has a great need, as well as the drive to 25
satisfy it, and great deeds proceed only from profound mental anguish.
It is here that we may trace the origin of evil etc. Thus, the animal is +
positively self-contained within a negative context, and higher natures
also have the privilege of existing as this contradiction. To an equal
extent, the animal also restores its lost harmony however, and finds 30
satisfaction within itself. Animal appetite is the idealism of objectivity,
whereby this objectivity loses its alien character.

The external manner of interpretation mentioned in the paragraph is
certainly rampant in the philosophy of *Schelling*, who often oversteps the
mark in drawing parallels. *Oken, Troxler* and others also fall into an empty +
formalism; we noticed above for example (§ 346 Addition III. 74, 1), that
Oken called the wood-fibres of plants their nerves, and that others have
called the roots their brain(see above § 348, Add. III. 92, 13): similarly, the

[1] Addition to the first and second edition, 'such as north-south, west-east polarity, or any other
material'.

brain is supposed to be the human Sun. In order to express the thought-determination of an organ of vegetable or animal life, the name is taken not from the sphere of that thought, but from another sphere. Forms must be created from the Notion if they are to be used for determining
5 other forms; they ought not to be derived a second time from the intuition.

§ 360

The need is specific, and its determinateness is a moment of its universal Notion, although it is particularized in an infinite variety of ways. The drive is the activity of overcoming the de-
10 ficiency of such a determinateness, i.e. of overcoming its form, which is initially merely subjective. In that the content of the determinateness is primary, and in that it maintains itself in the activity in which it is merely carried into effect, the drive consti-tutes purpose (§ 204), and confined solely to living existence,
15 instinct. This deficiency in form is inner stimulation, the specific determinateness of whose content appears at the same time as an animal's relation to the particular individualization of the various spheres of nature.

Remark

Instinct is supposed to be shrouded in mystery and difficult to
20 grasp, but the root of this difficulty is merely that purpose can only be grasped as the inner Notion, so that it soon becomes apparent that the relationships by which the mere understanding attempts to explain instinct, are inadequate. The fundamental determination of living existence is that it is to be regarded as acting purposively.
25 This has been grasped by Aristotle, but has been almost for-gotten in more recent times. Kant revived the concept in his own way however, with the doctrine of the inner purposiveness of living existence, which implies that this existence is to be regarded
+ as an end in itself. The main sources of the difficulty here, are
30 that the relation implied by purpose is usually imagined to be external, and that purpose is generally thought to exist only in a conscious manner. Instinct is purposive activity operating in an
+ unconscious manner.

Addition. Since the drive can only be fulfilled by wholly specific activities, it makes its appearance as instinct, in that it appears to be a choice made in accordance with a purpose—determination. As the drive is not a known purpose however, the animal is not yet aware of its ends as ends. *Aristotle* calls that which is activated unconsciously in accordance 5 with ends φύσις.

+

§ 361

In so far as need is a connectedness with the *universal* mechanism and abstract powers of nature, instinct is merely an internal stimulation which is not even sympathetic. It is this in sleeping and waking, climatic and other migrations etc. As a relation- 10 ship of the animal to its own inorganic and individualized nature however, instinct is generally determined, and in its further particularity, is restricted to no more than a limited range of universal inorganic nature. Instinct maintains a practical relation in the face of inorganic nature; its inner stimulation is 15 accompanied by the show of an external stimulation, and its activity is partly formal, and partly a real assimilation of inorganic nature.

Addition. Waking and sleep are not the result of a stimulus originating in something external. They are an unmediated participation in nature 20 and its changes, occurring as internal rest and retrenchment from the outer world. The migrations of animals constitute the same sort of participation, for they are a passage within the life of nature itself, as for example when fish migrate to other seas. Sleep is preceded by the awareness of a deficiency, not by a need; one falls asleep without trying to 25 do so. It may well be said that animals sleep and gather food for the winter instinctively, for they are also merely drawn to this, as they are to waking. The lower the organism, the fuller is its participation in this life of nature. +
Primitive peoples are sensitive to the course of nature, but the spirit turns night into day, so that the moods of the seasons are also less marked in 30 more highly organized beings. Intestinal worms, which are to be found in the liver, and the brain of hares or deer at certain times of the year, are a weakness of the organism, in which one part separates out into its +
own vitality. As the animal participates sympathetically in the universal course of nature, it is not so absurd to assume that there is a connection 35

between the life of the animal, and the moon, as well as terrestrial and sidereal life. For example, it is quite feasible that earthquakes may be + predicted from the flight of birds, and certain animals such as spiders and frogs have premonitions of the coming weather. Man will also be 5 aware of a future climatic change in a weak spot such as a scar, so that the change is present and manifests itself in man, even though it only shows itself later in the weather.

The drive is completely determinate in particular animals; each animal has as its own only a restricted range of inorganic nature, which is its 10 own domain, and which it must seek out by instinct from its complex environment. The mere sight of the object does not arouse the lion's desire for a deer, nor the eagle's desire for a hare, nor the desire of other animals for corn, rice, grass, oats etc. Yet these animals have no choice, for the drive is immanent in such a way, that this specific determinateness 15 of the grass, and indeed of this grass, and this corn etc., is present in the animal itself, and it is simply unconscious of the presence of anything else. As the universal thinking animal, man has a widely extended range, and can treat everything as his inorganic nature, and as the object of his knowledge. Undeveloped animals have only an elemental principle such 20 as water as their inorganic nature. Lilies, willows and fig trees have their own particular insects, whose inorganic nature is entirely restricted + to such growth. The animal can be stimulated only by means of *its* inorganic nature, because for the animal, the only opposite is its *own*. The animal does not recognize the other in general, for each animal recog- 25 nizes its *own* other, which is precisely an essential moment of the special nature of each.

§ 362

In so far as instinct accomplishes a formal assimilation, it forms its determination within externalities. It gives the material of these externalities an outer form appropriate to the purpose, 30 and leaves the objectivity of these things untouched, as in the building of nests and lairs etc. It is process of a real nature how- ever, in so far as it individualizes inorganic things, or relates itself to those already individualized, and assimilates them by consuming them and destroying their characteristic qualities, i.e. 35 through *air* entering into the process of respiration and of the skin, *water* into the process of thirst, and the particular formations of individualized *earth* into the process of hunger. Life, which is the subject of these moments of the totality, constitutes a state of tension between itself as Notion and the external reality of these moments, and maintains the perpetual conflict in which it overcomes ₅ this externality. **At this juncture,** the animal **functions as an** immediate singularity, and can only **overcome this externality** in the singular, **and by means of all the determinations of singularity, such as this place and this time etc. Consequently, this realization** of itself is not adequate to its Notion, and its ₁₀ satisfaction is[1] perpetually reverting to a state of need.

Addition. The animal itself determines where it will rest, sleep and bear its young; it not only changes its place, but decides upon it. The animal does something therefore, and by determining in a purposive manner, expresses its inner drive as activity. ₁₅

The real nature of the process is primarily a process with the elements, for in the first instance external being itself is universal. The plant stops at the process of the elements, but the animals go on to the process of singularity. The *relationship with light* might also be called an elemental process, for light is also an external and elemental potency. However, ₂₀ light as such is not the same power for the animal and man as it is for vegetable nature; men and animals see light, so that the self-manifesting of the objective form of light is external to them, although in the theoretical process their relation to it is of an ideal nature. Light only has an influence upon the colour of feathered creatures and of pelts; the ₂₅ black hair of the negro is also the result of the climate, an effect of the heat and the light. The blood and coloured fluids of animals are also to be considered at this juncture. Goethe has observed that the colour of + plumage is determined by the action of light, as well as by its internal organization. Speaking of the colours of organic beings generally, he ₃₀ says, 'White and black, yellow, orange and brown, alternate in a variety of ways; yet the manner in which they appear does not remind us of the elementary colours. They are to a much greater extent mixed colours, subdued by organic concoction, and they more or less indicate the level + of the creature which displays them. Markings on the skin are related ₃₅ to the internal parts they cover. The colours of shells and fish are more elementary. Warmer climates certainly have an effect upon the water also, and bring out the colours of fish, beautifying and heightening

[1] Addition to the first and second edition, 'therefore'.

them. On Otaheiti, *Forster* saw a wonderful display of colours on a certain kind of fish, especially when it was dying. When it is first exposed to the light and the air, the fluid in shell fish has the peculiar property of appearing yellowish and then greenish; it subsequently turns blue, and then violet, before assuming a deeper red. Through the action of the Sun, and especially when it is spread on cambric, it finally turns a pure deep red. The action of light upon the plumage and colours of birds is quite remarkable. For example, the breast feather of certain parrots is really yellow, but in the squamous part of it, which stands forth and catches the light, the yellow is intensified into red. Thus, although the breast of such a bird seems to be crimson, the yellow will appear if one blows into the feathers. There is therefore a very great difference between the exposed part of the plumage, and that part of it which is covered and unruffled. In ravens for example, it is in fact only the uncovered part of the plumage which displays colours. If we bear this in mind, it is quite easy to rearrange the raven's tail feathers in their natural order.'[1]

The process with light remains of an ideal nature, but the process with air and water involves material being. The cutaneous process is the extension of the vegetative process, which breaks out into hairs and feathers. Human skin has less hair than animal skin, but it is mainly in the plumage of birds that vegetable being is taken up into animal being. 'The quills become true feathers when they are fully barbed; many of these barbs and befeatherings are subdivided once again, so that the whole bears a striking resemblance to the plant. The surface of the human body is smooth and clear, so that in the most perfect human specimens, with the exception of a few places which are more decorated with hair than covered with it, the body shows forth the beauty of its form. An excessive amount of hair on the chest, arms and legs is evidence of weakness rather than strength. It is probably only the poets who, having been misled by the kind of strength displayed by animal nature, have created among us the reputations enjoyed by these hairy heroes.'[2]

The respiratory process is continuity displaying its interruptedness. Exhalation and inhalation bring about a vaporization of the blood, and so constitute the vaporization of irritability (§ 354 Add. III. 124, 18); the transition into air is started and retracted. '*Mud fish* (Cobitis fossilis) inhale through the mouth, and eject the air through the anus.'[3] Fish decompose

---

[1] *Goethe*, 'Theory of Colours', vol. I, § 664, 640, 660.
[2] *Goethe*, 'Theory of Colours', vol. I, § 655; § 669.
[3] *Treviranus*, loc. cit. vol. IV, p. 146.

the water by means of their gills, which are also a secondary respiratory organ analogous to the lungs. The tracheae of insects are distributed throughout the whole body, and have orifices on both sides of the venter. Some underwater insects collect a supply of air, and keep it under their elytra, or in the pubescence of the abdomen.[1] Now why does the blood + relate itself to the ideal nature of this digestion of the abstract element? It relates itself because it is this absolute thirst, and is in an incessant agitation, both within itself and in opposition to itself. The blood is motivated towards the differentiation of animation. More exactly, this digestion is at the same time a mediated process with the air; that is to say, 10 it is a conversion of air into carbon dioxide and dark carbonated venous blood, and into oxygenated arterial blood. I attribute the activity and vivification of the arterial blood to its satiation rather than to its material alteration. It seems to me in fact that the blood resembles other forms of digestion by perpetually appeasing what one may call its hunger or 15 its thirst, and achieving being-for-self by negating its otherness. The air is the implicitness of the fiery and negative element. The blood is the same element as a developed restlessness; it is the burning fire of the animal organism, which not only consumes itself, but which also preserves its fluidity, and finds its pabulum vitae in the air. Consequently, + the action of the organism may be paralysed by injecting venous blood in the place of arterial blood. When the organism is dead, the red blood is almost entirely replaced by venous blood; in the case of apoplexies, venous blood is found in the brain. This is not caused by a slight variation in the amount of oxygen and carbon.[2] In the case of scarlet fever however, 25 the venous blood is also a scarlet-red. Yet the true life of the blood is the incessant conversion of arterial and venous blood into each other. It is in this operation that the capillaries develop the greatest activity.[3] 'In certain organs, there is evidence that the arterial blood is converted into venous blood more rapidly. In many cases, the characteristic properties of venous 30 blood, such as its blackness and its lower density when coagulating, are present to a greater extent than they are elsewhere, for example in the spleen; yet the walls of the vessels in question bear no evidence of an abnormally high influx of oxygen through the arterial blood, on the contrary they are softer, and often almost pulpy. Taken as a whole, the 35 *thyroid gland* has more arteries than any other part of the human body. In the short course of this gland, a great deal of arterial blood is converted

---

[1] *Treviranus*, loc. cit. vol. IV, p. 150.
[2] Cf. *Bichat*, loc. cit. p. 329 et seq.
[3] *Autenrieth*, loc. cit., vol. III, Index, p. 370.

into venous blood.'[1] Since the vessels of this gland do not get harder, as they should, what becomes of the oxygen of the arterial blood? The gland brings about no external chemical action.

The process with water is the demand for the neutral element, the desire to drink. On the one hand, it counteracts the abstract heat within the organism, and on the other hand, it is used to remove a specific taste. Consequently, the drive is only instinct when it relates itself to an individualized object. In such a relation, the momentarily satisfied need is perpetually recurring. Spirit however, by developing its cognition of universal truths, finds its satisfaction in a much more universal manner.

§ 363

The process begins with the *mechanical seizure* of the external object. **Assimilation itself is the enveloping of the externality within the unity of the subject. Since the animal is**[2] **a subject,** a simple negativity, the nature of **this assimilation can be neither** mechanical **nor** chemical, for in these processes, the substances, as well as the conditions and the activity, *remain external* to one another, and lack an absolute and living unity.

Addition. Appetitive organic being, aware of itself as the unity of itself and of that confronting it, and so seeing through the determinate being of the object, is shape, which is orientated outwards, and armed. Its teeth derive from its bones and its claws from its skin; in these features the process is still mechanical, although in the *saliva* it is already organic. For a long time now, it has been the fashion to give a mechanical explanation of the process of assimilation and of the circulation of the blood. Similarly, although a nerve is quite slack, the action of the nerves has been envisaged and explained as a quivering of taut strings. The nerves are also supposed to be a series of globules, which by exerting pressure, strike and push one another until the last of the series strikes the soul. The soul is omnipresent within the body however, and the extrinsicality of bones, nerves and veins is of no significance to its ideality. When dealing with electricity, we saw that it was futile to expect laboratory experiments to reproduce atmospheric phenomena, but it is even more pointless to apply finite relationships to life. Attempts have also been made to explain

---

[1] *Autenrieth,* loc. cit. pt. I, § 512 (391); § 458–459.
[2] *Addition* to the first edition, 'thereby'.

digestion by means of impact and pumping etc. If it could be explained as such, it would be an external relationship of inner and outer. The animal is the absolute self-identity of animation however, it is not a mere composition. Use has recently been made of chemical relationships, but assimilation cannot be susceptible of a chemical interpretation either, for in living being we have a subject which maintains itself and negates the specific nature of the other, whereas the acid and alkaline being of the chemical process loses its quality, and either sinks into the neutral product of a salt, or reverts to an abstract radical. In this case, the activity is extinguished, whereas the animal is the persistent unrest within self-relatedness. Digesting may certainly be grasped as a neutralization of acid and alkali: it is correct to say that such finite relationships begin in life, but life interrupts them, and brings forth a product which is not chemism. It is like the moisture in the eye which refracts light. These finite relationships may be pursued to a certain point therefore, but then quite another order begins. A chemical analysis of the brain will certainly reveal a good deal of nitrogen, just as an analysis of exhaled air will reveal constituents other than those of the air that is breathed in. One is therefore able to trace the chemical process until even the separate parts of living being disintegrate. It should not be assumed however, that the processes themselves are chemical, for chemical being only accommodates that which is lifeless, whereas the animal processes are perpetually sublating the nature of chemical being. There is plenty of scope for tracing and indicating the mediations which occur in living being and in the meteorological process, but this mediation is not to be confused with the real nature of the phenomena.

§ 364

Living being is the *universal* power of its external and opposed nature; **initially therefore, assimilation** is the *immediate* fusion of animality with that which is taken up into it. That which is taken up is infected with animality, and a *simple transformation* occurs (§ 345 Rem. and § 346). In the second instance, assimilation consists of the *mediation of digestion*. Digestion is the opposition of the subject **to that which is external to it; it is further differentiated**[1] into the

---

[1] First edition, 'in opposition to its immediate assimilating, so that this assimilation stimulates itself into a negative opposition to it, and occurs as a process of opposition'.

aqueous process of the animal, i.e. gastric and pancreatic juice and animal lymph in general, and into the animal's
+ *igneous process* or *bile,* in which the organism has *returned into itself* from its concentration in the spleen, and is
5 determined as *being-for-self* and active consumption. **These processes are to an equal extent particularized infections however.**

§ 365

This involvement with external being, in stimulation and the process itself, is also determined as an *externality* however, being *opposed* to *universality,* and to the *simple* self-refer-
10 ence of living being. **Strictly speaking therefore, this involvement itself[1] constitutes the object and negative opposed to the subjectivity of the organism, an object and negative which the organism has to overcome and digest.** The change in its orientation constitutes **the principle of the organism's intro-reflec-**
15 **tion. The return-into-self is the negation of its[2]** outward-oriented activity. **There is a double determination here.[3]** On the one hand, the organism expels from itself[4] the activity **it has set in conflict with the** externality of the object, **and on the other, it has become for itself** through its immediate identity with
20 this **activity, and** by this means has reproduced itself. It is in this way that the process outwards is transformed into the first formal process of **simple** reproduction from itself, **into the uniting of itself with itself.**

Remark

The main moment in digestion is the *immediate* action of
25 life as the *power* over its inorganic object. Life presupposes

---

[1] First edition, 'In the first instance, this animal stimulation is directed against the external potency; by means of infection however, this potency is placed immediately on the side of the organism. Yet as the opposition and being-for-self of the process, this stimulation has, likewise, the determination of externality with regard to the universality and simple self-relatedness of living being. Initially, these two moments appear together on the side of the subject as a means, and so, strictly speaking, constitute the object and the negative opposed to the organism, an object and negative which the organism has to overcome and digest'.

[2] Addition to the first and second edition, 'own negativity or'.

[3] First edition, 'As natural being, the singularity which it reaches here consequently joins up with its universality as a loosening factor.'

[4] Addition to the first and second edition, 'the first negation, that is to say'.

this object[1] as its stimulus only in so far as it is *implicitly* identical with it, **although at the same time it is its ideality and being-for-self.** This action is *infection* and immediate trans- formation; **it corresponds to the immediate seizure of the object pointed out in the exposition of purposive activity** (§ 208). The researches of *Spallanzani* and others, as well as more recent physiology, have also demonstrated the immediacy with which living being as a *universal, employing no other means* than simple contact and the taking up of nutriment into its heat and its own sphere in general, *maintains its continuity within this nutriment.* **These researches have been carried out empirically, and have shown that the facts are in accordance with the Notion. They have exploded the fiction that digestion functions as a purely mechanical secretion and ex- cretion of[2] parts which are ready for use, or as a chemical process.** However, research on the *intermediary* actions has not revealed any more *determinate* moments of this trans- formation, as it has for example in vegetable matters, where a series of *fermentations* has been discovered. On the contrary, it has been shown for example, that a great deal of nutriment passes straight from the stomach into the mass of gastric juices without having passed through the further intermediary stages, and that the pancreatic juice is nothing more than saliva, so that it might[3] well be dis- pensed with etc. The final product is the chyle, which is taken up by the *thoracic duct* and *discharged* into the blood. It is the same lymph as that which is secreted by each separate intestine and organ, which is appropriated every- where by the skin and the lymphatic system in the immedi- ate process of transformation, and which is already prepared wherever it is appropriated. Certain lower animal organ- izations, which are however nothing more than a simple alimentary canal, or lymph curdled into a point or tube, do not progress beyond this immediate transformation. In the higher animal organizations, the *special product* of the *mediated* digestive process is just as *superfluous* as the plant's production of seeds by means of their so-called sexual

---

[1] Addition to the first edition, 'and sets it in opposition to itself'.
[2] First edition, 'homogeneous'.
[3] Addition to the first and second edition, 'very'.

differentiation. In faeces, the greater part of the food is usually unchanged, and mixed mainly with *animal* matters such as *bile* and phosphorus etc. This is particularly so in the faeces of children, who assimilate comparatively more
5 matter than other people; which shows that the main action of the organism consists of its overcoming and ridding itself of its own products. Consequently, the syllogism of the organism is not that of *external purposiveness*, for it does not stop at directing its activity and form
10 towards the outer object, but makes an object out of this process itself, which on account of its externality, is on the point of lapsing into mechanism and chemism. **This behaviour was expounded as the second premiss of the universal syllogism of purposiveness (§ 209).** The organism is the coal-
15 escence of itself with itself **in its outward process. It wins and takes over from this process nothing but chyle, which is its universal animalization. Consequently, as the being-for-self of the living Notion, it is to an equal extent** a disjunctive activity which rids itself of this process, separates itself from the
+ one-sided subjectivity of its *hostility* towards the object, and so becomes *explicitly* what it is implicitly. It therefore becomes the non-neutral identity of its Notion and its reality, and so finds the end and product of its activity to be the already established beginning and origin of its
25 being. It is thus that *satisfaction conforms to reason;* the process which enters into external differentiation turns into the process of the organism with itself, and the result is not the mere production of a means, but the bringing forth of an end, **the unity of the self.**

30 *Addition.* At this juncture, the *alimentary process* is the main factor. Organic being is in a state of tension with inorganic nature, which it negates, and posits as identical with itself. In this immediate bearing of organic upon inorganic being, the former is as it were the immediate dissolution of the latter into organic fluidity. The ground of all relation between them is
35 precisely this absolute unity of substance, which ensures that for organic being, inorganic being is simply transparent, of an ideal nature, and lacking in objectivity. The alimentary process is merely this transformation of inorganic nature into a soma belonging to the subject. Subsequently however, it also appears as process which passes through many phases, and which is

no longer an immediate transformation, but seems to employ media. Animal nature constitutes the universal facing the particular natures which have their truth and ideality within it, for it is the actuality of that which constitutes the implicitness of these figures. Similarly, as all men are implicitly rational, the man who appeals to their rational instinct has power over them, for what he reveals to them already corresponds to something in this instinct which is able to respond to the reason he makes explicit. The general public accepts what it comes across in an immediate manner, so that it exhibits rationality as a propagation and an infection; it is because of this that the former barrier or apparent separation disappears. This power of animality is the substantial relationship which constitutes the main factor in digestion. Consequently, if the animal organism is the substance, inorganic being is merely an accident, its specific nature being merely a form which it abandons immediately. 'We know from experience therefore, that sugar, vegetable gums and oils, nourish bodies which contain little or no nitrogen, and that in spite of this, they are converted into an animal substance which contains a great deal of nitrogen. For entire populations are completely vegetarian, just as others eat nothing but meat. The lack of malnutrition among these vegetarians makes it evident however, that their bodies do not merely retain the minute amount of apparently animal matter which is present in the plants they consume, and reject everything else, but that they elaborate a great deal of this vegetable diet into a nutriment appropriate to their organs.'[1] Although it is true that the animals and plants which an animal consumes are already organic, they constitute, in their relation to it, the animal's inorganic being. Such a particular and external being has no subsistence of its own, for it is a nullity as soon as it is touched by living being. This transformation merely reveals the relationship.

It is on this immediate transition and transformation that all chemical and mechanical explanations of the organism founder and find their limit. The precise reason for this is that their explanations are merely based on a datum which already possesses exterior equality. The truth is however, that both sides in their determinate being are completely free with regard to each other. Bread in itself for example, has no connection with the body, the chyle, or the blood, for it is something quite different. Try as they will, neither chemistry nor mechanics can trace empirically the transformation of the nutriment into blood. Chemistry certainly displays something similar in both of them; albumen perhaps, and certainly iron and suchlike, as well as oxy-

---

[1] *Autenrieth*, loc. cit. pt. II, § 557.

gen, hydrogen, nitrogen etc. It will certainly extract matters from the plant that are also present in water. Wood, blood and flesh do not remain the same thing as these matters however, because, quite simply, both sides are at the same time something else. Blood which has been broken down into
5 such constituents is no longer living blood. It is quite impossible to trace similarity any further and to find continuity here, for the existing substance completely disappears. By decomposing a salt, I obtain again the two matters which had combined to form it; consequently, this combination accounts for the salt, and the matters within it have not become something
10 else, but have remained the same. In organic being however, the existing substances are posited as becoming something else. However, as inorganic being is merely a moment which is sublated in the organic self, it comes into consideration not in accordance with its determinate being, but in accordance with its Notion. Yet in accordance with its Notion it is identical with
15 organic being.

This is evident in organic assimilation. The nutriment which enters into the sphere of organic life is steeped in this fluid, and changes into this solution. Just as a certain thing becomes odour, something dissolved, a simple atmosphere, so here it becomes a simple organic fluid, in which nothing more of it or its con-
20 stituents is to be discovered. This organic fluid, which persists in its self-equality, is the igneous essence of inorganic being, which here returns immediately, into its Notion; for inorganic things are turned into their implicit being by means of eating and drinking. Organic being is the unconscious Notion of inorganic things, and they are sublated into it because they constitute its implicit
25 nature. This transition also has to exhibit itself as a mediated process, and display the members of its opposition. The basis of it is however, that as organic being is the genus as a simple self, and so holds sway over inorganic being, it draws inorganic being into its organic matter in an immediate manner. If organic being,
+ as purpose, does gradually bring inorganic being into identity with itself by
30 means of the particular moments of this immediacy, then these extensive digestive preparations by means of various organs are certainly superfluous for *inorganic being*. The course of organic being within itself still *takes place however,*
+ *in order that organic being itself* may constitute movement, and so have actuality. It is the same with spirit, the strength of which is measured by the extent of
35 the opposition it has overcome. Nevertheless, the basic relationship of the organism is this simple contact, in which there is an immediate and instantaneous transformation of the other.

The lower animals are still completely devoid of special features such as bile and gastric juice, which are essential to the activities connected with the
40 assimilation of food. Water is already absorbed by the skin in the process

with the air, as may be seen in many worms and zoophytes. Polyps
provide an example of this, for the water on which they feed is transformed directly into lymph and jelly. 'The simplest form of nutrition
through a single mouth is to be found in Hydras, Brachiopoda and
Vorticella. The Hydra viridis feeds on small aquatic animalcules, which it +
seizes with its tentacles. The sac-like receptacle which comprises most of
its body opens and receives the prey, which is changed almost as soon as
it is swallowed. It is transformed into a homogeneous mass, and continually loses volume in the process. Finally, the mouth of the Polyp opens
again, and part of the ingested food is evacuated through precisely the same 10
orifice as that by which it had entered the hydra's stomach. Frequently,
the creatures swallowed are long worms, only half of which can be contained in the stomach. Even then however, there is still a rapid decomposition of whatever has entered the stomach, so that on many occasions
one half of the worm is still trying to escape, while the other half has 15
already been digested. What is more, the Polyp is also able to digest with
its outer surface. It can be turned inside out, "like a glove", so that the inside
of its stomach becomes its outer covering, and yet the phenomena referred
to still take place as before.'[1] An intestine of this kind is a mere canal, and +
is of so uncomplicated a structure, that there is no difference to be found 20
between oesophagus, stomach and intestines. But, 'after the alimentary
canal, there is no viscera so universal in its occurrence throughout the
whole of the animal kingdom, as is the *liver*. It is to be found in all mammals, birds, amphibia, fish and molluscs. Even in the vermian class, the
Aphrodites seem to possess bile-secreting organs, for the sacs arranged +
along either side of their intestinal canal contain a bitter dark green fluid.
Similar sacs are to be found in the alimentary canal of Holothuria. An +
actual liver occurs again in Asteriae. In insects, the vessels which may be +
regarded as biliary vessels, seem to take the place of the liver.'[2] Others +
attribute another function to these vessels. 'Although many Zoophytes 30
seem to produce no visible excretions, there can be no doubt that they all
evacuate gaseous matters through their skin and respiratory organs, and
that this evacuation is connected with their nutrition. There is therefore a
close connection between nutrition and respiration.'[3]

   This immediate digestion is also to be found higher up the scale in more 35
complex animals. It is well known to those who catch Thrushes and Fieldfares for example, that if these birds are quite thin, they will fatten up con-

---

[1] *Treviranus*, loc. cit. vol. IV, pp. 291–292.
[2] *Treviranus*, loc. cit. vol. IV, pp. 415–416.
[3] *Treviranus*, loc. cit. vol. IV, pp. 293–294.

+ siderably in the matter of a few hours, after a misty morning. In this case, an immediate transformation of this moisture into animal matter takes place, without any further secretion and passage through the separated moments of the assimilation process. Man also digests immediately, as is shown by the account
5 of the English ship, the crew of which ran out of water while it was on the high seas. The rain-water very laboriously collected in the sails also running out on them, they slaked their thirst by soaking their shirts, and dipping themselves in the sea, so that their skins absorbed only the water
+ from the sea, not its salt. In animals which have organs by means of which
10 they digest, the digestion which takes place is partly of this general and universal kind, and partly distinct and particular. In this latter case the assimilation is initiated by organic heat. The stomach and the intestinal canal themselves are nothing but the outer skin however, which is simply adapted, and which is developed and remoulded into a special form.
15 *Treviranus* makes a more detailed comparison of these various membranes
++ (loc. cit. vol. IV, p. 333 et seq.). If ipecacuanha and opium are rubbed in on the outside of the stomach, they have the same effect as when they are taken internally; but ipecacuanha has also been rubbed into the shoulder, and equally well digested. 'Tiny pieces of flesh, enclosed in small linen bags,
20 and placed in the abdominal cavity of a live cat, have been found to decompose into a pulp and tiny scraps of bone, as they do in the stomach. Precisely the same decomposition occurred when flesh of this kind was inserted under the skin of living animals next to their bare muscles, and left there for a time. An apparently similar phenomenon occurs in the case
25 of bone fractures; nature discharges a quantity of moisture around the fractured part, by which the sharp ends of the bones are softened and entirely dissolved. A further phenomenon of this kind occurs when the congealed blood in contused parts of the body is gradually dissolved again, becomes fluid, and is finally absorbed once again. The gastric juice does
30 not act therefore as a wholly special animal fluid, quite different from any other. It acts merely as a watery animal fluid, supplied in plenty to the reservoir of the stomach by the exhalatory arteries. It is secreted from the arterial blood, which just prior to this secretion, was exposed in the lungs to the action of oxygen.'[1] *Treviranus* also observes (loc. cit. vol. IV, pp.
35 348–349) that, 'The bones, flesh and other animal parts which *P. Smith* inserted into the abdominal cavity or under the skin of living animals, were entirely decomposed there (*Pfaff* and *Scheel's* "Nordic Archive for Natural
+ Science" etc. vol. III pt. 3, p. 134). This explains a remarkable phenomenon

---

[1] *Autenrieth*, loc. cit. vol. II, § 597–598.

which *Cuvier* discovered while observing the Salpa octofora. In many of these creatures, although not in their stomachs, he found parts of an Antifera, all of which had decomposed and vanished, apart from the outer skin, and which had probably come in through the orifice by which Salpas take in water ("Annales du Muséum d'Histoire naturelle" vol. IV, 5 p. 380). These creatures certainly have a stomach, but they may well digest as much outside it as they do inside. They constitute the transition to organisms in which respiration, digestion and various other functions take place through similar but distinct organs.'

The object of *Spallanzani's* experiments was to discover whether digestion 10 was brought about by solvent juices, by triturations effected through the muscles of the stomach, or by both means. In order to decide the matter, he administered food in metal tubes or spherical containers, to Turkeys, Ducks, Chickens etc. These tubes and containers were latticed or perforated, so that the gastric juice could reach the food. As the grain 15 was never digested, but merely became sourer, he concluded that digestion is brought about by the intense pressing and pushing of the inner walls of the stomach. In these experiments, the hardest things, such as metal tubes and glass containers, and even sharp and jagged objects, were ground by the stomachs of these animals. It was thought therefore, that the trituration 20 of the food was helped on by the numerous tiny stones, sometimes as many as two hundred, often to be found in the stomachs of such animals. In order to refute this hypothesis, *Spallanzani* took young pigeons, which could not yet have swallowed any stones from their parents' beaks, made certain that they obtained none with their food, and cooped them up to 25 prevent them from finding any. Although these birds had no stones, they were also able to digest. 'I began to mix hard objects into their food, some iron tubes, some glass beads, some small fragments of glass; yet although not a single tiny stone had been found in the stomachs of these pigeons, the metal tubes were ground (froissés), and the beads and fragments of 30 glass were broken up and worn down (émoussés), without leaving the slightest trace of injury on the walls of the stomach.'[1]   +

The two digestions are particularly to be distinguished in the case of drink. Drink exudes through the walls of the stomach and the cellular tissue into the urinary vessels, from which it is evacuated. Beer is a diuretic. 35 Asparagus plants impart a special odour to the urine only a few minutes after they have been eaten, which is the effect of immediate digestion by

---

[1] 'Expériences sur la digestion de l'homme et de differentes espèces d'animaux, par l'abbé *Spallanzani* (par Jean *Senebier*, Genève 1783).' pp. 1–27.

means of the cellular tissue. The odour subsequently passes off, and only reoccurs eight to twelve hours later, when the digestion proper and the
+ discharge of excrements is being completed. *Treviranus* cites another instance of this immediate digestion (loc. cit. vol. IV, p. 404). 'When five
5 ounces of water were injected into a dog, two were vomited, and one remained in its stomach; two ounces must therefore have found an exit
+ through the walls of the stomach.' If a diet consists solely of meat dishes for example, it will be so much easier to digest immediately, on account of its homogeneity. It is into the animal lymph, which is the universal
10 element of animality, that the inorganic being is immediately transformed. The animal digests the food from without, as well as it digests its own viscera, muscles, nerves and so on, and in the same way that it absorbs even the phosphate of lime constituting bones, as it does for example when it absorbs the splinters of bone in a fracture. It eradicates
15 the specific particularity of these formations, and turns it into the general lymph or blood; it then specifies this lymph into particular formations once again.

The *other form* of digestion involves mediation, and occurs first in higher organizations. Of course, its primary moments are also actions of the
20 organism opposed to external being, but it is no longer general, for it is a particular operation of particular animal formations such as the bile and the pancreatic juice etc. However, the activity of this mediation does not consist of merely passing through the organism, through the four stomachs of ruminants for example; nor does it entail various operations and
25 changes, different stages of processing, as if the foods were being softened and seasoned. What is more, it is not an alteration brought about by the action of one specific matter upon another, for then the relationship would be merely chemical, and its effect nothing more than a neutralization. Chemical researches into gastric juice and bile have shown no more than
30 that the chyme in the stomach is somewhat acidified (not putrid, but tending rather to resist putrefaction), and that the acidity is removed by the
+ bile. When the bile is mixed with the chyme, 'a white precipitate is formed, which resembles a thick mucilage,' although this no longer contains any acidity, milk will curdle in the stomach.[1] This is certainly not
35 beyond doubt however, and in any case it is by no means the specific principle of digestion, for if the precipitate were freed from acidity, it would be the same as it was before. The bile is therefore opposed to the juice which derives from the great gland or pancreas below the stomach.

[1] *Treviranus*, loc. cit. vol. IV, pp. 467-469.

In higher animals, this pancreatic juice takes the place of the lymph which occurs in the glands, although it does not differ from it in any essential respect.

Digestion as a whole is therefore as follows. By its hostility towards that external to it, the organism divides itself internally in two. The final product of digestion is the *chyle*, and this is the same as the animal lymph into which the animal in its immediate appropriation transforms its nutriment, which it acquires either fortuitously or on purpose. In the lower animals, immediate transformation prevails, but in developed animals, digestion consists of the organism's relating itself to external being through activity which is specified, not immediate. This stage is not much of an advance however. The food is first mixed with the general animality of the saliva; the pancreatic juice is added to the stomach, and then finally the bile, which is resinous and inflammable, and of prime importance. Chemical analysis of the bile indicates nothing more specific than that it is igneous. We know also that bile flows into the stomach when we are angry, and it is common knowledge that there is a connection between the bile, the stomach, and the liver. A physiology which investigated such connections would be extremely interesting; it might explain for example why a feeling of shame is accompanied by blushing in the face and bosom. Just as anger is the feeling of being-for-self which flares up when a person is offended, so bile is the being-for-self which the animal organism turns on this potency posited within it from without; for the pancreatic juice and the bile attack the chyme. The bile, which is this active destruction, in which the organism has returned into itself, originates in the spleen. The spleen presents physiologists with certain difficulties. It is a sluggish organ belonging to the venous system, and related to the liver. It seems to function solely as a focal point for venous inertia, in opposition to the lung. This sluggish being-for-self, which has its seat in the spleen becomes the bile when it is ignited. Animals possess liver and bile as soon as they are developed, that is to say, as soon as they do not merely digest immediately or simply remain at the lymphatic stage.

The main point is however, that although the organism is active in a mediatory and differentiated manner, it does not abandon its universality, while at the same time it operates chemically upon external objects. It therefore resembles fractured crystals, which display their characteristic inner formation as a particular mode of their determinate being. The animal becomes inwardly differentiated because it behaves in a differentiated manner. In other words, as the animal is involved in the struggle with external being, its relationship with it has no reality, because the in-

version of this external being has also been brought about implicitly through the power of the animal lymph. Consequently, the animal is not aware of its own self when it attacks this food. The immediate and precise result of this is however, that as the animal comes to itself, and recognizes
5 that it constitutes this power, it reproaches itself for having become involved with the external powers, and turns against itself and against its former illusion. By doing this however, it abandons its state of outward orientation, and returns to itself. By overcoming inorganic potency, the animal overcomes animality itself, it does not overcome inorganic potency
10 as such. The true externality of animal being is not the external object, but its irritated hostility towards external being. Animal being has to free itself from mistrusting itself in this way; it has to overcome this false bent, which makes the struggle with the object look like the work of the subject. In this struggle with that external to it, organic being is on the point
15 of putting itself at a disadvantage, for it hinders itself somewhat in the face of this inorganic being. It is its own process, its being involved with external being, that the organism has to overcome, and its activity therefore runs counter to its outward orientation. This activity is the means to which the organism reduces itself, although only in order to return to
20 itself through removing and discarding this means. If the organism were actively hostile to inorganic being, it would not get its due; in its precise constitution it is however the mediation of engaging itself with inorganic being, and yet returning into itself. This negation of outward orientated
+ activity has a double determination, for while the organism excerns its
25 hostile activity towards inorganic being, and posits its immediate self-identity, it also reproduces itself in this self-preservation.

The Notion of digestion is therefore as follows. After the mediation of digestion has simply posited that which is already implicit, and the nutriment which enters the atmosphere of living being has been overcome,
30 organic being returns into itself out of this opposition, and concludes the matter by laying hold of itself. The phenomena which correspond to this Notion have already been considered (p. 162). It is through this process of assimilation that the animal acquires its reality and individuality, for by specifying itself into the main differences of animal lymph and bile in its
35 relation with individual being, it has proved its animal individuality, and by negating its other, it has posited itself as subjectivity and real being-for-self. As animal being has now acquired the individuality of real being-for-self, this self-relatedness is immediate self-diremption and division, and the constituting of subjectivity is the immediate self-repulsion of the
40 organism. Consequently, differentiation does not occur solely within

organic being itself, but is rather a self, producing itself as a self-externality. The plant falls apart into its differentiation, and there can be no doubt that animal being also displays differences. In the case of animal being however, the independent being from which it distinguishes itself is not merely something external, but is at the same time posited as being identical with 5 it. This real production, in which the animal duplicates itself by repelling itself, constitutes the final stage of animality in general. This real process in its turn has three forms: (a) the form of abstract, formal repulsion, (b) the nisus formativus, and (c) the propagation of the species. In nature, these + three apparently heterogeneous processes are essentially inter-connected. 10 In many animals, the excretory and genital organs, which constitute the highest and lowest features of animal organization, are intimately connected: just as speech and kissing on the one hand, and eating, drinking and spitting on the other, all focus upon the mouth.

The conclusion of the process of assimilation is *excretion*, which is the 15 abstract repulsion of itself by which the animal constitutes its self-externality. As the animal only converts itself into an external being, this externality is inorganic; it is an abstract other which is not identical with the animal. In thus separating itself from itself, the organism expresses its loathing for its lack of self-reliance; it does this by giving up the struggle, 20 and ridding itself of the bile which it has discharged. Consequently, the significance of the excrements is merely that through them the organism acknowledges its error, and rids itself of its entanglement with external things. This is confirmed by the chemical composition of the excrements. The moment of excretion is usually regarded as nothing but the necessary 25 evacuation of useless and unusable material. The animal need not have ingested anything useless or superfluous however, and although there is such a thing as indigestible material, the material evacuated in the excrements is either mainly assimilated, or consists of whatever is added to the ingested matters by the organism itself, i.e. the bile, which has the function 30 of combining with the victuals. 'The healthier the animal, and the more digestible the food it consumes, the smaller will be the amount of undecomposed fodder evacuated through its rectum, and the more homogeneous will be the composition of its excrements. However, even the dung of the healthiest animals invariably contains a fibrous residue of in- 35 gested food. The *principal ingredients* of dung are however substances which originate in the *gastric juices*, especially the bile. When he analyzed human excrements, *Berzelius* found undecomposed bile, albumen, choloidic acid, and two peculiar substances, one of which looks like glue, and the other of which only forms from the choloidic acid and the biliary 40

+ albumen when the excrements are exposed to the air. Through its rectum, the human body excretes bile, albumen, two peculiar animal matters, biline, carbonate, muriate and phosphate of soda, phosphate of magnesia and phosphate of lime. Through its urinary organs it evacuates mucus,
5 lactic, uric and benzoic acid, muriate of soda, muriate of ammonia, phosphate and hydrofluate of lime etc. All these matters are not merely extraneous substances incapable of being assimilated; they are the very constituents of the animal organs. The constituents of the urine are to be
+ found elsewhere in the body, principally in the bones. Many of these
10 matters also enter into the composition of the hair, others into that of the
+ muscles and the brain. Superficially considered, this comparison seems to indicate that a greater amount of matter is assimilated through digestion than can be appropriated by the organs which are to be nourished by it, and that it is this unchanged surplus which is evacuated through the
15 excretory organs. Closer investigation will make it evident however, that there are disproportions between the constituents of the nutriment, the assimilated materials and the matters excreted, which cannot be brought into harmony with this conclusion.' The following is certainly evidence of disproportions between the nutriments and the assimilated materials,
20 though it is hardly evidence of disproportions between the assimilated materials and the matters excreted. 'These disproportions are particularly
+ evident in phosphoric acid and lime. *Fourcroy* and *Vauquelin* found more phosphate of lime in horse-dung, and more carbonate and phosphate of lime in bird-mute than could be extracted from the food consumed. In
25 the case of birds on the other hand, a certain quantity of the silica in their food disappears. Perhaps the same might also be true of sulphur,' which is also found in excrements. 'Natron however is found in the bodies of herbivorous animals, whose foods are devoid of any significant quantity of this salt. On the other hand, the urine of Lions and Tigers contains a
+ great deal of potash, instead of natron. It is more than likely therefore, that separations and combinations occur generally in all living bodies, and that they are more powerful than the chemical agents *known at present*'.[1] They are still supposed to be chemical therefore! Is there never to be any progression beyond the chemical sphere? The truth of the organism's
35 activity is that it is purposive however, for it consists precisely of attaining its end and then discarding its means. Consequently, bile and pancreatic juice etc. are nothing but the organism's own process, which it gets rid of in material shape. The result of the process is the satiation or sentience

[1] *Treviranus*, loc. cit. vol. IV, pp. 480–482; 614–618.

which is aware that completeness has countered its previous deficiency. The understanding will always keep to the mediations as such, and regard them as external relationships comparable with those of the mechanical and chemical spheres. These spheres are however completely subordinate to free animation and sentience. The understanding regards its knowledge 5 as being superior to speculation, which it looks down upon. It remains limited to the sphere of finite mediation however, and is therefore unable to grasp animation as such.

3. The nisus formativus

As *Blumenbach* defined it, the nisus formativus is principally reproduc- + tion, but here it is not to be understood as such. The *mechanical drive*, as + an instinct, constitutes the third moment; it is the unity of the ideal nature of the theoretical process, and of the real process of digestion. Primarily however, it is merely their relative totality, for the generic process is the true inner totality, the third moment of the whole. That which is assimi- lated here is an externality belonging to the inorganic nature of the 15 animal; in its assimilation however, it is at the same time allowed to remain as an external object. Consequently, the nisus formativus resembles ex- cretion by being a self-externalization, but by externalizing itself, it reproduces the form of the organism within the external world. The ob- ject is formed in a way that can satisfy the subjective need of the animal; 20 here however, appetite does not merely stand in a hostile relation to the external world, for peace prevails in the face of external existence. Ap- petite is satisfied and restrained at one and the same time therefore, and the organism only objectifies itself by disposing of inorganic material for its own purpose. Here therefore, the practical and theoretical relationships 25 are united. The form can satisfy the drive without the object's being sublated, but this is only one side of the nisus formativus. The other side consists of the animal's excreting formations from itself. It does not do this on account of a loathing, and a desire to be rid of them however; the excrements which are externalized are formed so as to satisfy the animal's 30 need.

This mechanical instinct makes its appearance as an intentional and knowing act of nature, and it is this determination of purposiveness which makes it difficult to grasp. It has always seemed most remarkable on account of its having been customary to grasp rationality only as external 35 purposiveness, and to get no further than a sensuous mode of intuition in

the general interpretation of animation. The nisus formativus is in fact *analogous* to the understanding as a self-conscious entity; but because of this, one must not think of the purposive action of nature as self-conscious understanding. Each step involved in the consideration of nature is out of
5 the question unless the end has been perceived. The end is precisely that which is predetermined and active, and which preserves itself by assimilating the other to which it relates itself. The Notion is the relation between these moments; it is a formation of the external being or the secretions, which have a connection with the animal's need. As mechanical instinct
10 however, this Notion is only the inner implicitness, the mere unconscious overseer of the animal; it first constitutes its being-for-self in thought, in the human artist. This explains the observation made by *Cuvier* that instinct is most prominent in insects, and diminishes in accordance with the
+ height of an animal's grading. By virtue of this internal Notion, every-
15 thing is a means, i.e. everything is related to a unity. It is related in such a way, that if the unity (which in this case is living being) were devoid of this means, it would have no being. The means is at the same time only a moment sublated within the whole, it is not independent, it has no being-in-and-for-itself. Similarly, for the Earth, even the Sun itself is a means,
20 and in the case of the crystal, each of its lines is a means serving the immanence of its form. Living being has this higher faculty of constituting the activity which forms things external to it, and at the same time, simply because they are related to the Notion as a purposive means, of respecting their externality.

25 The *primary* form of the mechanical instinct, which we have already touched upon, is the instinctive building of nests, burrows and lairs, whereby the general totality of the animal's surroundings is its own, although only in respect of its form (see above § 362). Then there is the migration of birds and fish, which is related to their climatic sensitivity,
30 and also the collecting of provisions for the winter, whereby that which is to be consumed later by the animal becomes part of its present habitat (see above § 361). Animals therefore have relationships with the ground on which they lie, and want to make it more comfortable. In satisfying the need to lie down therefore, they do not consume something, as they
35 do in the case of nutriment, but preserve it and merely form it. Nutriment is also formed of course, but it completely disappears. This theoretical aspect of the nisus formativus is a check on appetite; it does not occur in plants, which unlike the animal are unable to check their drives, because they do not possess the theoretical nature of sentience.

40 Many animals first *prepare* and *equip* themselves, and this constitutes the

practical aspect of the mechanical instinct. The spider weaves its web in order to catch its food for example, and other animals extend their powers of feeling and grasping prey by means of their claws and feet: in the case of the Polyp, by means of its tentacles. Animals of this kind excrete in order to equip themselves from their own bodies. The weapons they ex- 5 crete are certainly their own productions, and separate themselves from the animals at the same time as they are ejected by them. 'In Crabs and Brachiopoda, caecal appendages (*tufts*, villi) in the intestinal canal take the + place of the liver and the pancreas, and in general of the whole apparatus of glandular organs which promotes digestion and nutrition in higher 10 classes of animals.' (The oesophagus, stomach, intestinal canal, is one long tube, although it is, 'divided by contractions and sphincter muscles into several sections, varying in length, width and texture). In insects, not only does the same thing occur, but there is also no trace whatever of glands. In Spiders, these blind-sacs,' (inside the body) 'which resemble intestines, 15 provide the material for web-making, while in caterpillars and similar larvae, they provide the material for the cocoon,' the transformation into + the chrysalis. 'In the larva of the Puss moth, they supply the liquid it ejects + when it is irritated, and in Bees, the poison imparted by the sting of this insect. It is moreover in sacs such as these that insects elaborate all the 20 juices required for procreation. In the male, both sides of the body are equipped with an organ consisting of an extremely long but very delicate and narrow canal, which is coiled inwards, and which corresponds to the epididymus in mammals. From it, a further duct passes on to the penis. In + the female, there is a double ovary etc. All insects in their larval state are 25 completely devoid of genitals, and some insects such as Worker-bees lack them throughout the whole of their life-span.' The only way in which these asexual Bees produce themselves is by building cells and excreting honey; they are sterile flowers as it were, and do not attain to the propagation of the species. 'With regard to this point, there is the remarkable law 30 that in all cases of asexuality among insects, the genitals are replaced by other organs, which supply a material for constructional purposes. The converse of this law is not true however. Spiders for example, construct their webs from a material elaborated by their own organs, but they are not asexual.'[1] Caterpillars merely eat and excrete, and are devoid of any 35 external genitals; the nisus formativus comes into play at the second stage, when the cocoon is spun for the chrysalis, while the life of coupling belongs to the Butterfly. 'There are a few insects which retain the shape

---

[1] *Treviranus*, loc. cit. vol. I, pp. 366 (364)–367; 369–370.

they have when they emerge from the egg throughout the whole of their life-span. All the species of the Spider family have this characteristic, as well as many species from the orders of Woodlice and Mites. All other creatures of this class undergo a partial or total transformation during their
5 life-span. Where metamorphosis is only partial, the main difference between the larva and the pupa, and between the pupa and the adult insect, consists for the most part in nothing but their having fewer, or less completely developed organs. On the other hand, where total transformation occurs, the perfect insect no longer bears any trace of what it was in
10 its larval state. The innumerable muscles of the larva have disappeared, and quite different ones have taken their place; similarly, head, heart and
+ trachea etc. have a completely different structure'.[2]

In the nisus formativus, the creature has brought itself forth and yet remained in its initial immediacy; it is at this juncture therefore that it
15 first attains to the self-enjoyment of determinate sentience. Previously, the creature was the immediate sensation of a simply abstract being-in-self, a mere enjoyment of external things. As such, it merely has a sensation of the way in which it is determined. It certainly finds satisfaction in appeasing its hunger and thirst, but this is not yet the self-satisfaction of which it
20 now becomes capable. By adapting external being to itself, it possesses and enjoys itself in its environment. The mechanical instinct also accounts for the *voice*, in which the ideal nature of subjectivity is articulated into air, and the subject hears itself in the external world. It is the birds in particular which abandon themselves to this blithe self-enjoyment. A bird's vocal
25 faculty is not confined to expressing a need, and is not simply a cry, for its song is the free expression of what is ultimately an immediate self-enjoy-
+ ment.

§ 366

Through the process with external nature, the animal as a *single* individual endows its self-certainty or subjective
30 Notion with truth and objectivity. **Consequently, this** *production* **of itself is** a self-preservation or *reproduction*, **although as subjectivity has become a product, its immediacy is at the same time implicitly sublated. Linked up with itself in this way, the Notion is determined** as the *concrete universal* or *genus*, **which**

[2] *Treviranus*, ibid., pp. 372–374.

enters into a relationship and a process with the singularity of subjectivity.[1]

Addition. At this juncture, the significance of the appeased appetite is not that the individual brings itself forth as this particular being, but that it brings itself forth as a universal, as a ground of individuality, for which it is merely form. 5 The determinate appetite is therefore the universal which has returned to itself, and which contains individuality in an immediate manner. The theoretical return (of sense) into itself, only brings forth a general deficiency, while through the return of individuality into itself, the deficiency produced is positive. The deficient being is completed by itself, it is a dual individual. Initially, the 10 animal is restricted to itself; secondly, it brings itself forth at the expense of inorganic nature, by assimilating it. The third relationship, which is the union of the first two, is the generic process, in which the animal relates itself to itself by relating itself to one of its kind. As in the first process, it relates itself to a living being, and as in the second process, it relates itself 15 at the same time to a being which it finds before it.

C

Generic process[2]
(*The generic process*)

§ 367

The genus constitutes the concrete substance of the subject, and is in implicit and simple unity with its singularity. As the universal is basic division however, it may proceed from this its self-diremption as a unity which has being-for-self, and so posit 20

---

[1] Addition to the first and second edition, 'The *disjunction* of the singularity which comes to itself within the genus, constitutes *sexual differentiation*, which is the subject's relation to an object which is itself just such a subject.' This sentence was omitted from the third edition, in which the sex-relationship no longer followed on immediately after the nisus formativus. In the third edition, the genus and the species, as the object of zoology, formed the first member of the division which also included the sex-relationship and disease. The original order would seem to be more logical however, and I have therefore retained it. To quote the first edition, and the words are much the same in the second, 'The sex-relationship . . . has the universal Notion, as the essence of the individuals, as its universal extreme. *Primarily*, the genus exists within it only as this single individual, while in the *second instance*, it particularizes itself into the species, and finally into singularity itself, through the sinking away of which, it reveals itself as the true universal'.

Note by Michelet.

[2] Instead of making Generic process correspond to Shape and Assimilation as the third main division of The animal organism, it might have seemed more to the purpose to present the *Type of the individual* as sub-divided into the Process of formation, Assimilation, and The sex-relationship,

itself within existence as **subjective universality**. This process by which the universal links up with itself, contains both the negation of the merely internal universality of the genus, and that of the merely immediate singularity in which living being still belongs
5 to nature. The negation of this singularity exhibited in the preceding process (see § 366) is merely primary and immediate. In this generic process, it is only the being which merely lives that perishes, for as such it does not transcend naturality. As the moments of the generic process are not yet based on the subjective
10 universal of a single subject however, they fall apart and exist as various particular processes, which terminate in the various kinds of death suffered by living being.

Addition. Consolidated by means of its sentience, the individual has acquired breadth so to speak; its immediate singularity is sublated, and
15 singular being no longer needs to have a relationship with inorganic nature. With the disappearance of its determinations as an exclusive singularity, the Notion acquires the further determination of the subject's determining itself as a universal. This determination falls into a further basic division and exclusion of an other; it has the determination of being
20 identical for this other however, and of existing for it as this identity. It is thus that we have the genus, the determination of which is its coming into existence in distinct opposition to singularity, which is the generic process in general. It is certainly true that in the individual, the genus fails to attain to free existence and universality; at this juncture however,
25 although on the one hand the genus is also still identical with the individual in a merely immediate manner, on the other hand, the individual has already assumed a singular subjectivity, and is therefore also distinct from the genus. This difference constitutes a process, the result of which is that the universality of the genus asserts itself, and immediate singularity
30 is negated. This submergence constitutes the death of the individual. This

---

and to make Zoology and Medicine, which are two sub-divisions of Generic process, follow Anatomy and Physiology as the last two of four main divisions (see above p. 109 note.). In addition to the remark accompanying § 370 in the first and second edition (see below p. 177), it is made quite clear that the type of the individual, which was *first* presented merely as Notion completed within itself, has now in the *second instance* to unfold itself into the sequence of animal genera and species. To that which is subordinate in this sequence, that above it is invariably inorganic nature as a genus, and through this genus, that which is *subordinate* perishes. In the *third instance*, the animal dies in an immanent manner, and not into a genus which is external to it. It is thus that it then leaves itself behind in order that it may itself bring universality into actuality in a positive manner (cf. § 371, Add. III. 193, 25).

Note by Michelet

brings organic nature to a close, for by coming into its own through the death of the singular being, the genus becomes its own object, and it is this that constitutes the proceeding forth of spirit. We have still to consider this submergence of singularity within the genus. The relationship of the genus to the singular being is not always the same however, so that 5 we also have to distinguish between the particular processes which constitute the various kinds of death suffered by the living individual. Thus, the generic process has three forms. The *first* is the sex-relationship, through which the production of the kind consists of the procreation of individuals through the death of other individuals of the same kind, i.e. 10 the individual's dying after having reproduced itself as another individual. *Secondly*, the genus particularizes itself into its various species, and comporting themselves as individuals in opposition to other individuals, these species at the same time constitute inorganic nature for one another, for they comport themselves as a genus does to individuality, and so give rise 15 to violent death. The *third form* is the relationship of the individual to itself as genus, within a single subjectivity. This relationship is partly the transitory disproportion of an ailment, and partly the terminating state in which the genus as such maintains itself through the individual's passing over into existence as a universal, i.e. natural death. 20

1. The sex-relationship

§ 368[1]

This relationship is a process which begins with a need, for while the individual **as a** *singular being* **is not adequate to the immanent** genus,[2] **it is at the same time the identical self-relation of the genus in a single unity. It therefore** *feels* **this deficiency.[3] Consequently, the genus is present in the individual as** a strain opposed to the inadequacy of its single actuality; **it is present as an urge to attain** its sentience in the 25

---

[1] In the third edition, this and the following paragraph came after § 370. It began with the following reference to 'The genus and the species', which preceded it, 'This primary diremption of the genus into species, and the further determination of these species into the immediately exclusive being-for-self of singularity, is merely a negative and hostile attitude towards others. However, the genus is to the same extent singularity, as an essentially affirmative self-relatedness within the genus. In this self-relatedness, the singularity is an exclusive individual opposed to another of its kind, continues itself in this *other*, and is sensible of itself within *it*.'

[2] Addition to the first edition, 'this inadequacy still falls into an external reflection'.

[3] Addition to the first edition, 'and constitutes natural sexual differentiation'.

other of its genus, to integrate itself through union with this other, **and** by means of this mediation **to bring the genus**
₊ **into existence** by linking itself into it. **This constitutes generation.**[1]

Addition. Since the ideality of inorganic nature is posited through the
₅ process with it, the animal has consolidated its sentience and objectivity
in its own self. This is not merely implicit sentience, but a sentience which
is existent and animated. In the separateness of the two sexes, the extremes
constitute totalities of sentience, and in its sex-drive, the animal produces
itself as a sentience, as a totality. In the nisus formativus, organic being
₁₀ became a dead product; it was certainly freely released from organic
being, but it was only a superficial form imposed upon an external
material, so that this externality was not objective to it as a free and
indifferent subject. This case bears a resemblance to the process of assimilation however, for both sides are now independent individuals. The dif-
₁₅ ference is that they are not related to each other as organic and inorganic
beings however, for they are both organic beings belonging to the genus,
and they therefore exist only as a single kind. Their union is the disappearance of the sexes, in which the simple genus has come into being. The
animal has an object with which it feels an immediate identity; this
₂₀ identity is the moment of the first process (of formation), which is added
to the determination of the second process (of assimilation). The relation
of one individual to another of its kind is the substantial relationship of
the genus. The nature of each permeates both, and both find themselves
within the sphere of this universality. Both are implicitly a single genus,
₂₅ the same subjective vitality, and in the process they also posit this as being
so. At this juncture, the Idea of nature is actual in the male and female
couple; up till now their identity and their being-for-self merely had being
for us in our reflection, but they are now experienced by the sexes themselves in their infinite reflection into each other. This feeling of universal-
₃₀ ity is the supreme moment of the animal's capabilities, but within it, its
concrete universality never occurs for it as a theoretical object of intuition.
If it did, it would be thought or consciousness, in which alone the genus
attains to free existence. Consequently, a contradiction occurs; the universality of the genus, which is the identity of the individuals, is different
₃₅ from the particular individuality of these individuals. The individual is
only one of the two individuals, and exists merely as a singularity, not as

---

[1] First and second edition, 'and through this mediation, the concrete universal is linked up with itself, and assumes singular actuality.'

their unity. The animal sublates this difference by its activity. The basic genus constitutes the one extreme of the syllogism, for every process is syllogistic in form. The vitality which wants to bring itself forth, finds itself placed within the genus. The genus is the driving subjectivity and essence of the individuals, and by straining in opposition to the inadequacy of their singular actuality, it constitutes the mediation or middle term of the syllogism. It is precisely this that drives the individuals to realize their sentience only within another of their kind. As the actuality assumed by the genus has the form of an immediate existence, it is of course only a single actuality. By means of it, the genus links itself up with the other extreme of singularity.

As the *different sexes* constitute the sex-drive as differentials, there must be a *difference* in their *formation*; their mutual determinateness must exist as posited through the Notion. The implicitness of both sides is not merely neutral, as it is in chemism however, for on account of the original identity of their formation, the same type underlies both the *male and female genitals*. The difference is however, that in one or the other of these genitals, one or the other part is essential; in the female this is necessarily the undifferentiated element, while in the male it is the sundered element of opposition. This identity is most conspicuous in the lower animals. 'In some Grasshoppers, such as the Gryllus verruccivorus, the large testicles, which consist of fascicularly coiled vessels, resemble the ovaries, which are equally large, and which consist of oviducts coiled in a similarly fasciculate manner. Similarly, in the male *Gadfly*, the testicles not only have precisely the same general outline as the thicker and larger ovaries, but also consist of delicate vesicles, which are almost oviform and oblong, and which stand on end on the substance of the testicles, like ova on an ovary.'[1] The identification of the female uterus in the male parts has presented the greatest difficulty. The scrotum has ineptly been mistaken for it,[2] for it is actually the testicle which apparently corresponds to the female ovary. In the male, it is however the prostate which corresponds to the female uterus; in him therefore, the uterus is reduced to a gland, an indifferent generality. *Ackermann* has demonstrated this very well from his hermaphrodite, which has a uterus, although the formation of its other organs is male. This uterus not only occupies the position of the prostrate however, for the ejaculatory ducts also pass through its substance, and open into the urethra at the crista galli. What is more, the lips of the female pudendum are shrunken scrota, which accounts for the labia pudendi of *Ackermann's* hermaphrodite having been filled with a

---

[1] *Schubert*, 'Ideas for a general history of life' pt. I, p. 185.
[2] Op. cit., pp. 205–206.

kind of testicular formation. Finally, the medial line of the scrotum is split in the female, and forms the vagina. From this, it is quite understandable that one sex should change into the other. On the one hand, the uterus in the male is reduced to a mere gland, while on the other, the male testicle in the
5 female remains enclosed within the ovary, fails to emerge into opposition, and does not become an independent and active cerebrality. The clitoris moreover, is inactive feeling in general; in the male on the other hand, it has its counter-
+ part in active sensibility, the swelling vital, the effusion of blood into the corpora cavernosa and the meshes of the spongy tissue of the urethra. The female
10 counterpart of this effusion of blood in the male consists of the menstrual discharges. Thus, the simple retention of the conception in the uterus, is differentiated in the male into productive cerebrality and the external
+ vital. On account of this difference therefore, the male is the active principle; as the female remains in her undeveloped unity, she constitutes the principle of
15 conception.

+ *Conception* must not be regarded as consisting of nothing but the ovary and the male semen, as if the new formation were merely a composition of the forms or parts of both sides, for the female certainly contains the material element, while the male contains the subjectivity.[1] Conception
20 is the contraction of the whole individual into the simple self-abandoning unity of its representation. The seed is precisely this simple representation; it is a wholly singular point, as is its name and its entire self. Consequently, conception consists of nothing but the unification of these opposed and abstract represen-
+ tations.

§ 369

25 **The** product is the *negative identity* **of differentiated singularities, and as a** *resultant genus,* an asexual life. In its *natural*
aspect, **it is** merely the *implicitness* of this product which
constitutes this genus however. **This differs from the** singular
beings **whose differentiation** has subsided into it,[2] and is itself
30 an immediate *singular,* although it has the determination **of**
developing itself into the same natural individuality, and into a

+ [1] *Aristotle,* 'Metaphysics' VIII 4: 'What is the material cause of man? The menses. What is the moving cause? The semen.'

Note by Michelet.

[2] First edition, 'the singular beings which have subsided into it'.

corresponding sexual differentiation and transience. **This process of propagation issues forth into the progress of the spurious infinite. The genus preserves itself only through the perishing of the individuals, which fulfil their determination in the process of generation, and in so far as they have no higher determination than this, pass on to death.**[1]

Addition. Thus, the animal organism has run through its cycle, and now constitutes the asexual and fecundated universal. It has become the absolute genus, which is however the death of the particular individual. Lower animal organisms such as Butterflies die immediately after generation therefore, for their singularity is their life, and they have sublated it within the genus. Higher organisms survive the act of generation, for they have a higher degree of independence; their death is the developed dissolution of their shape, which we shall see presently as disease. The genus brings itself forth by negating its differentiation; it exists merely in a series of single living beings however, not in-and-for-itself. Consequently, the sublation of each contradiction invariably gives rise to a fresh one. The different individuals perish within the generic process, for it is only outside the unity of this process, which is the true actuality, that they are different. In the feeling of love however, the selfishness of the single being is negated, together with its self-contained aloofness. The single shape is no longer able to preserve itself therefore, and so perishes, for only that which is absolute in its self-identity, i.e. the universal which is for the universal, is self-preserving. The genus is merely implicit within the animal however, it does not exist within it, and it is only within spirit that it is eternal in its being-in-and-for-self. The transition to the existent genus takes place implicitly, in the Idea, in the Notion, that is to say, in the sphere of eternal creation. There however, the sphere of nature is closed.

---

[1] First edition, 'However, within this new life, in which the* singularity is sublated, the same subjectivity is at the same time positively preserved. This constitutes the return of the genus into itself. Within it, the genus as such has entered into the being-for-self of its reality, and has† transcended nature.'‡

* Addition to the second edition, 'immediate'.

† Addition to the second edition, 'nevertheless'.

‡ Addition to the second edition, 'It is this higher sphere which has subsequently to be considered.'

2. The genus and the species
(*Zoology*)

§ 370[1]

The universal *type of the animal* determined by the Notion, lies at the basis of the *various forms* and *orders of animals*. This type is exhibited by nature partly in the various *stages of its development* from the simplest organization to the most perfect, in which nature is the instrument of spirit, and partly in the various *circumstances* and *conditions* of *elemental nature*. **Developed into singularity, the animal species distinguishes itself from others both in itself and by means of itself, and has being-for-self through the negation of that from which it has distinguished itself. In this hostile relation to others, in which they are reduced to inorganic nature, violent death constitutes the natural fate of individuals.**

Remark[2]

In *zoology*, as in the natural sciences in general, the main concern has been the discovery of simple and unmistakable *characteristics* by which **classes and orders etc.** may be recognized. A wider prospect, **taking in the objective nature of the forms themselves,** has only opened up since there has been less preoccupation with the classification of animals

---

[1] In the third edition, this paragraph constituted the first subdivision of Generic process, and began with the following words, 'At first, the genus in its implicit universality simply *particularizes* itself into *species*.'

[2] In the first and second edition, this remark began with the following passage, 'As the animal is the actuality of the Idea of life, the essence of its Notion is the *Notion* itself. Through the nature of its *universality*, the Notion has the possibility of a determinate being which varies in simplicity and development, and which, to a varying extent, corresponds to it. Consequently, the Notion in its determinateness cannot be grasped by means of this determinate being. The developed Notion emerges into the full display of its moments in the classes, which appear as a particular *determinate being*, opposed to the others; but even here, its determinate being can be *imperfect*. In order to say that such a determinate being is *imperfect* however, it is necessary to have presupposed the Notion. When the empirical determinate being is presupposed* in order to recognize the nature and essential determinations of the animal, or to identify the essential organs of a class, it is impossible to establish a fixed determination,† and what is more, none of the particular characteristics seems to be indispensable. For example, Acephala have been cited to show that man also might live without a brain.'

* In the first edition, this read as follows, 'When, as was usually the case, the determinate being was presupposed . . .'

† Addition to the first edition, 'empirically'.

by means of what are called artificial systems. In recent times, all the empirical sciences have made great advances in the accumulation of observations, but in the extent to which its material has tended to conform to the Notion, scarcely one of them has advanced as much as zoology has by means of its auxiliary science, *comparative anatomy.* **Thoughtful observation of nature, primarily by French naturalists, has led to the division of plants into monocotyledons and dicotyledons, and in the animal world, to the cogent distinction based upon the absence or presence of vertebrae. By means of this distinction, the fundamental classification of animals has, in its essentials, been led back to that which had already been observed by Aristotle.—What is more,** particular importance has been attached to the *habit* of the individual forms, which has been regarded as a coherence determining the construction of *every part;* this has enabled *Cuvier,* the illustrious founder of comparative anatomy, to boast that from a single bone, he could make out the essential nature of the entire animal. In addition to this, the general type of the animal has been traced in its barest initial indication, as well as in the various formations, which appear in an extremely imperfect and disparate manner; it has also been possible to grasp the significance of the interrelated organs and functions. It is precisely by means of this that the general type of the animal has been lifted out of particularity, and raised into its universality.—An important aspect of this approach is the recognition of the way in which nature shapes and adapts this organism to the particular element in which it places it, to climate, to a range of nutrition, and in general, to the environment which it finds about it. This environment can also be a particular genus of plants or another genus of animals (see § 361 **Add.**). **For the determination of the species however, the distinguishing characteristics have, by a happy intuition, been selected from the animal's weapons, i.e. its teeth and claws etc. This is valuable, because it is by its weapons that the animal, in distinguishing itself from others, establishes and preserves itself as a being-for-self.**

The *immediacy* of the Idea of life consists of the Notion[1]

---

[1] Addition to the first and second edition, 'although it alone is that which is determined in and for itself.'

as such failing to *exist in life*, submitting itself therefore to the manifold conditions and circumstances of external nature, and being able to appear in the most stunted of forms; the *fruitfulness* of the earth allows life to break forth *everywhere*, and in all kinds of ways. The animal world is perhaps even less able than the other spheres of nature to present an immanently independent and rational system of organization, to keep to the *forms* which would be determined by the Notion, and to proof them in the face of the imperfection and mixing of conditions, against mingling, stuntedness and intermediaries. The feebleness of the Notion **in nature in general,**[1] **not only subjects the formation of individuals to external accidents, which in the developed animal, and particularly in man, give rise to monstrosities, but** also makes the genera themselves completely subservient to the changes of the external universal life of nature. The life of the animal shares in the vicissitudes of this universal life **(cf. Remark § 392), and consequently, it merely** alternates **between health and disease. The milieu of external contingency contains very little that is not alien, and as it is continually subjecting animal sensibility to** violence **and the threat of dangers, the animal cannot escape** a feeling of *insecurity, anxiety and misery*.[2]

Addition. In that it is a life belonging to nature, the animal is still essentially an immediate existence, and is therefore determinate, finite and particular. Bound as it is to the infinitely numerous particularizations of inorganic and vegetable nature, animation always exists as a limited species, and the living being is not able to overcome these limitations. Universality of existence would constitute thought, and the particular character is devoid of this determination; in its relationship to nature, living being attains to nothing more than particularity. The life which takes up these potencies is capable of the most diverse modifications of formation; it is able to put up with all kinds of conditions and to continue to pulsate among them, although the universal powers of nature within these conditions never relinquish their overall supremacy.

[1] Addition to the first and second edition, 'which also fails to exist in animals in the firm independence of its freedom.'

[2] In the first and second edition, this reads as follows, 'Consequently, the general life of the animal appears as a life of illness, and the animal's feelings are those of *insecurity, anxiety* and *misery*.'

The method used by research which has as its object the classification of animals, is to look for the common element to which the concrete forms can be reduced, i.e. for a simple sensuous determinateness, which moreover is also an external one. There are no such simple determinations however. For example, one might accept the general concept 'Fish', as the common element of what one includes under this name when one thinks about it, and then enquire as to the simple determinateness or objective characteristic of fish. The conclusion to be drawn from this enquiry would be that fish swim in water, but as a number of land animals also do this, it would be insufficient. What is more, swimming is neither an organ nor a formation; it is mode of the activity of Fish, and in no respect is it part of their shape. Simply as a universal, a universal such as fish is not bound in any particular mode to its external existence. If one now assumes that a common element must be present as a simple determinateness, such as fins for example, and such a determinateness is not to be found, classification will be difficult. In this classification, the features and habits of the individual genera and species are used as the basis and rule, but the untrammelled variety of life in this genera and species excludes all universality. Consequently, the infinity of forms exhibited by animal being is not to be pedantically regarded as conforming absolutely to the necessary principle of orders. The general determinations must be made to rule therefore, and the natural forms compared with them. If the natural forms do not tally with this rule, but exhibit certain correspondences, agreeing with it in one respect but not in another, then it is not the rule, the determinateness of the genus or class etc. which has to be altered. The rule does not have to conform to these existences, they ought to conform to the determinateness, and this actuality exhibits deficiency in so far as it fails to conform. Some Amphibia are viviparous for example, and like Mammals and Birds, breathe by means of lungs; in that they have no breasts, and their heart has a single ventricle, they resemble Fish however. If one is prepared to admit that the works of man are sometimes defective, it must follow that those of nature are more frequently so, for nature is the Idea in the mode of externality. In man, the basis of these defects lies in his whims, his caprice and his negligence, e.g. when he introduces painting into music, paints with stones in mosaics, or introduces the epic genre into drama. In nature, it is the external conditions which stunt the forms of living being; however, these conditions produce these effects because life is indeterminate, and also because it is from these externalities that it derives its particular determinations. The forms of nature cannot be brought into an absolute system therefore, and it is because of this that the animal species are exposed to contingency.

There is subsequently another aspect to this, which is of course that the Notion also asserts itself, although only to a certain degree. There is only one animal type (§ 352 Add. III. 108, 4), and all animal difference is merely a modification of it. The main varieties of it are based on the same determinations as those we saw earlier in inorganic nature as the elements. These stages are therefore also stages in the formation of the animal type in general, so that it is possible to recognize from these determinations the gradings of the various kinds of animal. Two principles are therefore effective in determining the difference between animal genera. The first principle of classification, which is closer to the Idea, is that each subsequent stage is merely a further development of the simple animal type; the second is, that the organic type's scale of development is essentially connected with the elements into which animal life is cast. Such a connection occurs only in more highly developed animal life however; lower animal life bears little relation to the elements, being indifferent to these great differences. These are the main moments in the grouping of animal classes, and their further determinateness is related to the climatic factor. We have already observed (§ 339 Add. III. 23, 19) that the comparative uniformity of the flora and fauna of the northern hemisphere is a result of the contiguity of the continents, and that as the continents of Africa and America taper away towards the south, their indigenous animal genera also break up, to an increasing extent, into species. Whereas animals are determined by climatic differences therefore, man lives everywhere; although even in the case of man, Eskimos and other extreme peoples differ from those of the temperate zone. The animal however is subject to a much greater extent to such determinations and localities, to mountain, forest and plain etc. In this case there is no need to search everywhere for determinations of the Notion, although traces of them are never absent.

In the graded scale of development formed by the genera and species, a beginning can now be made with the undeveloped animals, in which the three systems of sensibility, irritability and reproduction do not yet exist in differentiation. As animation's most perfect organism, man then constitutes the highest stage of the development. Particularly in recent times, classification of this kind, based upon the stage of development, has been introduced into zoology. It is natural to progress in this way from the undeveloped to the higher organism, but in order to understand the lower stages, one has to identify the developed organism, for it is this that constitutes the measure or prototype of its less developed counterparts. As everything in it has reached its developed activity, it is clear that it is primarily from this developed organism that the undeveloped being is to be understood. Infusoria cannot be taken as the basis, for in this subdued life, the rudiments of the organism are still so feeble, that they can only be recognized through prior knowledge of more developed animal life. It is dunder-headed to say that the animal is more perfect than man however, for although the animal may certainly be better formed, it is the harmony of the organization which is the precise constituent of its perfection. The universal type which forms the basis cannot exist as such of course; but as the animal *exists*, it does so in a *particularity*; just as the perfect beauty of art must always be individualized. It is only in spirit that the universal, as ideal or Idea, possesses the universality of its determinate being.

We now have to see how the organism determines itself for these particularities. The organism is alive, and its viscera are determined by the Notion, although it also develops entirely in accordance with this particularity. This particular determination pervades all the parts of the shape, and harmonizes them with one another. This harmony is mainly present in the limbs, not in the viscera, for the particularity is precisely outward orientation towards a determinate inorganic nature. The prevalence of this particularization becomes more marked in the higher and more completely formed animals however. It is *Cuvier* who has developed this aspect of the science, and he was led to do so as the result of his having concerned himself with fossil bones. In order to discover the animal to which these bones belonged, he had to study their formation, and through this, he was led to consider the purposiveness of the way in which the individual limbs are related to one another. In the 'Discours préliminaire' to his 'Recherches sur les ossements fossiles des quadrupèdes' (Paris 1812, p. 58 et seq.) he says, 'Every organized being forms a whole, a unified and closed system, all the parts of which mutually correspond, and by means of reciprocal action, contribute to a common purposive activity. None of these parts can alter without the others altering also; as the result of this, each of them, taken separately, implies and yields all the others.'

'Consequently, if the intestines of an animal are so organized that they are only able to digest raw meat, its jaw-bones must also be adapted to the swallowing of its prey, its claws to the seizure and tearing of it, and its teeth to the biting off and chewing of the flesh. What is more, the animal's whole system of motor organs must enable it to pursue and

overtake other animals, just as its eyes must enable it to see them at a distance. It is even necessary that nature should have implanted in the animal's brain the instinct by which it conceals itself and lays traps for its victims. These are the universal requisites of *carnivorous* animals, every
5 one of which has to combine all of them within itself. Particular conditions such as the size, the species and the haunt of the prey, also result from the particular circumstances within the general forms however, so that not only the class, but also the order, the genus and even the species, is expressed in the form of each part.'

10 'In fact, in order that the jaw-bone may seize the prey, the condyle,' the organ which moves the jaw-bone, and to which the muscles are attached, 'must have a particular shape. The temporal muscles must have a certain bulk; this requires a certain hollowing of the bone which receives them, and of the zygomatic arch (arcade zygomatique) under
15 which they pass. This zygomatic arch must also have a certain strength, in order to provide a requisite support for the masticatory muscle (masseter).'

The same principle applies throughout the entire organism, 'In order that the animal may be able to carry away its prey, there must be a certain
20 strength in the muscles which lift the head' (the cervical muscles), 'this in its turn is closely related to the form of vertebrae to which the muscles are attached, and to the form of the occiput, in which they are inserted. The teeth must be sharp in order to bite into the flesh, and must have a firm base to facilitate the crushing of bones. The claws must have a
25 certain mobility,'—so that their muscles and bones must be developed; the same is true of the feet etc.

What is more, this harmony also leads on to further points of correspondence, which have an inner connection of another kind. This con-
+ nection is not always so easy to recognize, 'It is easy to see why animals
30 with hoofs must be *herbivorous*, for they have no claws for seizing anything else. We can also see why they do not need such large shoulderblades, for they can only use their forefeet for supporting their bodies. Their herbivorous diet will necessitate teeth with a flat crown which will enable them to grind grain and grasses. Grinding requires that this
35 crown should move horizontally, so that the condyle of the jaw bone will not constitute such a tight ginglymus as it does in the carnivorous animals,' *Treviranus* says (loc. cit. vol. I, pp. 198–199), 'In the lower jaw-bone on the other hand, instead of incisors, there is a cartilaginous pad. Most horned beasts lack canine teeth, and in all of them, the molars
40 are grooved by serrated transverse furrows. The crowns of these molars

are not horizontal, for they are obliquely notched in such a way, that in the upper jaw, it is their outer side which is higher, while in the lower jaw, it is their inner side, i.e. that closest to the tongue.'

The following observations by *Cuvier* also present us with no difficulties, 'It is fitting that those animal species whose teeth are less perfect, should have a more complex digestive system.' Here he is referring to *Ruminants*, which need a more complex digestive system of this kind mainly because it is more difficult to digest herbivorous fodder. 'However, I doubt whether anyone who had not discovered the fact by observation, would have inferred that all Ruminants have cloven hoofs, and that therefore the dental system of Ungulata which are not ruminants, is more perfect than that of the cloven-hoofed or ruminant animals. It is also noticeable that the formation of the teeth and the larger formation of the osteology of the feet are generally related.' According to *Trevi-ranus* (loc. cit. vol. I, p. 200), most horned animals have no fibulas (*Coiter*: 'De quadrupedum sceletia' ch. 2; *Camper's* 'Natural History of the Orang-outang', p. 103). In the passage quoted above, Cuvier continues as follows, 'It is impossible to give reasons for these connections; it is evident that they are not fortuitous however, for an animal with cloven hoofs very often shows an approximation to the non-ruminants in the arrangement of its teeth and in the structure of its feet. Camels for example, which have eye-teeth (canines), and even have two or four incisors in their upper jaw-bone, have one bone more in their tarsus,' than other animals whose dental system is less formed. In the case of children moreover, their teething, and the development of their ability to walk and talk, all begin to take place during the course of their second year.

The particularity of the determination brings a harmony into all the formations of an animal therefore, 'The minutest facet of bone, the slightest apophysis, has a determinate character relative to the class, order, genus and species to which it belongs. Consequently, with nothing but the well-preserved end of a bone, it is often possible to determine the whole of an animal by means of analogy and comparison, and with as much certainty as one would have if one were in possession of the animal itself,'—ex ungue leonem, as the saying goes. 'I tried this method out on parts of known animals on many occasions, before I felt that I could use it with complete confidence in dealing with fossil bones; its success has always been so complete however, that I no longer entertain the slightest doubt as to the certainty of the results it has yielded.'

But although there is a basic and universal type, which nature puts

into effect in animals in such a way, that this effecting is in conformity
with particularity, everything occurring within an animal must not be
thought of as having a purpose. In many animals, there are rudiments of
organs which belong only to the universal type, not to the particularity
5 of these creatures, and which have not yet developed, because they are not
needed by the animal's particularity. What is more, they can be understood only by means of higher organisms, not by means of these lower
organisms. For example, Reptiles, Snakes and Fish will be found to have
the rudiments of feet, which are quite superfluous; similarly, the Whale
10 has teeth which are not developed, and which, as they are merely rudimentary and hidden in its jaw-bones, serve no purpose. On the other
hand, man has many features which are only necessary in lower animals;
he has in his neck the so-called thyroid gland for example, the function
of which, as it is actually obliterated and defunct, cannot be discovered;
15 in the pre-natal foetus however, and still more in inferior species of ani-
+ mals, this gland is an active organ.

It is then the graded scale of formation which provides the basis for
the main divisions in the general classification of animals. In its inner
formation, the animal is an unmediated self-production, but in its out-
20 wardly orientated articulation, it is a production mediated by its inorganic
nature. More closely considered therefore, the difference between the
forms of the animal world will be found to depend either upon an equilibrium between these two essential aspects, or upon the animal's existing
more in accordance with one aspect than with the other, in which case its
25 formation will be lop-sided. It is through this lop-sidedness that one
animal is subordinate to another, and yet no animal can be completely
devoid of either aspect. Man is the crowning type of the organism, and
as he is used as the instrument of spirit, all aspects must have reached
their most perfect development.

30 *Aristotle* was the originator of the traditional division of animals into
the two main groups of those with blood (ἔναιμα) and those without
+ it (ἄναιμα). To this division he adds the general proposition, based on
observation, that, 'all animals which have blood have an osseous or bony
spine.'[1] This is in fact the great division, but it has of course been possible
35 to raise many objections to it. It has been pointed out for example,
that there are animals such as Leeches and Earth-worms, which according
to their habit should be bloodless, but which do possess a red fluid or
blood. What is blood then? This is the main question, and in the last

[1] *Aristotle*, 'Hist. animal', I 4; III, 7: πάντα δέ τὰ ζῷα, ὅσα ἔναιμά ἐστιν, ἔχει ῥάχιν ἢ ὀστῶδη ἢ ἀκανθώδη.

resort the deciding factor is colour. This division has been abandoned on account of its vagueness therefore, and as is well known, *Linnaeus* has replaced it with his six classes. *Linnaeus'* systematic classification of plants + is merely a rigid product of the understanding, and by the French it has been discarded in favour of *Jussieu's* division of plants into mono- 5 cotyledons and dicotyledons. Through the brilliance of another French- + man, *Lamarque*, the French have also returned to the Aristotelian division of animals, although this now takes the form of a distinction between Vertebrata and Invertebrata (animaux avec vertébres, animaux sans vertébres). *Cuvier* brought together both principles of division, for while + Vertebrata are in fact red-blooded, other animals have white blood and no internal skeleton; at least, if they do have one, it is either simply in- + articulate, or articulate and external. The initial occurrence of a noto- chord is in the *Lamprey*; in this case it is still coriaceous however, and the + vertebrae are merely indicated, by means of striae. Vertebrae are to be 15 found in Mammals, Birds, Fish and Amphibia, and consequently distin- guish them from Mollusca and Crustacea, which have a carapace which is separated from their fleshy skin, and from Insects and Worms. The animal world is divided between these two groups, and a cursory glance at them immediately brings to light the enormous difference between 20 them.

This difference also fits in with the previously mentioned division based on the relationship between the organism's viscera and its outward- ly orientated articulation. This relationship in its turn is based on the important distinction between 'vie organique' and 'vie animale'. 'Animals + which lack a spinal column also lack the basis of a proper skeleton, and as they are also devoid of true lungs, consisting of cells, they have no voice or vocal organ.'[1] On the whole, this is also a confirmation of *Aristotle's* division according to blood. In the passage already quoted, Lamarque continues as follows, 'Invertebrata have no true blood, which should be 30 red,' and warm, but which in their case is more like lymph. 'Blood owes its colour to the intensity of its animalization,' which is also lacking in these animals therefore. 'On the whole, animals such as this also lack a genuine circulation of the blood; their eyes have no iris, and they are devoid of kidneys. They also lack a spinal cord, as well as the great 35 sympathetic nerve.' Vertebrata exhibit more formation therefore, and + an equilibrium between inner and outer; while in the other group, one aspect is formed at the expense of the other. Consequently, two classes

---

[1] *Lamarque*, 'Éléments de zoologie', vol. I, p. 159.

of Invertebrata in particular are to be mentioned, Worms, (Mollusca) and Insects. The viscera of the former are more highly formed than those of the latter, while it is the Insects which have the more delicately fashioned exterior. Polyps and Infusoria etc. are also Invertebrata, but as they consist merely of skin and jelly, they have the appearance of being completely unformed. Polyps, like plants, are composed of several individuals, and will survive shredding; even the Garden snail will grow a new head. This reproductiveness stems from a weakness in the organism's substantiality however. In the graded scale of Invertebrata, the heart, brain, gills, circulatory vessels, the organs of hearing, sight and sex, finally sensation in general, and even movement itself, all disappear.[1] Where there is a predominance of self-sufficing inwardness, it is the digestion and the reproductive organs, as the concrete universal lacking as yet in differentiation, which exhibit formation. It is only where the animal world falls into externality, that a differentiation takes place together with the emergence of sensibility and irritability. Thus, while organic and animal life stand opposed to each other in the Invertebrata, both moments have a single unity in Vertebrata, and consequently it is in them that the other essential basis of determination must come into play. They are therefore determined in accordance with their element, i.e. the land, the water or the air. As Invertebrata are already subject to the first basic division however, they do not exhibit this relation between their development and the elements. There are of course animals which cannot be clearly classified; the reason for this lies in nature's not having the power to remain true to the Notion, and to coalesce neatly with the determinations of thought.

(a) In *Worms, Mollusca* and *Shell-fish* etc., the inner organism is more fully formed, although outwardly these creatures are formless. 'In spite of the outer difference which distinguishes Mollusca from the higher classes of animals, inwardly they are by no means devoid of the organization of these higher classes. Although they have no spleen or pancreas, they have a brain resting on an oesophagus, and a heart with arteries and veins. Their blood is white or bluish in colour; their fibrin does not form in the cruor, but its filaments swim freely in the serum. Only in a few cases are the male and female sexual organs to be found in separate individuals, and in these cases, the structure of these organs is so peculiar, that it is often almost impossible to recognize them.'[2] 'They breathe by means

---

[1] *Lamarque,* loc. cit., p. 214.
[2] *Treviranus,* loc. cit. vol. I, pp. 306–307.

of gills and they also have a nervous system, although they do not have nodulated nerves forming a series of ganglia. They have one heart or more, and although these hearts only have a single ventricle, they are well-formed.'[1] In Mollusca, the system of external articulation is however much less fully formed than it is in Insects, 'In all Fish and Amphibia there are still traces of a distinct head, thorax and abdomen, but in Mollusca, this distinctness completely disappears. Mollusca also lack a nose; most of them have no external extremities at all, and either move by alternately contracting and relaxing their venter muscles, or are quite incapable of any forward movement.'[2]

(b) *Insects* are far superior to Mollusca in their organs of movement, and in general, Mollusca have only a few motor muscles. Insects on the other hand have feet and wings, as well as a distinct head, thorax and abdomen. Internally however, their structure is correspondingly undeveloped. Their respiratory system permeates their whole body, and as in some Fish, coincides with the digestive system. Their blood-system also has few formed organs, and those that are formed are scarcely to be distinguished from their digestive system. In the external articulation of Insects however, for example in their masticatory organs etc., formation is correspondingly more determinate. 'In insects and other lower classes of animals, there appears to be a movement of fluids which is not however a circulation. This takes place in the following way:—fluids are continually being taken up into the body from the surface of the alimentary canal, and after contributing to the growth of the parts, are gradually evacuated from the body again as waste matter, either through its surface or in other ways.'[3] These are the principal classes of Invertebrata; according to *Lamarque* (loc. cit., p. 128), they fall into fourteen divisions.

(c) In the further classification of animals, Vertebrata divide more simply, i.e. in accordance with the elements of inorganic nature. These are the elements of earth, air and water, and *Vertebrata* are therefore either land animals, Birds, or Fish. In the preceding classification, the importance of this difference became negligible, many Beetles for example are fin-footed, live on land equally well, and have wings with which they fly; at this juncture it is obvious however, and presents no difficulties to any candid consideration of nature. Among the higher animals of course, this difference is also nullified by transitions from one class to another. The precise reason for life in different elements uniting

---

[1] *Lamarque*, loc. cit., p. 165.
[2] *Treviranus*, loc. cit. vol. I, pp. 305–306.
[3] *Autenrieth*, loc. cit. pt. I, § 346.

is that it is unable to find, in the exposition of the Land-animal for example, the special determinateness which should contain its simple and essential character. Only thought or the understanding can establish fixed differences, and only spirit, because it is spirit, can produce works
5 conforming strictly to these differences. Artistic or scientific works are abstractly and essentially individualized in such a way, that they neither violate their individual determination, nor confuse essential differences. Genius can produce a genuine work of art only by expressing itself through a specific individuality, and the essential character of a work of
10 art is violated if this distinctness is not preserved. There is a failure to preserve it in poetic prose or prosaic poetry for example, in dramatized history, in the introduction of painting into music or the poetic art, or in the painting of stone, either in order to give a statue curly hair for example, or in bass-relief, which is also sculptural painting. The same in-
15 congruity occurs when a man wants to be poet, painter and philosopher; this is not the case with nature however, for an animal form can progress in two ways, and there are many examples of its doing so. In the case of Cetacea for example, the Land animal returns to the water. In Amphidae and Ophidia, the Fish climbs to the land again, and in that Snakes for
20 example, possess the rudiments of feet, which are however without
+ significance, they make a poor show of it. The Bird becomes aquatic, until in the case of the Duck-billed platypus (Ornithorhynchus), it passes
+ over into a Land animal; in the case of the Ostrich, it becomes a camel-
+ like animal covered more with hair than with feathers. The Land animal
25 and the Fish also take to the air, as we see in the case of Vampire-bats, Flitter-mice and Flying fish. All this does not efface the fundamental difference however, which is determined in and for itself, and should not be regarded as a matter of common denominators. The main differences must be recognized despite these imperfect productions of nature,
30 which like humid air or wet earth (i.e. mud), are merely mixtures of the main determinations. The transitions have to be interpolated as mixtures of the differences. The Mammals are the true Land animals, and are the most perfect; then come the Birds, and these are followed by Fish, which are the least perfect.
35   (i) The whole structure of *Fish* shows that the water is their natural element; their articulation is limited by it, and forced inwards. They are not warm-blooded to any great extent, for the temperature of their blood differs very little from the temperature of the medium in which they live. Fish either have a heart with a single ventricle, or with several
40 ventricles which are however directly inter-connected. When describing

the four higher classes of animal, *Lamarque* says (loc. cit., p. 140 et seq.) that, 'Fish respire by means of gills, have a smooth or scaly skin, fins, no tracheae, no larynx, no sense of touch, and evidently no sense of smell either.' Fish, like certain other animals, simply abandon their young, and right from the start, show no concern for them whatever; consequently, they do not yet attain to a feeling of unity with their young.

(*ii*) *Reptiles* or *Amphibia* are intermediate forms, belonging partly to land and partly to water; that is why there is something repugnant about them. They have only one cardiac ventricle, an imperfect pulmonary respiration, and a smooth or scaly skin. Frogs have gills instead of lungs before reaching maturity.

(*iii*) *Birds* resemble Mammals in that they are capable of feeling for their young. They provide them with nourishment in the egg. 'Their foetus is contained in the inorganic envelope of the egg-shell, and at an early stage ceases to have a connection with the mother bird, being able to develop within the shell without drawing nourishment from her.'[1] Birds warm their young with their own bodies, sharing their own food with them and also feeding their hens, but they do not give up their own lives for their young, as Insects do. They give evidence of the mechanical instinct and the nisus formativus in nest–building, and so reach a positive self-aware- ness by positing themselves as inorganic nature in the interests of another being. Thirdly, they produce their young by means of immediate ex- cretion. In this connection, *Lamarque* (loc. cit., p. 150) attempts to rank Birds in the following way, 'If one bears in mind that web-footed aquatic Birds, Waders and Gallinaceae have an advantage over all other Birds, in that their young can walk and feed themselves as soon as they have emerged from the egg, it will be apparent that they must form the first three orders. It will also be apparent that Pigeons, Passeres, Birds of prey and Creepers must form the last four orders of this class, for their young, when they have emerged from the egg, can neither walk nor feed them- selves.' It is precisely this circumstance which might be regarded as a reason for reversing the order however, not to mention the intermediate nature of web-footed Birds.—Birds are distinguished by the positive nature of their relation to the air, evidence of which is to be found in their lungs, the reservoirs of air contained by their skin, and the large marrow- less cavities of their bones. They do not suckle their young, so they have no breasts. They are bipeds, and their two arms or forefeet are converted into wings. As animal life is in this instance committed to the air, it is in

---

[1] *Lamarque*, loc. cit., p. 146.

the Birds that the animation of the abstract element comes into being;
Birds consequently pass over from animal life, and revert to the preponderance of vegetative nature, which forms on their skin as plumage.
The particular formation of their thoracic system is also due to their
5 belonging to the air. That is why many Birds not only have a voice, as
Mammals do, but also sing, the inner vibration forming in the air, as in
its element. The Horse neighs and the Ox bellows, but the Bird's cry is
+ trilled forth as the ideal nature of self-enjoyment. On the other hand, the
bird does not roll about on the ground in crude contentment, but aban-
10 dons itself solely to the air, in which it becomes aware of itself.

(iv) *Mammals* have breasts, four articulated extremities, and exhibit all
the organs in a formed state. As they have breasts, they suckle and feed
their young from their own bodies. These animals therefore attain to the
feeling of unity between one individual and another, i.e. to the feeling of
15 the genus, which comes to existence in the progeny. For the progeny,
it is precisely the two parental individuals which constitute the genus, even
though in nature, this unity of the individual with the genus sinks away
again into singularity. Higher animals such as the Mammals, and Birds
which are still hatching their young, continue to behave towards this
20 existence as a genus however, since it is in this way that they sense their
universality. Monkeys are the most adaptable of animals, and show the
most affection for their offspring; the satisfaction of their sexual drive
maintains its objectivity, for they themselves have passed over into another,
and are aware of this unity in the higher unselfishness of caring for the
25 needs of their young. In Mammals also, the skin certainly has something
of a vegetative nature about it, although this is not nearly so marked as it
is in Birds. The skin of the Mammal progresses into wool, hairs and
bristles, into the spines of the Hedgehog, and even into the scales and
armour of the Armadillo. Man on the other hand has a skin which is
30 smooth, clear, and much more animalized, and which sheds anything of
an osseous nature. In the female sex there is a stronger growth of hair. An
abundance of hair on the chest and elsewhere is regarded as a sign of
strength in the male; it is however a sign of weakness in the organization
+ of the skin (see above § 362 Add. III. 149, 25).

35 Further essential classifications have been based on the relation of
animals as individuals to other individual animals; they have been based
therefore upon the animals' teeth, feet, claws and snout. It was a happy
intuition which led to the choosing of these parts, for it is by means of
them that the animals distinguish themselves from one another. If the
40 difference is to be a true one however, it has to belong to the animal itself,

and should not be a distinguishing feature which is merely selected by us. The animal displays the being-for-self of its subjectivity by using its weapons in order to oppose itself, as an individual, to its inorganic nature. The various classes of Mammals distinguish themselves very accurately in this way. (i) There are the Mammals whose feet form *hands—man* and the 5 *Monkey* for example. The Monkey is a satire on man, and if man does not take himself too seriously, but is willing to make fun of himself, he can hardly help appreciating the parody. (ii) There are the Mammals whose extremities form *claws—Dogs* for example, and *carnivorous animals* such as the *Lion*, the king of the beasts. (iii) There are the *Rodents*, in which the 10 *teeth* in particular are highly formed. (iv) There are the *Bats*, which have a membrane stretched between their toes, as indeed do several Rodents. These animals have a closer affinity with Dogs and Monkeys however. (v) There are the *Sloths*, which in a way are quite devoid of toes, for in them, these features have changed into claws. (vi) There the *Cetacea*, the 15 limbs of which are fin-like. (vii) There are the *hoofed* animals such as *Swine*, *Elephants*, which have a trunk, *Cattle*, which have *horns*, and *Horses* etc. The strength of these animals lies in the upper part of their bodies, and most of them can be tamed to work. The formation of their extremities shows a particular relationship to their inorganic nature. If 20 the animals in the second, third, fourth and fifth classes are grouped together as having *claws*, there are four classes: (1) *animals with hands*, (2) animals with *claws*, (3) working animals with *hoofs*, and (4) animals with *fins*. It is in accordance with this that *Lamarque* (loc. cit., p. 142) grades Mammals in a descending order (dégradation) as follows, 'Mammals with 25 *claws* (mammifiéres onguiculés) have four limbs, and at the tips of their toes, uncovered claws which are either blunt or pointed. These limbs are generally fitted for seizing objects, or at least for clinging to them. It is in this class that the most perfectly organized animals are to be found. The *hoofed* (ongulés) Mammals have four limbs, the toes of which are com- 30 pletely covered at their extremities by a rounded body of horn (sabot). Their feet can be used only for walking or running on the ground; they cannot be used for climbing trees, seizing their prey or any other object, or for attacking and tearing other animals. They are completely herbi-vorous. The Mammals *without hoofs* (exongulés) have only two extremities, 35 which are very short and flat, and shaped like *fins*. Their toes are covered by skin, and have neither claws nor hoofs (corne). They are the least perfectly organized of all Mammals. They have neither a pelvis, nor hind legs. They swallow their food without chewing it first. In the usual way they live in the water, although they surface in order to breathe the air.' +

The further subdivisions here must be left to determination from without, i.e. to the chance and contingency proper to nature. The climates still constitute the great determining factor however. In the southern latitudes, the animal kingdom is particularized more in accordance with differences
5 of climate and country than it is in the north; consequently, the Asiatic
+ Elephant is essentially distinct from its African counterpart, while there
+ is no American Elephant. Lions and Tigers etc. are also quite distinct.

3. The genus and the individual
(*Medical Science*)

a. The disease of the individual
(*Nosology*)

§ 371

In the two relationships considered above, the self-mediation of the genus with itself is the process of its diremption into individuals
10 and the sublation of its differences. However, as the genus also (§ 357) assumes the shape of an inorganic nature which is opposed to the individual, it brings forth its existence within it in an abstract and negative manner. The determinate being of the individual organism is therefore involved in a relationship of ex-
15 ternality, and while the organism preserves itself by returning into itself in its genus, it may also, and with equal facility, fail to correspond to it (§ 366).—The organism is in a *diseased* state when one of its systems or organs is *stimulated* into conflict with the inorganic potency of the organism. Through this con-
20 flict, the system or organ establishes itself in isolation, and by persisting in its particular activity in opposition to the activity of the whole, obstructs the fluidity of this activity, as well as the process by which it pervades all the moments of the whole.

25 *Addition.* The animal type particularizes itself into the division of the animal world; when the individual organism is diseased, it resembles this particular type, for it also is then capable of a particularization which does

not conform to its Notion, i.e. to its total particularization. Consequently, at this juncture also, the deficiency of the individual subject as opposed to the genus is still not effaced, for the individual is in itself the genus which is opposed to it, the individual alone being that which constitutes its genus, and has this genus within itself. This is the scission to which the animal is 5 now subjected, and with which it reaches its conclusion.

In a state of *health*, there is *no disproportion* between the organic self and its determinate being; all its organs give free play to the fluidity of the universal. When this state prevails, there is a commensurate relationship between organic and inorganic being, as the result of which inorganic being does not offer any 10 insuperable resistance to the organism. Disease is not an irritation incommensurate with the susceptibility of the organism; its Notion consists of a *disproportion* between the organism's being and its self, and not of a disproportion between certain mutually dissociating factors within it. Factors are abstract moments, and cannot dissociate. When disease is spoken of as a heightening of 15 excitation and a lessening of excitability, as if this were a matter of qualitative contrast, and an increase in the one were accompanied by a corresponding decrease in the other, the interpretation is immediately suspect therefore. To bandy about the concept of *disposition*, as if it were possible to be implicitly ill without being infected and sick, is no improvement; the reason for this being 20 that the organism itself constitutes this reflection, within which that which is implicit is also actual. Disease occurs when the organism as a being separates itself, not from inner factors, but from inner aspects which are completely real. The cause of disease lies partly in the age, mortality and congenital defects of the organism itself, and partly in its susceptibility, as a being, to external in- 25 fluences. As a result of this susceptibility, there is a build up of a single aspect which does not accommodate the inner power of the organism, and the organism then exhibits the opposed forms of being and self, the self being precisely that for which the negative of itself has being. A stone cannot become ill, for as its form is unable to survive chemical decomposition, its negative involves its 30 destruction. A stone is therefore devoid of the self-negation found in sickness and sentience, which is capable of taking in its opposite. Appetite, which is awareness of a deficiency, is also self-relating in constituting its own opposite, for it is both itself and its state of deficiency. In this case however, the deficiency is something external, so that the self is not opposed to its shape as such, while in 35 the case of disease, the negative thing is the shape itself.

Disease is therefore a *disproportion* between *irritation* and the organism's *ability to operate*. As the organism is an individual being, it can maintain equilibrium in an outer aspect, while exceeding its proportionality in a particular aspect. To quote *Heraclitus*, 'Excess of heat constitutes fever, 40

excess of cold paralysis, and excess of air suffocation.'[1] The organism is susceptible to excessive irritation because it is as completely the unity of the possibility of substance, as it is of the actuality of the self, being fully subject to both
forms. Activity and susceptibility to stimulation are separated through the
5 opposition of the sexes, by means of which they are allotted to two organic
individuals. The organic individual itself consists of both however, and it is
because it breaks down into these forms of its own accord, that it holds within
itself the possibility of its death. Consequently, the possibility of disease is
rooted in the individual's consisting of both forms. In the sex-relationship, the
10 individual has surrendered its essential outwardly orientated determinations, in
so far as this determinateness enters into the relationship; at this juncture how-
+ ever, it has it within itself, as if it were mating with itself. As animation is
bound up with a single singularity, the union is not consummated in the
genus, and in many animals copulation even constitutes the termination
15 of existence. However, although other animals survive copulation, so
that the animal overcomes inorganic nature as well as its genus, the genus
still retains its mastery over it. Disease falls into this reversal of the relationship. When an organism is healthy all its vital functions are maintained within the ideality of its health; however, when its blood is diseased
20 for example, an activity of its own is developed, and it becomes heated
and inflamed. It is the same when the bile becomes over-active for example, and generates gall-stones. If the stomach is overloaded, the digestive activity is no longer a moment of the whole, but dominates the
whole by its being isolated and turning into itself. This isolation can
25 progress so far, that life is generated in the intestines; all animals, at certain
times, have worms in their heart, lungs and brain (see § 361 Add.). Generally speaking, the animal is weaker than man; but although man is the
strongest of the animals, one is not justified in assuming that the Tape-
worms which occur within him are the result of his having swallowed
+ their eggs. The restoration of health can consist only in the overcoming of
this particularization.

A certain *Dr. Göde* has attacked this doctrine in a rigmarole published
+ in 'Isis' (vol. VIII, 1819, p. 1127), in which he even proposes to, 'preserve
the unity of the Idea, the *essence*, the comprehension of the essence of life
35 and of disease' in a deeply philosophic manner. This is a theory concerned
only with *appearance* and *externality*, and to attempt to refute it thus, with
the arrogance and parrhesia proper to truth, is the height of pretension,

---

[1] *Heraclitus*, 144. b. ὅσα ἐν ἡμῖν ἑκάστου κράτος, νόσημα· ὑπερβολὴ θερμοῦ,
πυρετός· ὑπερβολὴ ψυχροῦ, παράλυσις· ὑπερβολὴ πνεύματος, πνῖγος.

'This definition of disease is erroneous; it applies only to the external appearance, the symptom of fever.' He continues (p. 1134), 'That which in life is unified, blended, and inwardly concealed, emerges into the phenomenal world as a particularity, i.e. in a characteristic way, forms and exhibits the essence of the one organism and of its idea. It is thus that life's inner essence appears externally as its character. Where everything is, living from a single Idea and a single essence, all opposition is merely apparent and external, and has being only for appearance and reflection, not for the inwardness of life and of the Idea.' Yet it is precisely in living being itself that reflection and distinctness are prominent. To appear is to have life; what the philosophers of nature have in mind however, is merely an external reflection. They are unable to comprehend life because they fail to reach it, and stop short at inanimate gravity. One of Mr. *Göde's* particular tenets seems to be that in the first instance, the diseased form enters into conflict with *its own essence*, not with the organism, 'The collective activity of the whole is primarily a consequence and reflex of the checking of free movement in its individual parts.' He considers this to be a truly speculative remark. But what is this essence if it is not anima- tion? And what constitutes actual animation, if it is not the organism as a whole? Consequently, when he says that the organ is in conflict with its essence, with itself, this must mean that it is in conflict with the totality which is within it as a general animation or universal. It is the organism itself which constitutes the reality of this universal however. Here we have true philosophers, for they are of the opinion that essence is what is true, and that in order to express what is internal and correct, they merely have to mention it! I can find nothing worth considering in their prattle about essence however, for they proffer nothing but abstract reflections, while if essence is to be made explicit, it has to be made apparent as a determinate being.

There are various ways in which activities can fall short of ideality, and so disturb subjectivity. The essential origins of disease are on the one hand air and dampness, and on the other hand the stomach and the cutaneous process. Considered more precisely, the *forms of disease* can be reduced to the following classification.

(a) *Noxiousness*, which is a form of disturbance, is in the *first instance* a *general* determinateness residing in inorganic nature as a whole. This simple determinateness must be regarded as external in origin, and as being inflicted upon the organism from without; but although it is manifest externally in the organism's environment, it can also be apparent simul- taneously, and with equal facility, in the organism itself. Diseases such as

epidemics or *plagues* are not to be regarded as a particular determination of the organism, but as an aspect of the determinateness of external nature, to which the organism itself also belongs. They may well be said to infect the organism. Various circumstances contribute to noxious determinations
5 of this kind, and as these circumstances are of an elemental or climatic nature, they also reside and have their origin in the elemental determinateness of the organism. Initially therefore, the presence of these diseases resembles that of the universal fundamentals of the organism, which do not yet constitute a developed and formed system. In this state, they
10 reside mainly in the skin, the lymph and the bones. Diseases of this kind are not simply climatic; they are also historical, for they occur at certain
+ periods of history, and then disappear again. They can also break out as the result of an organism's being removed into an alien climatic environment. Historical research has not thrown any reliable light upon this
15 matter. When syphilis or venereal disease first occurred for example, there was certainly contact between European and American organisms. It has merely been presumed that the disease was brought from America however, this has not been proved. The French call it 'mal de Naples'
+ because it broke out when they took that city, but no one knew where it
+ came from. *Herodotus* gives an account of a nation which caught a disease after migrating from the Caspian to Media; the disease being brought forth merely by the change of place. The same thing occurred recently when cattle were brought into southern Germany from the Ukraine; although they were all healthy animals, the mere change of place gave
25 rise to a murrain. The mephitic exhalations which were encountered in Russia by Germans and the animals they took with them, gave rise to
+ various nervous diseases; similar circumstances set off a frightful outbreak
+ of typhus among a thousand otherwise healthy Russian prisoners. Yellow fever occurs endemically in America, and in certain Spanish maritime
30 districts for example: it will not spread from these districts, and the local
+ inhabitants guard against it by going a few miles inland. As changes such as these also take place within the human organism, it cannot be said that this organism is infected when it participates in these dispositions of elemental nature, although infection is then also present of course. Con-
35 sequently, it is pointless to dispute whether these diseases break out of their own accord, or occur through infection. Both factors play a part, for if such a disease breaks out of its own accord, after it has penetrated into the lymphatic system, it also occurs through infection.

(*b*) *Another* general form of disease is that which is brought forth by the organism's entering into contact with certain *specific noxious influences* from without. In this case one of the organism's specific systems, such as that of its skin or its stomach, becomes particularly involved, and so isolates itself. At this juncture, a distinction has to be made between acute and chronic diseases. It is the former of these which *medicine* knows better how to treat.

(*i*) When one of the systems of the organism is affected by an *acute disease*, curing it depends mainly upon the entire organism's being susceptible to the ailment. The spread of this disease will then also enable the former freedom of the entire activity of the organism to come into play again, and this in its turn will facilitate the cure. In a case such as this, the organism is not open to its environment, and is lacking in appetite and muscular movement; in so far as it lives, it draws upon its own resources. It is precisely because these acute diseases have their seat in the organism as a whole, not being confined exclusively to a single organic system, but residing in the so-called humours, that the organism is able to rid itself of them.

(*ii*) If the disease is unable to spread to the whole organism, I regard it as being *chronic*; scirrhus of the liver and pulmonary consumption are examples of chronic ailments. Diseases such as these do not impair the appetite and the digestion, nor do they weaken the sexual impulse. As in this case a single system has isolated itself as a centre of activity, and the organism is no longer able to overcome this particular activity, the disease remains confined to a single organ, and the organism also is no longer able to assert itself as an independent whole. Curing such a disease is difficult therefore, and the difficulty increases in proportion to the extent of the attack and alteration inflicted upon the organ or system involved.

(*iii*) A *third form* of disease is that which is rooted in the universal subject, and especially in man. It consists of *diseases of the soul*, which are caused by terror and grief etc., and can also give rise to death.

§ 372

The characteristic feature of disease is that the identity of the whole organic **process**[1] exhibits itself as the *successive* course of the vital motion, i.e. as *fever*. It therefore exhibits itself through sensibility, irritability and reproduction, which are the distinct moments of this course. As a

---

[1] First edition, 'Notion'; second edition, 'system'.

course which is inherent in the *totality* of the organism however, and which is opposed to the *isolated* activity, fever constitutes to an equal extent, the organism's incipient inclination towards *recovery*.

Addition. We have seen that the Notion of disease consists in this implicit dissociation of the organism; consequently, we now have to consider the course of disease in *more detail*.

(*a*) In its *first stage*, disease is implicitly present, but not apparent.

(*b*) In its *second stage*, disease becomes effective for the self, i.e. the self as a universal is opposed by the determinateness which establishes itself within it, and organizes itself as a fixed self. In other words, the self of the organism becomes a fixed determinate being, a determinate part of the whole. Consequently, while hitherto the systems of the organism had a selfless subsistence, the *actual incipience* of disease at this juncture consists in the organism's being stimulated beyond its ability to operate, so that the individual system gains subsistence in opposition to the self, from a certain aspect of the part of the organism which is in question. This is in fact a matter of digestion, and it is possible for the disease to be a general indigestibility, and to begin either in the organism as a whole, or in the isolating of an individual aspect of it, such as the hepatic or pulmonary process. The isolated determinateness is an individual being, which takes possession of the whole in spite of the self. When it is still as immediate as it is isolated, the disease is said by the physicians to be in its *first stages*; it still constitutes nothing but the initial conflict, the exuberance of the individual system. Disease in the full sense of the word is established in so far as the determinateness has become the centre and self of the whole, so that a determinate self is dominant, instead of the free self. On the other hand, so long as only a single organ is stimulated or weakened, so that the disease is peculiar to one particular system, and is confined to the development of that system, it will be easier to effect a cure in a case such as this. The system has only to be freed from its involvement with inorganic being and established in its proper proportion. At this juncture therefore, external remedies are also useful; generally speaking, remedies in cases such as these can be restricted to the stimulation of the system concerned, use being made of emetics, purgatives, blood-lettings and the like.

(*c*) Disease also passes over into the general life of the organism however; for when a particular organ is affected, it is principally the general organism which is infected. The whole organism is involved in this therefore, and because one of its circulations has turned itself into a centre, its activity is disturbed. At the same time however, in order that the

isolated activity may not remain an excrescence, but may become a
moment of the whole, the whole animation of the organism also turns
against it. If the digestion isolates itself for example, the circulation of the
blood and muscular energy etc., will also be affected; in the case of
jaundice, the whole body secretes bile and is thoroughly hepatic etc. The 5
third stage of disease is therefore *coction*, in which the weakening of one
system becomes an affection of the whole organism. At this stage, disease +
is no longer confined to a particular organ and external to the whole, for
the entire life of the organism is concentrated into it. It is therefore comparatively easy to cure, for as we saw above (III. 198, 6), it is always easier 10
to cure acute diseases, than it is to cure chronic pulmonary diseases for
example, in which the lungs are no longer capable of infecting the whole
organism. As the entire organism is infected with a particularity, a *dual life*
begins to emerge. The whole becomes a *differentiating motion* opposed to the
stable universality of the self, and the organism posits itself as a whole in 15
opposition to the determinateness. In a case such as this, the physician can
do nothing; in general moreover, the whole art of medicine does no more
than aid the forces of nature. As the particular morbid affection transforms
itself into the whole, this very disease of the whole is at the same time a cure; for
it is the whole which is motivated, and which breaks itself apart in the sphere of 20
necessity. It is therefore the characteristic *constitution* of disease, that the organic
process now follows its course in this hardened and subsistent shape, so that the
harmonious processes of the organism now form a *succession*. What is more,
the general systems are torn apart, so that they no longer constitute an immediate
unity, but display it by passing into one another. Health can only be restored 25
by a succession of activities, but although this disruption is harmful to it,
it does not drive it out of the organism. Health consists of the whole process, and its abnormality is not implicit in or relative to the form of
disease or the system; it is relative only to this succession. This motion now
constitutes fever. Consequently, fever is disease in its purity, or rather the 30
ailing individual organism, freeing itself from its specific disease in the same way
as the healthy organism frees itself from its specific processes. As fever con- +
stitutes the pure life of the diseased organism therefore, it is actually only when
fever is present that the diagnosis of a distinct disease becomes possible. As fever
is both the constitution and fluidification of this succession of functions, the +
disease is simultaneously sublated by it, i.e. digested by its motion. This sublation
constitutes an interior circulation opposed to the inorganic nature of the
organism, a digestion of medicines. Consequently, although fever is certainly
a morbid state and a disease, it is also the means by which the organism
cures itself. This is only true of a severe and virulent fever which affects 40

the whole of the organism however, for a lingering and consuming fever which never really develops is a very dangerous sign in chronic diseases. Chronic illnesses are therefore of a kind which cannot be overcome by fever. In the course of a lingering fever, the disease does not dominate the digesting
5 organism, for all the individual processes of this organism merely produce themselves in an untrammelled manner, each operating of its own accord. In this case, fever merely follows a superficial course, and fails to subdue these individual parts of the organism. In the case of violent inflammatory fevers, it is mainly the vascular system which is attacked, while in the case of asthenic
10 fevers it is mainly the nervous system. When it is attacked by a true fever therefore, the organism subsides initially into the nervous system, which is the general organism; then into the internal organism, and finally into its shape.

+ (*i*) *Coldness*, heaviness in the head, headache, twinges in the spine, twitching
15 of the skin and shuddering, constitute the *first symptoms* of fever. In this activity of the nervous system, there is a relaxing of the muscles, so that through their own irritability they constitute an uncontrolled trembling, and lose their strength. A heaviness of the bones, tiredness of the limbs, a draining of the blood from the surface of the skin, and a sensation of cold set in. The simple
20 and wholly intro-reflected subsistence of the organism isolates itself and dominates the whole. The organism dissolves itself inwardly into the simplicity of its nervous system, and feels that it has withdrawn into the simple substance of its being.

(*ii*) In the *second instance* however, it is precisely this, as a dissolution of the
25 whole, which constitutes the negative power. The organism has dissolved into its nerves, and by means of the Notion of this negativity, passes over into the organism of inflamed blood—delirium. It is precisely the withdrawal into the nervous system which constitutes the transformation into *inflamed* negativity; in this, the blood is now the dominating factor.

30 (*iii*) In the *third instance*, this dissolution finally passes over into the shaping of a product. The reproducing organism reverts to lymph, and so gives rise to the fluid subsistence of *sweat*. The significance of this product is that within it, the isolated singularity of determinateness disappears, the organism as a whole having brought itself forth, and generally digested itself. Sweat is *concocted*
35 *morbid matter*; it was the physicians of antiquity who described it as such, and
+ they were fully justified in doing so. Sweat is the *critical secretion*; in it, the organism attains to a self-excretion, by means of which it eliminates its abnormality, and rids itself of its morbid activity. The crisis is the organism's mastering of itself, reproducing itself, and putting this power into effect
40 by excretion. It is not the *morbid matter* which is secreted of course; it is not the

case that the body would have been healthy if it had never contained this matter, or if it could have been ladled out of it. The crisis, like digestion in general, is at the same time a secretion. It has a dual product however, so that critical secretions differ widely from the secretions of exhaustion. These latter are not really secretions at all, they are dissolutions of the organism, and in significance they ₅ are therefore the direct antithesis of the critical secretions.

Fever facilitates recovery on account of its motivating the totality of the organism into activity. Once motivated in this way, the organism as a whole is animated, and lifts itself out of its submergence in a particularity. It rises above the particular activity before also excreting it, and by ₁₀ reasserting itself in this way, recovers the universality obstructed by the disease. In the first instance, its determinateness changes into motion, necessity and total process, and this in its turn changes into the whole product. Likewise, by means of this, and because this product is a simple negativity, the organism assumes the wholeness of its selfhood. ₁₅

b. Healing

(Therapy)

§ 373

It is by means of the **healing** agent that the organism is excited **into**[1] **annulling the particular excitement in which the formal activity of the whole is fixed, and restoring the fluidity of the particular** organ or system **within the whole.** This is effected by the agent by reason of its being a stimulus **which is how-** ₂₀ **ever difficult to** assimilate and overcome, **and which therefore presents the organism with an externality against which** it is compelled to exert its force. **By acting in opposition to an externality, the organism breaks out of** the limitation which had become identical with it, by which it was indisposed, **and** ₂₅ **against which it is unable to react so long as the limitation is not an object for it.**

---

[1] Addition to the first edition, 'ridding itself of the inorganic potency with which the activity of the individual organ or system is involved, and by means of which it is singularized'.

Remark

Medicaments **have mainly to be regarded as something which is** *indigestible*. Indigestibility is a relative property however, although not in the vague sense[1] **that only that which can be tolerated by weaker constitutions is** easily digestible, for the
5 stronger the individuality, the more difficulty it will find in digesting such substances. **The immanent relativity of the Notion, which has its actuality in life, is of a qualitative nature;** expressed in its quantitative aspect, in so far as this aspect is valid at this juncture, it consists in the intrinsic *indepen-*
10 *dence* of the opposed moments increasing in accordance with increased *homogeneity*.[2] The lower forms of animal life, which have not reached the stage of *internal differentiation*, resemble the plants in that they are **only** able to digest the unindividualized *neutrality* of water. Infants digest the
15 completely *homogeneous* animal lymph constituting mother's milk; this is a substance which has already been digested, or rather converted directly into animality in a general way and without any further internal differentiation. They also digest those differentiated substances which have matured
20 least in individuality. For invigorated constitutions, substances such as these are indigestible however. On the other hand, individualized animal substances, or those vegetable juices which have been mellowed by light into a more powerful individuality and are therefore said to be *spirit-*
+ *uous*, are more easily digested by such constitutions than vegetable productions which still exhibit the neutral colour for example, and which have a closer affinity with chemism as such. On account of their more intensive individuality, the former substances constitute a stronger opposition, but
30 it is precisely because of this that they are more homogeneous as stimuli.—In so far as they are *negative* stimuli, medicaments are poisons. When the *external* and alien substance of an indigestible stimulant is administered to an organism alienated from itself by disease, **this organism is**
35 **forced to counter its effect by drawing itself together and entering**

[1] First and second edition, 'in which this is usually understood i.e'.
[2] Addition to the first and second edition, 'The sex-relationship, in which independent individualities comport themselves as being identical, has shown itself to be the highest *qualitative* form of this living existence'.

into a process, by means of which it regains its sentience and sub-jectivity.—In the *Brunonian* system, diseases were classified as being sthenic and asthenic, the latter being subdivided into direct and indirect asthenia. **This system also reduced** the efficacy of healing agents to the principles of invigoration and debilitation. In order to give these distinctions an air of natural philosophy they were[1] traced back to carbon and nitrogen, and to oxygen and hydrogen,[2] or to magnetic electric and chemical factors etc. Regarded as a complete system of medicine, Brown's theory was merely an empty formalism, **but by tracing these distinctions back in this way, it served to direct** attention beyond what was merely specific and particular in diseases and healing agents, to a recogni-tion of their essential *universality*. By calling in question the traditional method, which on the whole had attached more importance to the healing power of *asthenia*,[3] Brown's **theory led to the discovery** that the organism does not react to extreme opposites of treatment in correspondingly opposite ways, but that at least in the final results of treat-ment, it often reacts in a similar and therefore *general* way. **It also led to the discovery that** the *simple* self-*identity* of the organism, **as the substantial and truly effective activity** opposed to a particular indisposition of one of its systems, displays itself in specific stimuli.—**In this paragraph and this remark, the determinations put forward are so general, that they are clearly inadequate to the extremely diverse phenomena of disease. Nevertheless, it is only the firm foundation of the Notion which is able to lead the way through particulars, and make fully intelligible those features of morbid phenomena and methods of healing which seem extravagant and bizarre to those who are steeped in the externalities of specific detail.**

Addition. Our treatment of digestion should be borne in mind when healing is being considered. The organism does not attempt to subdue an externality, but is healed by coming to itself, and abandoning its involvement with a particular determination which it has to regard as being subordinate to it. This can take place in various ways.

[1] Addition to the first and second edition, 'even'.
[2] Addition to the first and second edition, 'too'.
[3] Addition to the first edition, 'and by means of those of its transitions which were subsequently adopted'.

(a) One way is for the determinateness which holds sway within the organism to be administered to it as a selfless inorganic cause, with which it involves itself. Administered to the organism in this way, as something opposed to its health, this determinateness constitutes *medicine*. The animal is instinctively aware of the determinateness established within it, and the drive towards self-preservation, which motivates the whole self-relating organism, has a definite feeling of deficiency. The organism therefore proceeds to consume this determinateness, treating it as absorbable inorganic nature. It is therefore available to the organism in a less potent form, as a mere presence. *Homoeopathic* theory in particular treats illness by prescribing an agent capable of bringing forth the same disease in a healthy body. The effect of introducing this poison into the organism, and in general, of confronting it with something obnoxious, is that the particularity in which the organism is fixed becomes something external for it. When the organism is diseased however, this particularity is still one of its own properties. The medicine constitutes the same particularity therefore, the difference being that the determinateness with which it now brings the organism into conflict is an externality. Consequently, the healthful energy of the organism is now stimulated into an activity outwards; it is forced to rally, to emerge from its self-absorption, and not merely to concentrate itself inwardly, but to digest this externality. Every disease, and especially acute disease, is a hypochondria of the organism, in which the organism loathes the external world and repulses it. The reason for this is that it is restricted to itself while containing its own negative. As the medicine now stimulates it into digesting this negative however, the organism is restored to the general activity of assimilation. The precise way in which this effect is obtained is by administering to the organism something which is much more potently indigestible than its disease,[1] and so forcing it to draw itself together in order to overcome it. This results in the internal division of the organism; for as the initially immanent indisposition has now become external, the organism has been duplicated internally into its vital force and its diseased parts. This effect of medicine may well be regarded as magical. It resembles the effect of mesmerism in bringing the organism under the power of another person, for it is by means of the medicament that the whole organism is subjected to this specific determination, suc-

---

[1] This does not contradict the statement made just previously, that poison is available to the organism in a less potent form as medicine, for although poison is more powerful, the form in which it makes itself effective is less potent, being a merely external hostility, which is more easily overcome than the internal hostility of the disease itself.

Note by Michelet.

cumbing as it were to the power of a magician. However, even if the
organism, on account of its diseased condition, is under the power of
something other than itself; at the same time, as in the case of mesmerism,
it also has a world beyond, which is free from its diseased state, and by
means of which it can recover its vital force. Thus, the organism is 5
capable of internal repose; for in *sleep* it remains by itself. As the organism
has divided itself internally in this way, the force of its vitality endows it
with individuality, and in assuming this condition, the organism has
broadly re-established its general vitality, and removed the particularity
of its indisposition. As this particularity is no longer able to obstruct it, 10
the inner life of the organism has re-established itself by means of this
removal. In the case of mesmerism also, the organism's indisposition is
countered by the vitality of its inner life. It is just this liberation therefore,
which at the same time permits and effectuates the return of the organism
into itself by means of digestion; and it is precisely this state of being 15
withdrawn into itself which facilitates the self-digestion constituting the
organism's recovery.

Deciding which remedies are the right ones now presents us with a
difficulty. The *materia medica* has not yet uttered a single rational word on
the connection between a disease and its remedy; experience alone is 20
supposed to decide the matter. Experience with Chicken droppings is
therefore as valuable as that with the various officinal plants, for human
urine, and the droppings of Chickens and Peacocks were formerly used
medicinally, in order to produce nausea. Each particular disease does not +
have its specific remedy. If it did the connection here would have to be 25
found, i.e. the form in which a determinateness occurs within the organism, and the way in which it occurs in vegetable nature or elsewhere, as
an inanimate and external stimulant. Thus, cinchona, leaves and greenery
seem to have a cooling effect upon the blood. To counteract excessive
irritability, it seems to be necessary to administer soluble salt and salt- 30
petre. What is more, as disease merely obstructs the vitality of the organism, it is frequently the case that the mere sustaining of this vitality by
easily digested foods suffices to bring about a cure. When the disease is
located not in a particular system, but in the digestive system in general,
vomiting can occur of its own accord, as in the case of children, who 35
vomit very easily. An inorganic agent such as quicksilver for example,
gives rise to an inordinate heightening of a partial activity; although on
the one hand the effect here is specific, a general stimulation of the
organism also takes place. In general, it may be said that the relationship
between disease and medicine is a magical one.—*Brown* calls the stimulus 40

or poison which is administered, a *positive stimulus*, which is an acceptable
+ term for it.

(*b*) However, the remedy can also be more in the nature of a *negative
stimulus*, such as hydrochloric acid for example. It is then used to depress
5 the activity of the organism, so that by removing all its activity, that
which accrues from its morbid state is also eliminated. Thus, in the one
case, the organism has to exert its activity in order to direct itself outwards,
while in the other, the activity of the conflict is weakened, either by
means of blood-letting or ice, as in the case of inflammations for example,
10 or by paralysing the digestion by means of salts. In this way, the external
object is eliminated, and the organism's inner vitality is therefore encouraged to re-emerge. It is this that has suggested the fasting cure as a
method of debilitation, and in so far as homoeopathy is mainly concerned
with dieting, it also employs this kind of treatment. The purpose of the
15 simplest kind of nutriment, such as that received by an unborn child, is
to enable the organism to overcome abnormality by living from its own
resources. On the whole, remedies have tended to become more general
in character. In many cases, all that is necessary is a general shake-up, and
physicians themselves have admitted that one remedy may work as well
20 as its opposite. Thus, although the debilitating and restorative methods
are antithetical, they have both proved to be effective, and ailments
which prior to the teaching of Brown had been cured by means of emetics
and purging, have since been cured by means of opium, naphtha and
brandy.

25 (*c*) A *third* way of healing, corresponding to the third form of disease
(see § 371, Add. III. 198, 27), is that which also affects the organism in its
entirety. It is here that *mesmerism* has its place. As the organism in its
implicit entirety is to be brought into control of itself, this healing can
be effected from without. Thus, as the simplicity of the self falls outside the
30 diseased organism, it is the finger-tips of the mesmerizer which fluidize the
organism by conducting magnetism throughout the whole of it. Only sick
persons can be mesmerized, and put to sleep by this external means.
Precisely considered, mesmerization is the collection of the organism
+ into its implicit entirety. However, it is not only sleep brought about by a
35 mesmerizer which can elicit this turning-point in an illness, for a healthy
sleep has the same effect, and in this case the organism collects itself into
its substantiality entirely of its own accord.

§ 374

In its diseased state, the animal is involved with an inorganic potency, and held fast in one of its particular systems or organs in opposition to the unity of its vitality. As a determinate being, its organism has a certain quantitative strength, and is certainly capable of overcoming its division; however, this division is just 5 as likely to master it, and it will then succumb to one of the forms of its death. In the long run, the universal inadequacy of the individual is not removed by the suppression of its singular and transitory inadequacy. The individual is subject to this universal inadequacy because its Idea is only the Idea 10 in its *immediacy*, because as an animal it stands *within nature*, and because its subjectivity merely constitutes the implicitness of the Notion, not its *being-for-self*. Consequently, the inner universality remains opposed to the natural singularity of the living creature as a *negative* power. 15 From this negative power it suffers lethal violence, for its determinate being as such does not contain this universality, and is therefore not a reality which corresponds to it.

Addition. The organism which is abandoned by the self dies away within itself. In so far as disease as such is not fatal however, it constitutes the external 20 and existent course of this movement from singular to universal. Nothing in organic being subsists in singular causes, and the necessity of death is no exception to this, for it lies in the nature of the organism itself that externality should be the cause of its death. A singular cause may always be remedied, for it is weak, and cannot be the ground of death. This ground constitutes the 25 necessity of the transition of individuality into universality; for while the living creature in its animation is the exclusive existence of the self, the genus is the movement which comes into being by sublating the immediate singularity of the self, into which it relapses — a process in which the immediate singularity sinks away. In general, death in old age is due to lack of strength, a general and 30 simple state of wasting away. The outer signs of this are an increase in ossification and the slackening of muscles and tendons, bad digestion and feeble sensation, a retreat from the individual to the purely vegetative life. 'Although to a certain extent the steadiness of the heart increases in old age, its irritability diminishes and finally ceases completely.'[1] There is also a notice- 35

[1] *Autenrieth*, loc. cit. pt. I, § 157.

able 'shrinking in size in extreme old age.'[1] Disease properly so called was this merely quantitative relation as a qualitative relation and determinate process; to regard it as weakness or excessive strength is to interpret it in a wholly superficial manner.

+   *c.* The death of the individual of its own accord

§ 375

Universality, in the face of which the animal as a singularity is a finite existence, shows itself in the animal as the abstract power in the passing out of that which, in its preceding process (§ 356), is itself abstract. The *original disease* of the animal, and the inborn *germ of death*, is its being inadequate to universality. The annulment of this inadequacy is in itself the full maturing of this germ, and it is by imagining the universality of its singularity, that the individual effects this annulment. By this however, and in so far as the universality is abstract and immediate, the individual only achieves an *abstract objectivity*. Within this objectivity, the activity of the individual has blunted and ossified itself, and life has become a habitude devoid of process, the individual having therefore put an end to itself of its own accord.

Addition. The organism can recover from disease, but it is because it is diseased from its very nature, that death is a necessity, i.e. that this dissolution occurs, in which the series of processes becomes an empty process not turning back into itself. In the opposition of the sexes, it is only the excreted sexual elements which die in an immediate manner,— the plant-like parts. At this juncture they die on account of their one-sidedness, not as a whole. The sexual parts die as a whole on account of the opposition between male and female which each contains within itself. Just as the stamens of the plant swell into the passive receptacle, and the passivity of the pistil swells into the generative principle, so now at this juncture, each individual itself constitutes the unity of both sexes. It is this that constitutes its death however, for each is nothing more than individuality, individuality constituting its essential determinateness. Only the

[1] Ibidem, pt. II, § 767.

genus unifies complete wholes within a single unity. In the first instance therefore, the opposition between male and female fell within the organism in an unresolved state; now a similar but more determinate opposition falls within it, i.e. the opposition of the abstract forms of the whole which emerge in fever, and which contain nothing but the whole. Individuality is not a universal, and 5 is therefore unable to divide its self in this way. It is this general inadequacy which establishes the separability of soul and body; spirit is not mortal but eternal however, for as it is truth and therefore constitutes its own object, it is inseparable from its reality, i.e. the universal which exhibits itself as universal. In nature however, universality makes its appearance 10 only in this negative way, which involves the sublation of the subjectivity within nature. It is precisely the form in which this separation comes about that constitutes the consummation of the singular being which assumes a universal character, but is unable to sustain this universality. In life, the animal certainly maintains itself in the face of its inorganic 15 nature and its genus, but in the long run the universality of the genus retains its supremacy. As living being brings about the infusion of its living reality into its body, it dies as a singularity in the habitude of life. In that its activities become universal, animation endows itself with a universality which is for itself, and within this universality, it is precisely 20 animation which dies. It does not survive, because it is a process which needs opposition, and at this juncture, the other which it had formerly to overcome, is no longer an other. The physical sphere resembles the spiritual therefore, in which to an ever increasing extent, old people settle down within themselves and their genus, steadily becoming more 25 set in their general attitudes, and less aware of anything particular; as a result of this, there is also a dying away of tension or *interest*, (i.e. *to be between*) however, so that they are satisfied with this habitude devoid of 4 process. The lack of opposition to which the organism progresses constitutes the stillness of dead being, and the repose of death overcomes the 30 inadequacy of disease, which was therefore the primary origin of death.

§ 376

[1]**The identity with the universal which is achieved here is** the sublation of the *formal opposition* **between** the individuality **in its immediate singularity and** in its *universality;* **it is how-**

---

[1] Addition to the first and second edition, 'Essentially however, the subjectivity of living being is *implicitly* identical with the genus'.

ever the death of natural being, which is only one side, and moreover the abstract side of this sublation. In the Idea of life however, subjectivity is the Notion, and implicitly therefore, it constitutes the absolute *being-in-self* of *actuality*, as well
5 as concrete universality. Through this sublation of the *immediacy* of its reality, subjectivity has coincided with itself. The last *self-externality* of nature is sublated, so that the Notion, which in nature merely has implicit being, has become for itself.— With this, nature has passed over into its
10 truth, into the subjectivity of the Notion, whose *objectivity* is itself the sublated immediacy of singularity, i.e. *concrete universality*. Consequently, this Notion is posited as having the reality which corresponds to it, i.e. the Notion, as its *determinate being*. This is *spirit*.

15 *Addition.* Superseding this death of nature, *proceeding* from this dead
+ husk, there rises the finer nature of *spirit*. Living being ends with this separation, and this abstract coincidence with itself. The one moment contradicts the other however, for (*a*) that which coincides is necessarily identical, so that Notion or genus and reality, or subject and object, are
20 no longer separated; and (*b*) that which has repulsed and sundered itself is for that very reason not abstractly identical. Truth consists in their unity as distinct moments. It is because of the implicit identity of those moments therefore, that it is precisely and exclusively their formal opposition which has sublated itself in this coincidence and separation;
25 similarly, it is because of their separation, that it is only their formal identity which has negated itself. This may be expressed more concretely in the following way. The Notion of life, the genus, life in its universality, expels from itself its reality, which has become a totality within it. It is however identical with this reality, and because it is Idea, absolute in its
30 self-preservation, the Divine, the Eternal, it abides within it. That which has been sublated is only the form, the natural inadequacy, the merely persistent abstract externality of time and space. In living being, the Notion certainly exhibits the highest mode of its existence in nature; but here also, the Notion is merely implicit, for the Idea exists in nature as a
35 singular. By moving from one place to another, the animal has certainly released itself completely from gravity; it is aware of itself in sensation and hears itself in voice; the genus exists in the generic process, but also only as a singular. Now as this existence is still inadequate to the universality of the Idea, the Idea has to break out of this sphere, and draw breath

by shattering this inadequate existence. Consequently, instead of the third moment of the generic process lapsing again into singularity, the other side, which is death, constitutes the sublation of the singular, and is therefore the proceeding forth of the genus, of spirit. This is so because the negation of the immediate singularity of natural being consists in the positing of the universality of the genus, and moreover in the form of the genus. In spiritual *individuality*, this movement of the two sides is the self-sublating progression which *results in consciousness*, i.e. the unity which is in and for itself the unity of both, and which is this as self, not merely as genus in the inner Notion of the singular. It is in this way that the Idea exists in the independent subject, which as an organ of the Notion, finds everything to be fluid and of an ideal nature, i.e. it *thinks*, appropriates to itself all that is spatial and temporal, and so contains universality, i.e. itself. As the universal now has being for the universal, the Notion is for itself. This is first manifest in spirit, in which the Notion objectifies itself, although by this, the existence of the Notion is posited as Notion. As this universal which has being for itself, thought is *immortal being*, while mortal being consists on the universality of the Idea being inadequate to itself.

This is the *transition from natural being into spirit*; nature has found its consummation in living being, and has made its peace by shifting into a higher sphere. Spirit has therefore issued forth from nature. The purpose of nature is to extinguish itself, and to break through its rind of immediate and sensuous being, to consume itself like a Phoenix in order to emerge from this externality rejuvenated as spirit. Nature has become distinct from itself in order to recognize itself again as Idea, and to reconcile itself with itself. To regard spirit thus, as having come forth from implicitness, and as having *become* a mere being-for-self, is however a one-sided view. Nature is certainly that which is immediate, but as that which is distinct from spirit, it is nevertheless merely a relativity. As the negative of spirit, it is therefore merely a posited being. It is the power of free spirit which sublates this negativity; spirit is nature's antecedent and to an equal extent its consequent, it is not merely the metaphysical Idea of it. It is precisely because spirit constitutes the end of nature, that it is *antecedent* to it. Nature has gone forth from spirit; it has not done this empirically however, for while it presupposes nature, it is already constantly contained within it. In its infinite freedom however, spirit allows nature freedom, and opposes it by exhibiting within it the action of the Idea, as an inner necessity; just as a free man is certain that his action constitutes the activity of the world. Spirit itself therefore, proceeding forth in the first instance from immediate being, but *then* abstractly apprehending itself, wants to liberate itself by fashioning nature from within itself; this action of spirit is philosophy.

With this we have brought our consideration of nature to its limit. Spirit, which has apprehended itself, also wants to recognize itself in nature, to make good again the loss of itself. It is only by this reconciliation with nature and actuality that spirit is truly liberated, and sheds the particularity of its modes of thought and intuition. This liberation from nature and its necessity constitutes the Notion of the philosophy of nature. The shapes of nature are merely shapes of the Notion, although in the element of externality; it is true that their forms are grounded in the Notion as the stages of nature, but even where the Notion collects itself into sensation, it is still not yet present to itself as Notion. It is precisely because material being is so intractably opposed to the unity of the Notion, and because spirit has to deal with an ever increasing wealth of detail, that the philosophy of nature is so difficult. In spite of this difficulty however, reason must have confidence in itself, confidence that in nature the Notion speaks to the Notion, and that the true shape of the Notion, which lies concealed beneath the extrinsicality of infinitely numerous shapes, will reveal itself to it.—Let us briefly survey the field we have covered. In the primary sphere of gravity, the Idea was freely deployed into a body which has the free heavenly bodies as its members. This externality then shaped itself inwardly into the properties and qualities belonging to an individual unity, and having an immanent and physical movement in the chemical process. Finally, in animation, gravity is released into members possessing subjective unity. The aim of these lectures is to convey an image of nature, in order to subdue this Proteus: to find in this externality only the mirror of ourselves, to see in nature a free reflection of spirit: to understand God, not in the contemplation of spirit, but in this His immediate existence.

(Concluded: March 18, 1820; March 23, 1822; March 30, 1824; March 17, 1826; August 26, 1828; August 27, 1830).

NOTES

10, 21

‚Licᵇtig' is an obsolete Swabian word. Hegel evidently uses it in order to catch the shade of meaning implied by this complicated nexus of fact and theory. See Wilhelm Pfleiderer's supplements to Hermann Fischer's 'Schwäbisches Wörterbuch' vol. 6 pt. 2 (Tübingen, 1904–1936). He quotes from Nicodemus Frischlin (1547–1590) in order to clarify the meaning of the word, 'Lucidus, luminosus ḣell, liecᵇtig.'

Although the importance of light to the living organism was known at this time, it was by no means fully understood. Jean Senebier (1742–1809) spent six years (1782–1788) investigating the influence of light upon vegetation, and published the results of his labour in 'Expériences sur l'action de la lumière solaire dans la végétation' (Geneva, 1788), and in the five volumes of his 'Physiologie végétale' (Geneva, 1800). J. C. Reil (1759–1813) makes mention of its influence upon animals, ‚Auᵍ baß Licᵇt, bie äußerſt ſubtile Materie, ſᵍeint ein Beſtanbteil ber tieriſᵍen Körper ʒu ſein. Mangel beß Lichteß macᵇt fett; baᵇer ſperrt man Tiere, bie man mäſtet, an finſtere Örter ein" ('Von der Lebenskraft' 1796 ed. K. Sudhoff Leipzig 1910 I p. 16). Cf. E. Horn (1772–1848) 'Ueber die Wirkungen des Lichts auf den lebenden menschlichen Körper, mit Ausnahme des Sehens' (Königsberg, 1799).

11, 2

This may be a reference to Spinoza's 'Ethics' pt. 11 prop. XLV 'Every idea of every body or individual thing actually existing necessarily involves the eternal and infinite essence of God . . .' prop. XLVI 'The knowledge of the eternal and infinite essence of God which each idea involves is adequate and perfect.'

11, 33

'The Logic of Hegel' tr. W. Wallace. Second Edition Oxford University Press 1963 p. 336.

11, 36

Kant 'Critique of Judgement' tr. J. C. Meredith pt. II pp. 3–34 Oxford University Press 1964.

Cf. Aristotle's remark, 'It is manifest that the soul is also the final cause of the body. For Nature, like mind, always does whatever it does for the sake of something, which something is its end. To that something corresponds in the case of animals the soul, and in this it follows the order of nature; all natural bodies are organs of the soul,' 'De Anima' II 4 (415^b) tr. J. A. Smith Oxford University Press 1931.

12, 11

The division of the kingdoms of nature into a triad has been attributed to Aristotle, but in modern times it seems to have been the 'Gazophylacium Rerum Naturalium, e regno Vegetabili, Animali, et Minerali depromptarum' (Nuremberg, 1642) of M. R. Besler (1607–1661) which initiated its wide-spread acceptance. It had already become a commonplace by the end of the seventeenth century cf. the 'Regnum Animale' (1682), 'Regnum Minerale' (1686) and 'Regnum Vegetabile' (1688) of Emanuel König (1658–1731). Linnaeus makes use of it in his 'Systema naturae' (Leyden, 1735), and H. F. Link has an interesting assessment of it in his 'Ueber die Leiter der Nature' (Rostock and Leipzig, 1794) p. 21. ‚Schon seit langen Zeiten unterscheidet man die dren Reiche der Natur, und ungeachtet aller Künsteleyen der Systeme, hat sich diese Eintheilung bis jetzt erhalten, ja den Sieg über alle Veränderungen davon getragen. Ein Beweis, daß sie sich wenigstens dem gemeinen Menschenverstande sehr empfehlen muß.'

12, 33

In Hegel's day, crystals were of great importance in speculation and experiment concerned with the distinction between inanimate and animate being. Charles Bonnet (1720–1793), who seems to have initiated this line of research, distinguished between crystalline growth by means of accretion, and organic growth by means of intussusception, 'Les Etres organisés proviennent d'un germe où toutes leur parties essentielles sont concentrés, et ils croissent par intussusception. Les Etres crystallisés croissent par l'apposition successive de certaines molécules de figure determinée, qui se réunissent dans une masse commune. Ainsi, les Etres crystallisés ne croissent pas proprement; mais ils accroisent.' 'Oeuvres d'Histoire Naturelle' (8 vols. Neuchâtel, 1779–1783) Part III Ch. IV note 12 (p. 51).

Bonnet realized therefore, that as organizations of elements, crystalline and organic formations were closely related, but he was unable to give a precise definition of their common factor, and was therefore led to assert that at this juncture nature made a leap, 'Si le polype nous montre le passage du Végétal à l'Animal, d'un autre côté nous ne découvrons pas celui du Minéral au Végétal. Ici la Nature nous semble faire un saut; la gradation est pour nous interrompre, car l'organisation apparente de quelques pierres et des crystallisations ne répond que très-imparfaitement à celle des plantes.' See his 'Considerations sur les corps organisés' (Amsterdam, 1762) Ch. 12 § 209.

Various lines of research were opened up in geology, botany and animal physiology in order to discover this common factor. The geologist J. L. Heim

(1741–1819), in his 'Geologische Beschreibung des Thüringer Waldgeburgs' pt. II sect. IV (Meiningen, 1803) noted the close resemblance between the elongated mica crystals occurring in a certain coarse-grained conglomerate (Gemenge) found near Brottrode, and the reed- and rush-like figurations found in the greywack formations of the Kellbach area. Commenting upon this resemblance, he continues as follows (p. 290) ‚Ohne zu erwarten, daß wir jemals es dahin bringen werden, die Entstehung der ersten organischen Wesen zu enträthseln, wird doch jeder Naturforscher eingestehen müssen, daß dieses ein höchst interessanter Gegenstand, und wohl werth sey, daß Geognosten und Chemiker bey dessen Untersuchung sich einander die Hände bieten.' He then quotes with approval an article by Charles Hatchett (1765–1847) 'Chemical experiments on Zoophytes,' in 'Phil. Trans. of the Roy. Soc.' 1800 pp. 327–402.

The botanist K. H. Schultz (1798–1871), a colleague of Hegel's in Berlin, took the overcoming of chemical differentiation to be the common factor ('Die Nature der lebendigen Pflanze' Berlin 1823, I pp. 41–60). See especially § 58 of this work, ‚Krystalle gestalten sich, wie die Pflanzen und Thiere, aus innerer Macht, und zwar bilden sie sich, aus ursprünglich geformten Gegensätzen, die man ihre organischen Elemente nennen könnte . . . In diesen organischen Elementen ist jede chemische Differenz durchaus zur Ruhe gebracht, und aus dem chemischen Tode gehen sie erst ins individuelle Leben über.'

J. C. Reil (1759–1813), in his 'Von der Lebenskraft' vol. I 1796 (ed. K. Sudhoff, Leipzig, 1910) p. 37 emphasised the similarity between crystallisation and animal growth, ‚Die tierische Materie schießt in Gefäße, Nerven, Häute, Muskelfasern usw. an, wie das Kochsalz in einem würfeligen Kristall. Das Anschießen der fremden Materie an die schon vorhandene muß von außen geschehen, welches aus dem Begriff einer Kristallisation erhellt. Organische Wesen vermehren also, wie die Fossilien ihre Masse durch Zusatz von außen.'

F. Tiedemann (1781–1861), in his 'Physiologie des Menschen' vol. I pp. 105–106 (Darmstadt, 1830 Engl. tr., 'A Systematic Treatise on Comparative Physiology' tr. with notes by J. M. Gully and J. H. Lane. London, 1834) suggested that it was in their lines and surfaces that the essential difference between these inorganic and organic 'crystallisations' was to be found, ‚Alle organischen Körper, die Gewächse sowohl als die Thiere, haben eine mehr oder weniger rundliche und eyförmige, oder ästige und gegliederte Form, und sie sind durch krumme oder wellenförmige Linien, so wie durch convexe oder concave Flächen begränzt. Die unorganischen Körper dagegen, wenn sie eine reguläre Form haben, wie die Kristalle, sind durch ebene Flächen und gerade Linien, die in bestimmten Winkeln an den Ecken und Kanten zusammentreten, begränzt.'

These approaches towards the distinction between inanimate and animate being found a protagonist in Hans Przibram as late as the 1920's; see his 'Die anorganischen Grenzgebiete, insbesondere der Kristallvergleich' (Berlin, 1926), cf. E. Schrödinger 'What is Life?' (Cambridge, 1944). Schrödinger calls the gene or the chromosome an 'aperiodic crystal'. Hegel makes use of them on many occasions, and may have been encouraged to do so at this juncture as a result of the work of the geologist J. F. L. Hausmann (1782–1859); see his 'Entwurf des Systems der anorganischen Naturkörper' (Cassel, 1809), and 'Untersuchungen über die Formen der leblosen Nature' (Göttingen, 1822). E. Mendelsohn 'Physical Models and Physiological Concepts: explanation in nineteenth century biology' in 'Boston Studies in the Philosophy of Science' (ed. Cohen, Wartofsky, New York, 1965) vol. ii pp. 127–155.

13, 22

Cf. I.210,11. ‚die Unſchuld der Pflanze.' Light is thrown upon Hegel's attribution of *innocence* to plants by Johann Christoph Adelung (1732–1806), who, in his 'Grammatisch-kritisches Wörterbuch der Hochdeutschen Mundart' (ed. Soltau and Schönberger, 4 pts. Vienna, 1807–1808) IV col. 888, notes that the word 'is often used for innocuousness, to denote that state in which a thing does not contribute to the lessening of the perfection of something else.' The O.E.D. cites a contemporary English instance of its use in this sense (1828), 'The innocence of a medicine which can do no harm.' The Houstonia caerulea, a plant with small blue flowers, is known popularly as Innocence.

13, 31

Etheriality, das Aetheriſche, Greek αἰθήρ, formed on root of αἴθειν to burn, glow. Cf. Hölderlin's elegy 'An den Äther.'

> ‚Und es drängt ſich und rinnt aus deiner ewigen Fülle
> Die beſeelende Luft durch alle Röhren des Lebens.'

For Aristotle, the ether was the quintessence or fifth element after earth, water, air, and fire, it was the godlike in contradistinction to the terrestrial fire, and functioned as spirit and as the source of everything spiritual and living. For the postulation of ether in modern physical theories, see Sir Edmund Whittaker 'A History of the Theories of Aether and Electricity' (2 vols. London, 1951.) Cf. E. A. Underwood 'Science, Medicine and History' (2 vols. Oxford, 1953) vol. I pp. 247–265. W. Kern 'Eine Uebersetzung Hegels zu De Anima III, 4–5': in 'Hegel-Studien' (ed Nicolin and Pöggeler, Bonn, 1961) vol. I pp. 49–88.

16, 20

This paragraph almost certainly owes something to Kant's 'Kurzer Abriss der physischen Geographie' ('Sämtliche Werke' II ed. Hartenstein, Leipzig, 1867). Kant distinguishes between mathematical, political and physical geography, and if we consider his definitions of these branches of the subject, it becomes evident that they broadly correspond to what are now known as geodesy, human geography and geomorphology.

The geodetical background to geographical studies, as it is presented here by Hegel, was a commonplace at that time; see the introduction to 'A New Geographical, Historical and Commercial Grammar' (6th ed. London 1779) by William Guthrie (1708-1770), John Pinkerton's 'Modern Geography' (London, 1811), and Carl Ritter's 'Die Erdkunde im Verhältniss zur Nature und zur Geschichte des Menschen (Berlin, 1822).

16, 33

‚Die Erde ist unter allen Planeten der vortrefflichste, der mittlere." 'For a planet to be suitable for life, it must move in what is known as the parent sun's biosphere—that is to say, the region in which the temperature is neither too high nor too low. In our Solar System there are three planets in the biosphere: Venus (near the inner edge), Earth (more or less in the middle) and Mars (near the outer edge).' P. Moore, 'The Listener' vol. LXXIV p. 229.

17, 23

Geognosy (formed on Greek γεω (γῆ) earth + γνῶσις knowledge). This term seems to have been coined by J. C. Füchsel (1722-1773), who speaks of 'scientia geognostica' in his 'Historia terrae et maris' ('Acta Academiae electoralis Moguntinae' Erfurt, 1761 vol. II p. 44-209).

'Geognosy treats of the general structure of the earth. It makes us acquainted with the *common* and *particular beds* of fossils, with their probable origin, relative formation and arrangement in the Earth—with the *rocks* which compose mountains, and which constitute, if not the solid mass, at least the great shell of the Globe—with the various strata and veins which form the more particular repositories of fossils, and with their reciprocal relations to each other.' A. G. Werner 'A treatise on the external characters of fossils' (Leipzig 1774, tr. T. Weaver, Dublin 1805 p. 3).

In modern German 'Geognosie' may be used to cover mineralogy, petrology and economic geology, whereas 'Geologie' deals specifically with the history of the earth and the superficial crust.

F. Hoffmann 'Geschichte der Geognosie' (Berlin 1838); C. Keferstein 'Geschichte und Litteratur der Geognosie' (Halle, 1840).

17, 32

From about 1790 until about 1820, this controversy gave rise to two distinct schools of geology. Abraham Gottlob Werner (1749-1817), professor at the Freiberg Mining Academy and founder of the neptunist school, held that the sea had at one time covered the whole of the globe, and that rocks and their formations were the result of marine depositions and the recession of this universal ocean.

Robert Jameson (1774-1854), professor of natural history at Edinburgh, was one of the first to introduce Werner's ideas into Britain. In one of his earliest articles, 'Examination of the supposed igneous origin of the rocks of the Trapp formation' ('Nicholson's Journal' III Oct. 1802 pp. 111–119), he called in question the volcanic origin of basalt and attempted to show that it had been formed by the action of water. In 1805 (2nd ed. 1816), he published an English translation of Werner's 'Von den äusserlichen Kennzeichen der Fossilien' (Leipzig, 1774), and in 1804–1808 gave a full account of Werner's system in his 'System of Mineralogy' (3 vols. 3rd ed. Edinburgh, 1820). It was his enthusiasm which led to the formation of the 'Wernerian Natural History Society of Edinburgh' (1808–1839), the memoirs of which show how Werner's ideas were put to the test, modified and finally abandoned.

The founder of the vulcanist school was James Hutton (1726–1797) of Edinburgh. Hutton expounded the doctrine that the present rocks of the earth's surface have been formed mainly out of the waste of older rocks; that these materials, having been laid down under the sea, were consolidated there under great pressure, and subsequently disrupted and upheaved by the expansive power of subterranean heat; that during these convulsions, veins and masses of molten rock were injected into the rents of the dislocated strata; that every portion of the upraised land, as soon as it is exposed to the atmosphere, is subject to decay; and that this decay must tend to advance until the whole of the land has been worn away and laid down on the sea-floor, whence future upheavals will once more raise the consolidated sediments into new land. Hutton first communicated these views to the Royal Society of Edinburgh in 1785. Ten years later he gave a fuller account of them in his 'Theory of the Earth' (2 vols. Edinburgh, 1795), but the book was clumsily written and never finished, and it was John Playfair (1748–1819) who, by presenting Hutton's theories in a brilliantly lucid manner, gained widespread acceptance for them ('Illustrations of the Huttonian Theory of the Earth' Edinburgh, 1802, ed. G. W. White, New York, 1964).

The best contemporary English account of the neptunist-vulcanist controversy is John Murray's 'A Comparative View of the Huttonian and Neptunian Systems of Geology' (anon. Edinburgh, 1802).

As this controversy was thought to have theological implications, the two points of view were denigrated and defended with great vehemence: see C. C. Gillipsie 'Genesis and Geology' (Harvard University Press, 1951).

Goethe introduces the subject into 'Faust' pt. II Act II, in the interchanges between the Sphinxes and Seismos, and between Anaxagoras and Thales. Cf. Goethe 'Schriften zur Geologie und Mineralogie' ed. G. Schmid (Weimar, 1947, 1949).

18, 14

Matthew XXIV v. 35: Mark XIII v. 31: 2 Peter III vv. 4–10: Revelation XXI v. 1.

Cf. M. Stuart 'Remarks on a critical examination of some passages in Genesis

I; with remarks on difficulties that attend some of the present modes of geological reasoning.' ('The American Journal of Science and Arts' ed. Silliman vol. xxx pp. 114–130, 1836).

18, 27

Hutton's geological studies led him to the conclusion that the history of the world showed, 'no trace of a beginning and no prospect of an end.' In its day this was a revolutionary assertion, for natural scientists were then only beginning to become aware of the true extent of geological time.

George Buffon (1707–1788) drew attention to these 'prodigious revolutions' of the 'remote past', by distinguishing seven main epochs in the history of the earth: (i) the formation of the solar system, (ii) the cooling of matter and the interior formation of the earth, (iii) the universal ocean, (iv) the subsidence of the ocean and emergence of volcanoes, (v) the first appearance of animals, (vi) the separation of the continents, (vii) the appearance of man. ('Oeuvres Philosophiques de Buffon' ed. J. Piveteau, Paris, 1954: pp. 116–229 'Époques de la nature' 1778).

This new chronology, together with the systematic investigation of the animal remains discovered in geological formations, gave rise to great advances in palaeontology. The changes postulated as having taken place in the past were thought to have been the result of cataclysms however, 'The breaking to pieces, the raising up and overturning of the older strata, leave no doubt upon the mind that they have been reduced to the state in which we now see them by the action of sudden and violent causes . . . Life, therefore, has often been disturbed on this earth by terrible events.'—G. Cuvier (1769–1832) 'Theory of the Earth' tr. Jameson, 5th ed. 1827 pp. 14–16.

In his 'Essai sur la géographie minéralogique des environs de Paris' (Paris, 1808), Cuvier made the first exact contribution to stratigraphic geology, but he never abandoned this cataclysmic theory of change, and in geology, it was Hutton and Sir Charles Lyell (1797–1875) who, by their advocacy of uniformitarianism, did most to prepare the way for the evolutionism of Darwin. Nevertheless, it was also Cuvier who laid the foundations of vertebrate palaeontology in his 'Recherches sur les ossemens fossiles' (Paris, 1812).

J. B. Lamarck (1744–1829) brought geological uniformitarianism to bear upon palaeontological theory, and it was his 'Sur les fossiles des environs de Paris' (Paris, 1802–1806) which laid the foundation of all subsequent invertebrate palaeontology.

S. Toulmin and J. Goodfield 'The Discovery of Time' (London, 1965).

18, 29

Johann Gottfried Ebel (1764–1830) was a medical doctor by profession, and practised for some years at Frankfort-on-Main in this capacity. At one time, Goethe wanted to find him an appointment at Jena. After travelling widely in

Switzerland, he published a travel book on the country which was translated into French and English and ran into many editions: see 'Anleitung die Schweiz zu bereisen' (2 vols. Zürich, 1793; French tr. Paris, 1795; English tr. D. Wall London, 1818).

H. Escher 'J. G. Ebel, sein Leben und Wirken' (Trogen, 1836).

In his 'Ueber den Bau der Erde in dem Alpen-Gebirge zwischen 12 Längen- und 2-4 Breitengraden. Nebst einigen Betrachtungen über die Gebirge und den Bau der Erde überhaupt' (2 vols. Zürich, 1808), he drew to some extent upon the material he had collected for his first book, but added much that was new. It was evidently the detail of his observations rather than his theorizing which interested Hegel, and subsequent assessments of his work have tended to bear out the soundness of Hegel's judgement on this point. The primary object of the book was to present the Alps in their inter-related entirety. Ebel took the core of the whole system to be a series of more or less steeply inclined tables of primitive rock, which had been engendered by the chemical process and the prevailing force of crystallization. He distinguished between several parallel lateral ranges resting upon this central core, i.e. the fletz-formations, which he thought to be of mechanical origin, the limestone hills, and other stratified rocks such as molasse (tertiary sandstone). He regarded the globe of the earth as a huge voltaic pile, from which these particular formations had derived their basic animation.

Ebel also published a slender volume entitled, 'Ideen über die Organisation und das eigenthümliche Leben des Erdkörpers, und über die gewaltsamen Veränderungen seiner Oberfläche' (Vienna, 1811) which consists very largely of extracts from the work quoted by Hegel.

18, 31

Fletz-formations ‚Flötzgebirgen' The word ‚flöz' is cognate with the Anglo-Saxon 'flett', floor, ground, hall, dwelling. In Old High German 'flezzi' had the same meaning, and in Middle High German occurred as 'vlez', with the added general meaning of 'levelled ground'. The word was first used as a technical term by the miners of the Erz- and Riesengebirge in the sixteenth century (H. Veith 'Deutsches Bergwörterbuch' Breslau, 1871 p. 188, E. Göpfert 'Bergmannssprache' 1902 p. 26). As a geological term it is now obsolete, having given way in modern geological nomenclature to 'Secondary' and 'Tertiary', but it was widely used in Hegel's day, and the history of its origin covers some important advances in the development of geology.

Ultimately, its subsequent use by geologists may be traced back to the theories of rock-formation put forward by the Dane Nicolaus Steno (1638–1686) in his 'The Prodromus to a dissertation concerning Solids naturally contained within solids. Laying the foundation for the rendering a rational account . . . of the frame . . . of the Earth' (Florence, 1669 tr. H. Oldenburg London, 1671). As the result of his geological studies in Tuscany, Steno put forward the theory that geological strata are sediments which have been deposited in water, subsequently hardened to a greater or lesser degree, and then raised or convulsed by seismic disturbances.

A. L. Moro (1687–1740), in his, 'De Crostacei e degli altri marini corpi che si truovano su monti' (Venice, 1740, German tr. Leipzig, 1751), distinguished between 'montes primarii' which he regarded as primeval and volcanic in origin, and 'montes secundarii' which he regarded as derived from these primary rocks by the various processes of weathering, erosion and disintegration.

In the foreword to his 'Versuch einer Geschichte von Flötz-Gebürgen' (Berlin, 1756, French tr. 1759), J. G. Lehmann (d. 1767) distinguished between primitive and veined rocks (Ur-und Ganggebirge) devoid of fossils, and fletz-formations (Flötzgebirge), within which he distinguished between an older series consisting of old red sandstone, blue slate, coal etc., and a newer series consisting of new red sandstone, blue clay, upper earth (Dammerde) etc. Lehmann certainly did a great deal of original research upon the geology of north Germany, but in the ordering of his material he seems to have been influenced by Moro.

It was Lehmann who gave the term 'flötz' a general currency in Germany. A. G. Werner (1749–1817) adopted it in his 'Classification der Gebirgsarten' (Dresden, 1787), and it was mainly through the work of his disciple Robert Jameson (1774–1854), that it was introduced into English.

Werner's classification distinguished between primitive rocks such as granite, gneiss, mica- and argillaceous schist, porphyry, basalt etc.; fletz-formations such as limestone, marl, sandstone, greywack, coal, chalk, rock-salt, gypsum and iron-clay; volcanic rocks; and alluvial terrains. In his later system he inserted a further group, which he called 'transition rocks' (Uebergangsgebirge), between the primitive rocks and the fletz-formations, and enumerated twelve sub-divisions of fletz. C. Keferstein (1784–1866) published a critical analysis of this classification ('Tabellen über die vergleichende Geognosie' Halle, 1825), but he did not abandon the term 'fletz'.

19, 14

Ebel's source here seems to have been the 'Beobachtungen, Zweifel und Fragen die Mineralogie überhaupt und insbesondere ein natürliches Mineral system betreffend. Erster Versuch (Hanover and Osnabrück, 1792) of Franz von Beroldingen (1740–1798). ‚Der Holländische, der Friesländische, der Dänische und der meiste Englische Torf scheinen auf folgende Art, nemlich durch Ueberschwemmung und Zurückweichung des Meeres, entstanden zu seyn. Die natürliche flache Lage dieser Länder läßt dieses leicht begreifen, und zu geschweigen, daß der meiste Torf gedachter Länder Kochsalz, und wie in Norwegen, oft sehr vieles Kochsalz aus sich ausbringen läßt; so versichern auch die davon handelnden Schriftsteller, daß die, besonders in holländischen Torfmooren nicht selten vorkommende, umgestürzte Bäume einerlei Lage haben, so, daß sie ihre

Krone ober Gipfel nach ber Gegend zwischen Oft und Nord, ihre Wurzeln aber gegen Süd=West zukehren.' (vol. I pp. 43–44)

19, 28

'Voyage au sommet du Mont-Perdu' par le citoyen Ramond. ('Annales du Muséum National D'Histoire Naturelle' vol. III pp. 74–84, Paris, 1804). 'Tout est secondaire dans ces énormes amas. Les poudingues, les gris, le calcaire coquiller et fétide, tels en sont les matériaux; et dans le nombre des corps marins qui y sont enfermés, le genre qui l'emporte sur tous les autres, est celui des numismales que l'on rencontre par-tout dans une si prodigieuse abondance, qu'elle épouvante l'esprit le plus accoutumé à l'idee des grandes destructions de la nature' (pp. 82–83). Cf. 'Nicholson's Journal' vol. vi pp. 250–252 Dec. 1803.

19, 29

Most of the data here is taken from Ebel, but Hegel himself introduced this reference to Voltaire's 'Dissertation . . . sur les changemens arrivés dans notre globe, et sur les pétrifactions qui'on prétend en être encore les témoignages', which was addressed to the Academy of Boulogne in 1746 ('Oeuvres complètes de Voltaire' 2nd ed. Paris, 1828 vol. XLII pp. 227–244).

'On a vu aussi dans des provinces d'Italie, de France etc. de petits coquillages qui'on assure être originaires de la mer de Syrie. Je ne veux pas contester leur origine; mais ne pourrait-on pas se souvenir que cette foule innombrable de pèlerins et de croisés, qui porta son argent dans la Terre-Sainte, en rapporta des coquilles?'

This volume (pp. 282–303) contains a further discussion of these shells and of the theories built upon them, 'He! pauvres gens qui osez parler en maîtres, vous voulez m'enseigner la formation de l'univers, et vous ne savez pas celle d'un ciron, celle d'un paille' (p. 303).

19, 32

Thomas Jefferson (1743–1826) mentions these shells in a letter to a friend, 'Immense bodies of Schist with impressions of shells near the eastern foot of North mountain recall statements that shells have been found in the Andes 15,000 feet above sea level, which is considered by many writers both of the learned and unlearned as a proof of a universal deluge . . . We must be contented to acknowledge that this great phenomenon is as yet unsolved. Ignorance is preferable to error, and he is less remote from truth who believes nothing than he who believes what is wrong'. F. W. Hirst 'Life and Letters of Thomas Jefferson' (New York, 1926) p. 186.

20, 11

Throughout the eighteenth century, these animal remains attracted a great deal of interest, and most of the travel books of the time made mention of them.

J. B. Breyne's 'Observations, and a Description of some Mammoth's Bones dug up in Siberia, proving them to have belonged to Elephants' (Phil. Trans. Roy. Soc. 1737 pp. 124–128 London, 1741) is typical of speculation on the subject early in the century. Breyne set out to prove, 'that the extraordinary large Teeth and Bones found under Ground, and digged up in several Places of Siberia, by the Name of Mammoth's, or Mammut's, Teeth and Bones, were,

    I True Bones and Teeth of some large Animals once living; and,

    II That those animals were Elephants, by the Analogy of the Teeth and Bones, with the known ones of Elephants.

III That they were brought and left there by the universal Deluge'.

P. S. Pallas (1741–1811) frequently refers to these remains in his 'Reisen durch verschiedene Provinzen des Russischen Reichs' (3 vols. 1771–1776, Eng. tr. 'Travels through the Southern Provinces of the Russian Empire' 2 vols. London, 1802–1803), and was often quoted on the subject by the writers of Hegel's day.

For an account of A. von Humboldt's American travels between 1799 and 1804 see H. M. Williams' translation of his 'Personal Narrative of Travels to the Equinoctial Regions of the New Continent' (6 vols. London, 1818–1826). The fossils he discovered on these journeys are dealt with in detail in 'Annales du Museum d'Histoire Naturelle' vol. II p. 177 et seq., and 'Gilbert's Annalen der Physik' vol. XVI pp. 424–425. At the time of Hegel's delivering these lectures, the fullest account of the fossilized quadrupeds of the River Plate was to be found in 'Essais sur l'histoire naturelle de Quadrupèdes de la Province de Paraguay' by Felix d'Azara (tr. M. L. E. Moreau-Saint-Méry 2 vols. Paris, 1801).

By the turn of the century, the first competent attempts at dating rocks by means of these fossils were being made. As the Secondary and Tertiary formations of southern and eastern England and the Paris Basin are easily observable, and lie in undisturbed succession one above the other over hundreds of square miles, it was natural that English and French geologists should have taken the lead in this work.

As early as the seventeenth century, Martin Lister (1638–1712) had done systematic work on conchology, and had suggested that the shells and animal remains found in the different strata might be of prime importance in reaching an understanding of the formation of the earth: see his 'Historia Animalium Angliae' (London, 1678–1681). In 1799 William Smith (1769–1839) dictated his famous 'Order of Strata and their imbedded Organic Remains' to the rector of Pewsey; in 1816 he began his 'Strata identified by organized fossils'; and in 1817 his 'Stratigraphical System of Organized Fossils . . . explaining . . . their use in identifying the British Strata' appeared. John Farey (1766–1826) pointed out that Smith's work was in many ways the fulfilment of Lister's suggestions; 'A Stratigraphical or Smithian arrangement of the fossil shells described by Martin Lister in his 'Historia Animalium Angliae' (Tilloch's Philosophical Magazine 1819 pp. 133–138).

In France, George Cuvier's 'Recherches sur les Ossemens fossiles' (Paris, 1812), and 'Essai sur la Géographie minéralogique des environs de Paris' (Paris, 1811) opened up similar fields of research. German geologists soon began to produce corresponding works. E. F. Schlotheim (1764–1832) published his 'Beiträge zur Naturgeschichte der Versteinerungen' in 1813 ('Mineralogisches Taschenbuch von Leonhard' VII pp. 1–134), and in 1826 August Goldfuss (1782–1848) began to publish his 'Petrefacta Germaniae' in a series of magnificently produced folio volumes (Düsseldorf, 1826–1844).

These works brought the rapid advances then being made in palaeontology to bear upon stratigraphical geology. Hegel could have drawn upon a number of systematic palaeontological works in illustrating this subject therefore, but as he saw no teleological significance in these researches into the chronology of rock formation, he regarded them as philosophically unimportant, and chose to draw upon the comparatively random observations of Ebel.

20, 34

Cf. J. F. W. Charpentier (1738–1805) 'Beytrag zur geognostischen Kenntnis des Riesengebirgs schlesischen Antheils' (Leipzig, 1804), p. 54. ‚Ich habe oben gesagt, daß die Hauptgesteinart des Riesengebirgs Granit sey. Es findet sich aber auch noch Gneiß und Basalt, jedoch nur an einigen einzeln zur Zeit bekannten Stellen: den Gneiß fand ich auf der Schneekoppe, dem höchsten kegelförmigen Berge des ganzen Riesengebirgs, in einer Höhe von 4940 Par. Fuß über der Meeresfläche, abwechselnd in und zwischen dem Granit.'

21, 9

Hoffmeister ('Jenenser Realphilosophie II', Leipzig, 1931) p. 109 gives the words emphasized by Hegel, and corrects the tense of this passage, ‚Die Geschichte ist früher in die Erde gefallen; jetzt aber ist sie zur Ruhe gekommen, ein Leben, das in sich selbst gärend, die Zeit an ihm selbst hatte, der Erdgeist, der noch nicht zur Entgegensetzung gekommen, die Bewegung und Träume eines Schlafenden, bis er erwacht und im Menschen sein Bewußtsein erhalten (hat) und sich also als ruhige Gestaltung gegenübergetreten (ist)'.

He also prints Hegel's marginal note on this, ‚Allgemeiner Charakter der Gestalt. — Hat die Erde eine Geschichte? Was ist Geschichte? Zeit fällt in den Menschen dem Vernunftlosen gegenüber. — Form des Nacheinander neben dem Zugleich.'

21, 19

‚In die Spalten sey der Brei hineingelaufen'. Cf. the note III. 240.

21, 23

The nature of 'organic fermentation' was not known at this time, although it played as important a part as crystal formation in speculation and experiment concerning the distinction between inanimate and animate being.

L. J. Thénard (1774–1857) was the first to suggest that it was animal and not chemical in nature ('Annal. de Chimie' XLVI, 1803 pp. 224–320), but it was not until 1835 that C. C. Delatour (1777–1859) showed that it was caused by minute organisms ('L'Institut' III, 1835 pp. 133–134).

Prior to these advances, it was not uncommon to account for rock formation by means of 'fermentation'. F. W. H. von Trebra (1740–1819), in his 'Erfahrungen vom Innern der Gebirge' (Leipzig, 1786), attributed the formation of rocks to what he called 'fermentation' and 'decomposition', although in modern terminology the processes he had in mind would probably be referred to as 'metamorphism' and 'weathering'.

In the controversy between Werner and J. K. Voigt (1752–1821) concerning the origin of basalt (see Voigt's 'Mineralogische und bergmännische Abhandlungen' Weimar, 1789–1791), Werner insisted that the main factor in its formation had been water, and Voigt that it had been heat. This conflict of opinion gave rise to C. Keferstein's theory ('Beiträge zur Geschichte und Kenntniss des Basaltes' Halle, 1819), according to which basalt had been formed by a kind of fermentation. Keferstein was unable to give a precise description of this process however.

22, 9

Abraham Gottlob Werner (1749–1817) was appointed lecturer in mineralogy at the Freiberg Academy in 1775, and taught there for forty years. He wrote very little, and his first-hand knowledge of geological formations was confined to those of his native Saxony, but he had an immense influence on account of his lectures, and although not a few of those who heard them later abandoned many of the leading ideas they were meant to convey, they gave a great impetus to geological research throughout Europe. Several outstanding British geologists—George Greenough (1778–1855), Robert Jameson (1774–1854) and Thomas Weaver (1773–1855) studied under him.

His accurate and systematic work on the classification of minerals has proved to be his most lasting contribution to science. He took a comprehensive view of the subject, assessing opacity, colour, lustre, hardness, specific weight, chemical content, cleavage and crystal structure etc. See F. von Kobell 'Geschichte der Mineralogie' (Munich, 1865 pp. 85–96); Werner 'Von den äusserlichen Kennzeichen der Mineralogie' (Leipzig, 1774); 'Abraham Gottlob Werner's letztes Mineral-System' (Freiberg, 1817).

Systematic mineralogy was already well established when geologists began to suggest systematic classifications of strata in the closing decades of the eighteenth century, and it was natural therefore that they should have been influenced by the mineralogists. The working method generally adopted by the German geologists of the time was to make a detailed study of a certain area, noting the juxtaposition and sequence of the rocks, and then to attempt a classification by generalizing from this data. The assumption made was that if rocks are closely juxtaposed, they are almost certainly closely related in composition and origin, and have probably been subjected to similar aqueous and igneous processes.

The systems evolved by this method naturally tended to reflect the geological structure of north Germany, where most of the fieldwork was done. J. G. Lehmann's 'Versuch einer Geschichte von Flötz-Gebürgen' (Berlin, 1756) was the first work of this kind, and led to the general acceptance of the distinction between primitive rocks and fletz-formations. After studying the geology of Thüringia, J. C. Füchsel (1722–1773) drew up a series of fourteen formations grading from what he called basic rocks (Grundgebirge) to shell-limestone characterized by the presence of ammonites, nautilites and terebratulae etc. ('Historia terrae et maris, ex historia Thuringiae per montium descriptionem erecta' Act. Acad. elect. Moguntinae, Erfurt, 1762, vol. II pp. 44–209). J. F. W. Charpentier (1738–1805) also did his field-work in Thuringia, and in his 'Mineralogische Geographie der Chursächsischen Lande' (Leipzig, 1778) elaborated upon Lehmann's basic distinction between primitive rocks and fletz-formations.

J. L. Heim (1741–1819) and K. G. von Raumer (1783–1865), whose works are quoted elsewhere by Hegel, as well as Werner's disciples in France—A. H. Bonnard (1781–1857) and J. F. d'Aubuisson (1769–1819)—and England, also worked out classifications in which there was a general progression from primitive inorganic formations to rocks having a certain organic content. Hegel might therefore have quoted any of them as having drawn attention to the 'the sequence' which constitutes, 'the significance and spirit of the process'. The whole body of their work lent itself easily to the teleological interpretation he was looking for, and he probably mentions Werner specifically only because his classification was the best known.

The weakness of Werner's geological system was that it involved his theory of a primeval universal ocean, and that the field-work on which it was based had been carried out only in Saxony. The value of it lay in the accuracy and comprehensiveness with which he had noted the characteristics of the various rocks, and the neatness with which his graded assessment of them allowed Hegel to make the transition from 'the primary organism' constituting the subject matter of geodesy, geognosy and physical geography, to the 'animation' of the atmosphere, the sea and the land. Hegel has already pointed out that he is no Neptunist, so that when he says that Werner's assessment of the sequence is 'on the whole' correct, he probably has in mind Werner's controversy with J. K. Voigt (1752–1821) concerning the classification of basalt, C. Keferstein's critical analysis of the Wernerian classification of the fletz-formations ('Tabellen über die vergleichende Geognosie' Halle, 1825), and the dialectical imperfections in Werner's progression from the chemical and crystalline texture of granite, to the arborescent and conchyliaceous formations of coal–measures and limestone stratifications.

Werner produced two systems of geological classification. In the first ('Classification der Gebirgsarten' Dresden, 1787), he distinguished between (i) primitive rocks such as granite, gneiss, mica and argillaceous schist, porphyry, basalt etc.; (ii) fletz-formations such as limestone, marl, sandstone, greywack, coal, chalk, rock-salt, gypsum and iron-clay; (iii) volcanic rocks; and (iv) alluvial terrains. About 1796 he introduced a new class of 'transition' rocks into this system, so that his final classification distinguished between (i) primitive rocks, sub-divided according to their age into granite, gneiss, mica and argillaceous schist, which are uniformly deposited, and prophyry and syenite which accompany these uniform deposits in an irregular manner; (ii) transition rocks such as greywack, slate, chalk, trapp etc.; (iii) fletz-formations such as sandstone, fletz-chalk, gypsum, rock-salt, coal-formations, and trap rocks such as basalt etc.; (iv) alluvial rocks consisting of sand, brown-coal etc.; (v) volcanic rocks.

22, 13

,Die Geschichte der Erde ist also einerseits empirisch, andererseits ein Schließen aus empirischen Daten.'

22,21

Cf. Hegel 'Philosophy of Right' tr. T. M. Knox, Oxford, 1962. Introduction § 3.

22, 32

,Die Natur hat wesentlich Verstand'. The understanding is to be distinguished from reason on account of its failing to exhibit the unity of the Idea. In nature, as in the understanding, the Idea is divided and fragmentary. 'The understanding determines, and maintains the determinations; reason is negative and dialectical because it dissolves the determinations of the understanding into nothing; it is positive because it engenders the universal and grasps the particular within it.' ('Wissenschaft der Logik' Glockner's ed. vol. 4 p. 17).

22, 37

It is not clear why Hegel should refer to these gods by their Latin names. Pallas Athena was the daughter of Zeus and Metis. Her father had swallowed her mother before her birth, and she sprang forth from his head fully armed. She was the pre-Hellenic patroness of the Minoan and Mycenaean princes in their fortress palaces, and was probably thought of as protecting and guiding the handicrafts carried on there. In the more complex economic life of Athens her functions tended to embrace every kind of skill, until she came to be regarded as presiding over the purely *intellectual* activity of the citizens.

The Stoics put forward various allegorical interpretations of her birth; see H. Diels 'Doxographi Graeci' (Berlin, 1879) pp. 548–549. Hegel may have in mind Plato's 'Republic' 508, 509 and the interpretation of the myth mentioned by Macrobius in his 'Saturnalia' (Bk. I, 17, 66 et seq.), 'Porphyrius too asserts that Minerva is the sun's virtue, which furnishes the minds of men with wisdom. Indeed that is why the goddess is said to have sprung from the head of Jupiter, in other words, to have arisen in the topmost portion of the upper air, where the sun originated'.

The representation of her birth on the magnificent Etruscan mirror from Arezzo, which is now in the museum of Bologna, was illustrated in F.Inghirami's 'Monumenti Etruschi o di Etrusco nome disegnati' (Fiesole, 1824) vol. II plate 10. Philipp Buttmann (1764–1829), in his 'Mythologus, oder gesammelte Abhandlungen über die Sagen des Alterthums' (2 vols. Berlin, 1828) vol. I p. 28 asks, ,Ist es nun nicht natürlich, daß die Nation welche den Verstand in der Pallas personificirte, und diese, als göttlichen Verstand, aus dem Haupte der obersten Gottheit entstehen ließ, daß sie, sage ich, eben dieser Pallas den höchsten Rang nach Juppiter einräumte?' Alexander Ross (1590–1654) interprets the myth in a similar way in his delightful 'Mystagogus Poeticus' (2nd ed. London, 1653) p. 284. Cf. E. Rückert 'Der Dienst der Athena' (Hildburghausen, 1829) pp. 63, 193 etc. Dictionaries and handbooks had spread this edifying doctrine, and in Hegel's day no gentleman's library was complete without a bust of the goddess. See A. B. Cook 'Zeus: a study in ancient religion' (3 vols. Cambridge, 1914–1940) vol. III pp. 656–739.

23, 8

Hegel is here expressing his views on certain eighteenth century controversies respecting embryology and evolution; there is no evidence that he was aware of the important advances being made in these fields in the first decades of the last century by Meckel, Döllinger, Pander, von Baer etc. His opinions are by no means worthless, but his knowledge seems to have been second-hand, and was probably based upon the various philosophical interpretations of these controversies current at the time.

By not accepting 'a revolution out of chaos' as an explanation of the production of living being, he is evidently rejecting the theory of *epigenesis* put forward by C. F. Wolff (1733–1794) in his 'Theoria Generationis' (Halle, 1759), according to which, in the process of reproduction, the germ is not merely developed, but is brought into existence by successive accretions. This theory found difficulty in accounting for heredity and the formative power of the organism, and in asserting that an individual at birth, 'is already the real possibility of everything it will become', Hegel shows a tendency to accept the opposing theory of *preformation*, according to which all parts of the perfect organism exist previously formed in the germ, and are merely developed or unfolded in the process of reproduction. Swammerdam and Leibnitz had put forward this theory in the seventeenth century, but its classical formulation is to be found in the 'Elementa physiologiae corporis humani' (vols. 7 and 8, Berne, 1764–1766) of Albrecht von Haller. W. Cullen published an English version of this book: 'First lines of physiology' (Edinburgh, 1779).

When he says that such an individual, 'evolves in certain ways', and that, 'at birth', it is the real possibility of everything it will become, Hegel is evidently avoiding the *encasement* (emboîtement) theory accepted by most preformationists. According to this hypothesis, which was worked out by Charles Bonnet (1720–1793) in his 'Considérations sur les corps organisés' (Amsterdam, 1762), successive generations proceed from germs, and contain the germs of all future generations.

The theory of preformation strengthened belief in the fixity of the species. Linnaeus thought that, 'There are as many species as issued in pairs from the hands of the Creator', and it was one of Haller's tenets that, 'God has created all structures; they do not develop, but only grow.' Hegel falls in with this line of thought when he says that a determinate and complete formation is present, 'as soon as the flash of living being strikes into matter.' In denying that, 'man has formed himself out of the animal' etc., he is evidently rejecting the theory of evolution put forward by J. B. Lamarck (1744–1829) see especially the introduction to his 'Histoire naturelle des animaux sans vertèbres' (Paris, 1815).

In taking 'the point at which the soul is present' to be the principle of living being, Hegel is evidently accepting Harvey's doctrine of the 'punctum sanguineum saliens': see 'Anatomical Exercises on the Generation of Animals' no. 17, in 'The Works of William Harvey' (tr. Willis, London, 1847) p. 235, and the note on crystals III. 215.

'The general living existence which has dispersed into the various species' etc. is evidently a reference to the postulations of G. L. Buffon (1707–1788); see his 'Histoire Naturelle' (Paris, 1750) vol. 2 p. 306) 'La matière qui sert à la nutrition et à la reproduction des animaux et des végétaux est la même; c'est une substance productive et universelle composée de molécules organiques toujours existantes, toujour actives, dont la réunion produit les corps organisés. La nature travaille toujours sur le même fond, et ce fond est inépuisable; mais les moyens qu'elle emploie pour le mettre en valeur, sont différens les uns des autres.' Hegel probably knew of Buffon's theories through the works of G. R. Treviranus (1776–1837): see his 'Biologie oder Philosophie der lebenden Natur' (Göttingen, 1802–1822) vol. II p. 403. Cf. Erasmus Darwin 'Zoonomia' (2 vols. London, 1794–1796). 'Would it be too bold to imagine that all warm-blooded animals have arisen from one living filament, which the great First Cause endued with animality!'

When he says that 'natural and living being is not mixed', Hegel is evidently rejecting the theory of *animism* worked out by G. E. Stahl (1660–1734) in his 'Theoria medica vera physiologiam et pathologiam . . . sistens' (Halle, 1708), according to which the phenomena of animal life are produced by an immaterial anima or soul, which is distinct from matter. Stahl was of the opinion that any true conception of the phenomenon of life must be based upon knowledge of the mixture of the body and its parts, i.e. its chemical constituents: see 'De vera diversitate corporis mixti et vivi . . . demonstratio' (Halle, 1707): 'Philosophical Principles of Universal Chemistry. Drawn from the Collegium Jenense of G. E. Stahl. By P. Shaw.' (London, 1730): J. R. Partington 'A History of Chemistry' vol. II pp. 664–665 (London, 1961).

About 1810 J. F. Meckel (1781–1833) of Halle began to call attention to the epigenesist theories of Wolff, and in a remarkable essay published in 1811, he suggested that it might be profitable to introduce Lamarck's theory of evolution into embryological studies, 'There is no good physiologist who has not been struck by the observation that the original form of all organisms is one and the same, and that out of this one form, all, the lowest as well as the highest, are developed in such a manner that the latter pass through the permanent forms of the former as transitory stages.' ('Entwurf einer Darstellung der zwischen dem Embryozustande der höheren Thiere und den permanenten der niederen statt-findenden Parallele' in 'Beyträge zur vergleichenden Anatomie' vol. II pt. I Halle, 1811.)

While Hegel was at Heidelberg, the Russian biologist C. H. Pander (1794–1865), who had been working under professor I. Döllinger at Würzburg, published his 'Historia metamorphoseos quam ovum incubatum prioribus quinque diebus subit' (Würzburg, 1817), in which a clear description of the developing blastoderm was given for the first time, and the origin, in its three layers, of the principal rudimentary organs and systems of the embryonic chick, was noted. K. E. von Baer (1792–1876) was also studying under Döllinger at this time, and took up Pander's researches. In 1819 he moved to Königsberg, and his work there laid the foundations of modern embryology. In 1827 he announced the discovery of the mammalian ovum, and in 1829 published the first part of his 'Beobachtungen und Reflexionen über die Entwicklungsgeschichte der Thiere' (Königsberg, 2nd part 1837), in which he distinguished between the animal and vegetal layers and their intermediaries, i.e. the endoderm, ectoderm and mesoderm, and pointed out the organs which develop from them.

Unfortunately, although the work of Wolff, Pander and von Baer outdated eighteenth century speculations on embryology and evolution, and has been the basis of all subsequent developments in these fields, Hegel seems to have been completely ignorant of it. Since Hans Driesch showed by experiment in 1891, that if two blastomeres are separated at the two-cell stage, each half is able to form a pluteus, epigenesis can no longer be denied. On the other hand, Sven Hörstadius (b. 1898) has shown that the eggs of Sea Urchins contain two qualitatively different agents or substances, both of which show concentration gradients, the peak of one being the animal and the peak of the other the vegetal pole, and that the proper *ratio* of both is necessary for the formation of a normal larva. In this way, preformation has also found its place in modern embryological theory.

E. Radl 'Geschichte der Biologischen Theorien' (Leipzig, 1905–1909) tr. E. J. Hatfield (O.U.P., 1930).

L. R. Wheeler 'Vitalism: its history and validity' (London, 1930).

Joseph Needham 'A History of Embryology' 2nd ed (Cambridge, 1959).

S. J. Holmes 'K. E. von Baer's perplexities over evolution' ('Isis' 1947 pp. 7–14).

23, 36

This attempt to explain the origin of the continents and oceans bears some resemblance to the tetrahedral theory put forward by W. L. Green ('Vestiges of the molten Globe as exhibited in the figure of the earth, volcanic action and physiography' London, 1875). Green attempted to explain the apparent symmetry of the great land masses and the oceans, and suggested that as the earth cools, its outer crust is warping towards a tetrahedral shape. He pointed out that in the western hemisphere there is a large triangle of land with its apex to the south and its base to the north; that in the eastern hemisphere two triangular land masses unite at their bases to the north and have separate apices to the south; and that there is a fourth land mass around the South Pole. These four triangular land masses he took to be the four points of the tetrahedron, and pointed out that between them lie three triangular oceans, with their apices to the north and their united bases to the south. Ch. Jean Reynaud 'Terre et ciel' (Paris, 1854), J. N. Møller (1777–1862) 'Forsøg til en Characteristik af de fire Verdensdele' (C. Molbech's 'Athene' II pp. 322–344, Copenhagen, 1814, Swedish tr. Stockholm, 1815). Møller and Hegel taught together at the Grammar School in Nuremberg for a while in 1812 (note II. 307).

24, 12

,Eine ungeheure Vegetation (ist) darin vorhanden.' Michelet seems to have substituted ,ungeheure' (vast, immense, prodigious) for ,üppige' (exuberant, luxuriant, luscious). In the lectures of 1803/4 Hegel speaks of ,die ftarke Vegeta-tion' of the Americas, i.e. vigorous. See 'Jenenser Realphilosophie' I p. 95; II p. 108 n. 2.

,Üppige' is a common adjective for tropical vegetation; see Spix and Martius 'Reise in Brasilien' pt. II p. 190, ,in den üppigen Urwalbungen . . .' etc. Cf. the note II. 298.

24, 21

,der nicht ins Bewußtfeyn tretende ftumme Geift.' Michelet evidently misread the manuscript. Hegel wrote ,der nicht ins Bewußtfein tretende ſtumpfe Geiſt'. ‚Stumm' has the meaning of mute, speechless inarticulate, ‚ſtumpf' that of obtuse, dull, stupid.

24, 23

A marginal note ('Jenenser Realphilosophie' II p. 108 n. 3) may help to clarify the meaning here. Hegel writes, ‚Entſtehung, Werden, wilde Ver= wüſtung des Menſchengeſ(chlechtes)'.

For a fuller exposition of Hegel's views on geographical anthropology, see his 'Philosophy of History' (tr. Sibree, Dover Publications, 1956) pp. 79–102.

24, 28

On the state of geography and related studies at the beginning of the nine-teenth century, see Oscar Peschel 'Geschichte der Erdkunde bis A. v. Humboldt und Carl Ritter' (Munich, 1865), and K. A. von Zittel 'Geschichte der Geologie und Paläontologie bis Ende des 19. Jahrhunderts' (Munich, 1899).

John Pinkerton (1758–1826), at the beginning of his 'Modern Geography' (3 vols. London, 1807) gives a lucid account of what was at that time considered to be the scope of the subject, 'What is called General Geography embraces a wide view of the subject, regarding the earth astronomically as a planet, the grand divisions of land and water, the winds, tides and meteorology etc. and may extend to what is called the mechanical part of geography, in directions for the construction of globes, maps, and charts . . .

Among other divisions of this science may be named Sacred Geography and Physical Geography, or Geology, which investigates the interior of the earth . . .

But Geography, popularly considered, is occupied in the description of the various regions of this globe as being divided among various nations, and improved by human art and industry.'

25, 11

Oryctognosy (Greek ὀρυκτός 'dug up' γνῶσις 'knowledge'). An eight-eenth century term for the science of fossils, or whatever is dug from the earth. 'Oryctognosy teaches us to know fossils, to recognize them whenever they occur to us. For this purpose it exhibits the subjects of the mineral kingdom to our view arranged in an *order* corresponding as nearly as possible with that of their *affinities*, and distinguished from each other by *appropriate denominations* and by determinate and *defined characters*.' A. G. Werner 'A Treatise on the External Characters of Fossils', (tr. T. Weaver, Dublin, 1805) p. 2.

Cf. also Werner's 'Oryktognosie, oder Handbuch für die Liebhaber der Mineralogie' (Leipzig, 1792); James Parkinson 'Outlines of Oryctology' (London, 1822). In his 'Elements of Geology' (1838), Sir Charles Lyell (1797–1875) referred to this science as 'palaeontology', and as it became more special-ized and differentiated, the older term fell out of use.

25, 19

Werner's account of this distinction is to be found in his 'Neue Theorie von der Entstehung der Gänge' (Freiberg, 1791, Eng. tr. C. Anderson 'New Theory of the Formation of Veins', Edinburgh, 1809).

Werner was not the first to make the distinction however, for it is also to be found in 'Anleitung zur Markscheidekunst nach ihren Anfangsgründen und Ausübungen kürzlich entworfen' (Dresden, 1749) by F. W. von Oppel (1720–1769). Part two of this work is entitled ‚Von den Streichen und Fallen derer Gänge und Klüfte.'

‚Ein Gang (vena) . . . ist ein in einem Gebürge sich weit ausbreitender Riß und Trennung des Gesteins, welche mit einem von dem Gebürge unterschiedenen Gestein angefüllet ist.

Weder eine Kluft noch Gang richten sich nach der Lage des Gesteins, und sie können die Lager eines Gebürges durchsetzen.

Das Gestein, mit welchem eine solche Trennung und Spaltung des Gebürges angefüllet ist, und welches in Ansehung des Gebürges, durch welches der Gang setzet, jederzeit frembartig befunden wird, wird dessen Gangart genennet.

Es ist also ein Gang mit einem andern Gestein angefüllet, als mit demjenigen, aus welchem das Gebürge bestehet, und welches man die Bergart nennet.' (pp. 233–234).

25, 35

Werner 'Neue Theorie von der Enstehung der Gänge' (Freiberg, 1791) § 2 ‚Gänge sind plattenförmiche besondere Lagerstädte der Fossilien, welche fast immer die Schichten des Gesteins durchschneiden, und in soferne eine von diesen abweichende Lage haben, auch mit einer von der Gebirgsart mehr oder weniger verschiedenen Maße angefüllet sind.'

26, 2

Cf. F. M. Bullard 'Volcanoes in history, in theory, in eruption' (Univ. of Texas 1962); F. Hoffmann 'Geschichte der Geognosie' (Berlin, 1838) pp. 271–596.

Werner supported the conjecture that most volcanoes arise from the combustion of underground seams of coal, and in 1826 C. G. B. Daubeny (1795–1867) put forward a chemical theory of volcanic activity ('A Description of Active and Extinct Volcanoes' London, 1826). In Hegel's day however, the formation of volcanoes was generally explained in terms of von Humboldt's and von Buch's crater-elevation hypothesis, according to which molten material rises from below and arches the earth's crust into a blister or dome. This theory was challenged in 1825 by G. J. P. Scrope (1797–1876), who after studying Vesuvius, Etna and the volcanic regions of Central France, published 'Considerations on Volcanos', (London, 1825, German tr. Berlin, 1872). This book was dedicated to Lyell, and had as its object, 'to dispel that signal delusion as to the mode of action of subtelluric forces with which the crater- elevation theory has mystified the geological world.' Scrope's 'craters of accumulation' theory laid the foundation of modern vulcanology.

26,18

Werner and the neptunists regarded granite as a chemical precipitate from a universal ocean, on the bed of which it had served as a foundation for the stratified rocks. Hutton and the vulcanists regarded it as the consolidation of matter made fluid by heat. Lyell agreed with Hutton as to its origin, but suggested that as it is so frequently associated with transformed rocks (which he was the first to call 'metamorphic'), it may itself be metamorphic in origin.

Although he insists upon the 'primary' nature of granite, Hegel avoids discussing its origin, and his exposition of its significance accords well with H. H. Read's conclusion in 'The Granite Controversy' (London, 1957): 'Each granite is a unit to be discussed by itself, to be related to its setting and to be interpreted on its intrinsic evidence' (p. xix).

26, 36

Heinrich Steffens (1773–1845) 'Geognostische-geologische Aufsätze' (Hamburg, 1810) p. 205, , Am meisten von den übrigen Lagern der Urgebirge getrennt in sich am einfachsten erscheint der Urkalk, indes die übrigen Gebirgsmassen, und wenn sie auch noch so verschieden sind, durch den alles verbindenden Feldspath oder durch den Quarz ein vermittelndes Glied erhalten. In den Urgebirgen scheint sich der Gegensatz zwischen den Kalkgebergen und den übrigen Gebirgsarten am reinsten erhalten zu haben.'

Some of Steffens' views may have been undisciplined, but this did not prevent him from producing some extremely valuable, systematic and detailed work on geological subjects cf. his 'Handbuch der Oryktognosie' (4 vols. Halle, 1811–1824): note II. 253.

27, 15

J. G. Ebel (1764–1830) 'Ueber den Bau der Erde in dem Alpen-Gebirge' (2 vols. Zürich, 1808) vol. I pp. 63–64. Ebel speaks of 'a series of extremely diverse (mannigfaltigsten) relationships' between the constituents of gneiss, but Hegel omits the adjective.

27, 25

In a marginal note at this point, Hegel writes, ,Heim ganz abgesondert.' 'Jenenser Realphilosophie' II p. 112 n. 3.

27, 33

Johann Ludwig Heim (1741–1819), councillor to the Duke of Saxe-Meiningen, brother of the popular Berlin doctor Ernst Ludwig Heim (1747–1834).

Hegel is here referring to his 'Geologische Beschreibung des Thüringer Waldge-bürgs. Von der innern Einrichtung des Gebürgs nach seinen Gebürgslagern' (3 parts Meiningen, 1796–1812).

This work was the result of a very careful geological survey of the Thüringerwald, which occupied Heim for twenty years. As a hand-book for field-work in the area it proved to be indispensable, although its usefulness in this respect was somewhat limited by Heim's failure to provide any accompanying maps. It is remarkable on account of the accuracy and detail of the observations it contains, its freedom from the Wernerianism prevalent when it was being written, and, as Hegel notes, on account of the attention it draws to the related-ness of certain rocks.

Heim regarded basalt as volcanic in origin, he was the first to draw attention to the close relationship between granite and porphyry, and he made useful suggestions as to the origin of dolomite.

28, 10

Greywack (German ‚Grauwacke'). This term was introduced into English by Robert Jameson ('Elements of Geognosy' Edinburgh, 1808). As he used it, it covered practically all Werner's 'transition' rocks (Upper pre-Cambrian and Lower Palaeozoic), sedimentary rocks other than limestone, and hard schistous mudstones. It was used so loosely, that by 1839 it had become useless as a means of mineralogical definition: see R. I. Murchison 'The Silurian System' (London, 1839). Fairly recently, (Bailey, 'Geological Magazine' 1930) it has been proposed to revive it as a term for certain sandstones.

In German geological terminology the term has retained a more precise meaning however, and signifies a conglomeratic breccia, grey or red in colour and granular or schistous in texture, consisting of fragments of quartz, argillac-eous and siliceous schist, and grains of felspar and micaceous lamina, set in a siliceous, argillaceous or calcareous matrix.

28, 11

Greenstone (German ‚Grünstein'). This term was brought into use towards the end of the eighteenth century to cover all those varieties of dark, greenish, igneous rocks which in more recent terminology would be referred to as diorites, dolerites and somewhat altered basalts. It is now obsolete in German also.

28, 13

Trappean formation. (Swedish 'trapp', so named from the stairlike appearance often presented by the rock, formed on 'trappa' stair.) The term was used by Swedish miners long before it was introduced into the written language about the middle of the eighteenth century. The first mineralogist to classify it was Axel von Cronstedt (1722–1765): see 'Försök til Mineralogie eller Mineral

Rikets Upställning' (Stockholm, 1758, Eng. tr. G. von Engström ed. J. H. Magellen, London, 1788 p. 880). At that time however, Swedish mineralogists were not agreed as to the exact meaning of the term or the origin of the rocks covered by it. Sven Rinman (1720–1792), in his 'Bergwerkslexicon' (2 vols. Stockholm 1788–1789) p. 1023, noted that it was used to refer to rocks differing widely in texture and hardness, but generally consisting of clay hardened with silica and iron, and usually occurring in considerable gangues. He mentions the 'rowly-ragg' found in England, and the 'Schwarze Wacke' found in Germany as rocks corresponding to Swedish trap.

From the local names for it, it is clear that Swedish miners regarded it as aqueous in origin; the 'Saxum Danemorense' found in the Dannemora iron-mines and mentioned in the English translation of Cronstedt's book (op. cit.), was known locally as 'vattband' (water-band) for example. T. O. Bergman (1735–1784) submitted 'trap' to chemical analysis, and came to the conclusion that it differed very little from basalt, although he was convinced that unlike basalt, it had never been affected by heat: 'De Productis Vulcanicis' (Uppsala, 1783) p. 213: 'T. Bergmann . . . Kleine Physische und Chymische Werke' iii p. 259, (tr. H. Tabor, Frankfurt-on-Main, 1785).

This uncertainty as to the use of the term and the origin of the rocks it referred to gave rise to further controversies once it was taken over into German geological nomenclature.

In his assessment of this formation Hegel keeps to Werner's first system (1787), in which trap rocks were classified as primitive, although in his second system, they were classified as a fletz-formation. Werner did not regard them as an independent rock-type, but as a distinct group of rocks composed mainly of felspar and hornblend. He distinguished between (i) primitive trap, including greenstone, hornblend, green porphyry and diorite etc.; (ii) transition trap, including amygdaloid and wacke; and (iii) fletz-trap, including basalt formations. The term has since been extended to include all igneous rocks which are neither granitic nor of recent volcanic formation.

28, 15

In the lectures of 1805–6 Hegel takes porphyry to be the 'limit of these absolute rocks'. ‚Der Glimmer wird aber zum Ton vorzüglich in Porphyr, (der) die Grenze dieser absoluten Gebirge (ist).' 'Jenenser Realphilosophie' II p. 110.

28, 24

N. Desmarest (1735–1815) was the first to establish the plausibility of the proposition that basalt is volcanic in origin: see 'Mémoire sur l'origine et la nature du Basalte . . . observé en Auvergne' ('Histoire de l'Academie Royale des Sciences' 1771 pp. 705–775, Paris, 1774).

T. O. Bergman (1735-1784) submitted the rock to chemical analysis, and came to the conclusion that Swedish basalt from Hunneberg in Västergötland did not differ from that found on the island of Staffa. He argued that as the rock has none of the porous and slaggy texture of lava, and that as marl also is frequently separated into columns, it was probably not volcanic in origin: see 'De productis vulcanicis' (Uppsala, 1783): 'T. Bergmann . . . Kleine Physische und Chymische Werke' vol. III p. 259 (tr. H. Tabor, Frankfurt-on-Main, 1785). Werner's later classification of basalt was almost certainly influenced by Bergman's work.

Werner's re-classification gave rise to the controversy concerning the origin of basalt: see C. Keferstein 'Geschichte des Basaltes' (Halle, 1819). J. F. d'Aubuisson (1769-1819) began his career as an orthodox neptunist, but a first-hand study of the basalts of Auvergne convinced him of their volcanic origin: see 'Sur les volcans et les basaltes de l'Auvergne' ('Bulletin des Sciences de la Société Philomathique de Paris' 1804 p. 182). L. von Buch (1774-1853) also began his career as a Wernerian, but was convinced of their volcanic origin by 1809: see 'Geognostische Beobachtungen auf Reisen' pt. II.

It was the opposition these men encountered from orthodox neptunists which more than any advance in the geological sciences, served to lessen Werner's authority. Hegel retains Werner's original classification because he regards basalt as being related to the 'absolute' rocks by reason of its composition and structure. He therefore regards its origin as a matter of comparative indifference.

28, 40

Talc, serpentine, steatite, soapstone, olivine, peridotite etc. are all magnesium silicates, and olivine and peridotite are certainly igneous in origin. In his dialectical interpretation of the primitive rocks, Hegel takes the formations of this silicate to be the mediating moment in the progression from siliceous graniticity to the calcareousness of primitive limestone. 'The property of bitterness' possessed by these rocks is due to their magnesia content; dolomite was once known as 'bitter-spar' for example, and it was in allusion to its magnesia content that J. F. L. Hausmann (1782-1859) called serpentine of a columnar or coarsely fibrous kind 'picrolite' (Greek πικρός, bitter).

Light may be thrown upon Hegel's formulation of this moment by comparing it with the account of the 'Magnesian Earth' given by A. F. Cronstedt (1722-1765): 'An Essay towards a System of Mineralogy' (Stockholm 1768; Eng. tr. G. von Engström London, 1788 pp. 93-119). Pierre Bayen (1725-1798) analysed serpentine chemically: 'Opuscules Chimiques' vol. II p. 128 (Paris, 1798).

A progression similar to that made by Hegel at this juncture is made by Alexandre Brongniart (1770-1847), in his 'Tableau des Terrains qui composent l'écorce du globe' pp. 311-312 (Paris, 1829), i.e. from what he calls 'terrains hemilysiens talqueux' to 'terrain primordiaux de cristallisation', which include calcareous formations.

Dolomite, which is a double-salt consisting of calcium and magnesium carbonate, may be regarded as the moment realizing the transition from granite to calcareousness. It was chemically analyzed by M. H. Klaproth (1743–1817) in 1804. Cf. Leopold von Buch (1774–1853) 'Ueber Dolomit als Gebirgsart' ('Abhandlungen der Berliner Akademie' 1822–1823, pp. 93–136.)

29, 12

Karl Georg von Raumer (1783–1865) studied under Werner at the Freiberg Mining Academy, and was later councillor of mines at Breslau. The war years took him to France and England, and enabled him to acquaint himself with the geologists and geological structures of these countries (see his 'Geognostische Umrisse von Frankreich, England, einem Theil von Deutschland' etc. Berlin, 1816). From 1811 until 1813 he was professor of mineralogy at Breslau, and from 1819 until 1823 member of the chief mining office and professor of mineralogy at Halle. He then taught at Nuremberg for a time, and in 1827 was appointed professor of natural history at Erlangen.

While he was still a student at Freiberg, his discovery of a granite lying *above* younger rock strata caused Werner to reconsider his views on granite formation. In 1808, together with Engelhardt, he investigated the granites and syenites on the north eastern edge of the Erzgebirge, where these hills dip away into the valley of the Elbe, and in his 'Geognostische Fragmente' (Nuremberg, 1811), he was able to point out that in this area Werner's 'transition rocks' often underlie his 'primitive rocks'. This was of course a great blow to the orthodox neptunist theory of rock-formation, and the book caused a great stir.

By assessing rocks by concentrating upon their composition and structure rather than upon the chronological sequence of their formation, and insufficiently substantiated theories of their general history, Hegel avoided becoming involved in open questions of this kind.

The work Hegel quotes at this juncture, ('Geognostische Versuche von Moritz von Engelhardt und Karl von Raumer' Berlin, 1815) falls into two parts: (1) ‚Das Schiefergebirge des nordwestlichen Teutschlands, der Niederlände und des nordöstlichen Frankreichs,' and (2) ‚Das Kreide ... und Sand-Gebilde — besonders in der Gegend von Paris.'

It may be of value to quote at length the passage Hegel refers to here, because where Hegel speaks of primitive limestone (Urkalk), Raumer speaks of a close-textured calcareous stone (dichten Kalkstein).

‚§ 7 Kalkstein. So erscheinen die Schiefer als ein Gestein, in welchem die Keime anderer Gebirgsarten schlummern, aus denen sich diese entwickeln; oder — mögte vielmehr der Oryktognost sagen — in welche sich die eigenthümliche Natur der Quarz-, Feldspath-, Glimmer- und Hornblende-Bildungen auflöst und verliert. In einem ganz anderen Verhältniß stehen die Schiefer zum dichten Kalkstein, welcher nächst ihnen in unserm Gebirgszuge vorwaltet. Seine Natur ist durchaus verschieden von der Natur der Schiefer; er mengt sich aber mit ihnen, wechselt mit ihnen in dünnen Lagen, in Schichten, in mächtigen Lagern, bis er zuweilen Stücke Gebirge bildet in welchen der Schiefer fast ganz unterdrückt ist.' (p. 13).

Cf. p. 19 ‚Der Thonschiefer wechselt zwar häufig mit dem Kalksteine, ist aber im Ganzen nicht so mächtig. Bemerkenswerth sind Dachschiefer-Brüche von Steenkerken unweit Enghien.'

30, 4

'The metallic magma' (‚der aufgelöste Brei von Metallen') Cf. Werner's 'Neue Theorie von der Entstehung der Gänge' (Freiberg, 1791), '§ 28 Alle wahre Gänge sind ... von oben herein ausgefüllte Spalten ... § 62 (Ch. VI) Beweise über die Ausfüllung der offenen Gang-Räume durch nassen Niederschlag von oben herein.'

Bearing in mind the neptunist theory, one might translate Hegel's ‚Brei' (which is not a term peculiar to him) and Werner's ‚nassen Niederschlag' as 'solution' or 'sludge'. If 'magma' is understood here in its original Greek sense however, i.e. as a plastic mass or a paste of solid and liquid matter, and not in its modern sense, i.e. as a subterranean lava, the word will cover Hegel's meaning.

30, 12

Friedrich Wilhelm Heinrich von Trebra (1740–1819) was born in the Palatinate. From 1769 until 1773 he was chief mining officer at Marienberg in the Erzgebirge. In 1780 he was appointed deputy director of mines at Zellerfeld in the Harz, in 1791 director of mines at Klausthal, and in 1801 chief director of mines at Freiberg. Apart from numerous articles on geology, which appeared in various periodicals, he wrote 'Erfahrungen vom Innern der Gebirge' (Leipzig, 1786) and 'Die Bergbaukunde' (2 vols. Leipzig, 1789–1790).

His reputation rests mainly on the first of these books, which is elegantly and charmingly written, and well supplied with good plates. Only a year after its publication in German, a magnificent French edition of it appeared at Paris: 'Observations de M. de Trébra sur L'Intérieur des Montagnes, précédées d'un plan d'un Histoire générale de la Mineralogie par M. de Veltheim. ed. M. le Baron de Dietrich.'

In this work, Trebra gives a geological description of the Harz, and it was his account of the greywack of this area, of the rocks, that occur with it, and of the fossilized animals and plants which it contains, which led Werner to introduce the new classification of 'transition rocks' into his later system. Trebra tries to account for the formation of rocks by means of 'fermentation' and 'decomposition'; he regards gneiss as a transformation of granite, argillaceous schist as a transformation of greywack, and clay as a transformation of quartz etc.

Trebra has many references to the gentle slopes of lodes (French ed. pp. 21, 97, 182, 246 etc.). Hegel may well have had in mind the passage which occurs on page 246 of the French edition, 'Pour saisir d'un coup d'oeil l'ensemble d'une chaîne de filon principale, suivant les trois dimensions, longueur, largeur et profondeur, il faut rapprocher toutes les figures de nos planches . . . La planche III prouve ce que nous avons déjà observé à plusiers reprises, que les points les plus puissons se trouvent dans les vallons à pentes douces.'

30, 18

Knowledge of the paragenesis of metals is still very incomplete, so that in many cases this determining is still a matter of *experience*, and cannot be *explained*. 'In each of these two classes' (of isomorphism, or the formation of mixed crystals) 'the association is natural and what might be expected to occur on general chemical and physical grounds. There are however other instances of metal associations, many of them of great economic importance, for which no reason can as yet be assigned.' —R. H. Rastall 'The Geology of Metalliferous Deposits' (Cambridge, 1923).

30, 21

C. T. Delius (1728–1779) 'Abhandlung von dem Ursprunge der Gebürge und der darinne befindlichen Erzadern, oder der sogenannten Gänge und Klüfte; ingleichen von der Vererzung der Metalle und insonderheit des Goldes' (Leipzig, 1770).

Delius regards rocks and lodes as aqueous in origin. He assumes that the mother rock split while drying out, and that the fissures were subsequently filled with the aqueous magma now forming the lodes. He discusses the occurrence of gold at some length (pp. 87–157), and is almost certainly the ultimate source of Hegel's information on the subject. Cf. F. von Kobell 'Geschichte der Mineralogie' pp. 559–564 (Munich, 1864); E. J. Dunn 'Geology of Gold' ch. XV (London, 1929).

30, 37

‚Die alte (tobtliegende) Sandstein-Formation.' The rock Hegel is referring to forms part of the sandy conglomeratic subdivision of the Permian system, which flanks the Harz and is also found in the Rhine Provinces, Saxony, Thuringia, Bavaria and Bohemia. It was called the red-dead-layer (Rothtobtliegende) by the miners who worked the cobalt and copper-bearing slate (Kupferschiefer) of these areas, because it was into these red rocks lying beneath the slate that the lodes they worked tended to disappear.

Heinrich Veith, in his 'Deutsches Bergwörterbuch' (Breslau, 1870) pp. 493–4 observes that, 'the terms red-layer or dead layer are not exactly some of the most brilliant to be found in geological nomenclature; the term red-dead-layer, from which they originate, is however a nomenclatural monstrosity which quite clearly originates in the language of the miners of Thuringia.' In England, the millstone grit into which the coal seams disappear was known to the miners as 'farewell-rock', and in France the unproductive rocks flanking these seams were known as 'les terrains d'adieu.' Cf. C. F. Naumann 'Lehrbuch der Geognosie' (Leipzig, 1850) II 583: F. A. Römer 'Synopsis der Mineralogie und Geognosie' (Hanover, 1853) 337.

As the pioneer work of William Smith (1769-1839) enabled his countrymen to become more intimately acquainted with the English fletz-formations, attempts were made to identify them with the German formations which were already well-known in England as the result of Werner's disciples. There was some doubt as to the identity of this 'primordial and moribund sandstone formation.' J. C. Prichard, in his 'Remarks on the older floetz strata of England' (T. Thomson's 'Annals of Philosophy' First Series vol. VI pp. 20-26, 1815) is of the opinion that although there is little correspondence between German and English formations, this German rock may be identified with the old red sandstone of the west Midlands etc. W. Buckland (1784-1856) paid several visits to Germany in order to settle the matter, and in his 'On the structure of the Alps . . . and their relation to the Secondary and Transition rocks of England' (T. Thomson's 'Annals of Phil.' Second Series vol. I pp. 450-468, 1821) comes to the conclusion that the closest English equivalent is the 'Exeter conglomerate'.

Thomas Weaver (1773-1855), who was well acquainted with the German geological literature of his day, supported Prichard's view in his 'Additional remarks on the Rothe Todte Liegende of German geologists', and defended it when it was challenged by Conybeare and Phillips (T. Thomson's 'Annals of Phil.' Second Series vol. V pp. 321-340, 1823; vol. VIII pp. 11-22, 1824).

31, 10

For details concerning these mining areas and mineral deposits see Carl Hintze 'Handbuch der Mineralogie' (7 vols. Leipzig, 1897-1933): J. F. Zückert 'Die Naturgeschichte und Bergwerksverfassung des Unterharzes' (Berlin, 1763) 'Die Naturgeschichte und Bergwerksverfassung des Oberharzes' (Berlin, 1762); Joseph von Sperges 'Tyrolische Bergwerksgeschichte' (Vienna, 1765); C. F. Mosche 'Zur Geschichte des Bergbaues in Deutschland' (Liegnitz, 1829); F. A. Römer 'Synopsis der Mineralogie und Geognosie' (Hanover, 1853).

31, 22

'Reise in Brasilien auf Befehl Sr. Majestät Maximilien Joseph I Königs von Baiern in den Jahren 1817 bis 1820 gemacht' vol. I p. 332.

This book was prepared by J. B. Spix (1781-1826), a friend of Schelling's and K. F. P. Martius (1794-1868), from the records of their travels, and published by subscription in three volumes quarto (Munich, 1823, 1828, 1831). As Spix died during the preparation of the second volume, the greater part of the work was carried out by Martius, who was director of the botanical garden at Munich from 1832 until 1864.

Cf. Jakob Frischholz 'Ueber den Salzburger Smaragd.' (K. E. von Moll 'Neue Jahrbücher' IV pp. 382–385, 1821.)

32, 15

From 1804 until 1806 Henrik Steffens (1773–1845) was professor of Philosophy, Mineralogy, Physiology and Natural History at Halle. His 'Grundzüge der Philosophischen Naturwissenschaft' (Berlin, 1806) was written as a textbook for his lectures there, and it is evidently to pp. 115–116 of this work that Hegel is here referring. ,Die Animalisation schließt sich in den Flötzgebirgen an die Kalklager, die Vegetation an die Flötztrappgebirge und Sandsteinformationen — die letztern als Fortsetzung der Schieferbildung. Daher alle Thierversteinerungen kalkig, alle Pflanzenversteinerungen kieselig ... Kalk und Kiesel sind organische Residuen der Animalisation und Vegetation, und nicht als solche von außen in die Organisation hineingetreten.'

33, 12

Hegel's opinions on the origin of these shells were conventional and traditional rather than well informed. As he regarded the new geological chronology of his day as philosophically insignificant (§ 339), he found it difficult to grasp its importance in the development of palaeontology being pioneered by Lamarck ('Histoire naturelle des animaux sans vertèbres' 1815–1822), James Parkinson ('Outlines of Oryctology' London, 1822), and E. F. Schlotheim ('Die Petrefaktenkunde' Gotha, 1820–1823). He therefore based his interpretation of these shells upon the generally accepted theories of the seventeenth and eighteenth centuries.

James Woodward (1665–1728), in 'Fossils of all Kinds, digested into a Method' (London, 1728), distinguished between 'native' formations, which he took to be mineral in origin, and 'extraneous' formations, which he regarded as the remains of living creatures.

Robert Plot (1640–1696), in his 'Natural History of Oxfordshire' (Oxford, 1705 p. 112) mentions an 'organic-plasticity' in connection with the origin of fossilized shells, 'This brings me to consider the great question, now so much controverted in the World, whether the Stones we find in the Forms of Shellfish, be Lapides sui generis, naturally produced by some extraordinary plastic virtue, latent in the Earth or Quarries where they are found? Or, whether they rather owe their Form and Figuration to the Shells of the Fishes they present, brought to the places where they are now found by Deluge, Earth-quake, or some other means.'

At the beginning of the last century 'plasticity' was still regarded as an attribute of a formative principle giving rise to organisms, and corresponding to the 'vis formativa' of Aristotle: see A. von Humboldt, 'Versuche über die Gereizte Muskel und Nervenfaser' (Berlin, 1797) vol. I p. 180: Reil's 'Archiv für die Physiologie' vol. 1 sect. ii p. 281: Sprengel 'Instit. med.' vol. 1 p. 104. Hegel evidently regarded it as a link between crystallization and organic formation.

34, 7

'Generatio aequivoca', i.e. spontaneous generation, the development of living organisms without the agency of pre-existing living matter. This development was usually considered to be the result of changes taking place in some inorganic substance.

Prior to Pasteur (1822–1895), the concept was used to account for internal parasites, infusoria and bacteria. Towards the close of the nineteenth century it gave rise to hypotheses such as abiogenesis, autogeny and plasmogeny, which were used in the attempt to explain the simplest forms of life.

Francesco Redi (1626–1698) had called the doctrine of spontaneous generation in question by showing that flies were the cause of maggots in rotten meat: see 'Esperienze Intorno Alla Generazione Degl' Insetti' (Florence, 1668: Eng. tr. M. Bigelow Chicago, 1909 'Experiments on the Generation of Insects.'). John T. Needham (1713–1781) defended it in his, 'Observations upon the generation, composition and decomposition of Animal and Vegetable Substances' (London, 1749), but was worsted by L. Spallanzani (1729–1799) in the controversy which followed the publication of this book.

Priestley's discovery of oxygen in 1774 gave the doctrine a new lease of life, but by the early years of the nineteenth century it was again being questioned: see T. A. Knight's discussion (1813) of the supposed generation of mushrooms from horse-dung by vital powers, 'For, if a mass of horse-dung can generate a mushroom, it can scarcely be denied that a mass of animal matter, an old cheese may generate a mite; and if the organs of a mite can be thus formed, there can be little difficulty in believing that a larger mass of decomposing matter might generate an elephant, or a man.' ('Transactions of the Horticultural Society of London' vol. II p. 83 London, 1818).

34, 25

‚Indem die Erde aber auch ein besonderer Körper gegen ihrer Trabanten,' (sic) ‚die Sonne und die Kometen ist'.

36, 3

‚theils verwandelt sie sich in Meteore als vergängliche Kometen — in Erden, die sie erzeugt, d.h. Atmosphärilien.' The original text differs from this somewhat, ‚teils in die vergänglichen Kometen (und) Meteore, teils in Erden, die sie erzeugt, Atmosphärilien'. ('Jenenser Realphilosophie' II p. 106).

36, 5

Aerolites. When he regards them as atmospheric formations, Hegel is keeping to the traditional opinion as to the origin of aerolites. E. F. F. Chladni (1756–1827), in his consideration of the iron masses found by P. S. Pallas (1741–1811) in Russia, came to the correct conclusion that they were extra-terrestrial and not atmospheric in origin: 'Ueber den Ursprung der von Pallas gefundenen und anderer ähnlicher Eisenmassen' (Leipzig, 1794). Chladni subsequently backed up his thesis with a wealth of detail from a wide range of sources, and so initiated the modern approach to this subject: 'Ueber Feuer-Meteore und über die mit denselben herabgefallenen Massen' (Vienna, 1819).

Miasmata. (Greek μιασμα, pollution). 'The Edinburgh Medical and Physical Dictionary' by R. Morris and J. Kendrick (2 vols. Edinburgh, 1807) gives the following information on 'miasma', and shows that microbiology had not as yet given any very precise meaning to the term, 'Miasma . . . is a particle of poison, in a volatile state, borne on the wings of the atmosphere, and capable of attaching itself to an animal body so as to produce disease. Miasmata, as they relate to diseases, are productive of some of the febrile kinds, and of them only, as in the case of Contagion. They are, in the atmosphere, not observed to act, except when a healthy body approaches the sources from whence they arise; or else is brought into contact with some substances, which are imbued with the noxious effluvia. The idea of *contagion* properly implies a matter arising from a body under disease; and that of miasma, a matter arising from other substances, so from putrefying vegetables etc.' Cf. 'Sur les differens miasmes contagieux' ('Mém. de Turin' 1805–1808. vol. IX p. 92); Michael Underwood (1736–1820), 'A treatise on disorders of childhood' (4th ed. London, 1799, I p. 288), 'I have attended where children born in an air, saturated as it were, with the miasma of this disease,' (small-pox) 'and even lying continually in a cradle in which another child has died a few days before, have, nevertheless escaped the disease.' Cf. J. S. T. Gehler's 'Physikalisches Wörterbuch' vol. I pp. 475–488 (Leipzig, 1825).

Honey-dew. R. A. F. Réaumur (1683–1757), in his 'Mémoires pour servir à l'histoire des insectes' (6 vols. Amsterdam, 1734–1742, vol. 3 pt. 2 p. 46), had shown that aphides are the principal cause of honey-dew. Towards the end of the century Gilbert White (1720–1793) was still speculating on its origin however; see 'The Natural History of Selbourne' ed. Allen, 1898, p. 471, 'June 4th 1783. Fast honey-dews this week. The reason of these seems to be that in hot days the effluvia of flowers are drawn up by a brisk evaporation, and then in the night fall down with the dews with which they are entangled.' By 1802 however, Réaumur's views were generally accepted in England; see W. Curtis 'Observations on Aphides, chiefly intended to show that they are the principal Cause of Blights in Plants, and the sole cause of Honey-dew.' ('Trans. of the Linnean Soc.' vol. vi pp. 75–95, London, 1802). L. C. Treviranus (1779–1864) regarded honey-dew as the natural excretion of leaves; see, 'Ueber die süssen Ausschwitzungen der Blätter,' in 'Vermischte Schriften' (Göttingen, 1816, vol. vi, p. 89).

Aphides and Coccideae are the most frequent, but not the *sole* cause of honey-dew. A fungus—Claviceps—also causes it, and in some tropical plants such as Caesalpina and Calliandra, it appears to be excreted by the ordinary processes of overturgescence pressing the liquid through the water-pores.

Mildew. See T. A. Knight 'On the Prevention of Mildew in particular cases' (a paper read to the Horticultural Society of London on May 4, 1813, published in the 'Transactions' of this Society vol. II p. 82 in 1818), 'This disease originates in a minute species of parasitical fungus, which is propagated, like other plants, by seeds.' Cf. James Robertson 'On the Mildew' etc. ('Transactions of the Horticultural Society of London' vol. V pp. 175-179, 1824) 'It has been a question, whether it was of animal or vegetable origin, or a fortuitous produc-tion, but it is now generally admitted to be a parasitic fungus, and that those parts of it which are apparent, form the fructification.'

36, 8

See Newton's 'Mathematical Principles' (ed. Cajori, Berkeley, 1947) bk. iii prop. 36 prob. 16, prop. 37 prob. 18: 'System of the World' par. 38–54.

36, 24

This is probably a reference to the 'nymphs called Naiads of the windring brooks', the tutelary spirits of springs and rivers. (Greek Ναϊάς, Ναϊάδ, related to νάειν to flow, νᾶμα running water). Nevertheless, Hegel could be referring to the generative powers of *Naididae* (Naiden, Wasserschlängelchen): Abraham Trembley (1700–1784), in his 'Mémoires pour servir à l'histoire d'un genre de Polypes d'eau douce (Leyden, 1744, Germ. tr. J. A. E. Goeze, Quedlinburg, 1775) first described the multiplication of these Water-worms by means of *voluntary division,* and O. F. Müller (1730–1784), in his 'Von Würmern des süssen und salzigen Wassers' (Copenhagen, 1771) gave a detailed and precise description of this form of generation.

Cf. W. H. Roscher 'Ausführliches Lexikon der Griechischen und Römischen Mythologie' (Leipzig, 1897–1909) vol. iii cols. 507–515.

36, 26

Aristotle took the sources of spring water to be percolated rain water, the condensation of air within the earth and the condensation of vapours which have risen from the earth. He observed that, 'We do not call water that flows anyhow a river, even if there is a great quantity of it, but only if the flow comes from a spring' ('Meteorologica' Book I ch. 13 2–20). Until the close of the eighteenth century, these views, together with the difficulties which hydrologists encoun-tered in their attempts to explain artesian wells etc., coloured most theories as to the origin of springs and rivers.

However, Bernard Palissy (1510–1589) suggested that springs might be caused solely by water percolating down and collecting between non-porous strata:

'Discours admirable de la nature des eaux et fontaines tant naturelles qu'artificielles' (Paris, 1580, Eng. tr. E. E. Willett, Brighton, 1876), and E. Mariotte (1620–1684) confirmed this hypothesis by experiment: 'Traité de mouvement des eaux' (Paris, 1668, 2nd ed. 1700, Eng. tr. 'The Motion of Water and other Fluids' by J. T. Desaguiliers, London, 1718).

By the end of the eighteenth century John Dalton (1766–1844) had shown beyond reasonable doubt that the rain and dew of the areas he had investigated were equivalent to the quantity of water carried from them by evaporation and rivers: 'Experiments and Observations to determine whether the quantity of Rains and Dew is equal to the quantity of Water carried off by the Rivers and raised by Evaporation, with an Enquiry into the origin of Springs.' ('The Literary and Philosophical Society of Manchester,' March 1, 1799).

Hegel may have revived Aristotle's views on this subject on account of the hypothesis put forward by Prof. J. K. P. Grimm of Breslau, that subterranean water is formed chemically from hydrogen and oxygen: 'Ueber den Ursprung des unterirdischen Wassers' ('Gilbert's Annalen der Physik' 1799 vol. II pp. 336–345). G. H. O. Volger (1822–1897) attempted to revive the Aristotelian hypotheses as recently as 1877: 'Zeitschrift des Vereins deutscher Ingenieure' vol. XXI, but the theoretical basis of his argument was demolished soon afterwards by J. Hann: 'Zeitschrift für Meteorologie,' 1887 p. 388.

In the geological literature of his day, the closest approximation to Hegel's views on the origin and nature of springs and on the 'organic' nature of the earth, is to be found in C. Keferstein's 'Teutschland geognostisch-geologisch dargestellt' (vol. V pt. i, 1827). For a detailed survey of the subject see J. S. T. Gehler's 'Physikalisches Wörterbuch' (ed. Brandes, Muncke etc. 11 vols. Leipzig, 1825–1845) vol. 7 pp. 1023–1125.

Cf. G. Wachsmuth 'Die Erde als lebender Organismus', in his 'Goethe in unserer Zeit' (Basel, 1949) pp. 29–50.

36, 36

'Generatio univoca' (universal generation) i.e. normal generation between members of the same species.

36, 37

'Omne vivum ex ovo.' This saying is generally attributed to William Harvey (1578–1657), although he seems never to have expressed the idea in precisely these words. It may well have originated from the frontispiece of his 'Exercitationes de generatione animalium' (London, 1651) however, in which Zeus is depicted holding an egg, from which all kinds of living creatures are issuing forth, and on which is inscribed 'Ex ovo omnia'.

37, 14

Olaf Wäsström, 'Versuch über einen besonderen Schein im Wasser der

Ost-See' tr. from the Swedish ('Gilbert's Annalen der Physik' vol. II p. 352 1799). Cf. F. Tiedemann (1781–1861) 'Physiologie des Menschen (1830, tr. Gully and Lane, London, 1834) Book II Pt. ii Sect. 2 Ch. 2. Tiedemann is profuse in his references to the periodicals of his time. Cf. E. N. Harvey 'A History of Luminescence from the earliest times until 1900.' (Philadelphia, 1957).

37, 23

This account of the spontaneous generation of the sea may owe something to J. T. Needham's assertion that water breeds its microscopic animals from a vegetative force. 'Needham imagined that there was a vegetative force in every microscopical point of water, and (sic) every visible filament of which the whole vegetable contexture consists; that the several species of microscopic animals may subside, resolve again into gelatinous filaments, and again give lesser animals, and so on, till they can be no longer pursued by glasses.' George Adams 'Essays on the Microscope' (2nd ed. London, 1798 p. 421).

37, 27

O. F. Müller (1730–1784) of Copenhagen first distinguished and classified many of these 'determinate formations', and his 'Animalcula infusoria, fluviatilia, et Marina' (Copenhagen, 1786) became a standard work on the subject. C. G. Ehrenberg (1795–1876), in his monumental 'Infusionsthierchen als vollkommene Organismen' (Leipzig, 1838, English adaptation by A. Pritchard, 'A History of Infusoria' London, 1842), produced a more exact classification, but even his work has since been largely superseded. He distinguished between (i) Desmids, Diatoms and Schizomycetes, now regarded as essentially Plant Protista or Protophytes; (ii) Sarcodina (excluding Foraminifera, as well as Radiolaria, which were only as yet known by their skeletons, and termed Polycystina), and (iii) Rotifers, as well as (iv) Flagellates and Infusoria in our present sense.

37, 31

Adelbert von Chamisso (1781–1838) came of a French emigré family which had settled in Berlin soon after the Revolution. His reputation now rests mainly upon his work as a novelist and poet, but in the Berlin scientific circles of his day he was also well known as a botanist.

In 1815 he was appointed botanist to the Russian ship 'Rurik', which Otto von Kotzebue commanded on a scientific voyage round the world. On his return in 1818 he was made custodian of the botanical gardens in Berlin, and was elected member of the Berlin Academy of Sciences. See E. H. du Bois-Reymond 'Adelbert von Chamisso als Naturforscher' (Leipzig, 1889).

Salpae constitute a family of Hemimyaria, which are a sub-order of the Tunicata. Their most striking characteristic is that they exhibit alternation of generations in their life history. Each species occurs in two forms, which are usually quite unlike one another, the solitary asexual (proles solitaria), and the aggregated sexual (proles gregaria). The solitary form gives rise by internal gemmation to a complex tubular stolon, which becomes segmented into a series of buds or embryos. As this stolon elongates, the embryos near the free end which have become advanced in their development are set free in groups, which remain attached together by processes of the test, each enclosing a diverticulum from the mantle so as to form 'chains'. Each member of the chain is a Salpa of the sexual or aggregated form, and when mature may produce one or several embryos, which develop into the solitary Salpa. Thus the two forms alternate regularly.

Chamisso and J. F. von Eschscholtz (1793–1831), who accompanied him on the voyage around the world, were the first to observe this alternation of generations in salpae. Their 'fine discovery' as Hegel calls it was made on October 23, 1815, while the 'Rurik' was becalmed just north of the Canary Islands (30°36'N. 15°20'W.). Chamisso gives the following account of it in his 'Reise um die Welt mit der Romanzoffischen Entdeckungs-Expedition in den Jahren 1815–1818,' ‚Hier beschäftigten mich und Eschscholtz besonders die Salpen, und hier war es, wo wir an diesen durchsichtigen Weichthieren des hohen Meeres die uns wichtig dünkende Entdeckung machten, daß bei denselben eine und dieselbe Art sich in abwechselnden Generationen unter zwei sehr wesentlich verschiedenen Formen darstellt; daß nämlich eine einzeln frei-schwimmende Salpa anders gestaltete, fast polypenartig an einander gekettete Jungen lebendig gebiert, deren jedes in der zusammen aufgewachsenen Republik wiederum einzeln freischwimmende Thiere zur Welt setzt, in denen die Form der vorvorigen Generation wiederkehrt. Es ist, als gebäre die Raupe den Schmetterling und der Schmetterling hinwiederum die Raupe.' ('Werke' ed. J. E. Hitzig, Leipzig, 1842, vol. I b. 43).

Chamisso published two Latin works on Salpae: 'De animalibus quibusdam e classe vermium linnaeana in circumnavigatione terrae auspicante Comite N. Romanzoff duce Ottone de Kotzebue annis 1815. 1816. 1817. 1818. peracta observatis Adelbertus de Chamisso. Fasciculus Primus. De Salpa. Berolini 1819' and 'De animalibus e classe vermium linneana Fasciculus secundus, requos vermes continens,' which was published in 'Verhandlungen der Kaiserlichen Leopoldinisch-Carolinischen Academie der Naturforscher' (vol. ii, Bonn, 1821). It was probably on these publications that Hegel based his account of the discovery. An anonymous and somewhat critical review of the first of these works appeared in Oken's 'Isis' (1819, pp. 652–653).

38, 4

The analogy between the discoveries made with the help of the microscope and those made with the help of the telescope also occurred to George Adams (1750–1795), 'By the help of magnifying glasses we are brought into a kind of new world; and numberless animals are discovered, which from their minuteness, must otherwise for ever have escaped our observation: and how many kinds of these invisibles there may be, is yet unknown; as they are observed of all sizes, from those which are barely visible to the naked eye, to such as resist the action of the microscope, as the fixed stars do that of the telescope, and with the best magnifier hitherto invented, appear only as so many moving points.' ('Essays on the Microscope' 2nd ed. London, 1798, pp. 415–416).

38, 20

In Greek mythology for example, Oceanus was the seat of all dark and mysterious things, and the origin of gods and men. See Juno's words in the Iliad (XIV 200–201),

> 'For lo, I haste to those remote abodes,
> Where the great parents (sacred source of Gods!)
> Ocean and Tethys their old Empires keep,
> On the last limits of the land and deep.' (Pope)

Cf. M. Leach 'Dictionary of Folklore, Mythology, and Legend' (2 vols. New York, 1950) vol. 2 p. 1167. Stith Thompson 'Motif-Index of Folk Literature' (5 vols. Copenhagen, 1955) A 1232.2, A 1261.

39, 2

Between 1802 and 1846 approximately 500 new species of lichen were described, but because of tardiness in the use of the microscope, investigation into the nature and structure of these plants did not keep pace with the advances made in classifying them.

C. F. W. Wallroth (1792–1857), in his 'Naturgeschichte der Flechten' (2 vols. Frankfurt-on-Main, 1825) supposed them to be propagated by means of gonidia and spores, but G. F. W. Meyer (1782–1856), whose 'Die Entwicklung, Metamorphose and Fortpflanzung der Flechten' appeared at the same time (Göttingen, 1825), thought them capable of the 'generatio originaria' here ascribed to them by Hegel, and he was by no means alone in holding this opinion. See A. L. Smith 'Lichens' (Cambridge, 1921); A. von Krempelhuber (1813–1882) 'Geschichte und Litteratur der Lichenologie' (3 vol. Munich, 1867–1872).

39, 2

Informed opinion of Hegel's day would not have regarded mosses as 'universal vegetation' on account of their being devoid of 'seeds', although at that time the propagation of moss was certainly a matter of controversy.

J. J. Hedwig (1730–1799), who laid the foundations of modern bryology, realized that the archegonium and antheridium of bryophyta correspond to the pistil and anthers of flowering plants. C. G. Nees von Esenbeck (1776–1858), on seeing the capsule of the Sphagnum burst and throw off the operculum and spores, was surprised that, ‚fich aus ihnen ein Heer lebender Monaden ergoß‘ (1823), although it was not until 1834 that F. Unger (1800–1870) showed that these 'monads' were in fact spermatozoids. By the 1820's therefore, bryologists were well on the way to understanding the sexual generation of mosses.

Hedwig also described the germination of the spores and the development of the protonema correctly, although it was not until 1830 that Wallroth recognized the true significance of the protonema in the asexual propagation of these plants. C. G. Nees von Esenbeck, F. Hornschuch, J. Sturm 'Bryologia Germanica' (Nuremberg, 1813); M. Möbius 'Geschichte der Botanik' ch. 26 (Jena, 1937).

39, 5

Cf. the note on III. 246 Hegel evidently regarded mildew as being vegetable in nature and atmospheric in origin.

39, 36

Carl Asmund Rudolphi (1771–1832) was born in Stockholm, but when his father died in 1778, his mother moved to Swedish Pomerania, and it was there that he grew up. In 1790 he began his studies at the university of Greifswald, where he took his doctorate in 1795. He taught in the medical and veterinary faculties of the university until 1808, when he left for a six-month tour, taking in Brussels, Paris and Lyons. On his return to Greifswald he was appointed professor of medicine. In 1810 he accepted the offer of the chair of anatomy and physiology at the newly founded university of Berlin. He settled in the city, and finally took Prussian citizenship.

He did his best work as a biologist not as a botanist, and published important works on physiology ('Elements of Physiology' tr. W. D. How, London, 1825), intestinal worms ('Entozoorum synopsis' Berlin, 1819) and embryology ('Ueber den Embryo der Affen' Abhandlungen der Berliner Akademie, 1831). His 'Anatomie der Pflanzen' (Berlin, 1807) was one of the three essays accepted by the Royal Academy of Sciences at Göttingen as answering a prize-question on plant anatomy. Those who judged the entries evidently knew as little of the subject as the competitors however, for the two winning essays (Rudolphi's, and H. F. Link's 'Grundlehren der Anatomie und Physiologie der Pflanzen') contradicted each other on several important points, while the best of the three (L. C. Treviranus's 'Vom inwendigen Bau der Gewächse') was deemed to be worthy of a mere 'proxime accessit'.

Luigi Galvani (1737–1798) had published his account of muscular irritability in 1786, and the 'Versuche über die gereizte Muskel- und Nervenfaser, nebst Vermuthungen über den chemischen Process des Lebens in der Thier- und

Pflanzenwelt' (Berlin, 1797) of Alexander von Humboldt (1769–1859) contained the results of a prolonged course of experiments in which the nature of this phenomena had been investigated.

P. A. Micheli (1679–1737) had given an excellent description of the growth of fungi from spores a full century before Hegel delivered the last of these lectures: 'Nova Plantarum Genera juxta Tournefortii Methodum disposita' (Florence, 1729), and Linnaeus' assessment of fungi as plants without leaves was widely accepted by the turn of the century.

Hegel's choice of these works by Rudolphi and von Humboldt as the authorities on which to base his views on the nature of lichens and fungi was therefore most unfortunate, although some of his contemporaries outdid him in the singularity of their opinions on this subject. Otto von Münchhausen (1716–1774) thought of fungi as being intermediate between animals and plants ('Der Hausvater' vols. II and III, Hannover, 1765–1766), 'The black powder in the Lycoperdon and Mucor was taken for animalcules by Baron Münchhausen, and thus the Fungi were on the verge of migrating into the class of Zoophytes' (P. Miller and T. Martyn 'The Gardener's and Botanist's Dictionary' 2 vols. London, 1807). Robert Scott, in his 'Account of crystallized Oxalic Acid produced from the Boletus sulphureus' ('Transactions of the Linnean Society of London' vol. VIII 1808 pp. 262–263) throws an interesting sidelight on one of the reasons for Münchhausen's opinion, 'That the oxalic acid is produced or evolved in the course of vegetation in many plants of the higher ranks is well known, but that it should be found in any of the fungus tribe, (which have hitherto been supposed to produce only an ammoniacal salt, and on that account considered as a link between vegetables and animals,) is a curious, and, I believe, isolated fact'.

Other naturalists, concentrating upon the rapidity with which fungi grow, regarded them as intermediate between crystals and plants: see F. K. Medicus (1736–1808), 'Über den Ursprung und die Bildungsart der Schwämme' ('Vorlesungen der kurpfälzischen physikalisch-ökonomischen Gesellschaft zu Heidelberg' vol. 8); N. J. de Necker (1729–1793), 'Traité sur la Mycetologie' (Mannheim, 1793); K. H. Schultz (1798–1871), ‚Der Krystall bildet sich, wie der Pilz und das Infusionsthier, durch seine eigene totale Macht, und wie bei den letzteren, so kann auch bei ihm die Bildung durch äußere Einflüße gehindert und begünstigt werden, ohne daß jedoch der Grund dieser ursprünglichen Erzeugung in den äußern Verhältnissen des allgemeinen Naturlebens begründet wäre.' ('Die Natur der Lebendigen Pflanze' vol. I p. 58, Berlin, 1823).

C. A. J. A. Oudemans, in his monumental 'Enumeratio Systematica Fungorum' (5 vols. Hague, 1919–1924) makes no mention of either the 'Boletus cetatophorus' mentioned by Rudolphi, or the 'Clavaria militaris' mentioned by von Humboldt. E. J. Corner's 'A Monograph of Clavaria and Allied Genera' (Oxford, 1950) also makes no mention of the 'Clavaria militaris'.

40, 1

Intestinal worms were thought to be formed from the matter contained in the intestines: see G. R. Treviranus (1776–1837) 'Biologie' vol. II p. 366 (Göttingen, 1803); Matthew Baillie (1761–1823) 'The Morbid anatomy of some of the most important parts of the human body' (3rd ed. London, 1807 p. 192). The theory that they reproduced themselves by eggs was widespread, but had not yet been substantiated, 'There is every reason to believe that Taeniae produce ova, and that their ova, as well as those of other intestinal worms, are so constructed as to be very little perishable'—A. Carlisle 'Observations upon the Structure and Oeconomy of those Intestinal Worms called Taeniae' ('Transactions of the Linnean Society' vol. II pp. 147–262. London, 1794). Cf. 'Einiges über Einge-weide-Würmer' by H. W. Eysenhardt 'Verhandlungen der Gesellschaft Natur-forschender Freunde zu Berlin' (Berlin, 1829, p. 144). J. F. Blumenbach (1752–1840), in his 'Beyträge zur Naturgeschichte' (2nd ed. pt. I Göttingen, 1806, Eng. tr. by Thomas Bendyshe, London, 1865) discusses the origin of *swine-gargets*, 'The pimple-worm in pigs, which Malpighi was the first to discover, is quite as real and perfect an animal in its kind as man and the elephant in theirs. But, as is well known, this animal is only found in tame swine, and never in any way in the wild pig, from which however the former is descended. It would seem there-fore that this worm was no more created at the same time as the original stock of the hog than, according to probability, the allied species of bladder worms, which have been lately discovered, just like those hydatids, in the flesh and among the entrails of human bodies, which must needs have been created after the original parents of mankind.'

R. W. Dickson, in his 'An improved system of management of Livestock and Cattle' (London, 1822–1824, vol. II p. 329), proposes to cure a hog of the garget by mixing sublimed sulphur and powdered root of madder into its swill.

45, 22

Cf. 'The Logic' tr. Wallace §§ 95–96. The geological organism does not attain to this ideality, although as a bare system of shape (des Geſtaltens) it has an implicit ideality which becomes explicit in plant-life. The causal relationship falls away here, because although inorganic nature provides the matter of organic being, life is self-engendering, its ideality consisting in its transforming this matter in accordance with its own organic forms.

45, 25

'Everything lives in nature.' This is evidently a reference to Schelling's 'Von der Weltseele, eine Hypothese der höheren Physik zur Erklärung des allgemeinen Organismus' (1798, 2nd ed. 1806, 3rd ed. 1809; 'Schellings Werke' ed. M. Schröter vol. I Munich, 1958). ‚Da nun dieſes Princip die Continuität der anorganiſchen und der organiſchen Welt unterhält und die ganze Natur zu einem allgemeinen Organismus verknüpft, ſo erkennen wir aufsneue in ihm jenes Wesen, das die älteste Philosophie als die gemeinschaftliche Seele der Natur ahndend begrüßte, und das einige Physiker jener Zeit mit dem formenden und bildenden Aether ... für eines hielten.' (loc. cit. p. 637).

46, 12

The infinite form of living being constitutes the end of nature (Add. to § 337). Consequently, this process of physical properties is subordinate to it, and in the production of living being it is the form which determines the properties, not the properties which determine the form. Cf. 'The Logic' tr. Wallace § 219.

46, 14

,das schwache kindische Leben.'

46, 35

The translation of the first two sentences of this quotation has been made from the version of them printed by Michelet in his edition of 'The Philosophy of Nature'. In Goethe's 'Zur Morphologie' (vol. I pp. x–xi, Stuttgart and Tübingen, 1817), they appear in a slightly different form however, ,Je unvollkommener das Geschöpf ist, destomehr sind diese Theile einander gleich oder ähnlich, und destomehr gleichen sie dem Ganzen. Je vollkommener das Geschöpf wird, desto unähnlicher werden die Theile einander.'

47, 9

Karl Heinrich Schultz (1798–1871) was trained at the Frederick William Institute in Berlin as an army doctor. In 1822 he left the army for an academic career, writing his thesis on the circulation of the sap in Celandines. He was appointed extraordinary professor of medicine at Berlin 1825, and in 1833 became a full member of the professorial staff of the university. In 1830 his essay 'Sur la circulation et sur les vaisseaux lactifères dans les plantes' was awarded a prize by the French Academy. Hugo von Mohl (1805–1872), professor of botany at Tübingen, called in question Schultz's mistaken contention that the lactescence of plants corresponds to the blood of animals and circulates, and the ensuing controversy degenerated into a series of abusive exchanges. 'Über den Milchsaft und seine Bewegung' Botanische Zeitung I, 1843 col. 553–558, 593–598; Annals of Natural History XIII 1844, pp. 441–444; Annales des Sciences Naturelles I (Bot.) 1844 pp. 4–24.

J. B. D. Boussingault (1802–1887), professor of chemistry at Lyons, took the trouble to check many of Schultz's experiments, and found them to be faulty. 'Über die gegen seine Versuche über Pflanzenernährung gemachten Einwend-. ungen' Neue Notizen, von L. F. und Rob. Froriep vol. XXXIII, 1845 col. 39–41.

'Die Natur der lebendigen Pflanze', which is a rambling but basically competent work, was published in two parts (Part I, Berlin, 1823; Part II Stuttgart and Tübingen, 1828). The sentence here referred to by Hegel reads as follows in its entirety, ‚Das Wachstum der Pflanzen ist ein ewiges Hinzubilden neuer, vorher nicht vorhandener Theile, zu den alten, und unterscheidet sich dadurch wesentlich von dem thierischen Wachstum, welches bloß in einer Vergrößerung ursprünglich vorhandener Theile besteht, zu denen keine neue hinzugebildet werden.'

48, 6

‚Noch ins processualische Außereinander versenkt.' i.e. the vital principle of the plant is confined to *external* development, to the engendering of products united only by the process of this development, and in themselves external to one another.

48, 20

‚Wie der Mensch den Menschen sucht.' Hegel wrote, ‚wie der einsame Mensch den Menschen sucht.' ('Jenenser Realphilosophie' II p. 126). Cf. Johann Georg Zimmerman (1728–1795) 'Über die Einsamkeit' (4 pts. Leipzig, 1784, Eng. tr. London, 1791).

48, 24

Schelling certainly *implies* this in the following passage, 'Kein Wunder, daß (die Wärme) für (den Menschen), den alle ihre Wirkungen unmittelbar rühren, das Erste ist, was ihn zur Anbetung der Sonne hinreißt . . . Die Pflanze durch den Einfluß der Wärme hervorgetrieben, vertvelkt doch wieder, sobald Licht und Wärme aufhören zu entwickeln, wovon sie sich nährte.' 'Ideen zu einer Philosophie der Natur' (1797, 2nd ed. 1803): 'Schellings Werke' First Supplementary volume pp. 174–175 (Munich, 1958). Cf. James Hervey (1714–1758) 'Meditations' (London, 1746, 42nd ed. 1824, Germ. tr. Hamburg, 1762) pt. I sect. 2, "To an attentive mind the garden turns preacher, and its blooming tenants are so many lively sermons . . . Let us all be heliotropes . . . to the Sun of righteousness." Macrobius 'Saturnalia' I xvii 66 et seq.

48, 36

Cf. Hegel's 'Philosophy of Right' § 33 Addition (tr. Knox pp. 233–234): 'Philosophy of History' (tr. Sibree, Dover ed. 1956 pp. 108–110).

49, 3

The ultimate source of this information is to be found in the 'Memoirs of the American Academy of Arts and Sciences' vol. II pp. 146–147 (Boston, 1793). James Warren (1726–1808), wrote to the Academy from Milton, Massachusetts on January 25, 1786, 'I therefore beg leave to communicate an extraordinary instance, related to me by a gentleman of undoubted veracity in my neighbourhood. The account is as follows: On going into a cellar, which he used for the preservation of roots in the winter, and kept close and dark, he discovered, in the south east corner, a very small hole, which admitted a little light; and that a vine proceeding from a potato, accidentally left in the north west corner, had pursued a direct course to the aperture in the wall; and after running twenty feet on the cellar floor, ascended the wall, and without any deviation in its whole course, went out at the hole. This is the strongest instance of the effect of light on the growth of plants, that has fallen under my observation; and being so extraordinary, will, I hope, apologize for this communication, if it produces no other effect, than amusement to the curious.' Cf. 'Transactions of the Linnean Society' (II p. 267, 1794).

49, 10

Carl Ludwig Willdenow (1765–1812) was born in Berlin, and was introduced to botanical studies by his uncle J. G. Gleditsch (1714–1786) who was director of the Berlin botanical garden. After studying chemistry under M. H. Klaproth (1743–1817), he qualified in medicine at Halle, but through the influence of his friend A. von Humboldt, geographical botany soon became his main interest. In 1790 he was offered the position of botanist on a Russian ship about to start on a world voyage, but as he had planned to marry in the autumn of that year, he eventually decided not to accept it.

His 'Grundriss der Kräuterkunde' was first published at Berlin in 1792, and on account of the admirably lucid manner in which its subject-matter was presented, was widely read. A large part of the book is devoted to the definition of botanical terms. Willdenow was appointed professor of botany when the university of Berlin was founded in 1810.

Hegel might have added Oenothera tetraptera, molissima, Silene noctiflora, Mirabilis longiflora, Gladiolus tristis and Cactus trianguloris as further examples of flowers which open only at night. Willdenow continues here as follows, 'Für Oenothera biennis scheint der Reiz des Tageslichts zu heftig zu sein, und sie kann sich nicht eher öffnen als bis kein starkes Licht mehr auf sie wirkt, daher steht sie von Abend die Nacht hindurch bis zum Morgen offen.'

49, 13

The Portulacca Oleracea is also known as the Garden Purslane. It is an annual and herbaceous plant, a native of the East and West Indies, China, Indo-China, Japan, Ascension and many parts of Europe. In Hegel's day it was prescribed as a salad for scorbutic disorders.

The Drosera Rotundifolia or Round-leaved Sundew, is also known as Sundew, Youthwort, and in Northern England as Red-rot. In Hegel's day its juice was mixed with milk and applied to the skin in order to remove freckles or cure sun-burn.

The *Cactus Grandiflorus* is a native of Jamaica and Vera Cruz. 'This species, when arrived to a sufficient strength, will produce many exceedingly large, beautiful, sweet-scented flowers; like most of this kind, of very short duration, scarcely continuing six hours full blown; nor do the flowers ever open again when once closed. They begin to open between seven and eight o'clock in the evening, are fully blown by eleven, and by three or four in the morning they fade, and hang down quite decayed.' Thomas Green 'The Universal Herbal; or, botanical, medical and agricultural dictionary' (2 vols. 2nd ed. London, 1824) vol. I p. 219. Green also supplies a fine illustration of the flower (p. 220).

49, 22

‚Indem die Pflanze so das Sinnliche noch nicht ganz vernichten kann, ist sie noch nicht reine Zeit in sich.‘ In this sentence, and in the passage which follows, Hegel clearly has in mind his analysis of space, time and motion (cf. §§ 253–271).

In the plant *space* is dominant, in that the parts of the plant are external to one another and confined to the space they occupy in the process of growth. In the animal however, *time* is dominant, in that the animal's ego, while functioning as the ideal unity of its body, is able to *nullify* its spatial fixity by willing *movement*, which involves time.

The progression from vegetable to animal being is therefore analogous to the progression from space to time and motion. The time involved in animal movement is 'pure' because it is determined by the animal's *ego*, whereas the time of the solar system involves the *laws* of that system.

50, 4

Gottfried Reinhold Treviranus (1776–1837) was born at Bremen, and studied medicine and mathematics at Göttingen. While still a student, he contributed an important article on neurology to 'Reil's Archive for Physiology' (1796 pt. I sect. ii), and at the age of twenty-one was appointed professor of mathematics and medicine at Bremen.

His 'Biologie, oder Philosophie der lebenden Natur für Naturforscher und Aerzte' (6 vols. Göttingen, 1802–1822), which is based upon a great deal of reading and a certain amount of research, provides an admirably detailed and comprehensive survey of the botanical and biological studies of his time. Hegel often uses the book without referring to it. Treviranus's second great work was, 'Die Erscheinungen und Gesetze des organischen Lebens' (2 vols. Bremen, 1831–1833).

The Hedysarum gyrans was discovered in the Dacca lowlands of Eastern Bengal in 1775, by Lady Monson (d. 1776), wife of George Monson (1730–1776), the opponent of Warren Hastings. J. E. Pohl (1746–1800) gave an account of the strange movements of its leaves in 'Vorläufige Nachricht von einer bis jetzt noch unbekannten sich bewegenden Pflanze' ('Sammlungen der Physik und

Naturgeschichte' Leipzig, 1779, vol. I p. 502), as did the younger Linnaeus (1741–1783) in his 'Supplementum plantarum' (Braunschweig, 1781): cf. 'Mémoires de l'Academie des sciences de Paris' 1784 p. 616; 'Vorlesungen der kurpfälzischen physikalisch-ökonomischen Gesellschaft' (Mannheim, 1785, vol. I p. 391).

At the beginning of book sixteen of 'Dichtung und Wahrheit', Goethe speaks of the consternation caused by our discovering an apparent exception to what we had accepted as a general law of nature, when we find for example that plants are not devoid of movement, and that the Hedysarum gyrans, ,feine Blättchen ohne sichtbare Veranlaßung auf und niedersenkt und mit sich selbst wie mit unseren Begriffen zu spielen scheint'.

50, 12

Christoph Wilhelm Hufeland (1762–1836), the well known doctor. Both his father and his grandfather were physicians in ordinary at the court of Weimar, and for ten years (1783–1793), he also lived in the town, making the acquaintance of Wieland, Herder, Goethe and Schiller. He moved first to Jena, and in 1798 to Berlin, where he threw himself energetically into the organizing of hospital facilities for the poor. He was one of the most uncompromising opponents of the Brunonian system, and was one of the first to introduce Jenner's method of vaccination into Germany.

Treviranus is here referring to his, 'Ueber die Bewegungen des Hedysarum gyrans und die Wirkung der Elektrizität auf dasselbe', which appeared in J. H. Voigt's 'Magazin für das Neueste aus der Physik und Naturgeschichte' (Gotha, 1790, vol. VI pt. iii pp. 5–27). Hufeland discovered that when the leaves of the plant were touched by an electric spark, they would not move again until the following day, and that although a minute or two of continuous electrification would stimulate their movements, it would also bring about their death. ,Ja zum Erstaunen war mirs zu sehen, wie so gar der blasse Wiederschein der Sonne auf eine ohngefähr 20 Schritt entfernte Mauer, ein sehr deutliches Aufrichten der Blätter bewirken konnte... Ließ ich den Focus des Sonnenlichts durch ein Brennglas auf das Blatt oder den Stiel fallen, so war die schon oben bemerkte zitternde Bewegung im Sonnenschein viel stärker.' (p. 12).

50, 22

Treviranus had observed this movement in the zoospores of the 'Rivularia endiviaefolia R.' in 1803. J. P. Vaucher (1763–1841) in his 'Histoire des conferves d'eau douce' (Geneva, 1803), suggested that it was voluntary in nature, and J. Girod Chantrans (1750–1841), whose 'Recherches chimiques et microscopiques sur les Conferves, Bysses, Tremelles' was published at Paris in 1802, and whose preliminary article on the subject (1797) is quoted by Treviranus, suggested that the movement might indicate the link between vegetable and animal being.

For subsequent attempts to explain the movement see M. Möbius 'Geschichte der Botanik' (Jena, 1937, pp. 75–76).

51, 8

Auguste Pyrame de Candolle (1778–1841) was born at Geneva. From 1798 until 1808 he studied at Paris, where he made the acquaintance of Desfontaines, Cuvier and Lamarck. From 1808 until 1816 he was professor of botany at Montpellier, and in these years he also travelled widely in Europe.

In 1813 he published 'Théorie élémentaire de la botanique', and in 1817 'Système naturel des végétaux'. These are his best known works, and by showing that the affinities of plants are to be sought by the comparative study of the *form* and *development* of organs (morphology), not of their *functions* (physiology), they did much to further the acceptance of Jussieu's natural system of classification, and to prepare the way for Darwin.

In 1816 a chair of botany was founded for him at Geneva, and he returned, for the rest of his life, to his native city. In 1824 he began the monumental 'Prodromus systematis naturalis regni vegetabilis', which was continued by his son, and which had as its object the classification of all the known species of plants in accordance with Jussieu's system.

His account of the experiment mentioned by Hegel is to be found in 'Journal de Physique' vol. 52 p. 124. He discovered that the movements of the Convolvulus arvensis, Convolvulus Cneorum, Silene fructicosa and Mimosa leucocephola were not affected by the artificial light, but that after three days of treatment, the Mimosa pudica was open at night and closed by day, and that it returned to its former rhythm once it was placed in the open again. He also discovered that artificial light at night lengthened the blossoming period of the Convolvulus purpureus, and caused the Anthemis maritima to stay open continuously.

Linnaeus concerned himself with this phenomenon: see 'Dissertatio de somno plantarum, resp. P. Bremer' (Uppsala, 1755: Amoenitat. academic. vol. 4 p. 333). John Hill (1716–1775) published his letter to Linnaeus on this subject as 'The Sleep of Plants and cause of Motion in the Sensitive Plant explained' (London, 1757, German tr. Nuremberg, 1768), and evidently inspired much of the subsequent research. Hill's conclusion was that, 'We know that in these experiments, light alone is the cause, we are therefore certain, that what is called the sleep of plants, is the effect of the absence of light alone, and that their various intermediate states are owing to its different degrees' (op. cit. p. 21). Cf. 'Observations upon the sleep of plants, and an account of that faculty, which Linnaeus calls "Vigiliae florum"' (Phil. Trans. Roy. Soc. vol. 50 p. 506) by R. Pulteney (1730–1801).

51, 17

Sigismund Hermbstädt (1760–1833) was born in Erfurt, and trained as a doctor and pharmacist. In 1791 he was appointed professor of chemistry and pharmacy at the Berlin Collegium Medico-Chirurgicum, and in 1810 professor of chemistry and technology at the newly founded university of Berlin. He was interested in industrial chemistry, and published works on brewing, distillation and tobacco, and on improving the quality of soap.

Hegel is evidently referring to his 'Über die Fähigkeit der lebenden Pflanzen im Winter Wärme zu erzeugen' which was published in 'Der Gesellschaft Naturforschender Freunde zu Berlin. Magazin für die Neuesten Entdeckungen in der Gesammten Naturkunde' (vol. II pp. 316–319, Berlin, 1808). He describes experiments made with plane-trees in January 1796, in which he investigated the sugar content of their saps, and discovered that the saps were warmer than the air. He also discovered that although apples and pears remained the same temperature as the air surrounding them, beetroots, carrots, turnips and potatoes were somewhat warmer. He concludes, ‚Vielleicht hängt jene Wärmezeugende Kraft der lebenden Vegetabilien von einer wirklichen Respirationsfähigkeit derselben ab, welche der Respiration der Thiere ähnlich ist? welches gleichfalls näher untersucht zu werden verbient'.

John Hunter and Jean Senebier (1742–1809) also came to the conclusion that plants had power of generating heat: see 'Phil. Trans. Roy. Soc.' 1775 p. 116; 1778 pt. I p. 6: 'Journal de Physique' vol. 40 p. 173.

51, 24

Cf. F. Tiedemann 'Physiologie des Menschen' (Darmstadt, 1830, p. 449). Those who wrote on this subject used the thermometric scales of Réaumur, Fahrenheit, Celsius and De Luc, so that when summarizing and comparing their arguments, it became usual to convert all the temperatures quoted to the Celsius scale. In this case $-5°R = 21°F = -6°C: -10°R = 9°F = -12°C: 1°R = 34°F = 1·25°C.$

51, 30

Felice Fontana (1730–1805) was born at Pomarole in the Tyrol. He studied the humanities at Verona and Parma, and the sciences at Bologna and Padua. After finishing his studies at Florence and Rome, the grand-duke of Tuscany appointed him professor of theoretical philosophy at the university of Pisa. He published a great number of works on physics, chemistry and physiology, his best known book being, 'Richerche filosofiche sopra la fisica animale' (Florence, 1775), in which he formulated the laws of animal irritability. A German translation was published at Leipzig in 1785.

For thirty years he was curator of the museum of physics and natural history at Florence, and under his direction it became one of the most outstanding institutions of its kind in Europe.

He wrote the article to which Treviranus refers in November 1804, and died only four months later, on March 9, 1805. It was published by Harless and

Ritter in their 'Neues Journal der ausländischen medizinisch-chirurgischen Litteratur' vol. v pt. ii pp. 45–68, Erlangen, 1806). In order to discover whether or not plants had the power of producing heat, he placed them in a cellar, so that he could regulate and check their temperature, and some weeks later brought in fresh plants, ‚Ich unterſuchte hierauf dieſe Pflanzen nach einigen Stunden, den ganzen Tag hindurch, und fand nun, daß die Wärme derſelben genau mit der Wärme der übrigen aufgehangenen Vegetabilien, die ſchon ſeit mehrere Wochen in dem Keller ſich befanden, übereinkamen; zum klaren Beweis das alle übrigen Pflanzen im Keller das nemliche Vermögen beibehalten, entweder ihre Wärme zu erhalten, oder ſolche zu erzeugen . . . Das Endreſultat von mehr als 4600 Verſuchen die mit einer ſo großen Menge vegetabiliſcher Subſtanzen von ſo verſchiedener Art im Zuſtande ihres Lebens angeſtellt worden ſind, ſetzt es vollkommen außer allen Zweifel, daß die Vegetabilien das Vermögen, Wärme zu erzeugen, nicht beſitzen, welches den warmblutigen Thieren beſtimmt zukommt.'

Schuebler and Halder, in their 'Ueber die Temperatur der Vegetabilien' (Tübingen, 1826) agreed with Fontana that although plants are unable to *generate* heat, they are certainly able to *conduct* it from the earth.

51, 37

Arum Maculatum, i.e. the Common Arum, native of all except the most northern parts of Europe.

52, 3

Jean Senebier (1742–1809) gives an account of this generation of heat by the Arum maculatum in his 'Physiologie végétale' (Geneva, 1800) vol. iii p. 314. J. B. Bory de St. Vincent (1780–1846), in his 'Voyage dans les quatre principales îles des mers d'Afrique' (Paris, 1804) vol. ii p. 66, mentions the generation of heat by the Arum cordifolium, and the fact that the male parts of its blossom become warmer than the female. In the instance of this recorded by St. Vincent, the temperature rose from 23·33°C to 56·67°C in the male parts.

N. T. de Saussure (1767–1845) investigated this phenomenon, and came to the conclusion that it was the rapid combination of oxygen with the carbon of the plant which gave rise to the generation of heat ('Annales de chimie et physique' vol. 21 Nov. 1822 p. 286).

John Murray (1786–1851) showed that the colour of a flower has an effect upon its temperature ('Experimental Researches' Glasgow, 1826, p. 9).

This reference to Link's 'Grundlehren der Anatomie und Physiologie der Pflanzen' is somewhat misleading, as Link is referring to the Arum italicum in the passage quoted.

52, 8

Mesembryanthemum Crystallinum, 'This plant is an annual, and is distinguished by its leaves and stalks, being closely covered with pellucid pimples full of moisture, which when the sun shines on them reflect the light, and appear like small bubbles of ice; whence it has been called by some the *Ice Plant*, and by others the *Diamond Plant*.' Thomas Green 'The Universal Herbal' (2 vols. 2nd ed. London, 1824) vol. 11 p. 118.

52, 11

Cf. §§ 354 and 364.

52, 34

Friedrich Kasimir Medicus (1736–1808) was born at Grumbach in the Rhineland. He studied medicine at Tübingen, Strassburg and Heidelberg, and in 1758 settled in Mannheim as a general practitioner.

He published several important medical works, including 'Sammlung von Beobachtungen aus der Arzneywissenschaft' (Zürich, 1764–1766), and 'Vorlesung von der Lebenskraft' (Mannheim, 1774), but through his friendship with J. G. Kölreuter (1733–1806), who was supervisor of the court gardens at Karlsruhe, he also developed an interest in botany.

In 1763 he became a member of the Palatinate Academy of Sciences. In 1765 he started a botanical garden at Mannheim, but during the French occupation of the town in 1794, and the subsequent Austrian counter-offensive in 1795, it was destroyed.

The reference here is to his 'Pflanzen-physiologische Abhandlungen. Von Friedrich Kasimir Medicus. Erstes Bändchen. Fortpflanzung der Pflanzen durch Saamen. Erzeugung des Saamens.' (Leipzig, 1803) p. 29, ‚Auch bei der Kühlung sind diese Blüthen (Cistus helianthemum) am reizbarsten, bei trockner und starker Hitze hingegen gänzlich, und zu allen Zeiten unempfindlich. Bei der starken Hitze, die wir zu Anfange und in der Mitte des Junius 1773 hatten, konnte ich zu keiner Tagesstunde nur die geringste Bewegung wahrnehmen; da aber mit den 20sten Junius heftiges Regenwetter einfiel, erwachte diese Reizbarkeit auf einmal, und zeigte sich in ihrer größten Stärke.' Cf. loc. cit. p. 139 et seq.

53, 11

On the Dionaea muscipula, see J. Ellis (1710–1776), 'Directions for bringing over Seeds and Plants from the East Indies' (London, 1770); 'Dionaea muscipula descripta' (Nov. Act. Societat. Upsaliens. vol. i p. 98).

On the Oxalis sensitiva, see G. E. Rumphius (1627–1602), 'Herbarium amboinense' (ed. Burmann, 6 vols. Amsterdam, 1741–1755; vol. v p. 302); and 'Phil. Trans. Roy.' Soc. 1729, vol. 36 p. 377.

On the Averrhoa carambola, see R. Bruce, 'An account of the sensitive quality of the tree Averrhoa carambola' ('Phil. Trans. Roy.' Soc. 1785, vol.75 pt. ii p. 356).

53, 12

Heinrich Friedrich Link (1767–1851) was born at Hildesheim, and studied the natural sciences at Göttingen, where J. F. Blumenbach (1752–1840) was his tutor. In 1792 he was appointed professor of natural history at Rostock. He was interested in Kant, and for some years his writings had a distinctly philosophical bent. His 'Ueber die Leiter der Natur' (1794) touches upon many of the ideas taken up by Hegel in 'Die Naturphilosophie', and in 'Ueber Naturphilosophie' (1806) and 'Natur und Philosophie, ein Versuch' (1811) he shows that he continued to concern himself with the problems involved in a philosophical interpretation of the natural sciences, although he never advanced much beyond the Kantian position.

From 1797 until 1799 he travelled extensively in France, Spain and Portugal, and wrote an account of his journeyings (Eng. tr. by J. Hinckley, 'Travels in Portugal and through France and Spain' London, 1801). In 1811 he was appointed professor of botany at Breslau, and in 1815 professor of natural history at Berlin. As his interest in philosophy waned, he turned to history as a means of synthesizing knowledge, and expressed this change of view in a popular form in his 'Die Urwelt und das Altertum, erläutert durch die Naturkunde' (1820–1822). In his old age he came to regard inductive empiricism as the only sound means of grasping philosophical truths. He expressed this view in 'Philosophie der gesunden Vernunft' (1850), and near the end of his life, in a private conversation with his friend K. F. P. Martius (1794–1868), he said proudly but not with complete accuracy, 'Jch bin fünfzig Jahre lang den induktiven Weg gegangen.'

Hegel is here referring to his 'Grundlehren der Anatomie und Physiologie der Pflanzen' (Göttingen, 1807). Despite improvements in the microscope, very few advances in the sphere of plant anatomy had been made during the eighteenth century, and in the early years of the nineteenth century, phytotomists still knew very little about the nature and functions of the vascular structure of plants; attempts were made to ascribe a circulation to the sap, and the plant's vessels were therefore regarded as being analogous to the veins and lymphatic vessels of animal bodies. There was in fact no clear understanding of the structure, origin and function of these vessels, and in 1804 therefore, the Royal Academy of Sciences at Göttingen decided to invite prize-essays on the following subject, 'Although it has generally been accepted that plants are truly vascular in structure, some modern physiologists have denied this. A fresh microscopical investigation should be made therefore, either in order to confirm the observations of Malpighi, Grew, Duhamel, Mustel and Hedwig, or to demonstrate that the simpler organization of plants differs from that of the animal kingdom, and that it has its origin either in incomposite and distinct fibres and threads (Medicus), or in cellular and tubular tissue (Mirbel).'

Link's 'Grundlehren' and Rudolphi's 'Anatomie der Pflanzen' were awarded the prize, although they contradicted one another on several important points, whereas L. C. Treviranus's 'Vom inwendigen Bau der Gewächse', which most botanists would now consider to have been the best of these essays, was awarded a mere 'proxime accessit'.

In this work Link denies that receptacles such as the lactiferous and resiniferous ducts are vessels, and regards only the ducts in wood as being vascular. He notes that cells containing coloured sap occur between colourless cells, and concludes from this that the cells are sealed. With regard to the relationship between cells, threads and vessels, he comes to the conclusion that all these parts originate in the cellular tissue. Although he has no doubt that the threads develop from cells, he has no very clear conception of the way in which cells give rise to vessels.

53, 27

Charles François Brisseau de Mirbel (1776–1854) was professor at the Sorbonne, and Napoleon's 'Director of gardens and conservatories.' Réné Louiche Desfontaines (1750–1833) travelled for two years in north west Africa and discovered more than three hundred new plants, which he described in his 'Flora Atlantica' (2 vols. Paris, 1798).

Mirbel's account of Desfontaines' experience occurs in his 'Histoire naturelle, génerale et particulière des plantes' (vol. i pp. 263–264, Paris, 1802), 'Le hasard a rendu le célèbre Desfontaines témoin d'un phénomène très singulier; il étoit en voiture et transportait d'un lieu dans un autre un pied de sensitive; le mouvement communiqué à la plante fit d'abord fermer toutes les feuilles, mais elles se rouvrirent insensiblement et ne se fermèrent plus pendant la route, comme si elles se fussent accountumées au balancement de la voiture.'

54, 9

Goethe's 'Versuch die Metamorphose der Pflanzen zu erklären' was first published at Gotha in 1790, and then re-issued, together with other related writings, in his 'Zur Morphologie' (Stuttgart and Tübingen, 1817). The 'Deutsche Akademie der Naturforscher' has recently published a critical edition of these works: 'Goethe, die Schriften zur Naturwissenschaft' (vols. viii, ix, x, ed. D. Kuhn, Weimar, 1962, 1954, 1964).

Goethe said that because of the opposition to which it stimulated him, the 'Philosophia botanica' of Linnaeus (1751, Eng. tr. 'The elements of Botany' H. Rose, London, 1775), had the greatest influence upon his intellectual development after the writings of Shakespeare and Spinoza, 'For the innermost necessity of my being made it imperative, that what he had tried forcibly to keep apart, should tend towards unity.'

The general argument of the 'Metamorphosis of Plants' is not easy to follow, for while Goethe agrees with C. F. Wolff (1733–1794) in regarding the plant as a development from a basic leaf, he also thinks of it as a variation of a basic plant-type. He probably formulated his 'category of metamorphosis' by asking himself how it is that such a variety of living forms, ranging from the minutest mosses to the greatest trees, may be regarded as having a common factor, and coming to the conclusion that as all these forms have leaves, the leaf must constitute the basic organ of plant-life.

Goethe's great contribution to botany consists, as Hegel notes, in his having treated the plant as a living and developing unity (cf. M. Möbius 'Geschichte der Botanik' Jena, 1937 p. 150).

Literature in English on this subject is limited, but the following works will be found to be useful:—'Essay on the Metamorphosis of Plants. By J. W. von Goethe' tr. E. M. Cox ed. M. T. Masters in 'The Journal of Botany' ed. B. Seemann vol. I pp. 327–345 and 360–374 (London, 1863): M. T. Masters 'Vegetable Morphology' ('British and Foreign Medico-Chirurgical Review' vol. xxix pp. 202–218, Jan. 1862): W. Whewell 'History of the inductive sciences' vol. III pp. 433–441 (Cambridge, 1837): W. Darlington 'An essay on . . . plants; compiled chiefly from the writings of . . . Goethe' (West Chester Pa., 1839): K. Goebel 'The fundamental problems of present day plant morphology' ('Science' N. S. vol. xxii no. 550 pp. 33–45, July, 1905): B. Hayata 'An interpretation of Goethe's Blatt in his "Metamorphose der Pflanzen"' (Tokyo, 1921): W. B. Crow 'Contributions to the principles of morphology' (London, 1929).

54, 25

‚Es tritt ein Punkt ein, wo die Verfolgung der Vermittlung, es sey in chemischer oder in Weise mechanischer Allmählichkeit (graduality), abgebrochen und unmöglich wird'.

55, 8

See Schelling, 'Erster Entwurf eines Systems der Naturphilosophie' (1799, Schellings Werke ed. M. Schröter vol. ii p. 253, Munich, 1958). ‚Diese Identität der Sensibilität und des Magnetismus in Ansehung ihrer Ursache vorausgesetzt, so muß der Magnetismus, ebenso wie die Sensibilität das Bestimmende aller organischen Kräfte, das Bestimmende aller dynamischen Kräfte seyn.'

55, 29

Albrecht Wilhelm Roth (1757–1834) was born at Dötlingen in Oldenburg. He was the son of a clergyman, and it was his father who first interested him in botany. In 1775 he began to study medicine at Halle, and after taking his doctorate at Erlangen in 1778, he settled down as a general practitioner at Vegesack on the Weser, not far from Bremen.

He interested himself in the improvement of science instruction in the schools ('Ueber die Art und Nothwendigkeit, Naturgeschichte auf Schulen zu behandeln' Nuremberg, 1779), looked after a busy practice with great efficiency, botanized energetically in the surrounding countryside, and developed a small botanical garden for himself.

'Tentamen florae Germanicae', which is his main work, was published in three parts at Leipzig between 1788 and 1801. As a result of this book he was offered professorships at Jena and Erlangen, but as he could not bring himself to leave his garden, he refused them, and ended his days at Vegesack.

He made a number of important discoveries, being the first to note, for example, that the Drosera rotundifolia is insectivorous (1782). He did important work on the classification of aquatic Cryptogamia, being the first to apply the word 'Algae' to the class of plants to which it now refers (1797), and to define the genus Batrachospermum (1800), which Linnaeus had classified as a Fucus.

His definition of the genus Ceramium, which Treviranus refers to here, is to be found in his 'Catalecta Botanica quibus plantae novae et minus cognitae describuntur atque illustrantur'. (Fasc. primus, Leipzig, 1797 pp. 154–156). Roth also published a short survey of this work in German, 'Bemerkungen über das Studium der cryptogamischen Wassergewächse' (Hanover, 1797, see pp. 33–36).

56, 18

Treviranus cites Roth's Conferva scalaris as evidence of this, ‚Der Bildung dieser Eyer oder Samenkörner nun geht ein höchst merkwürdiges Phänomen, die Conjugation oder Copulation der Conferven, vorher. Gegen die Zeit nehmlich, wo sich jene Fruchtkeime bilden wollen, schwillt die Conferve etwas an, und aus den einzelnen Gliedern derselben schießen an den Seiten kurze, offenstehende Röhren hervor. Vermittelst dieser Röhren vereinigt sich jener Wasserfaden mit einer andern Conferve, die ebenfalls mit solchen Seiten= canälen versehen ist.'

In the Chlorophyceae group of algae, the subdivision Conjugatae effects reproduction solely by means of conjugation.

56, 30

Treviranus took this account of the Tillandsia usneoides from E. A. W. Zimmermann's translation of 'Travels through North and South Carolina, Georgia, East and West Florida' etc. (Philadelphia, 1791), by William Bartram (1739–1823). Zimmermann's translation appeared in volume ten of the 'Magazin von merkwürdigen neuen Reisebeschreibungen' (Berlin, 1793).

Francis Harper has recently published an excellent edition of 'The Travels of William Bartram' (Yale Univ. Press, 1958).

While describing his journey along the eastern side of St. John's River Florida, Bartram writes (Zimmermann p. 88, Harper p. 56), 'The long moss, so called (Tillandsea usneascites)'—Zimmermann standardizes the Latin—'is a singular and surprising vegetable production: it grows from the limbs and twigs of all trees in these southern regions, from N. lat. 35 down as far as 28, and I believe everywhere within the tropics. Wherever it fixes itself, on a limb, or branch, it spreads into short and intricate divarications; these in time collect dust, wafted by the wind, and which, probably by the moisture it absorbs, softens the bark and sappy part of the tree, about the roots of the plant, and renders it more fit for it to establish itself; and from this small beginning, it increases, by sending downwards and obliquely, on all sides, long pendant branches, which divide and subdivide themselves ad infinitum. It is common to find the spaces betwixt the limbs of large trees, almost occupied by this plant; it also hangs waving in the wind, like streamers, from the lower limbs, to a length of fifteen or twenty feet, and of bulk and weight more than several men could carry; and in some places, cart loads of it are lying on the ground, torn off, by the violence of the wind. Any part of the living plant, torn off and caught, in the limbs of a tree, will presently take root, and grow and increase, in the same degree of perfection, as if it has sprung up from the seed.'

57, 4

Louis Marie Aubert Dupetit-Thouars (1758–1831) was a native of Anjou. He was educated at a military academy, and at sixteen joined the regular army as a second lieutenant. The revolution unsettled him. In 1792 he was held in custody for six weeks by the local authorities at Quimper, who had found him botanizing in the district, and had regarded this activity with suspicion.

In September 1792 he fled the country, and spent the next ten years 'augmentant sans cesse son herbier' on Madagascar and the Mascarene Islands. When he arrived back in France in September 1802, he brought a collection of over two thousand species with him. He was appointed director of a nursery in Paris in 1807, and published several books on his work abroad, 'Histoire des végétaux recueilles dans les îles de France, de Bourbon et de Madagascar' (Paris, 1804); 'Esquisse de la flore de Tristan d'Acugna, précédés de la description de cette île, avec 15 planches et une carte' (Paris, 1815). He never systematized his work with any thoroughness, but he was highly thought of by several British botanists, including T. A. Knight (1759–1838) and John Lindley (1799–1865).

The development of the annual rings was very imperfectly understood at this time. C. F. Wolff (1733–1794) had attempted to explain their formation by postulating the growth of threads passing down from the new leaves and then combining to form these zones of new wood. The explanation of them offered by Dupetit-Thouars and C. A. Agardh (1785–1859), and assumed here by Willdenow, was even more fantastic. J. N. La Hire (1685–1727) had first formulated it in 'Mémoires de l'Academie des Sciences' 1719. Dupetit-Thouars drew upon La Hire's work, and expressed his own views on the subject in 'Essais sur la Végétation considerée dans le developpement des Bourgeons' (Paris, 1809). He defended them in 'Histoire d'un Morceau de Bois' (Paris,

1815). He evidently thought that the new wood was formed by 'root-fibres' passing down from the buds.

It was not until the middle of the nineteenth century that any clear conception of the function of the cambium in the formation of new wood was arrived at. See M. Möbius 'Geschichte der Botanik' (Jena, 1937, pp. 216–219).

57, 10

Willdenow noticed it in Robina Pseudacacia, which had had twigs of Robinia viscosa grafted upon it. He is evidently referring here to Link's 'Grundlehren der Anatomie und Physiologie der Pflanzen' (Nachträge i p. 50), ‚Eben so bey Propfreisern zwischen dem Holze des alten Stammes und dem Propfreise war eine neue Schicht von Parenchym gebildet worden, darüber war das Holz des Propfreises hingewachsen und die Rinde des alten Stammes umkleibete das Ganze.'

57, 14

Georg Andrea Agricola (1672–1738) was born and died in Regensburg, where he practised as a doctor. He made a great deal of money by advertising his skill in grafting and propagating plants from buds and roots, and claimed to have discovered a vegetable mummy (consisting largely of copal and turpentine) which with the aid of fire, would cause trees to sprout forth at the rate of sixty an hour.

Willdenow is here referring to his, 'Neu- und nie erhörter, doch in der Natur und Vernunft wohlgegründeter Versuch der universal Vermehrung aller Bäume, Stauden, und Blumen- Gewächse, das erste mahl theoretice als practice experimentiret' (Regensburg, 1716), in which he gives an account of his 'skills'. The book is well-produced and printed, and supplied with well-executed plates: see R. Bradley's Eng. tr. 'The Experimental Husbandman and Gardener' (London, 1721).

57, 14

Thomas Barnes was gardener to William Thomson Esq., at Elsham just north of Brigg in Lincolnshire. In 1758 he published, 'A New Method of propagating fruit-trees and flowering shrubs from their parts: Whereby the common kinds may be raised more expeditiously; and several curious exotics increased, which will not take root from cuttings or layers. Confirmed by successful and repeated experience.' (London, published by R. Baldwin at 1s 6d). Three editions of the pamphlet had appeared by 1762.

Barnes mentions that it was John Hill (1716–1775) who proposed the experiments he describes. Although Hill was never elected fellow of the Royal Society, and although his appointment as superintendent of the Royal Gardens at Kew was never confirmed, he was an industrious and learned botanist. He evidently knew of Agricola's book, because Barnes mentions it when describing the preparation of the mummy.

The preparation of this vegetable mummy was an important part of the whole procedure, 'Melt together, in a large earthen pipkin, two pound and a half of common pitch, and half a pound of turpentine. When they are melted, put in three quarters of an ounce of powder of aloes; stir them all together, and then set the matter on fire; . . . November the third, 1757, I took off four dozen leaves of the common Laurel, with the Bud entire in the bosom of each leaf; and everything being in readiness, I cut the wounded part smooth, wiped it dry, and covered it with some of the dressing . . . I planted them in four pretty large pots, one dozen in each. The mould in these pots was made extremely fine; and I planted them by making very small openings, and letting in the base of the leaf just so far that the top of the bud might not be wholly excluded from the benefit of the air.' He mentions similar experiments with White Poplars and Common and White Willow.

57, 23

This apple was named after the village of Borsdorf, which is situated on the river Parthe a few miles to the east of Leipzig. A. F. A. Diel (1756–1833), in his 'Ueber die Anlegung einer Obstorangerie in Scherben und die Vegetation der Gewächse' (Frankfurt-on-Main, 1798, p. 459) distinguishes between three varieties of Borsdorfer, largely on account of their periods of ripening.

Eduard Lucas (1816–1882), who founded the pomological institute at Reutlingen, and whose system of pomology replaced Diel's, classified Borsdorfers as the ninth of his fifteen classes of apples; see 'Die Lehre vom Obstbau' (1st ed. 1844/5, 8th ed. 1898).

The apple is a very fine German Rennet; it is a good keeper, and has a firm aromatic flesh.

58, 13

Lilium bulbiferum, the Bulb-bearing or Orange Lily, is found wild in Austria and the south of Europe, Siberia and Japan. It may be increased without digging up the plants, by means of the little bulbs that grow in plenty on the axils of the leaves.

Poa Bulbosa or Bulbous Meadow Grass is found in Sweden, Germany, Spain and North Africa. In England it is found only on sandy sea-coast, over which its little dry bulbs are blown in summer, until the autumn rains make them vegetate and take root.

Bryophyllum calycinum was sometimes known as the Cotyledon calycina. Oken, in his 'Lehrbuch der Naturgeschichte' (pt. ii sect. ii p. 851 (Jena), 1826) has the following note on it, ‚Jnſel Moritz, ſeit kurzem in allen Gärten und Zimmern; 2-3 Fuß hoch, mit breiten Fettblättern, welche das Eigenthümliche haben, daß die Kerben, wo ſie nur die Erde berühren, Wurzel ſchlagen und zu einer neuen Pflanze werden.'

58, 14

Agostino Mandirola (d. 1661) was born at Castelfidardo, a picturesque fortified town in the Italian province of Ancona. The date of his birth is unknown. He was a doctor of theology and a *conventual*, that is to say, a Franciscan following a mitigated form of the rules of his order. Like most of the botanists and horticulturalists of his day, he was also interested in the medicinal properties of plants. Little is known of him, see however Giovanni Cinelli (1625–1706) 'Biblioteca volante di Gio' (ed. Sancassani, 4 vols. Venice, 1734–1747) vol. iii p. 249: G. Panelli 'Memorie d'uomini illustri del Piceno' (Ascoli, 1757–1758): 'Novelle letterarie' (1759), col. 329: 'Miscellanea Francescana di storia, di lettere, di arti' (1926) pp. 88–89: P. A. Saccardo 'La botanica in Italia' (2 vols. Venice, 1895–1901) vol. i p. 101: C. Trinci 'L'Agricoltore' (Venice, 1796).

He was evidently the first to propagate orange and lemon trees from leaves, and he gave an account of the method he used in a well-written and widely read book, 'Manuale di giardinieri. 1. il modo di connoscere e coltivare li fiori di bulbi piu rari, 2. la cultura delli fiori de radiche piu rigardevoli, 3. il modo di cultivare gli agrumi.' (Vicenza, 1652).

Further editions of the book were published at Macerata (1658), Vicenza (1661), Venice (1675 and 1684), and Roveredo (1733). A French translation also appeared, 'Manuel du jardinier . . . par Sieur Mandirola, traduit sur l'original italien' (tr. M. Raudi, Paris, 1765). There are two German translations, the first published at Nuremberg in 1670, and the second, which is a great improvement on its predecessor, nine years later: see 'Der Italiänische Blumen- und Pomeranzen- Garten. F. Agustini Mandirolae. Nunmehro zum andern mal in unserer Mutter-Sprache aufgelegt, und mit Anmerkungen und schönen Figuren ausgezieret' (tr. W.A.S.U.R., Nuremberg, 1679).

The account of this method of propagation occurs in book iii ch. v (p. 374) of this second German edition, 'I put the best earth through a fine sieve and filled a tub with it. Taking the stalked leaves of these trees, I planted them in the tub so as to leave about two-thirds of their length above ground. I then filled a small pitcher with water, and placed it so that the drops should fall, in the abovementioned manner, into the middle of the tub. As soon as the drops had worn out a hole, I was careful to fill it again with fresh earth. In this way I not only obtained saplings easily, but also saplings with fine shoots.'

Link knew of Mandirola's book from 'Versuch einer Gründlichen Erläuterung der Merckwürdigsten Begebenheiten in der Natur' (Marburg, 1735) by L. P. Thummig (1697–1728). Chapter seventeen of this work treats 'Of trees, which are propagated from leaves': see especially pp. 108–9, where Thummig specifies the process into propagation from buds, stalks and calluses.

58, 34

Goethe analyzes the reception of this book in the following way ('Zur Morphologie' 1817, p. 66), ,Das Publikum stußte: denn nach seinem Wunsch ſich gut und gleichförmig bedient zu ſehen, verlangt es an jeden daß er in ſeinem Fach bleibe und dieſes Anſinnen hat auch guten Grund: denn wer das Vortreffliche leiſten will, welches nach allen Seiten hin unendlich iſt, ſoll es nicht, wie Gott und die Natur wohl thun dürfen, auf mancherley Wegen verſuchen. Daher will man daß ein Talent das ſich in einem gewiſſen Feld hervorthat, deſſen Art und Weiſe allgemein anerkannt und beliebet iſt, aus ſeinem Kreiſe ſich nicht entferne, oder wohl gar in einem weit abgelegenen hinüberſpringe. Wagt es einer, ſo weiß man ihm keinen Dank, ja man gewährt ihm, wenn er es auch recht macht, keinen beſondern Beyfall.' On pp. 69–79 and 117–127 he gives an account of its subsequent fate.

J. Sachs ('Geschichte der Botanik' Munich, 1875 pp. 168–172) regards Goethe's botanical writings as somewhat muddled, but since the appearance of A. Hansen's 'Metamorphose der Pflanze' (Giessen, 1907): G. Lakon's 'Goethe's physiologische Erklärung der Pflanzenmetamorphose' (Beiheften zum Bot. Zbl., vol. 38, ii, 1921): J. Schuster's annotated edition of 'Versuch die Metamorphose der Pflanzen zu erklären' (Berlin, 1924): W. Troll's 'Goethe's morphologische Schriften' (Jena, 1926): and D. Kuhn's edition of the morphological works (Weimar, 1954, 1962, 1964), a fuller understanding of his significance as a botanist has become possible.

59, 9

'Zur Morphologie' (1817 ed.), ‚So wie wir nun die verſchiedenen ſcheinenden Organe der ſproſſenden und blühenden Pflanze alle aus einem einzigen nehmlich dem Blatte, welches ſich gewöhnlich an jedem Knoten entwickelt, zu erklären geſucht haben; ſo haben wir auch diejenigen Früchte, welche ihre Samen feſt in ſich zu verſchließen pflegen, aus der Blattgeſtalt herzuleiten gewagt' (p. 59) . . . Wenn alſo alle Theile der Pflanze, den Stengel ausgenommen, auf die Form des Blattes zurückgeführt werden können, und nichts als Modification derſelben ſind: ſo ergiebt ſich leicht, daß die Generationstheorie der Pflanzen nicht ſehr ſchwer zu entwickeln iſt; und zugleich iſt der Weg bezeichnet, den man einſchlagen muß, wenn man dieſe Theorie liefern will' (pp. 85–86).

59, 29

Willdenow says that the *richness* of the *soil* is the deciding factor here, not cultivation as such, ‚Birnen, Citronen und mehrere Gewächſe haben in mageren Boden Dornen, die ſich in fetterem verlieren.' Link, in his edition of the book (1821), questions this fact, and this probably accounts for Hegel's modification of Willdenow's statement.

61, 7

The Sorbus Hybrida is the Bastard Service, or Mountain Ash. The Sorbus Aucuparia is the Mountain Service or Rowan Tree. The name Aucuparia originated from the fact that the German fowlers of Hegel's day used the

berries of this tree to bait the springes or nooses of hair with which they en-
trapped Redwings and Fieldfares (see the note on III. 340).

61, 9

Friedrich Joseph Schelver (1778–1832) was born at Osnabrück, and studied
medicine at Göttingen, where he graduated in 1798 with a thesis 'De irrita-
bilitate'. He then returned to his home town, and worked as a general practitioner until 1802, when he became a private tutor at Halle. In 1803 he was
appointed professor of philosophy at Jena, where he remained until 1806, and
where he must have become acquainted with Hegel. In 1806 he took up the
appointment of professor of medicine at Heidelberg, where he remained for
the rest of his life. He was director of the Heidelberg botanical garden from
1811 until 1827.

Early in his career he produced several works on entomology and also inter-
ested himself in the writings of Schelling and Oken, but after his move to
Heidelberg, he concerned himself almost exclusively with botanical studies.
During his stay at Jena, he persuaded Goethe that the formation of pollen has
nothing to do with fertilization, but although this opinion fitted in well with
Goethe's theory of metamorphosis, it was so unorthodox that he asked
Schelver not to publish the fact that he had begun to question the doctrine of
the sexuality of plants.

Schelver felt at liberty to express his views once he had left Jena however,
and did so in his 'Kritik der Lehre von den Geschlechtern der Pflanzen' (Heidelberg, 1812), to which he added two supplements (Karlsruhe, 1814 and 1823).
His doctrine was championed by his son-in-law August Wilhelm Henschel
(1790–1856) in 'Von der Sexualität der Pflanzen' (Breslau, 1820).

61, 10

The following passage was based largely on Goethe's observation of the
Stinking Hellebore (Helleborus foetidus).

61, 29

Goethe gives 'Folia floria' as the Latin equivalent.

63, 29

Four species of the genus Sarracenia were known at that time, the Sarracenia
Flava, Minor, Rubra, and Purpurea. See Thomas Green 'The Universal Herbal'
(2 vols. 2nd ed. London, 1824) vol. 11 p. 529.

63, 38

Hermann Friedrich Autenrieth (1799–1874) was the son of J. H. Autenrieth
(1772–1835), chancellor of Tübingen university. He was educated at Stuttgart
Grammar School, and in 1816 began his medical studies at Tübingen. As early
as October 1816, he had an article, 'Observations on some cases of deafness,

with the means of removing them', published in the Edinburgh Medical and Surgical Journal (vol. 12 pp. 498–500). Hegel quotes from his doctoral thesis, 'De Discrimine Sexuali Jam In Seminibus Plantarum Dioïcarum Apparente Praemio Regio Ornata. Additis De Sexu Plantarum Argumentis Generalibus' (Tübingen, 1821), and as he makes his own translation of Autenrieth's Latin, it may be of interest to give the original.

'In antherarum quidem formatione foliolorum margines per longitudinem introrsum convolvebantur, ita ut duplex idemque cavus primum cylindrus exoriretur, in quo medio perspicue saepe unum folioli calcini marginum, non mutatum, longitudine decurrere conspexi (xi et xii), cujusque apici fasciculus pilorum impositus erat (xiii), qui certe ex incremento lanae folioli calcini originem ducebat. Verum simul ac anthera magis ad perfectum statum accedebat et pulposa materia repleri coepit, fasciculus ille, sensim exarescens, postremo decidit, anthera justam legitimamque conditionem tunc adepta (xiv).

Similis, quamvis minus perspicua, mutatio quoque in germinis stilique formatione apparuit, cum foliola calicina, et saepe quidem plura (xvi) invicem connata, ex margine introrsum arcuarentur (xv); quo facto simplex modo cavitas orta est, posthac in ovarium mutata. Pilorum autem ille fasciculus, cavitatis apici impostus, idemque solidiore telae cellulosae obturamento a primitiarum germinis cavitate separatus, non, ut in antheris, exaruit, sed, prolongatus, perfecti stigmatis naturam assecutus est (xv et xvi).' The numerals refer to six of the diagrams on plate one of this book; the quotation occurs on pages 29–30.

Immediately after taking his doctorate, Autenrieth left for the Low Countries and Great Britain. He contributed another article to the Edinburgh Medical and Surgical Journal (vol. 18 pp. 325–34, July, 1822), 'On the sporadic abdominal typhus of young people', and collected material for his, 'Uebersicht über die Volkskrankheiten in Grossbritannien, mit Hinweisung auf ihre Ursachen und die daraus entstehenden Eigenthümlichkeiten der englischen Heilkunde' (Tübingen, 1823; reviewed in Edin. Med. and Surg. Journal vol. 23, pp. 308–35, 1825).

In 1823 he became a private tutor in medicine at Tübingen, and in 1834 just before the death of his father, he was appointed to a professorship at the university, where he continued to teach until he retired on account of illness in 1859. During his teaching period at Tübingen he wrote numerous articles and books on medical subjects, and edited his father's 'Ansichten über Natur-und Seelenleben' (Tübingen, 1836).

64, 35

'Versuch die Metamorphose der Pflanzen zu erklären' (Gotha, 1790, p. 3), ‚Die regelmäßige Metamorphose, können wir auch die fortschreitende nennen: denn sie ist es, welche sich von den ersten Samenblättern bis zur letzten Ausbildung der Frucht immer stufenweise wirksam bemerken läßt, und

durch Umwandlung einer Gestalt in die andere, gleichsam auf einer geistigen
Leiter, zu jenem Gipfel der Natur, der Fortpflanzung durch zwey Geschlechter
hinauf steigt'.

This passage shows to what extent Hegel's *overall* view of botanical phenomena coincided with Goethe's.

66, 8

Cf. 'Faust' pt. I lines 1936–1939: the study scene, where the student meets
Mephistopheles:

> ,Wer will was Lebendiges erkennen und beschreiben,
> Sucht erst den Geist heraus zu treiben,
> Dann hat er die Teile in seiner Hand,
> Fehlt leider! nur das geistige Band.'

68, 37

Antoin Galland (1646–1715), the French orientalist, was the first to translate
the story of Aladdin and his wonderful lamp from the Arabic; see 'Les Mille et
une Nuits' (12 vols. Paris, 1704–8). In Hegel's day, the best edition of this work
was Caussin's (9 vols. Paris, 1806), and both German translations, 'Arabische
Märchen' (4 parts, Gotha, 1790–1) and 'Der Tausend und einen Nacht' (tr.
Zinserling, 3 vols., Stuttgart, 1823–4) were from the French. Cf. R. F. Burton's
eccentric version: 'The Book of the Thousand Nights and a Night' (ed. Smithers,
12 vols. London, 1897) vol. X pp. 33–140.

The Danish romantic poet Adam Oehlenschlaeger (1779–1850) published
his 'Aladdin' in 1805, and like Hegel, took the lamp to be a symbol of

> ,Den hemmelige Urkraft: Lyset selv,
> Som virker alt, hvad der er Liv og Lykke.'

69, 32

The *Trapa Natans* or Four-horned Water Caltrops occurs over a considerable
part of Europe, the Caucasus and Siberia. It has been used from early times for
food, medicine and magic, and is supposed to have been introduced into
Switzerland as long ago as the period of the lake dwellings, although it is now
nearly exterminated in that country. In Hegel's day it was sold in the market
at Venice under the name of the *Jesuit Nut*. At Vercelli it was called *Galarin*,
and was much eaten by the children and the poor of the city.

Willdenow made this 'discovery' in 1788, and published his first account of
it in vol. XVII (p. 19) of the 'Annalen der Botanick' edited by P. Usteri (1768–
1831). He was wrong in regarding this 'long plumule' as foliar in nature however. It is by means of this finely divided submerged organ that gaseous change
takes place as the result of the intimate contact achieved with the water. The
organ probably assists not only assimilation but also respiration. 'In the Water

Chestnut, Trapa natans, the later *roots*, developed adventitiously below the leaf-bases are free-floating and branched. These feathery structures have been supposed by some authors to be of foliar nature; this is erroneous, although physiologically they correspond to the divided leaves of *Myriophyllum*.' Agnes Arber 'Water Plants, a study of aquatic angiosperms' (Cambridge, 1920) p. 207.

69, 35
Hegel inserted this description of the middle caudex. He took it from the first part of Willdenow's work (§ 13, p. 31), which is devoted to the definition of botanical terms.

69, 39
The pagination of the 'Grundlehren der Anatomie und Physiologie der Pflanzen' (Göttingen, 1807) is faulty at this point. Hegel does not correct it in this reference. The page referred to in parenthesis is actually p. 246 of the text.

70, 1
Ranunculus Bulbosus, i.e. Bulbous Crowfoot or Buttercup. Shakespeare's 'Cuckoo-buds of yellow hue'.

70, 15
The system of plant-classification proposed by Linnaeus (1707–1778) in his 'Systema naturae' (Leyden, 1735) was based on the number, proportion, figure and situation of the stamens and pistils, the so-called sexual organs of the flower. By means of it, he enumerated twenty five classes, *Triandria*, which have three fertile stamens constituting the third, and *Hexandria*, which have six, the sixth. Linnaeus' was a binary system, the first name indicating the plant's genus, and the second its species, and as it was easily grasped and readily applicable, it was soon widely accepted.

Linnaeus himself admitted that it was not a natural system however, that is to say, that it took into account only a few marked characters in plants, and did not propose to unite them by natural affinities. However, in his 'Fragmenta methodi naturalis' (Halle, 1747), and his 'Philosophia Botanica' (1751), he drew upon the system put forward by John Ray (1627–1705) in his 'Methodus Plantarum Nova' (London, 1682), and suggested that a division of plants in accordance with the number of seed-leaves they exhibit, i.e. into acotyledons, monocotyledons and dicotyledons might provide the basis for a more natural method of classification. 'Vegetables may be divided into the three following tribes, viz. 1. Monocotyledons; 2. Dicotyledons; and 3. Acotyledons. The first have only one seminal leaf, valve, or lobe; and therefore the leaves they put forth, at their first springing out of the ground, are entirely similar in the succeeding one. This tribe comprehends the three families of 1. palms, 2. grasses, and 3. bulbous plants of the lily kind etc.' ('Philosophia Botanica' 1751 pt. I, ch. iii, sect. 78, tr. H. Rose, London, 1775). Linnaeus never worked this suggestion out into a complete system however, and Hegel's statement that Jussieu was the first to draw attention to the difference between monocotyledons and dicotyledons is therefore only partly incorrect.

Antoine Laurent de Jussieu (1748–1836) came of a family distinguished for a century and a half by the botanists it produced. He was born at Lyons, but at an early age he was invited to Paris by his uncle Bernard de Jussieu (1699–1777), who gave him an excellent training in medicine and botany. In 1759 his uncle was asked to arrange the plants in the royal garden of the Trianon at Versailles, and did so on the basis of the natural system of classification recently outlined by Linnaeus ('Histoire de l'Academie Royale des Sciences' Paris, 1777).

Antoine de Jussieu began work on his, 'Genera plantarum secundum ordines naturales disposita, juxta methodum in horto regio Parisiensi exaratum' the year after his uncle's death, and saw the last sheets of it through the press as the revolution was sweeping the French capital. In this book, which is generally accepted as laying the foundation of modern botanical classification, he draws upon his uncle's work (see pp. lxiii–lxx), and divides the whole vegetable kingdom into acotyledons (Cryptogamia), monocotyledons and dicotyledons. He accepts many of the families formulated by Linnaeus and his uncle, diagnoses them with much greater precision, and groups them into fifteen classes. Instead of merely enumerating smaller co-ordinated groups of plants, he attempts to grasp the *actual* division of the whole vegetable kingdom as a series of gradually subordinated groups.

In 1790 Jussieu was made a member of the municipality of Paris, in 1792 he was put in charge of the hospitals of the city, and in 1793 he was given the task of organizing the Natural History Museum. It was not until 1802 that he was able to resume his botanical studies.

Although his system rapidly replaced that of Linnaeus in France and Germany, it was not so readily accepted in Britain, and Sir James Edward Smith (1759–1828) was purveying Linnean principles in his 'Introduction to Botany' as late as 1824. Robert Brown (1773–1858) employed Jussieu's system of classification in his 'Prodromus Florae Novae Hollandiae et insulae Van-Diemen' (London, 1810) however, and in 1830 John Lindley (1799–1865) introduced de Candolle's version of it to the British public in his 'Introduction to a Natural System of Classification'.

Once systems of classification based on natural affinities had replaced the old artificial systems, it was not long before the immutability of the species assumed by Linnaeus and his predecessors was questioned. Goethe's doctrine of morphology had also drawn attention to plant development (W. von Wasielewski, 'Goethe und die Descendenztheorie' Frankfurt-on-Main, 1903), and when the work of Franz Unger (1800–1870) on fossil plants, and of Wilhelm Hofmeister (1824–1877) on the morphology of mosses appeared in the early 1850's, the scene was set for the acceptance of Darwin's doctrine.

70, 32

Hegel mentions the Musa paradisiaca as an instance of this. ('Jenenser Realphilosophie' II p. 139).

71, 8

Hegel mentions the Cactus as an instance of this. ('Jenenser Realphilosophie' II p. 140).

71, 22

‚Der Träger'. Hegel is evidently referring here to the gynophore (der Stempelträger) or the torus (der Blumenboden).

72, 9

K. H. Schultz (1798–1871) 'Die Natur der lebendigen Pflanze' pt. I (Berlin, 1823) pp. 508–526, ‚Von den Lebensgefäßen (vasa laticis), ‚Die verschiedenartigen Dinge, welche seit Malpighi unter dem Namen der eigenen Gefäße begriffen worden sind, sind theils Sekretionsorgane, und theils Gefäße, in denen der Kreislauf vor sich geht. Diese letzteren haben auch einen ganz verschiedenen Bau von den Sekretionsorganen, und ich nenne sie zum Unterschiede von allen Dingen womit sie verwechselt worden sind, Lebensgefäße (vasa laticis), weil sie den Lebensaft (latex) führen'.

In this work Schultz attaches too much importance to the laticiferous vessels, and overestimates the extent of their distribution. To the lacteal juice he attributes the function of a vital-sap, and an independent movement which he calls a 'cyclosis'. The analogy with the functioning of an animal body which these assertions were meant to imply was questioned by a number of botanists and finally rejected. Hugo von Mohl (1805–1872), professor of botany at Tübingen, demolished Schultz's arguments and so became involved in an acrimonious debate ('Botanische Zeitung' I, 1843). J. B. D. Boussingault (1802–1887), professor of chemistry at Lyons, took the trouble to check Schultz's experiments, and found many of them to be faulty. Hermann Schacht (1814–1864), professor of botany at Bonn, examined the lactiferous vessels very carefully, and showed conclusively that they do not form a continuous system ('Die sogenannten Milchsaft-Gefässe der Euphorbiaceen, u.s.w. sind Milchsaft führende, nicht selten verzweigte Bastzellen' Botanische Zeitung 1851, col. 513–521; cf. his 'Physiologische Botanik,' Berlin, 1852).

One hundred and thirty-three pages of the first volume of Schultz's book are devoted to 'a philosophic confirmation' of its subject-matter, so he may well deserve the qualified compliment paid him by Hegel on this account. As Hegel indicates however, this is not to be confused with the tribute paid to the thoroughness of his empiricism.

73, 9

Kurt Polykarp Joachim Sprengel (1766–1833) was the son of a clergyman, and in 1783 began to study theology at Greifswald. In 1785 however, he began to study medicine at Halle, and in 1789 was appointed to a professorship at the university. His main interests were botany and the history of medicine. In 1797 he was appointed director of the botanical garden at Halle, and for almost forty years worked at his great 'Versuch einer pragmatischen Geschichte der Arznei-kunde' (5 vols. Halle, 1792–1828).

He was remarkable as a linguist, and mastered Swedish, French, Italian and Spanish, as well as Hebrew and the classical languages.

He published a number of important botanical works. His 'Historia rei herbariae' (Amsterdam, 1807–1808) was translated into German in 1817; his 'Grundzüge der wissenschaftlichen Pflanzenkunde' (Leipzig, 1820) was translated into English as 'Elements of the philosophy of plants' (Edinburgh, 1821), and C. D. E. Koenig published an English translation of another of his works: see 'An introduction to the study of Cryptogamous Plants' (London, 1807).

Link is here referring to his 'Anleitung zur Kenntniss der Gewächse, in Briefen von Kurt Sprengel, Professor der Botanik in Halle. Erste Sammlung. Von dem Bau der Gewächse und der Bestimmung ihrer Theile' (Halle, 1802). This work is written in the style of 'Botanical dialogues between Hortensia and her four children, Charles, Harriet, Juliet and Henry, designed for the use of schools. By a Lady'. (London, 1799), but by raising the question of the origin of cellular-tissue and spiral vessels, and by postulating a kind of peristaltic vascular movement, it awoke interest in plant anatomy, which since the days of Marcello Malpighi (1628–1694) and Nehemiah Grew (1641–1712) had been somewhat neglected.

‚Die erste und wichtigste Frage, die aber auch am schwersten zu beantworten ist, wird immer die seyn: Worauf, auf welche Form führt uns alle Zergliederung der Gewächse zurück? Was ist das erste, woraus sich die Theile des Gewächses bilden, und was das letzte, was uns die Zergliederung als Gränze der vegetabilischen Bildung zeigt?

So viel ich bis itzt weiß, meine Gnädige, scheint sich die Natur bey Pflanzen wie bey Thieren in der Bildung eines Gewebes zu gefallen, welches wir am besten mit den Bienenzellen vergleichen und, um kurz zu seyn, Zellgewebe nennen können.' (loc. cit. p. 88).

74, 1

Lorenz Oken (1779–1851) was born at Bohlsbach near Offenburg in Baden, and educated at the Franciscan Grammar School at Offenburg. He studied natural history and medicine at Freiburg im Breisgau, Würzburg and Göttingen, and in 1807 was appointed professor of medicine at Jena.

His inaugural lecture at Jena was 'On the significance of the skull bones', it was delivered in the presence of Goethe, who was rector of the university, and gave rise to the famous controversy concerning the origin of the idea of the vertebral analogies of the skull (see III. 305).

Oken's interest in the natural sciences had been awakened by Schelling, Steffens and D. G. Kieser (1779–1862), and it was because of his philosophical attitude towards the subjects he was teaching at Jena that he was not accepted as professor of medicine at Rostock in 1811. He was an excellent teacher in that he was able to stimulate enthusiasm, but he never developed the habit of testing his ideas by research and genuine induction. In his 'Lehrbuch der Naturphilosophie' (3 vols. Jena, 1809, 1810, 1811, Eng. tr. A. Tulk 'Elements of Physio-philosophy' The Ray Society, London, 1848), he systematized the natural sciences in much the same general way as Hegel, but his logic was flimsy, and his systematization was therefore arbitrary and frequently irresponsible.

In 1816 he began the journal 'Isis, eine encyclopädische Zeitschrift, vorzüglich für Naturgeschichte, vergleichende Anatomie und Physiologie'. Articles were admitted on politics as well as on the natural sciences however, and it was because of its political line that the court of Weimar, in 1819, gave Oken the choice of discontinuing the journal or resigning his professorship. He chose the latter alternative, and continued to publish it until 1848.

He lectured at Basel from 1821 until 1822, and in 1822 organized the first of the annual meetings of German naturalists and medical practitioners, at Leipzig. He had been impressed by the meetings of the corresponding Swiss association and the German meetings in their turn gave rise (1831) to the foundation of the British Association for the Advancement of Science. He was professor of physiology at Munich from 1827 until 1832, when he accepted the appointment of professor of natural history at Zürich.

In his essay on generation (1805) he put forward the proposition that, 'all the parts of higher animals are made up of an aggregate of Infusoria or animated globular monads', but it was the microscopical observations of Brown, Schleiden and Schwann which were to confirm this. In his 'Erste Ideen zur Theorie des Lichts' (1808) he suggested that, 'light could be nothing but a polar tension of the ether evoked by a central body in antagonism with the planets, and heat was more than a motion of this ether', and so anticipated the experimental discoveries of H. C. Oersted and M. Faraday. Sir Richard Owen, in his 'Archetype and Homologies of the Vertebrate Skeleton' worked out inductively Oken's vertebral theory of the skull. Oken played his part in the advancement of the sciences therefore, but as Hegel notes, most of his constructions were mere assertions, and it was left to others to stabilize his system by logic, and verify or reject his suggestions by means of experiment.

75, 11

'Philosophia Botanica' (1751) tr. Hugh Rose, London, 1775 p. 66 (pt. I ch. iii sect. 81), 'The second part of the vegetable is the herb or main body of the plant, which rises from the root, and is terminated by the fructification. It consists of the trunk, the leaves, the fulcra, props or supports, and the hybernacula or winter quarters . . . The leaves transpire and draw the air, as the lungs in animals, and also afford the shade . . .'

75, 37

Spix and Martius are here describing the *Locust Tree*, the beans in the pods of which, 'are enclosed in a whitish substance of fine filamenta as sweet as honey. This substance . . . is eaten by the Indians with great avidity. The wild bees are fond of building their nests in this tree . . . From between the principal roots of the tree a fine yellowish or red transparent resin, called gumamine, exudes. It is collected in large lumps, and makes a varnish superior to Chinese Lacca, when dissolved in the highest rectified spirits of wine. It burns readily, and with a clear flame, emitting a grateful fragrant smell, on which account it is sometimes ordered by way of fumigation, in the chambers of persons labouring with asthmas or suffocating catarrhs.' Thomas Green 'The Universal Herbal' (2 vols. 2nd ed. London, 1824) vol. I p. 724.

76, 8

Bonaventura Corti (1729–1813) was professor at Modena. He was born near Milan and died at Reggio. He published two accounts of this discovery: 'Osservazioni microscopiche sulla Tremella e sulla circolazione del fluido in una pianta acquajola' (Lucca, 1774), and 'Lettera sulla circolazione del fluido scoperta in varie piante' (Modena, 1775). He tells us that the sight of the plasma streaming in the cells so amazed him, that it took his breath away ('rimasi senza spirito'). Opinions differ as to the identity of the 'aquatic plant' in which he observed this movement. Hegel thought that it was the Water-horsetail, but F. Tiedemann ('Physiologie des Menschen' Darmstadt, 1830 § 279) thought that it was probably Willdenow's Caulinia fragilis.

76, 9

Giovanni Battista Amici (1786–1863) was a native of Modena. After studying at Bologna, he started an optical workshop, and in 1811 produced the first really effective reflecting-microscope, for which he was awarded a medal by the Institute of Milan. He was appointed professor of geometry and algebra at the university of Modena in 1810, and in 1815 began to teach in the philosophical faculty of the university. In 1825 he was appointed director of the astronomical observatory at Florence and held the post until 1859.

He effected several improvements in the construction of the microscope, and pursued his botanical studies mainly in order to demonstrate the excellence of the instruments he was producing. He read this account of his investigations into the functions of the Chara in 1818, see 'Memorie della Societa Italiana della Scienza, XVIII, Fisica' (Modena, 1820) pp. 183–204.

Hugo von Mohl wrote an obituary notice on him for 'Die Botanische Zeitung' (vol. XXI pp. 1–8, Leipzig, 1863). The article in the 'Jahrbücher der Literatur' vol. V pp. 203–215 (Vienna, 1819) seems to have been Hegel's main source of information on the subject. It is a review, evidently by K. F. A. von Schreiber (1775–1852) the Austrian naturalist, of two works by Amici: 'Memoria . . . de' Micropscopj catadiottrici' (Modena, 1818), and the published version of the paper read to the Society, 'Osservazioni sulla circolazione del Succhio nella Chara' (Modena, 1818).

77, 1

F. Tiedemann, in his 'Physiologie des Menschen' (Darmstadt, 1830, Eng. tr. 1834) §§ 278–290 discusses this subject at some length, and assesses the various books and articles dealing with it. For a contemporary English account of it see T. A. Knight (1759–1838). 'On the motion of the Sap of trees' ('Phil. Trans. Roy. Soc.' 1801–1808).

Hegel, in a footnote, presents the pros and cons of the case by making mention of the 'Wiener Jahrbücher' (1819, vol. V p. 203), and, in parenthesis, of two crucial articles.

L. C. Treviranus (1779–1864) published his, 'Beobachtungen über die Bewegung des körnigen Wesens in einigen Conferven und einer Chara' in a periodical which had been started by F. Weber (1781–1823) and D. M. H. Mohr (d. 1808), and which after the latter's death was published as 'Beiträge zur Naturkunde'. In Verbindung mit meinen Freunden verfasst und herausgegeben von Dr. und Prof. Friedr. Weber (vol. II, Kiel, 1810, pp. 126–141). He gives an account of an observation he made on June 24, 1803, while watching the Conferva glomerata L. through a microscope, ‚Ich hatte nun das mir unbeschreibliche Vergnügen, zwei Glieder eines Fadens neben einander zu sehen, worin zahllose Körper, etwas mehr angeschwollen wie gewöhnlich, in einer kreisenden und drehenden Bewegung sich befanden . . . In dem einen Gliede waren alle Körner in Bewegung in dem andern bewegten sie sich nur in der einen Hälfte desselben, während sie in der andern ruhten: doch kamen auch diese zuletzt in Bewegung.'

K. F. P. Martius (1794–1864) read his paper, 'Über den Bau und die Natur der Charen' to a meeting of the Royal Academy of Sciences at Munich in October 1815; it was published in 'Nova Acta Physico Medica Academiae Caesareae Leopoldino-Carolinae naturae curiosorum' (vol. IX, Erlangen. 1818, pp. 181–214). In it, he mentions the publications of Corti and Treviranus, and then speaks of his own observations (p. 175), ‚Ich gestehe, daß, obgleich ich die Chara flexiles im Frühling, Sommer und Herbste unter dem Mikroscop untersucht habe, ich doch nie so glücklich war, eine Bewegung in ihr zu entdecken, die nur im geringsten Grade den Schein von Regelmäßigkeit für sich gehabt hatte'.

77, 3

Schultz's doctoral disputation was concerned with this: see, 'Ueber den Kreislauf des Saftes im Schöllkraut und in mehreren andern Pflanzen' (Berlin, 1822).

77, 12

,Die Blutkügelchen in Thierischen.' Hegel is here referring to blood corpuscles (Körperchen) of course, but this term had not yet come into use.

77, 20

Corti, Amici, Treviranus, and on some occasions Schultz also, had evidently observed the movement of the plant's cytoplasm and nuclei, which is in many cases of a circulatory or rotatory kind. This first clear description in English of this rotary movement was given by Robert Brown (1773–1858) in 1831, who had observed it in the staminal hairs of Tradescantia virginica, the cells of which contain a large sap-cavity, across which numerous protoplasmic bridges run in all directions. In forms such as Elodea, Nitella, Chara etc., where the cytoplasm is restricted mainly to the periphery of the sap vacuole and lining the cell wall, the streaming movement is exhibited in one direction only. In some cases both the nucleus and the chromatophores may be carried along in the rotating stream, but in others, such as Nitella, the chloroplasts may remain motionless in a non-motile layer of the cytoplasm in direct contact with the cell wall. See A. J. Ewart 'On the Physics and Physiology of Protoplasmic Streaming in Plants' (Oxford, 1903).

Schultz's fault lay in his failing to distinguish between these protoplasmic movements and the functioning of the lactiferous tissue. M. J. Schleiden (1804–1881) was the first to point out the true analogy between the plant and the animal, by showing ('Grundzüge der wissenschaftlichen Botanik', Leipzig, 1842-3), that all the organs of plants are built up of cells, that the plant embryo originates from a single cell, and that the physiological activities of the plant are dependent upon the individual activities of these vital units.

78, 18

Johann Christian Friedrich Meyer (1777–1854) was the son of an orphanage inspector in the employ of the grand-duke of Saxe-Weimar-Eisenach. He was born at Eisenach, and attended the grammar school there before studying the law and cameralistics at Jena. Theoretical and experimental physics interested him as much as forestry, and after finishing his studies in 1799, he taught these subjects at the school of estate management run by H. Cotta (1763–1844) at Zillbach near Meiningen.

In 1803 he took his doctorate at Jena, the title of his thesis being 'Abhandlung über Forst und Jagdrecht', and in the following year he was appointed to a lectureship in forestry management at the newly founded institute of forestry at Dreissigacker near Meiningen. J. M. Bechstein (1757–1822) was then in charge of this establishment, which was in the process of becoming the most outstanding of its kind in Germany. Meyer was gifted as a teacher, but it was mainly on account of his books that his fame spread. He was influenced by the philosophical attitude towards the natural sciences being cultivated at Jena, and this is particularly apparent in his first book, 'System einer auf Theorie und Erfahrung gestützten Lehre über die Einwirkung der Naturkräfte auf die Erziehung, das Wachstum und die Ernährung der Forstgewächse' (Coburg and Leipzig, 1806). In 1807 he published 'Abhandlungen über die Waldhut, in ökonomischer, forstwirtschaftlicher und politischer Hinsicht'. In the preface to the book quoted here by Link, 'Naturgetreue Darstellung der Entwikkelung, Ausbildung, und des Wachstums der Pflanzen, und der Bewegung und Functionen ihrer Säfte; mit vorzüglicher Hinsicht auf Holzgewächse' (Leipzig, 1808), he shows that he is still intent upon defending the philosophers of nature; very little of their influence is apparent in the main body of the work however, which considering that the investigations described did not involve the use of chemical analysis or the microscope, gives a competent account of the formation of bast and sap-wood.

In 1808 he accepted the offer of a post on the Bavarian forestry commission, and it was in Munich that he made the acquaintance of Link. In 1810 he published his main work 'Forstdirektionslehre, nach den Grundsätzen der Regierungspolitik und Forstwissenschaft', on the strength of which he was appointed counsellor to the forestry board at Ansbach in 1818. He remained at Ansbach for the rest of his life. He made no attempt to keep pace with developments in plant physiology, but cultivated his early interest in the philosophy of the natural sciences, and towards the end of his life published two important works on estate and forestry management. See C. Fraas 'Geschichte der Landbau und Forstwissenschaft' pp. 577–578 592–594 (Munich, 1865).

Link is evidently referring to § 17 of the 'Naturgetreue Darstellung' etc., in which Meyer shows that ‚Der Saft steigt eben so wenig auch in der Rinde oder in der Oberhaut auf', see pp. 49–50: ‚Zur Prüfung dieser Angabe bot sich mir im verflossenen Jahr an einem in zwey Theile geberstenen, als Kopfholz behandelten Weidenstamm, der übrigens noch freudig im Sommer vegetirte, eine schöne Gelegenheit dar. An beyden Theilen war inwendig weniger Splint' (alburnum, sap-wood). ‚Ich nahm daher von der einen Hälfte auf 5 Zoll Breite sämmtlichen Splint weg, und vermied so viel wie möglich die Basthaut zu verletzen. An der andern Hälfte that ich dasselbe mit der Rinde, — und überließ sie, nachdem ich sie schon vorher unterstützt hatte, — ihrem Schicksal, welches folgendes war:

Der seiner Holztheile beraubte Stammtheil blieb zwar den Sommer des verflossenen Jahres hindurch so ziemlich grün, die Blätter veränderten jedoch zeitig im Herbste ihre Farbe, blieben eine lange Zeit im Winter hängen, und die Knospen fingen zwar an sich in diesem Frühjahr zu entfalten, wurden inzwischen, noch ehe sie ihre Größe erreicht hatten, schon welk, — und ein Trieb der Zweige war gar nicht zu bemerken.

Die ihrer Rinde beraubte Hälfte des Stamms aber vegetirte nicht nur denselben Sommer hindurch, die Blätter fielen zur gehörigen Zeit ab, sondern die Knospen entwickelten sich auch in diesem Frühjahr, trieben Zweige und Blätter, legten letztere in diesem Herbste wieder ab, und es ist zu hoffen, daß die gebildeten Knospen im künftigen Jahre noch einmal den selben Proceß bestehen ...

Dieser Versuch ... beweißt ... das in der Rinde kein Aufsteigen des Nahrungssaftes Statt findet, denn daß er bey der Beraubung der Holztheile noch eine Zeitlang grünte, hat seinen Grund in dem Bau und der Bestimmung der Knospen.'

80, 24

,Die Wurzel ist eine solche Verkrümmung.' In the original ('Jenenser Realphilosophie' II p. 129), Hegel speaks of ,die Wurzelung' (radication).

80, 28

'Lehrbuch der Naturphilosophie' vol. II p. 112 (Jena, 1810). '1424 Dagegen stirbt eine Pflanze nicht sobald, wenn der Bast durchschnitten, die Spiralfasern aber erhalten sind.

1425. Die Spiralfasern bedingen mithin die Bewegung und die Erregung der organischen Processe.

1426. Die Spiralfasern sind für die Pflanze das, was die Nerven für das Thier sind. Sie können mit vollem Rechte Pflanzennerven heißen, und ich freue mich, sie in dieses Recht einsetzen zu dürfen.'

83, 23

Bearing in mind the state of knowledge at the time and the sources upon which Hegel draws, it has to be admitted that he gives a perfectly competent and plausible exposition of plant anatomy. At the turn of the century, Sprengel, Mirbel, Treviranus and Link had revived interest in the nature and origin of vessels and in the functions of the various tissues, and as a result of their work, these features came to play a rôle in botanical research which was out of all proportion to their real significance in the construction of the vascular plant. What is more, plant anatomists began to develop a false confidence in the conclusiveness of their researches. In 1824 for example, R. H. J. Dutrochet (1776–1847) asked, 'Que pourrait-on, en effet, attendre de nouveau de l'observation microscopique des organes des végétaux, après les recherches de Leuwenhoeck, de Grew, de Malpighi, d'Hedwig; après les travaux recents de messieurs Mirbel, Link, Treviranus, Sprengel etc.?' ('Recherches anatomiques et physiologiques sur la structure intime des animaux et des végétaux, et sur leur motilité.' Paris, 1824, p. 8.)

By sharpening the antithesis between cells and their 'fluid content' in the cellular tissue, between 'life-vessels' and 'vital sap' in the vascular system, and between spiral-vessels and wood-sap in the assimilative system (III 77, 78), Hegel seems to be preparing the way for the discovery that the vessels also have their origin in cells. After having studied the Marchantia polymorpha, Mirbel reached this conclusion in 1831; see 'Recherches anatomiques et physiologiques sur le Marchantia polymorpha, pour servir à l'histoire du tissu cellulaire de l'epiderme et des stomates' ('Annales des Sciences Naturelles' vol. xxv, 1832 pp. 73–87). Hugo von Mohl (1805–1872) developed similar views at almost the same time, as the result of having submitted the trunk of a Cycad to a microscopical investigation; see 'Ueber den Bau des Cycaden-Stammes' ('Abhandlungen der . . . Königl. Baierischen Akademie der Wissenschaften' 1829–1830 pp. 397–442). M. J. Schleiden took up their suggestions, and in his 'Grundzüge der wissenschaftlichen Botanik' (Leipzig, 1842–3), attempted to show that all the organs of plants are built up of cells, that the plant embryo originates from a single cell, and that the physiological activities of the plant are dependent upon the individual activities of these vital units.

As the result of these researches, the decade following Hegel's death saw the foundations of plant cytology laid. It is true that Hegel would have found little that might have suggested a radical reconstruction of this paragraph in L. C. Treviranus's 'Physiologie der Gewächse' (2 vols. Bonn, 1835–1838), but when this book appeared, it was already out of date. Michelet was evidently so delighted with the neatness of Hegel's dialectical exposition of a difficult subject (III 79), that he failed to note that the information on which it was based was already obsolete.

85, 5

Hoffmeister ('Jenenser Realphilosophie' II p. 134) gives the emphasized words here. Michelet fails to indicate the emphasis, and also omits the word ,reine' (pure) from ,die reine egiſtierende Negativität'. He took the sentence from a passage in which Hegel is discussing the flower, and the sexuality and pigmentation of plants. It is difficult to grasp Hegel's precise meaning here, but Augusto Vera (1813–1885) evidently had no difficulty in doing so. He writes 'Pour entendre ce passage, il faut avoir présente la théorie de la lumière de Hégel, et l'ensemble de la philosophie de la nature. La lumière, cet élément simple, identique et universel qui manifeste, et dans lequel la nature se manifeste, reparaît sous des formes diverses dans les différentes sphères de la nature, en se combinant avec ces sphères, et se transforment avec elles. On peut dire qu'avant d'arriver à la sphère de l'organisme la lumière manifeste et éclaire, mais qu'elle ne se manifeste pas à elle-même, et ne s'éclaire pas elle-même, ou, si l'on veut, qu'elle n'est pas à elle-même son propre objet. C'est dans la vie que se produit d'abord cette réflexion de la lumière sur elle-même, cette manifestation réciproque du sujet et de l'objet, laquelle a sa racine dans l'unité interne et consubstantielle des deux termes, unité qui se pose et se réalise dans l'organisme. Or la plante aspire à cette unité, sans l'atteindre, elle y touche de près, sans la réaliser. Elle est dans la lumière, suivant les expressions du texte, et elle devient lumière; mais elle ne le devient pas pour elle-même, ce qui fait qu'elle est un objet de la vision, mais qu'elle ne voit point, et que, dans l'obscurité et le sommeil de sa vie, il n'y a point ce principe qui l'éclaire à la fois intérieurement et extérieurement, parce qu'en lui le dedans et le dehors, le moi et le non-moi viennent s'unir et se compénétrer;—cette lumière spiritualisée, cette négation réalisée (vergeistigte Licht, als die existirende Negativität) qui forme l'unité de la nature par cela même qu'elle nie tout ce qui n'est pas elle, et qu'elle le nie en le contenant.—Maintenant ce que Hégel dit de la lumière, il faut l'étendre à l'air, à l'eau et à la nature en général, car la pensée de Hégel est que l'organisme est l'unité de la nature, et que la plante constitue un moment de cette unité. S'il insiste ici surtout sur la lumière, c'est d'abord que de tous les éléments la lumière paraît être le plus essentiel à la plante; c'est ensuite que la vie, et surtout la vie animale (l'âme proprement dite) est cette lumière concrète où la nature se perçoit elle-même et devient transparente à elle-meme, si l'on peut ainsi s'exprimer. Voy. ci-dessous, I, plus haut, §§ 275, 337, 344, et plus loin, § 350.'— 'Philosophie de la Nature de Hégel' vol. III p. 142 (Paris, 1866).

86, 17

Cf. C. F. A. Morren (1807–1858), 'Essai pour déterminer l'influence qu'exerce la lumière sur la manifestation et le developpement des êtres organisés' ('Annales des sciences naturelles' Zoologie, 1822, vol. III).

86, 22

Hoffmeister (Jenenser Realphilosophie' II p. 134 note 3) indicates that this sentence was taken by Michelet from a marginal note which *he* reads as follows: ‚Feuerfarbe-Kornfeldgelb, Kornblume (Blau), Mohn (Rot). Viele Arten durchlaufen alle diese Farben. Fürstliche' (sic) ‚Gärtnerei(en versuchen,) sie durch alle diese Farben und ihre Vermischung durchzutreiben. Wenn die wilde Blume rot (ist, ist es) schwer, (sie) zum Blau hinüberzutreiben. Wenn eine Pflanze nicht blüht, färbt sie leicht ihre Blätter, malt auch die Pistille daraufhin'.

88, 5

Nicolas-Théodore de Saussure (1767–1845) was born at Geneva, into a family which for generations had produced outstanding scientists as well as members of the representative council of the city. He lived quietly and avoided society, and in the latter part of his life became more of a recluse than ever, but he was true to the family tradition, in that the attention he gave to public affairs was matched only by that which he devoted to scientific research. His father was

H. B. Saussure (1740–1799), the famous physicist and Alpine traveller, and it was by accompanying his father on his expeditions among the Alps that he got the grounding of his education in the natural sciences.

Saussure turned his attention to the chemistry of vegetable physiology when great advances were being made in chemistry through the application of Lavoisier's principle that the total weight of all the products of a chemical reaction must be exactly equal to the total weight of the reacting substances. John Ingenhousz (1730–1799), in his 'Experiments upon Vegetables, discovering their great power of purifying the common air in the sun-shine, and of injuring it in the shade and at night' (London, 1799), had shown that the green parts of a plant exhale oxygen in the light and carbon dioxide in the dark, but that the parts that are not green give off nothing but carbon dioxide. Priestley discovered oxygen in 1774, and Lavoisier discovered the constituents of carbon dioxide in 1779, so that in a German edition of Ingenhousz's book (Leipzig, 1798), F. A. von Humboldt was able to show, as did Ingenhousz in 'On the food of plants' (London, 1797), that the entire carbon content of the plant is derived from the carbon dioxide of the air, and that the absorption of it is a process of nutrition, in which the carbon is assimilated and the oxygen discharged, while the absorption of oxygen and the discharging of carbon dioxide correspond to the respiration of animals. Jean Senebier's researches into the influence of light upon the plant's leaves showed why the assimilative process took place during the day, and the respiratory process at night.

When Saussure began his experiments therefore, the assimilative and respiratory functions of the leaves were known, although Link, as Hegel's quotation shows, was still able to misassess them to some extent. As is apparent from Hegel's subsequent comment however, the functioning of the roots was not always taken to account for the presence in the plant of certain minerals. It was still thought that the plant had the power of engendering these minerals from pure water and air, and Saussure was the first to show that this was not the case. His experiments led him to suggest that these minerals were taken in through the roots, and that it was also by means of the roots that the nitrogen necessary to plant life was assimilated from the processes of vegetable and animal decomposition in the soil. Hegel evidently failed to see the significance of this part of his work.

Saussure published an account of his experiments in 1804: 'Recherches chimiques sur la végétation' (facsimile ed. Paris, 1957, ed. M. Solovine in 'Les Maîtres de la Pensée Scientifique' series.) He says of his work that, 'Les recherches dont je m'occupe dans cet Ouvrage, ont pour objet l'influence de l'eau, de l'air et du terreau sur la végétation'. Link is evidently referring to § VI (p. 104) and § VII (p. 109) of this book.

89, 7

Jean Baptiste van Helmont (1577–1644) has been called the Faust of the seventeenth century. He was born at Brussels, educated by the Jesuits, and took his M.A. at Louvain when he was only seventeen. From 1600 until 1602 he travelled widely, visiting France, Italy, Switzerland, Spain, England, and even Russia, and after contracting a rich marriage, settled at Vilvorde near Brussels in 1609 where he occupied himself with chemical experiments and medical practice until his death.

Like many other seventeenth century men of science, he presents curious contradictions. He was a careful observer of nature and an exact experimenter, and took part in the general criticism of Aristotelianism then in vogue, but on the other hand he was a disciple of Paracelsus, a Rosicrucian and a mystic, and based much of his general outlook on life on his reading of Thomas à Kempis and Johannes Tauler. From 1634 until 1635 he was imprisoned for supposedly denying the power of religion to effect physical healing.

As a chemist he deserves to be remembered as the founder of pneumatic chemistry, even though it made no substantial progress for a century after his time. He was one of the first to realize that there are gases distinct in kind from atmospheric air; in fact he claims to have been the inventor of the word 'gas': 'Hunc spiritum incognitum hactenus (Carbon dioxide), novo nomine GAS voco, qui nec vasis cogi, nec in corpus visibile reduci, nisi extincto prius semine, potest.' 'Ortus medicinae' (Amsterdam, 1652, Eng. tr. J. Chandler, London, 1662, Germ tr. Rosenroth, Sultzbach, 1683) no. 18 § 14.

He regarded air and water as being the two primitive elements of things. He explicitly denied that fire is an element, and thought that earth can be reduced to water. In order to show that plants are composed of water, he conducted the following experiment, which he describes in his 'Ortus Medicinae' (op. cit. no. 18 § 30; Eng. tr. p. 109), 'I took an earthen vessel, in which I put 200 pounds of Earth that had been dried in a Furnace, which I moystened with Rain-water, and I implanted therein the trunk or Stem of a Willow Tree, weighing five pounds; and at length five years being finished, the Tree sprung from thence did weigh 169 pounds, and about three ounces: But I moystened the Earthen Vessel with Rain-water, or distilled water (always when there was need) and it was large, and implanted into the Earth, and least the dust that flew about should be co-mingled with the Earth, I covered the lip or mouth of the Vessel, with an Iron plate covered with Tin (lamina ferrea, stanno abducta) and easily passable with many holes. I computed not the weight of the leaves that fell off in the four Automnes. At length, I again dried the Earth of the Vessel, and there were found the same 200 pounds, wanting about two ounces. Therefore 164 pounds of Wood Barks, and Roots, arose out of water onely'.

The conclusion is mainly correct, for about fifty per cent of fresh Willow wood consists of free water, but van Helmont knew nothing of the nutrition the plant had gained from the carbon dioxide in the air, and there was evidently some inaccuracy in his weighing of the earth. Hermann Kopp (1817–1892) gives an account of this experiment in his 'Geschichte der Chemie' (Braunschweig, 1843) pt. I p. 120; see also an excellent account of van Helmont in J. R. Partington's 'A History of Chemistry' (London, 1961) vol. II pp. 209–243.

H. M. Howe, in 'A Root of van Helmont's Tree' ('Isis' 1965 pp. 408–419), points out that Nicholas of Cusa (c. 1400–1464), in his 'De staticis experimentis' (1450), mentions the same experiment: see 'D. Nicolai de Cusa Cardinalis . . . Opera' (3 vols. Basel, 1565) p. 176.

89, 10

Henri Louis *Duhamel* du Monceau (1700–1782) was born and died at Paris. He had ample private means, which enabled him to devote himself whole-heartedly to his scientific interests. He was a member of the French Academy of Sciences and of the Royal Society of London, and when asked, patronisingly, what he considered to be the point of these memberships, is said to have replied, 'Monsieur, vous voyez à quoi il sert d'être de l'Academie: c'est à ne parler que de ce qu'on sait'.

His interests were wide, and he published works on physiology, botany, agriculture, economics and the navy. The excellence of his botanical works was somewhat marred by his failure to take into account certain of the other workers in the fields which interested him. In his 'Traité des arbres et arbastes' (2 vols. Paris, 1755) for example, although he listed many American species for the first time, he failed to use the improved system of nomenclature recently introduced by Linnaeus, and kept to the older system of Tournefort.

Link is here referring to an experiment mentioned by Duhamel in vol. II (p. 198) of his, 'De la physique des arbres, de l'anatomie des plantes, et de l'oeconomie vegetale' (2 vols., Paris, 1758). The merit of this book consists in the detail of its observations concerning the structure, anatomy and physiology of plants, and Haller, in his 'Bibliotheca Botanica', refers to it as, 'Nobile opus, cujus merita non possumus in nostram brevitatem contrahere.' However, although Edme Mariotte (1620–1684) of Dijon had shown in 1679 that plants form many of their constituents and do not find them ready-made in the soil, and although Stephen Hales (1677–1761), in his 'Vegetable Staticks' (1727) had shown that the air plays a part in this formation, Duhamel repeated Helmont's experiment with an oak, in order to prove that water alone is capable of pro-viding all the material necessary for plant growth.

89, 13

Johann Christian Carl Schrader (1762–1826) was born in Altmark, where his father was an apothecary, and was educated at home by his maternal grand-father. At the age of fifteen he left home to study pharmacy at Osterburg, but his teacher was so bad, that he spent most of his time there reading Klopstock and writing verse.

He taught himself botany while serving as an apothecary's assistant at

Altona, and in order to finish his training, went to study chemistry and mineralogy under Meyer at Stettin. In 1790 he took a job as a dispenser at the 'Elephant' apothec in Berlin, and in 1791 as the employee of M. H. Klaproth (1743–1817), under whom he greatly improved his professional training.

In 1794 he married, and so gained an apothec of his own. He took an active part in Berlin life, and soon became well-known there. He was elected member of the Berlin 'Gesellschaft Naturforschender Freunde', in 1807, adviser to the Berlin Board of Public Health in 1816, and member of the Royal Commission of Court Apothecaries in 1817. He also played an important part in the organization of the Sunday schools of the city.

Between 1796 and 1821 he published thirty five articles in various periodicals, most of them on the chemical and bio-chemical constituents of plants. He also published two botanical works: 'Die Norddeutschen Arzneypflanzen für Anfänger der Apothekerkunst' (Berlin, 1791), and 'Flora oder ländliche Gemälde' (Berlin, 1796).

In 1797 the Berlin Royal Academy of Sciences invited prize essays on the following subject, 'De quelle nature sont les principes terreux qu'on trouve, à l'aide de l'analyse chemique, dans les différentes sortes de blé indigénes? Ces principes entrent-ils dans les végétaux tels qu'on les y trouve? ou bien sont-ils produits par la force vitale et l'action des organes du végétal?'

Schrader's essay was awarded the prize, and an essay by Johann Samuel Benjamin Neumann, a clergyman from Templin, proxime accessit. The Academy published these essays in 1800 as, 'Zwei Preisschriften über die eigentliche Beschaffenheit und Erzeugung der erdigen Bestandtheile in den verschiedenen Getreidearten', and it is to this publication that Link is referring. Schrader came to the conclusion that the 'vital force' of the plant *was* able to generate these substances. That an essay defending such a point of view should have been awarded the prize is not so surprising if we remember that it was not until the middle of the last century that J. B. D. Boussingault (1802–1887) showed that most plants supply their nitrogen needs from the nitrates in the soil, and not until the end of it that S. Winogradsky (1856–1934) pointed out the functions performed by bacteria in plant nutrition.

In referring to this work by Schrader, Link evidently has the following passage in mind (op. cit. pp. 27–28), „ . . . ber sublimirte Schwefel, welcher alle Eigenschaften vereinigte, die mein künstlicher Pflanzenboden haben mußte. Er enthielt keine Erde und kein Metall, wie mir eine Digestion desselben mit Säuren bewies. Ich wusch ihn mit hinlänglichem destillirten Wasser ab, und saete darein vorzüglich Roggen . . . Ich nahm dazu Glas= und Porzelangefäße, und stellte sie der freien Luft und Sonne in einem Garten aus . . . Die Körner keimten und wuchsen sehr gut unter Anwendung des oben angeführten Wassers . . . Da aber durch die vielen kleinen vorläufigen Versuche, viel Zeit verloren war, verspätete sich mein letzter Versuch mit Schwefel, und meine Halme mußten bis in den spätesten Herbst wachsen, wo der herannahende

Froſt und die Beendigung meiner Arbeit, es nothwendig machten die Halme aufzuziehn. In dieſer Zeit hatten einige derſelben, eine Höhe von 12—14 Zoll erreicht, und mehrere davon . . . Ähren angeſetzt. Die Spelzen, welche mit ihren gehörigen Grannen verſehn waren, enthielten auch die Blütentheile ſchon deutlich entwickelt'.

For contemporary British views on plant nutrition see Richard Kirwan (1733–1812), in 'Transactions of the Royal Irish Academy' vol. 5 p. 160; John Murray (d. 1820), in 'The Edinburgh Philosophical Journal' no. xiv p. 328; John Ingenhousz (1730–1799), 'On the food of plants' (London, 1797); Sir Humphrey Davy (1778–1829), 'Elements of Agricultural Chemistry' (London, 1813); Sir James Edward Smith (1759–1828), 'Introduction to Botany' (London, 1809).

92, 10

In Michelet's edition this sentence reads as follows, ,. . . dieſer Verlauf iſt aber im ganzen ein Ueberfluß, da der Geſtaltungs= und Aſſimilationsproceß ſchon ſelbſt Reprobuction, als Probuction neuer Indibibuen, ſind'.

The translation has been made from the revised version of it given by Nicolin and Pöggeler in their edition of the 'Enzyklopädie' (Hamburg, 1959).

92, 15

Lorenz Oken 'Lehrbuch der Naturphilosophie' vol. II p. 113 (Jena, 1810). ‚§ 1433 Die Blühte iſt das Hirn der Pflanze, die Blume das Sinnenſyſtem, der Taſtſinn.'

Schelling 'Zeitschrift für speculative Physik' vol. II pts. i and ii (Jena and Leipzig, 1801). Most of this edition consists of Schelling's 'Darstellung meines Systems der Philosophie', in § 156 of which he writes, ‚Der potenzirteſte poſitive Pol der Erde iſt das Gehirn der Thiere und unter dieſen des Menſchen'.

Zuſ. 1 Das Geſchlecht iſt die Wurzel des Thiers. Die Blüthe das Gehirn der Pflanzen,

Zuſ. 2 Wie die Pflanze in der Blüthe ſich ſchließt, ſo die ganze Erde im Gehirn des Menſchen, welche die höchſte Blüthe der ganzen organiſchen Meta= morphoſe iſt.'

93, 3

Michelet has evidently made some important changes in the text at this point. Hegel (Jenenser Realphilosophie' II p. 135) speaks of the ‚unbefruchteten Germen' (germ), not the ‚unbefruchteten Samen' (seed). He says that, ‚Die Veränderung (mutation) entgeht den groben Händen der Chemie', not that ‚Betrachtung' (interpretation, speculation, reflection) from a chemical standpoint will be of no avail.

93, 10

Linnaeus based his system of plant-classification on the number, proportion, figure and situation of the stamens and pistils, the so-called sexual organs of the flower. See his 'Philosophia Botanica' (1751), Eng. tr. by Hugh Rose 'The Elements of Botany' (London, 1775). It is mainly in pt. I, ch. V, sects 132–150 of this work that he emphasizes the importance of this sexual process. See especially sect. 146, 'The calyx then is the marriage bed, in which the stamina and pistilla, the male and the female organs, celebrate the nuptials of the plants; and here also those tender organs are cherished and defended from external injuries'.

94, 2

Michelet makes 'determinateness' singular, whereas the verb in Hegel's sentence shows that he meant it to be plural, ',. . . beren Beſtimmtheit(en), in ſich vollfommen reflektiert, ſich über bas Ganze verbreiten.' ('Jenenser Realphilosophie' II p. 136).

94, 37

Chæmerops humilis, i.e. the Dwarf Fan Palm, which grows naturally in Italy, Sicily, Spain, and particularly in Andalusia, where, in a sandy soil, the roots will spread and propagate so quickly, that the plants cover the ground in the same manner as Fern in England.

94, 39

The Great Bosian garden at Leipzig, to which Hegel is referring, was founded by Caspar Bose (1645–1700), a wealthy merchant of the city, and during the late seventeenth century and the early eighteenth it contained one of the finest collections of rare plants in Germany. It took on its eighteenth-century form about 1690, when Bose had it laid out by the Brunswick architect Leonhard Christoph Sturm.

Its contents were catalogued on several occasions. Paul Amman (1634–1691) classified its plants in accordance with the system proposed by Robert Morison (1620–1683); see his 'Hortus Bosianus' (Leipzig, 1686). Elias Peine's 'Hortulanus, der Bosische Garten in Leipzig' (Halle, 1690), proved so popular, that four further editions of it were published at Leipzig (1699, 1705, 1713, 1723). On p. 89 of the 1713 edition of this book, mention is made of a, "Palma humilis Hispanica, spinosa, sive Chamaeriphes', and among the Palms mentioned in the 1723 edition (ed. F. A. Wehmann) is a, 'Palma dactylifera, minor: vulgo Palma foemina: it. Chamaeriphes.' J. E. Probst seems to have published the last of these catalogues, see his, 'Wörterbuch . . . nebst einem Verzeichniss der Pflanzen des Casp. Bosischen Gartens' (Leipzig, 1747).

Caspar Bose's brother also founded a garden at Leipzig, which was known as the 'Lesser Bosian'. On the death of the founder, the 'Great Bosian' passed into the hands of his son, Caspar Bose (1672–1730). Gleditsch worked in the garden from about 1730 until about 1733, when it was owned by the younger Bose's widow. This woman's son, Caspar Bose (1704-1733), made something of a name for himself as a doctor and botanist and was well known to Gleditsch. At the age of twenty-four he published 'Dissertatio de motu plantarum sensus aemulo' (Leipzig, 1728), in which he tried to explain the movements of Mimosa and the Rose of Jericho etc. by postulating a plant soul. Early in 1733 he was appointed professor of botany at the university of Leipzig on the strength of his 'Calycem Tournefortii explicat' (Leipzig, 1733), in which he defended Tournefort's theory of plant sexuality against the criticisms of Pontedera. He died, unmarried, on April 22, 1733, but the address books in the Leipzig archives show that his grandfather's foundation was known as 'Caspar Bose's Garden' until much later in the eighteenth century.

95, 3

Heinrich Jakob Eckleben (d. 1778) was one of the many Germans who contributed to the modernization of Russia during the eighteenth century. He first entered the service of the Empress as a gardener on May 13th 1757, and by his industry and ingenuity, but above all by the *success* of his experiments, he soon established his reputation. He was appointed head gardener at St. Petersburg on June 29th 1762. On June 3rd 1766 his outstanding contributions to Russian agriculture and horticulture were rewarded by his being summoned to take the oath of office as a member of the Civil Council.

He conducted experiments which enabled him to indicate methods for improving the production of wheat, rye and cattle fodder, and eventually published the details of these researches in 1772. M. V. Lomonósov (1711-1765), professor of chemistry at the university of St. Petersburg, seeing that this work was a means to improving the grain yield in northern Russia, brought it to the notice of the Empress. Patronage was granted as early as September 7th 1764, but since the promised financial support never materialized, the improvements were never made. In order to please his imperial patron, he subsequently concentrated upon hothouse production: despite the severity of the winter of 1767-8 for example he managed to astonish and delight her by presenting Spanish cherries on February 10th, a green cucumber at the end of the month, and on March 6th, ripe peaches. He was elected one of the fifteen members of the Free Imperial Economic Society, in the papers of which he is referred to as *Eikleben*. Curiously enough, in his official publications he signed himself either *Andrej Ekleben* or *H. J. Eklenberg*.

His two-year contract of March 28th 1759 required that he should undertake the *training* of students, but it was not until 1764 that the elementary school nearby provided him with four suitably literate pupils. His limited knowledge of Russian, his evident lack of interest in teaching, and the stringency of the financial situation hindered the development of this proposed 'Garden Training School.' In 1774 he reported that two students had completed the course successfully, that three continued to study satisfactorily, and that a sixth, who wanted to marry, was a complete failure, and had been transferred, as a worker, to another garden.

In January 1767 Eckleben received $\frac{2}{3}$ of a grain of the previous year's pollen from Kölreuter, and in March $\frac{1}{3}$ of a grain of the current year's pollen. The St. Petersburg palm, which had been acquired by Peter the Great, was then about 140 years old, and had never borne dates. That year it began to sprout on April 1st, and from the opening of the lower flowers in mid-April until the end of the month, Eckleben dusted on the pollen three times a day. By June the complete success of the experiment was fully evident. The old pollen yielded only 40 dates, but that of the current year was so effective that not one fruit fell. The dates were so clustered that it was impossible to count them, but there were not less than 600. Accounts of the experiment appeared in the local papers, and the palm was viewed by the general public on Wednesdays and Saturdays.

P. Stolpiansky 'Gardener Eckleben and the first School of Gardening at St. Petersburg' ('ВѢСТНИКЪ САДОВОДСТВА, ПЛОДОВОДСТВА И ОГОРОДНИЧЕСТВА' no. 5 May 1914 pp. 409–435).

95, 5

Nehemiah Grew (1641–1712), in a paper which he read to the Royal Society of London in November 1676, described the functions of the stamens and pistils as follows, 'When the attire or apices break or open, the globules or dust falls down on the seedcase or uterus, and touches it with a prolific virtue'. He said however that it was Sir Thomas Millington (1628–1704), who had suggested to him that sexuality might play a part in vegetable reproduction. The line of research opened up by this paper was developed by R. J. Camerarius (1665–1721), professor of botany at Tübingen, who demonstrated the existence of distinct sexes in the plant world by isolating female Mercurialis annua, Ricinus communis, Mulberry and Spinach plants, and then showing that they were unable to produce fertile seeds. From his experiments with dioecious, or at least with diclinous plants, and by regarding monoclinous flowers as self-fertilizing, Camerarius concluded that in the plant world there can be no generation from seeds unless the anthers of the female flowers have been fertilized. He expressed this view in a letter which he wrote to a friend in 1694, 'De sexu plantarum epistola' (tr. and ed. M. Möbius, Leipzig, 1899).

Many eighteenth-century botanists attempted to prove or disprove the existence of sexuality in plants. Willdenow is here referring to the famous 'Experimentum berolinense', first carried out by Gleditsch in 1749, and confirmed by further experiments in 1750, 1751 and 1767. Johann Gottlieb Gleditsch (1714–1786) was professor of botany at the Berlin Collegium Medico Chirurgicum, and director of the city's botanical garden. In 1770 he was appointed head of the Berlin institute of forestry. He was a close friend of Linnaeus, whose system of plant-classification was based upon the assumed sexuality of the vegetable kingdom. Gleditsch published an account of this experiment in 'Histoire de l'Academie Royale des Sciences et Belles Lettres' (Berlin, 1749, pub. 1751, pp. 103–108).

In 1749 Gleditsch received the pollen of a male Chæmerops humilis then growing at Leipzig, and used it to fertilize a female palm of this species which was at that time about eighty years old, which had been brought to Berlin from Holland about thirty years before, but which had never borne dates. A similar result was achieved in 1751.

Joseph Gottlieb Kölreuter (1733–1806) was supervisor of the court-gardens at Karlsruhe, and about 1760 he also began to interest himself in the sexuality of plants. The result of this interest was a series of excellent articles on experiments and observations relating to the subject, 'Vorläufige Nachricht von einigen das Geschlecht der Pflanzen betreffenden Versuchen und Beobachtungen' (Leipzig, 1761–1766, ed. W. Pfeffer, 1893). In 1767 he sent some pollen from the male Chæmerops humilis at Karlsruhe to Gleditsch at Berlin and to Eckleben at St. Petersburg. At Berlin, the experiment was successful again after an interval of sixteen years. Kölreuter published an account of this experiment in 'Historia et commentationes Academiae electoralis scientarum et elegantiorum literarum Theodoro-Palatinae' vol. III Physicum pp. 21–40, Mannheim, 1775). Gleditsch also published an account in 'Histoire de l'Academie Royale des Sciences et Belles-Lettres' pp. 3–19 (Berlin, 1769).

Kölreuter's 'Vorläufige Nachricht' is important, because in it he points out the significance of the nectaries and the function performed by insects in pollination. He considers the actual fertilization to be a mixing of two different oleaginous materials, which unite on the stigma.

95, 22

Lazaro Spallanzani (1729–1799) was born at Scandiano in Modena. He was educated by his father and the Jesuits, and then studied at the university of Bologna under his kinswoman L. M. C. Bassi (1711–1778) who first awakened his interest in the natural sciences.

In 1754 he was appointed professor of logic, metaphysics and Greek at the university of Reggio, and in 1760 was translated to Modena, where he continued to teach with great assiduity and success. He declined many offers from other Italian universities and from St. Petersburg, until in 1768 he accepted the invitation of Maria Theresa to the chair of natural history at Pavia. His fame grew, mainly as the result of his work on physiology, although he also made valuable contributions to vulcanology, meteorology and embryology. He was immensely popular with the students, and when he returned to Pavia after a year's sabbatical in Turkey in 1786, his entry into the city had the nature of a triumphal progress.

His main work is the 'Dissertazioni de fisica animale e vegetabile' (Modena, 1780). It was soon translated into English as 'Dissertations relative to the natural history of animals and vegetables' (London, 1784), and C. F. Michaelis translated the French version of it into German, 'Versuche über die Erzeugung der Thiere und Pflanzen' (Leipzig, 1786).

Link is referring here to vol. 3 p. 305 of the original Italian edition, where Spallanzani describes the experiments he made at Scandiano in 1777, 1778 and 1779. He tells us that he removed the male flowers from monoecious plants such as Melons, enclosed the female flowers of dioecious plants in glass vessels, and yet still obtained fertile seeds from the non-pollinated fruits. (Michaelis's tr. pt. II sect. iii ch. 3 § xv).

The parthenogenesis of aphides was discovered by Leeuwenhoek in 1702, and first described at length by Charles Bonnet (1720–1793), in his 'Observations sur les Puçerons' ('Oeuvres d'Histoire Naturelle' vol. I pp. 1–113 Neuchâtel, 1779). George Adams mentions it in his 'Essays on the Microscope' (London, 1798) p. 274, 'Their habits are very singular: an aphis or puceron, brought up in most perfect solitude from the very moment of its birth, in a few days will be found in the midst of a numerous family; repeat the experiment on one of the individuals of this family, and you will find this second generation will multiply like its parents; and this you may pursue through many generations'.

96, 3

Hegel is here referring to the following observation by Link ('Grundlehren' p. 219), ‚Es ist kein Einwurf, daß der Staub dieser Antheren nicht zum Pistill kommen könne — in manchen liegen doch Antheren und Pistill deutlich zu Tage — denn sonst dürfte es gar keine Antheren in den Asklepiadeen geben, weil man nicht einsieht, wie an einigen der Pollen auf das Pistill kommen kann'.

96, 16

Hegel wrote, ‚Reifen des Holzes überhaupt' in the margin at this point ('Jenenser Realphilosophie' II p. 136 n. 1).

96, 32

Hegel ('Jenenser Realphilosophie' II p. 137) speaks of ‚der Fruchtboden' (receptacle). Michelet prints ‚der Fruchtknoten' (ovary).

97, 32

Michaelis's translation (op. cit. pp. 384–390), which gives the Latin names of these fruits, is Schelver's source here. The Clypeiform Musk Melon (Schild-melone) is Spallanzi's 'Cucumis Melo fructu clypeiformi'. Six varieties of the Cucumis Melo, i.e. Common or Musk-Melon were recognized at that time.

Spallanzani is probably referring to the Cantaloup, so named from a place near Rome, where it had been long cultivated. It is a native of Armenia, where it is very plentiful. In Hegel's day it was also very popular in Holland. It is of middling size, long rather than round, and its flesh is for the most part of an orange colour. The Water Melon (Wassermelone) is Spallanzani's 'Cucurbita Citrulus', not Citrullus vulgaris.

99, 3

Michelet's version reads as follows, ‚Dieser aber ist die verdaute Pflanze; und in der Frucht stellt sich die Pflanze dar, ihre eigene organische Natur aus ihr selbst und durch sie hervorgebracht zu haben.' Hegel ('Jenenser Realphilosophie' II p. 137) wrote, ‚Dieser ist aber die unverdaute Pflanze, und Frucht, welche sich eben darstellt, sich als ihre eigne organische Natur aus ihr selbst und durch sie hervorgebracht zu haben.'

99, 21

Julius Pontedera (1688–1757) was born at Perusia, and studied Cartesian philosophy, medicine and natural history at Padua. As a boy he had taken a keen interest in botany however, and after finishing his university studies, he took up his botanical studies once again. In 1719 he took his doctorate at Padua, and in the same year was appointed professor of botany at the university.

He was one of the few botanists of his day who refused to accept the evidence of the sexuality of plants provided by R. J. Camerarius (1665–1721) of Tübingen, and this probably accounts for Schelver's interest in his writings. As a patriot, if not as a scientist, he felt obliged to support the views of Marcello Malpighi (1628–1694), who had denied the existence of sexual difference in plants.

His two most important works are, 'Compendium tabularum botanicarum, in quo plantae 273 ab eo in Italia nuper detectae recensentur' (Padua, 1718), and 'Anthologia, sive de floris natura libri tres' (Padua, 1720). Schelver is here referring to the second book of this latter work. As he quotes Pontedera's Latin, and Hegel makes his *own* version of it, it may be of interest to give the original, 'Quemadmodum apud nos in quam plurimis plantis, fructus externis injuriis affecti jamjam maturi decidunt, et aliquando etiam ob dissimiles et ineptos stirpium succos. Hinc etiam ars excogitata est, qua plantis fructum ante maturitatem amittentibus succuratur. Pomiferis et quibuscunque aliis stirpibus fructus acerbi decidunt, fixa radice, lapides indundur: hoc remedio saepe ne fructus amittat, prohibetur. Amygdalis cuneo e robere adacto idem praestant coloni. In aliis etiam usque ad medullam terebratos caulices prodesse vel incisum corticem rusticarum rerum scriptores testantur ... Hinc itaque peculiare culicum genus creatum fuisse opinor, qui sterilium (palmarum) floribus innascerentur: hi ad fructiferarum embryones delati eos terebrant, ... partesque medico veluit quodam morsu ita officiunt, ut poma omnia retineantur, et perfectionem habeant.'

100, 3

Johan Bauhin (1541–1613) came of a family which produced several out-standing botanists. His father, Jean Bauhin (1511–1582) had had to leave France on becoming a convert to Protestantism, and after living in England for three years (1532–1535), had finally settled in Switzerland. His brother, Gaspard Bauhin (1560–1624) was professor of botany at Basel, and produced several important botanical works, including 'Pinax Theatri Botanici, siue index in Theophrasti, Dioscoridis, Plinii et Botanicorum, qui a seculo scripserunt, opera' etc. (Basel, 1623). His nephew, John Gaspard Bauhin (1606–1685) was professor of botany at Basel for thirty years.

Johan B. was educated by his father, he then studied botany under Leonhard Fuchs (1501–1566) at Tübingen, and continued his studies at Montpellier, Padua, Lyons and Geneva. He also accompanied Konrad von Gesner (1516–1565) on some of his journeys. It was probably the example of Fuchs's 'Neu Kreüterbuch' (Basel, 1543) and of Gesner's 'Historia Plantarum' (Basel, 1541), which inspired Bauhin with the idea of writing a universal, critical history of plants.

Having finished his studies, he began to practise medicine at Basel, and in 1566 was elected professor of rhetoric at the university there. Four years later he accepted the post of physician to Duke Ulrich of Württemberg, and settled at Montbeliard, where he remained for the rest of his life.

His great work, 'Historia Plantarum Universalis' (Yverdon, 1619, 1650, 1651), which is in effect an encyclopaedia of all that was known about botany at that time, took him fifty years to compile. His son-in-law J. H. Cherler published the prodromus to it in 1619, and the work was completed thirty years later through the generosity of L. A. Graffenried of Berne, who contri-buted four thousand gulden towards the printing costs.

The passage given by Schelver is an adaptation of what Bauhin has to say 'de caprifico' in book I p. 135 col. I of this work. As Hegel makes his own translation of the Latin, it may be of interest to print it here, 'E putrescente caprifici fructu culices geniti in urbanae fructus euolant, easque morsu aperientes superfluan humiditatem depascuntur, radiosque una solares intromittunt, adeoque non tantum impediunt, ne decidant, sed et earundem concoctionem promovent et accelerant'.

100, 6

The Elder Pliny (A.D. 23–79). Books xii–xxv of his 'Naturalis historia' are devoted to botany, agriculture and horticulture. Schelver is here referring to book XV chap. 21 (Pliny, 'Natural History' tr. H. Rackham and W. H. S. Jones vol. 4 pp. 343–345 London, 1945) 'A remarkable fact about the fig is that this alone among all the fruits hastens to ripen with a rapidity due to the skill of nature. There is a wild variety of fig called the goat-fig which never ripens, but bestows on another tree what it has not got itself, since it is a natural sequence of causation, just as from things that decay something is generated. Consequently this fig engenders gnats which, being cheated out of nutriment in their mother tree, fly away from its decaying rottenness to the kindred tree, and by repeatedly nibbling at the figs—that is by feeding on them too greedily —they open their orifices and so make a way into them, bringing with them the sun into the fruit for the first time and introducing the fertilizing air through the passages thus opened. Then they consume the milky juice—this is the symptom of the fruit's infancy—which also dries up of its own accord; and because of this in fig orchards a goat-fig is allowed to grow on the windward side, so that when a wind blows the gnats may fly off and be carried to the fig-trees.'

101, 13

The meaning of this sentence is clearer in Hoffmeister's version of it ('Jenenser Realphilosophie' II p. 137), ‚Bis zu dieser Verdauung bringt es die Pflanze. Sie bietet sich als (Nahrung) höhern Organismen dar, um genossen zu werden'.

101, 20

‚Die Pflanze ist selbst die Bewegung des Feurigen in sich selbst, sie geht in Gährung über.' Hegel wrote ('Jenenser Realphilosophie' II p. 138), ‚Sie selbst ist die Bewegung des Feuers in sich selbst. Sie geht in Gärung über.'

101, 31

This transition from the vegetable organism to the animal organism would appear to be highly unsatisfactory. Hegel was never able to formulate it very clearly, and the differences between his successive attempts to do so show that he was aware of the inadequacy of his exposition. In the lectures of 1803–4 ('Jenenser Realphilosophie' I p. 145) he fastened upon the significance of the *fruit*, in those of 1805–6 he concentrated upon the *leaf* ('Jenenser Realphilosophie' II p. 140), and in the Heidelberg Encyclopaedia (1817) § 272, he drew attention to the *generic process* of the plant.

It was evidently Goethe's conception of a metamorphic progression in plants, culminating in reproduction by means of sexual differentiation (note III. 273), which finally led Hegel to conclude his dialectical assessment of vegetable phenomena in this way. Had he lived another ten years, and seen M. J. Schleiden lay the foundations of plant cytology in his 'Beiträge zur Phytogenesis' (J. Müller 'Archiv für Anatomie' 1838 pp. 137–177: R. Taylor 'Scientific Memoirs' ii, 1841 pp. 281–312), and Theodor Schwann apply Schleiden's discoveries in the field of animal physiology ('Mikroskopische Untersuchungen über die Uebereinstimmung in der Struktur und dem Wachstum der Tiere und Pflanzen', Berlin,

1839), he would almost certainly have illustrated the transition from vegetable to animal being in a different manner.

His transition from the animal organism to subjective spirit by means of the sex-relationship, zoology, disease and death (§§ 367-377) is much more successful, and he would undoubtedly have paralleled it at this juncture had he known that the subject-matter was tractable. Unicellular vegetable organisms such as Schizomycetes (Bacteria), several important forms of which were known to O. F. Müller as early as 1773, could have provided him with a very neat transition to the unicellular Protozoa which he knew as 'Infusoria'. This transition would have been especially effective if he had preceded it with an exposition of plant pathology, as this would have involved an assessment of various micro-organisms. Tournefort had attempted to systematize plant diseases as early as 1705. J. B. Zallinger (1731-1785) had continued this line of research in his 'De morbis plantarum' (Oeniponti, 1773, German tr. 1779), and A. J. Batsch had given it a high degree of precision in his 'Versuch einer Anleitung zur Kenntnis und Geschichte der Pflanzen' (Halle, 1787-8).

Hegel could easily have linked this up with a treatment of plant-like animals such as Porifera (Sponges), and Coelenterata such as Hydrozoa and Anthozoa, or a closely related division such as Ctenophora, the locomotive organs of which could have provided the link with his zoological classification (§ 370). At the beginning of the nineteenth century several naturalists were concerning themselves with possible connections between vegetable and animal being (see note III. 258), and as early as 1751, the Royal Society of London (Transactions, 1752 p. 445) had accepted a paper by Jean Antoine Peyssonel (b. 1694) containing the suggestion that coral-forming Anthozoa are animal and not vegetable in nature.

See N. E. Stevens 'Plant Pathology in the Penultimate Century' ('Isis' 1934 pp. 98-122).

103, 21

This definition of the soul is in substantial agreement with that given by Aristotle, who regarded it as the primary entelechy of an organic individual: see 'De Anima' II, (412^b) tr. J. A. Smith (Oxford, 1931).

Plato ('The Republic' 435 et seq.) finds three elements in the constitution of the soul, reason (logistikon), will (thymos) and desire (epithymia), and regards them as being functions of the head, breast and abdomen respectively. The seat of the soul was taken to be the frontal cavity by Heraclitus and Galen, and the pineal gland by Descartes. S. T. von Sömmerring (1755-1830), the most outstanding German anatomist of Hegel's day, in his 'Über das Organ der Seele' (Königsberg, 1796), put forward the theory that the vapour occurring in the ventricles of the brain constitutes the organ of the soul.

Hobbes evidently inspired the numerous materialistic interpretations of the soul put forward in the eighteenth century: see J. O. de Lamettrie (1709-1751)

'Histoire naturelle de l'âme' (Hague, 1745), P. J. G. Cabanis, (1757–1808) 'Traité de physique et de morale de l'homme' (Paris, 1802). Cf. M. Planck 'Scheinprobleme der Wissenschaft' (Leipzig, 1946).

104, 28

‚das Subject als Selbst-selbst, als Selbstgefühl.' See R. Adamson (1852–1902) 'Fichte' (London, 1881) pp. 153–163 'Only in and for a consciousness that is aware of its own identity can the law A = A have validity. The unity and identity of self-consciousness thus lies at the basis of all empirical consciousness, for all empirical consciousness falls under the rule, A = A. But if the proposition A = A, valid for all empirical consciousness, has validity only because it is grounded on the fact of the identity of self-consciousness, Ego = Ego, this identity must be the pure act of the Ego itself, the mere expression or product of the activity by which the Ego is Ego at all. Self-affirmation, then, is given simply, unconditionally, as the being the Ego. The Ego is, because it posits itself as being; it posits itself as being, because it is. The fundamental activity of all consciousness is thus the affirmation of itself by the Ego.' (pp. 155–156.)

107, 7

'De Anima' (tr. J. A. Smith, Oxford, 1931) 414^{a}28–414^b 20. Aristotle distinguishes between the nutritive, the appetitive, the sensory and the thinking powers of the soul. He then says that plants have only the nutritive power, that animals have the nutritive, the appetitive and the sensory powers, and that man 'and possibly another order like man or superior to him' has in addition the power of thinking.

107, 10

‚Als in sich reflectirte Einheit verschiedener Einzelnheiten, existirt das Thier als Zweck, das sich selbst sich selbst hervorbringt.' Hoffmeister ('Jenenser Real-philosophie' II p. 141) takes this repetition of ‚sich selbst' to be a slip on Hegel's part. If it is interpreted as meaning *spontaneous* self-production however, there is no need to accept this view.

108, 36

‚das Urtheil des Lebendigen, der thätige Begriff desselben ist.' The process of assimilation involves the basic division between the organism and that which it assimilates. The usual meaning of 'Urteil' is 'judgement', so that by using the word in this unusual and literal manner, Hegel is perhaps implying that the organism is *selective* in its assimilative process. Cf. 'The Shorter Logic' (tr. Wallace, Oxford, 1963) §§ 166–179.

110, 2

Michelet alters and misreads this sentence somewhat. The translation has been made from Hoffmeister's version of it ('Jenenser Realphilosophie' II p. 142), ‚das Tier (aber) ist die Negativität seiner selbst, das über seine Gestalt übergreift und das Aufhören des Wachstums nicht in seinem Verdauungs- und Geschlechtsprozeß unterbricht'.

112, 27

This assessment of sensibility and irritability derives from the work of Albrecht von Haller (1708–1777), who first discussed the cause of muscular motion in his commentaries on Boerhaave's 'Praelectiones academicae in proprias institutiones' (4 vols. Göttingen, 1740–1744) II p. 429. His pupil J. G. Zimmermann (1728–1795) published an account of their joint researches on the subject in his 'Dissertatio de irritabilite' (Göttingen, 1751), and Haller communicated the full results of their work to the Göttingen Society of Sciences on April 22, 1752: 'Sermones de partibus corporis humani sentienti-bus et irritabilibus' (French tr. Lausanne, 1754; English tr. London, 1755; German tr. Leipzig, 1756).

These publications gave rise to an extensive literature on the subject in Latin, French, Italian, German and English: see for example Robert Whytt (1714–1766) 'Physiological Essays . . . with observations on the sensibility and irrit-ability of the parts of man and other animals' (Edinburgh, 1755). An excellent survey of this literature was published by H. Dedial in his 'Succincta recensio historico-critica doctrinae Alb. Halleri, principis physiologorum, de irritabili-tate' (Bonn, 1854).

According to the writers of Hegel's day, *sensibility* was a term denoting the capability that a *nerve* possesses of conveying the sensation produced by the contact of another body along with it. All parts of the body possessing the power to produce a change so as to excite a sensation were said to be *sensible*. *Irritability* was 'the contractility of muscular fibres, or a property peculiar to *muscles*, by which they contract upon the application of certain stimuli, with-out a consciousness of action.' ('The Edinburgh Medical and Physical Diction-ary' R. Morris and J. Kendrick, 2 vols. Edinburgh, 1807).

According to Haller, the brain and the nerves are possessed of sensibility, and impart it to the skin, the muscles, the intestines, the urinary bladder, the ureters, the uterus, the penis, the tongue and the retina, and to a lesser extent to the heart, lungs, liver, spleen, glands etc. Irritability he regarded as characteristic of the heart, the muscles, the diaphragm, the stomach, the lymphatic vessels of the intestine, the Ductus thoracicus, the urinary bladder, the pituitary gland, the uterus and the genitals. See H. Haeser 'Geschichte der Medicin' vol. II pp. 575–583, (Jena, 1881); K. F. Burdach 'Die Literatur der Heilwissenschaft' (3 vols. Gotha 1810–1821) vol. I pp. 423–432; A. von Haller 'A dissertion on the sensible and irritable parts of animals' (tr. M. Tissort, London, 1755, ed. O. Temkin, Baltimore, 1936).

Irritability and sensibility were taken to be modifications of *reproduction*, which was regarded as predominating in the lower organisms, and as becoming subordinate to its modifications in more complex animals. See J. F. Pierer 'Anatomisch-physiologisches Realwörterbuch' vol. VI pp. 846–850 (Altenburg, 1825).

113, 36

Johann Heinrich Autenrieth (1772–1835) was the son of J. F. Autenrieth (1740–1800), professor of cameralistics at the Caroline Academy in Stuttgart. His brother Christian Friedrich A. was matriculated with Hegel at Tübingen on May 11, 1788 ('Die Matrikeln der Universität Tübingen' ed. A. Bürk and W. Wille vol III p. 342, Tübingen, 1953).

He took his doctorate in medicine at Stuttgart in 1792, and then went to Pavia to hear the lectures of A. Scarpa (1752–1832) on anatomy, and of J. P. Frank (1745–1821) on medicine. On the way back to Stuttgart he visited Trieste, Hungary and Vienna, and in 1794 left for Baltimore with his father. The main result of this journey was 'Bemerkungen über die Seekrankheit', which appeared in 'Hufeland's Journal' (1796). In 1796 he also published a translation of a work by Benjamin Rush (1745–1813), 'An Account of the bilious remittent yellow fever as it appeared in the city of Philadelphia in the year 1793' (Philadelphia, 1794). In 1797 he was appointed professor of anatomy at Tübingen, an academic post which also entailed practical work as an obstetrician in the town clinics.

Hegel has here quoted his, 'Handbuch der empirischen menschlichen Physiologie' (3 vols. Tübingen, 1801–2), which was the outcome of his early work at Tübingen, and which sought to rid physiology of its prevailing tendency towards Schellingianism and to emphasize that empiricism and experimentation were of prime importance to it.

About 1811 his interest in anatomy and physiology began to wane and he concerned himself to an increasing extent with pathology and therapy. He had learnt from J. P. Frank that theorizing about diseases was less important than exact observation of their symptoms, developments and consequences. He applied this teaching and his clinic at Tübingen became one of the most progressive in Germany. It was widely known on account of the 'Tübinger Blätter für Naturwissenschaften und Heilkunde' (Tübingen, 1815–1817), which Autenrieth helped to edit.

In 1819 he was appointed vice-chancellor of the university, and in 1822 chancellor. His son H. F. Autenrieth (1799–1874) also taught at the university and edited some of his father's works (see note III. 272).

114, 12

'The Edinburgh Medical and Physical Dictionary' (2 vols. Edinburgh, 1807)

by R. Morris and J. Kendrick gives the following account of this membrane:—
'*Periosteum* (περιοστεον from περι, about, and ὀστέον, a bone); that membrane which invests the external surface of all the bones except the crowns of the teeth. It is of a fibrous texture, and well supplied with arteries, veins, nerves, and absorbents . . . Its use appears to be, to distribute blood-vessels on the external surfaces of bones, and to protect the bones themselves from friction, and occasionally to afford a medium of attachment for the muscles.'

115, 8

The translation of these sentences has been made from Michelet's version of them. Hegel's version is as follows, ‚Den Schädelknochen liegt die Form der Rückenwirbel zum Grunde. (Diese) können darin auseinandergelegt werden (os spenoideum), geht aber darauf, den Mittelpunkt ganz zu überwinden und sie ganz zu verflächen ohne eignen Mittelpunkt'. ('Jenenser Realphilosophie' II p. 145). In the manuscript, Hegel wrote ‚Fledermaus' (Bat) above 'os spenoideum'.

'Sphaenoides Os (from σφην, a wedge, and εἶδος, likeness; because it is fixed in the cranium like a wedge), also named *os cuneiforme*, and os *multiforme* the sphenoid or pterygoid bone. This is called by the above name, from its wedge-like situation amidst the other bones of the head. It is however of a more irregular figure than any other bone, and has been compared to a bat with its wings extended. Yet this resemblance is but faint, though it would be difficult perhaps to find any better comparison . . . ' (R. Morris and James Kendrick 'The Edinburgh Medical and Physical Dictionary' 2 vols. Edinburgh, 1807).

At the end of the eighteenth century most handbooks of osteology described the sphenoid as a separate bone supporting the bones of the skull. S. T. von Sömmerring ('Knochenlehre' p. 109 note) called this conception of it in question however, and regarded it as a mere extension of the occipital bone. Many early nineteenth-century anatomists such as J. F. Meckel ('Handbuch der menschlichen Anatomie' § 528) accepted this new interpretation of it, and spoke either of the 'basilary' (Grundbein) or of the 'spheno–occipital bones'. Hegel, like later anatomists, rejected this view.

115, 14

Hegel ('Jenenser Realphilosophie' II p. 145) has a marginal note on toothache at this point, ‚Zahnschmerzen (gehören) zum vegetabilischen unmittelbaren Prozeß= rheumatische Schmerzen'. He has just defined (loc. cit. p. 142) one moment of animal being; ‚Als sich gegen die physischen Elemente verhaltend ist es vegetabilischer Prozeß, eine gestaltlose Gallerte, ein tätiger Schleim, der in sich reflektiert ist. Manche Tiere sind nichts als dieser Schleim'. He was aware therefore, that the tooth pulp enclosed by the dentine and the alveolar periosteum contains the dental nerve. When he says that toothache is rheumatic, he is probably thinking of 'Abhandlung vom rheumatischen

Zahnwehe' (Würzburg, 1801), by C. F. Ringelmann (1776–1833?), ‚Die Beantwortung der Frage: Was denn rheumatisches Zahnwehe sey, — wie man es erkenne? setzt eine andere voraus, nämlich: Was ist Rheumatism? ... Spüren wir den Ursachen von Rheumatism genau nach, so finden sich hauptsächlich folgende: veränderliche Witterung ... der Genuß stark gewürzter Speisen und geistiger Getränke; Leidenschaften, als Zorn, Schrecken, Kummer, u.s.f.' (op. cit. pp. 14–15).

P. Fauchard may well be regarded as the founder of modern scientific dentistry, see his 'Le chirurgien dentiste ou traité des dents' (Paris, 1728, German tr. Berlin, 1733); cf. J. C. F. Maury 'Traité complet de l'art du dentiste' (Paris, 1828, German tr. Weimar, 1830). John Hunter (1728–1793) helped to set British dentistry on a scientific basis with his 'The natural history of the human teeth' (London, 1771) and 'Practical treatise on the diseases of the teeth' (London, 1778), and in Hegel's day the 'Praktische Darstellung aller Operationen der Zahnheilkunst' (Berlin, 1804) by J. J. J. Serre (d. 1830) was the standard German work on this subject.

115, 15

In a marginal note at this point ('Jenenser Realphilosophie' II p. 145), Hegel draws attention to the nature of the marrow, and the formation of new bones, ‚Mark der Knochen ist Fett. Wird die Beinhaut abgetrennt, so bildet sich um sie ein neuer Knochen. Mark des Knochens (ist) bloßes Fett, wenig in magern, viel in fetten Menschen'.

Chronic ostitis and periostitis may be due to injury, rheumatism, or *syphilis*. There is a dull pain in the bone, which is worse at night, and the inflamed piece of bone is thickened and tender. Cf. Adolph Murray (1751–1803) 'Dissertation de sensibilitate ossium morbosa' (Uppsala, 1780) 'Acta med. suec.' I p. 393; J. F. Böttcher (fl. c. 1781–1800) 'Abhandlung von den Krankheiten der Knochen, Knorpel und Sehnen' (Königsberg and Leipzig, 1796); C. F. Clossius (1768–1797) 'Ueber die Krankheiten der Knochen' (Tübingen, 1798); C. F. Ringelmann 'De Ossium morbis, eorumque, in specie dentium, carie' (Würzburg, 1804).

115, 19

‚hat besonders Göthe mit feinem organischen Natursinn gesehen'. In the second edition of Michelet's text (Berlin, 1847) pp. 567–8 ‚feinem' is replaced by ‚seinem' i.e. 'Guided by his organic feeling for nature ...'

See Günther Schmid 'Goethe und die Naturwissenschaften' (Halle, 1940) no. 2235.

115, 24

As the facts given here are not strictly accurate, and as they complicated still further a bitter controversy well known to English readers on account of Sir

Richard Owen's article on Oken in the 'Encyclopaedia Britannica' (8th ed. 1853-60, 11th ed. 1911) and G. H. Lewes' 'The Life and Works of Goethe' (Everyman ed. 1949) pp. 369-377, it may be of value to give their background in some detail.

The treatise Hegel is referring to here is Goethe's 'Ueber den Zwischenkieferknochen des Menschen und der Thiere', in which he announces his discovery of the *intermaxillary bone* in man. This was composed at Jena between March 27, 1784, when he wrote excitedly to Herder about the discovery ('Goethes Werke' Weimarer Ausgabe pt. IV vol vi p. 264), and October 31, 1784 when J. C. Loder (1753-1832) wrote to thank him for sending a copy of the work (Karl von Bardeleben 'Goethe als Anatom' Frankfurt-on-Main, 1892 p. 168). Another copy was circulated via J. H. Merck (1741-1791) and S. T. Sömmerring (1755-1830) and finally reached Peter Camper (1722-1789) the famous Dutch anatomist on Sept. 16, 1785. The treatise was therefore well known to anatomists (see G. Schmid 'Goethe und die Naturwissenschaften' Halle, 1940 pp. 51-58), and was frequently cited by them prior to its being *printed* in Goethe's 'Zur Naturwissenschaft überhaupt, besonders zur Morphologie' (Stuttgart and Tübingen, 1820) vol. I sect. ii pp. 199-251. In this work it is dated 1786.

There is no evidence in this treatise that Goethe possessed any idea of the vertebral analogies of the skull. When he had it printed in 1820 however he added an appendix to the original text (loc. cit. pp. 248-251) entitled 'Inwiefern von den Wirbelknochen die Schädelknochen abzuleiten seyen, und auch Gestalt und Function dorther zu erklären seyn möchte?' This was written in *1819*, and apart from the publisher's notice, which appeared on January 11, 1820, was the first *published* evidence of Goethe's having concerned himself with this subject. Its appearance together with the earlier thesis evidently misled Hegel into thinking that it was also written about 1785.

Oken's inaugural lecture at Jena 'Über die Bedeutung der Schädelknochen' (Jena, 1807) contains a clear presentation of his theory concerning the vertebral analogies of the skull, which he says occurred to him when he came across the blanched skull of a deer while walking near Ilsenstein in the Harz in August 1806. This statement is confirmed by a letter he wrote to Schelling on December 27, 1806 (A. Ecker 'Lorenz Oken' Stuttgart, 1880 p. 199) and by the evidence provided by D. G. Kieser (1779-1862) in September 1836 ('Amtlicher Bericht über die Versammlung deutscher Naturforscher' Weimar, 1837 pp. 95-96).

Goethe had arranged for Oken to be invited to Jena, and in his capacity as privy-councillor and rector of the university, was present at the lecture. It was well-known by 1811-1815 that Oken's claiming the discovery had displeased him: see Henrik Steffens 'Was ich erlebte' (Breslau, 1842) vol. VI p. 252; George Ticknor (1791-1871) 'Life, letters and journals' (ed. Hillard and Ticknor, 2 vols. London, 1876) vol. I p. 115, but it was not until 1830 that he *printed* the passage in which he clearly accuses him of plagiarism ('Tag-und Jahreshefte'

Stuttgart and Tübingen, 1830 pp. 6–7). With these facts before him, it is only natural that Owen (op. cit.) should have concluded that Hegel was utterly wrong in attributing the discovery to Goethe. There can at least be no doubt that the publications quoted by Hegel do *not* provide evidence of Goethe's having developed the theory prior to Oken's having delivered his lecture.

Oken made no printed contribution to the controversy until 1836, when some anonymous articles in the 'Allgemeine Zeitung' (nos. 142–152, Stuttgart, March–April, 1836) stung him into calling anyone who said that he had borrowed the idea from Goethe 'a wicked liar, slanderer and traducer' (einen boshaften Lügner, Verläumder und Ehrabschneider): op. cit. nos. 282 and 283 (June 30, 1836). The publication of these lectures by Michelet in 1842, and the references to the controversy in K. P. Fischer's 'Speculative Charakteristik und Kritik des Hegel'schen Systems' (Erlangen, 1845) pp. 356–362, livened up the matter even further, and it was while passions were still running high that Owen and Lewes interested themselves in it and presented their first accounts of it to the English public.

It is now known however that a theory concerning the vertebral analogies of the skull, which would in any case have been a natural development of the studies he made known in 1784, occurred to Goethe as early as *April 30, 1790*, when he wrote about it from Venice to Charlotte von Kalb (E. Köpke 'Charlotte von Kalb und ihre Beziehungen zu Schiller und Goethe' Berlin, 1852); see also his letter to Caroline Herder (Venice, May 4, 1790) in 'Aus Herders Nachlass' (ed. Düntzer and Herder, Frankfurt-on-Main, 1856) vol. I. Hegel may therefore have *heard* about the matter from Goethe or his friends before it became a real issue in 1830, and may simply have cited the 1820 publication in order to confirm his knowledge. He should however have investigated the matter more carefully before making this statement in public.

115, 28

See T. H. Huxley's critical analysis of this view in his 'Lectures on the elements of comparative anatomy' (London, 1864): see also his Croonian Lecture delivered to the Royal Society on June 17, 1858: 'The fallacy involved in the vertebral theory of the skull is like that which before von Baer infested our notions of the relations between fishes and mammals. The mammal was imagined to be a modified fish, whereas, in truth, both fish and mammal start from a common point, and each follows its own road thence. So I conceive what the facts teach us is this:—the spinal column and the skull start from the same primitive condition—a common central plate with its lamiae dorsales and ventrales—whence they immediately begin to diverge. The spinal column, in all cases, becomes segmented into its somatomes; and in the great majority of cases distinct centra and intercentra are developed, enclosing the notocord more or less completely. The cranium never becomes segmented into somatomes; distinct centra and intercentra, like those of the spinal column, and never developed in it. Much of the basis cranii lies beyond the notocord. In the process of ossification there is a certain analogy between the spinal column and the cranium, but the analogy becomes weaker as we proceed towards the anterior end of the skull.'

116, 3

For a general account of Oken's life and works see the note III. 278. The development of his views upon the spinal column as being basic to the formation of the whole osseous system is to be traced in the following publications: 'Lehrbuch der Naturphilosophie' pt. III sect. iii (Jena, 1811) pp. 61–79; 'Isis' vol. I sect. ii cols. 157–159 (Jena, 1817); 'Allgemeine Naturgeschichte für alle Stände' (Stuttgart, 1833) vol. IV pp. 28, 163–172.

Oken's ideas clearly influenced Sir Richard Owen's 'On the archetype and homologies of the vertebrate skeleton' (London, 1848), Cf. William Whewell 'History of the inductive sciences' (London and Cambridge, 1837, Germ. tr. Stuttgart 1841) vol. III pp. 444–455.

See C. Güttler 'Lorenz Oken und sein Verhältniss zur modernen Entwickelungslehre' (Leipzig, 1885): H. Wohlbold 'Die Wirbelmetamorphose des Schädels von Goethe und Oken' (Munich, 1924).

117, 11

Hegel is here referring to Autenrieth (loc. cit. pt. III § 869), ,Die Nerven bilden je und je Nervenknoten, welche inwendig eine dem Hirn einigermaßen ähnliche Substanz haben'.

117, 13

For contemporary German views on the causes of headaches see; 'Ueber Kopf- und Zahnschmerzen und über die Mittel dagegen' (Hannover, 1806): 'Von den Kopfschmerzen und besonders der Migräne' (J. G. Krünitz 'Encyklopädie' Prague, 1794).

British doctors of that time tended to draw a distinction between headaches caused by disorders of the head itself, and 'cephalalgia spasmodica' or sick head-ache, which was considered to be incident to 'sedentary and inactive persons of relaxed habits, who are incautious respecting their diet'. This second form of the complaint was regarded as having its origin in the stomach. See R. Morris and James Kendrick 'The Edinburgh Medical and Physical Dictionary' (Edinburgh, 1807).

117, 25

In Hegel's day, the developments in psychotherapy brought about by F. A. Mesmer (1734–1815) through his doctrine of animal magnetism gave rise to a great interest in somnambulism. O. Goldsmith (1728–1774) in his 'History of the Earth and Animated Nature' (8 vols. London, 1774), collected some remarkable cases of this activity. In Germany some doctors such as Arnold Wienholt (1749–1804) 'Beiträge zu den Erfahrungen über den thierischen Magnetismus' (Hamburg, 1782), 'Heilkraft des thierischen Magnetismus' (3 pts. Lemgo, 1802–1806) saw mystical and religious implications in somnambulistic and hypnotic phenomena, others, such as J. L. Böckmann (1741–1802) 'Archiv für thierischen Magnetismus and Somnambulismus' (8 pts. Strassburg, 1787–1788), and A. E. Kessler 'Ueber die innere Form der Medicin' (Jena, 1807) attempted to provide physiological explanations of the activity. Hegel is evidently citing Kessler's theory that somnambulism is caused by the activity of the ganglia increasing in relation to that of the brain.

In 1812 the Prussian government set up a commission under C. W. Hufeland (1762–1836) to investigate Mesmer's doctrines. The result of this move was the publication, by C. C. Wolfart (d. 1832) of 'Mesmerismus oder System der Wechselwirkungen' (Berlin, 1814). See also J. C. L. Ziermann 'Geschichtliche Darstellung des thierischen Magnetismus als Heilmittel, mit besonderer Berücksichtigung des Somnambulismus' (Berlin, 1824); A. Gauthier 'Histoire de somnambulisme' (2 vols. Paris, 1842); H. Schwarzschild 'Magnetismus, Somnambulismus und Clairvoyance' (Cassel, 1853).

117, 27
Anthelme-Balthasar Richerand (1779–1840) studied at Paris, and at the age of twenty-three was already widely known throughout Europe on account of the work quoted here by Hegel, 'Nouveaux élémens de physiologie' (Paris, 1801). Thirteen French editions of this book were published, and seventeen translations of it appeared including one into Chinese. The first English translation appeared in 1807, the best was that edited by J. Copland in 1829.

Richerand was also successful with two further publications: 'Leçons de Boyer sur les maladies des os' (2 vols. Paris, 1803; German tr. G. A. Spangenberg, 2 vols. Leipzig, 1804; English tr. R. Farrel, London, 1804), and 'Nosographie et thérapeutique chirurgicales' (3 vols. Paris, 1805–6).

In 1806 he was appointed chirurgeon in chief to the Departmental Guard in Paris. In the following year he was made director of chirurgical pathology in the medical faculty of the university. He was ennobled in 1815, and in 1829 was appointed chirurgeon to Louis XVIII. In 1832 he began to relinquish his practice, and from then on he spent the greater part of his time on his estate at Villecresne.

Hegel is here referring to the following passage, 'Le système des nerfs grands-sympathiques a non-seulement pour usage d'établir une connexion plus intime, une liaison plus étroite entre tous les organes qui remplissent les fonctions nutritives; ils soustrait encore ces actions importantes à l'empire de la volonté: faculté de l'âme si mobile et tellement variable, que la vie courrait à chaque instant de grands dangers, s'il était en notre pouvoir d'arrêter ou de

suspendre l'exercice des fonctions auxquelles l'existence est essentiellement liée.'
'Nouveaux élémens de Physiologie' (11th ed. Brussels, 1833) p. 32.

117, 28

Marie François Xavier Bichat (1771–1802) the most outstanding French
anatomist and physiologist of the revolutionary period. He was born at Thoi-
rette in the Jura, and received his early training as a physician from his father.
He began his university studies at Lyons in 1791, and although he made rapid
progress in mathematics and the physical sciences, he finally devoted himself
to the study of anatomy and surgery.

In 1793 the revolutionary disturbances compelled him to flee from Lyons
and take refuge in Paris, where he became the pupil of P. J. Desault (1744–1795),
whose labours had made the Hôtel Dieu at Paris one of the finest chirurgical
clinics in Europe. In 1798/9 he brought out an edition of Desault's works, but
these years immediately following the death of his master were also spent on
his own researches in anatomy and physiology. He published the results of his
work in 'Traité des membranes' (Paris, 1800, German tr. Tübingen, 1802), in
which he gave a brilliant account of the structure of cellular tissue and the part
it plays in cicatrization and the formation of tumours, polypi, cysts etc.

In 1797 he began a course of anatomical demonstrations, and they were so
successful that he was encouraged to announce a course of operative surgery.
In 1798 he gave in addition a separate course on physiology. In 1799 he was
appointed physician to the Hôtel Dieu, a situation which opened an immense
field to his ardent spirit of enquiry.

'Anatomie générale appliquée à la physiologie et à la médecine' (Paris, 1801,
English tr. C. Coffyn, London, 1824), gave a fuller account of the researches
assessed in the 'Traité des membranes', and had as its main object the removal
of a postulated 'hidden force' from physiological theory, and the introduction
into this branch of science of the strictly anatomical method of Desault. Nevertheless, he was aware of the inadequacy of many of the contemporary attempts
to explain organic life in purely physical terms, 'Dans les corps organisés
l'esprit des théories doit être tout différent de l'esprit des théories appliquées
aux sciences physiques. Il faut dans celles-ci, que tout phénomène soit rigou-
reusement expliquée . . . Au contraire toute explication physiologique ne doit
offrir que des aperçus, des approximations . . . parce que nous conoissons
encore si peu les lois vitales.' (op. cit. I p. 535).

'La vie est l'ensemble des fonctions, qui resistent à la mort.' This is Bichat's
famous definition of life, and in his 'Traité de la vie et de la mort' (Paris, 1800,
Eng, tr. F. Gold, London, 1815), as Hegel points out (III. 126), he elaborates
upon it by distinguishing between the merely *organic* life of growth, nutrition
and propagation, which is dominant in plants, and the *animal* life involving
sensibility and contractility, by which the organism enters into active relations with its environment. This book was the result of a series of examina-

tions carried out with a view to ascertain the changes induced in the various organs by disease, and the effects of remedial agents. In one period of six months, while collecting material for it, he dissected more than six hundred bodies.

A fall from a staircase at the Hôtel Dieu resulted in a fever, and, exhausted by his excessive labours and by constantly breathing the tainted atmosphere of the dissecting room, he died on July 22, 1802. Napoleon ordered that his bust should be placed in the Hôtel Dieu. His physiological theories had a great influence upon Schopenhauer.

Hegel is here translating from 'Recherches physiologiques sur la vie et la mort' (4th ed. Paris, 1822) p. 91 'J'examinerai d'abord les divisions du système cérébral; je traiterai ensuite du système des ganglions, qu'on peut subdiviser en ceux de la tête, du cou, du thorax, d'abdomen et du bassin'.

118, 14

Hegel is here translating from Bichat (loc. cit. pp. 90, 92). The original French is as follows, 'Il est des sujets, par exemple où l'on trouve un intervalle très-distinct entre les portions pectorale et lombaire de ce qu'on appelle grand sympathique, qui semble coupé en cet endroit . . . Qui ne sait . . . qu'après avoir fourni une foule de divisions, le sympathique est plus gros qu'avant d'en avoir distribué aucune?

Quel anatomiste n'a pas été frappé, en effet, des différences qui se trouvent entre les nerfs de l'un et de l'autre? Ceux du cerveau sont plus gros, moins nombreux, plus blancs, plus denses dans leur tissu, exposés à des variétés assez peu fréquentes. Au contraire, ténuité extrême, nombre très-considérable, surtout vers le plexus, couleur grisâtre, mollesse de tissu remarquable, variétés extrêmement communes, voilà les caractères des nerfs venant des ganglions'.

118, 36

Paul Erman (1764–1851) was born in Berlin. His father, who had come to the city from Alsace, was a Huguenot pastor and director of the Collége français. Erman was educated in Berlin, and in 1791 was appointed professor of physics at the military academy. In 1806 he became a member of the Berlin academy, and in 1810 professor of physics at the newly founded university.

He was a determined opponent of Schellingianism, and was generally known on account of his experiments with animal magnetism, for which he was awarded a prize of three thousand francs by the National Institute of France in 1807. Research on this subject had been popularized by Luigi Galvani (1737–1798), who had published an account of muscular irritability in 1786. In his 'De viribus electricitatis in motu musculari commentarius' (1791, Mutinae, 1792), Galvani had shown that the living animal body generates electricity, and had put forward the view that this electricity has its origin in the brain, from which it is conducted, by means of the nerves, to all parts of the body, and especially to the muscles.

The experiment mentioned here by Hegel was devised by Sir Gilbert Blane (1749–1834), but Blane was unable to draw any satisfactory conclusions from the data he collected; see 'Phil. Trans. Roy. Soc.' vol. LXXIX, 1789. 'A lecture on muscular motion' (London, 1791). F. P. von Gruithuisen (1774–1852) was the first to conduct the experiment successfully, 'Resultate der Versuche über die Volums-Verminderung, welche die Muskeln bei ihrer Contraction erleiden' ('Salzburger medicinische und chirurgische Zeitung' 1811 no. 84 pp. 91–95).

Erman's findings confirmed those made by Gruithuisen, and he published his account of them as, 'Einige Bemerkungen über Muskular-Contraction' ('Gilberts Annalen der Physik' vol. 40 pp. 1–30, Leipzig, 1812). In this article he criticizes William Croone's (1633–1684) 'De ratione motus Musculorum' (London, 1664).

Hegel tells us that the water fell ‚ſtoßweiſe' (jerkily); Erman writes that it fell ‚mit einem einzigen Ruck, der ſo inſtantan war, wie das Contrahiren des Muſkels ſelbſt' (loc. cit. p. 14).

119, 11
The English line is equal to 2·54mm., the Rhenish to 2·179mm., and the Viennese to 2·95mm. It is to be presumed that Erman made use of the Viennese measure, in which case the water in the tube fell a little more than half an inch.

119, 19
Treviranus formulated this hypothesis in one of the earliest of published articles; 'Reils Archiv für Physiologie' (1796 pt. I sect. ii), and in part one of his 'Physiologische Fragmente' (Hanover, 1797–9).

119, 31
‚dieß absolute Jn-ſich-Erzittern'. Hegel wrote, ‚dies absolute Jn-ſich-Pulſieren und Erzittern' ('Jenenser Realphilosophie' II p. 148). The whole of this extract is merely an adaptation of Hegel's text.

119, 34
Linnaeus was evidently the originator of this idea cf. the note on III. 280.

120, 24
The translation of this sentence has been made from Michelet's version of it, Hegel wrote as follows, ‚a) das Blut; im Lungenkreislauf iſt es dies rein negative immaterielle Leben, eigne Bewegung, für welches die Natur Luft iſt und ſich hier die reine Überwindung derſelben hat.'

120, 35

‚Die lymphatiſchen Gefäße bilden ſich allenthalben eigene Knoten, Magen.'
Michelet reproduces Hegel here, Hoffmeister ('Jenenser Realphilosophie' II
p. 150 n. 1) makes ‚Magen' plural, and his emendation has been incorporated
into the translation.

Cf. Eduard Farber 'The Colour of Venous Blood' ('Isis' 1954 pp. 9–20).

121, 6

W. Cullen (1712–1790), in his system of nosology, 'Synopsis nosologiae
methodicae in usum studiosorum' (Edinburgh, 1769, English tr. 1800, German
tr. Leipzig, 1786), classified *hypochondriasis* as a disease belonging to the class
neuroses and the order *adynamiae*. He regarded *hypochondriasis melancholica* as
the only idiopathic species of it, and took all others (e.g. hysterica, asthmatica,
biliosa, pituitosa etc.) to be merely symptomatic. The disease was thought to
originate in the region of the spleen, and to be caused by plethora and preternatural thickness of the blood.

Then as now, there was some doubt as to the precise functions of the spleen.
It was thought, ‚daß eine beträchtliche Menge Blutes welche die Milzpulſader
führt, beſorybirt durch die Milzvene zurückkehrt, . . . und daß dieſes nicht
ohne wichtigen Einfluß auf den ganzen Körper geſchehen kann.' (J. F. Pierer's
'Anatomisch–physiologisches Realwörterbuch' Altenburg, 1823) vol. V p. 330.
Hegel is evidently questioning the adequacy of this chemical explanation of
the changes brought about in the blood by this organ, and the curious references
to 'sleep' and 'nocturnal force' (mitternächtige Kraft) might be interpreted as
anticipations of the hypothesis that useless or worn-out red blood corpuscles
are broken up by it, and the discovery that it plays some part in the formation
of the white blood corpuscles.

121, 32

‚Das ſchwache Blumenvolk, die Indier': i.e. 'the feeble flowery folk of
India'. Vegetarianism is of course wide spread in India, where the general
tenderness towards animals, based on the principle of 'ahimsa', or inflicting
no injury on sentient beings, may have originated in Buddhist teaching. See
the Laws of Manu, which in their present form date from about the time of
Christ, V. 46–48, 'He who does not willingly cause the pain of confinement
and death to living beings, but desires the good of all, obtains endless bliss.
He who injures no creature obtains without effort what he thinks of, what he
strives for, and what he fixes his mind on. Flesh-meat cannot be procured
without injury to animals, and the slaughter of animals is not conducive to
heavenly bliss: from flesh-meat, therefore, let man abstain.' (tr. Bühler ed.
F. M. Müller 'Sacred Books of the East' 50 vols. Oxford, 1879–1925, vol XXV).

Hegel's second reference is evidently to Genesis IX vv. 3–4, 'Every moving
thing that liveth shall be meat for you; even as the green herb have I given you

all things. But flesh with the life thereof, which is the blood thereof, shall ye not eat.'

George Cheyne (1671–1743) made known the merits of vegetarianism in his 'Essay on Regimen' (London, 1740). Cf. John Frank Newton 'The return to nature, or, a defence of the vegetable regimen' (London, 1811).

122, 7

Hegel is evidently referring to the following passage, in K. H. Schultz's 'Die Natur der lebendigen Pflanze' pt. I p. 534 (Berlin, 1823), ‚Betrachtet man den Lebensaft, so wie er eben aus den Gefäßen der lebendigen Pflanze ausgeströmt ist, in einem hellen Lichte, so bemerkt man, daß er durch und durch aus Theilen besteht, welche in einer lebendigen gegenseitigen Wechselthätigkeit, und somit in einem ewigen Entstehen und Vergehen, und einer unaufhörlichen Veränderung ihrer Gestalt begriffen sind, so daß sich immer je zwei und zwei mit einander vereinigen, aber augenblicklich wieder theilen und mit andern vereinigen, und so fort. Dieß ist nicht etwa eine bloße Anziehung und Abstoßung, sondern eine wirkliche Durchdringung und Vermischung der Substanz zweier Safttheile, so daß im Fall die einzelnen einen verschiedenen Inhalt haben, dieser sich gleichmäßig unter beide vertheilen muß, sobald sie sich wieder von einander trennen, wie ich dieß schon früher beschrieben habe.' Schultz is referring here to his 'Der Lebensprozess im Blute' (Berlin, 1822).

If Hegel and Schultz are of the opinion that the red and white corpuscles are only to be distinguished from the plasma when the blood is dying, they are of course mistaken. It seems likely however (cf. Vera op. cit. vol. III pp. 264–266) that they are merely opposing the idea that the basic constituents of the blood are these atomlike corpuscles, and attempting to make the perfectly valid point that the blood is *alive*.

See William Hewson (1739–1774) 'Experimental Inquiry into the Properties of the Blood' (3 pts. London, 1771–1777); John Hunter (1728–1793) 'Treatise on the Blood' (1794. ed. Home, London, 1812); J. F. Blumenbach 'Commentatio de vi vitali sanguinis' (Commentat. Soc. Gottingensis. vol. 9 pt. i p. 3).

122, 19

A. Haller (1708–1777) was the first to announce that the activity of the heart is not dependent upon the nervous system but is stimulated by the blood. See, 'Dissertatio de motu sanguinis per cor' (Göttingen, 1737); 'Elementa physiologiae corporis humani' vols. I and II (Lausanne, 1757–8).

122, 25

Bichat ('Anatomie générale, appliquée à la physiologie et à la médecine' (4 vols. Paris, 1801, Germ. tr. 2 vols. Leipzig, 1802, 1803) was of the opinion that the influence of the heart upon the movement of the blood was confined to the arteries and veins, and that in the capillaries the movement was to be attributed to the tonicity of these vessels.

Even in the lectures of 1803–4, Hegel opposed this theory, ‚Der Kreislauf des Blutes ist ein allgemeiner, realer des ganzen gestalteten Organismus; es ist der tätige absolute Begriff, der seine Lebendigkeit im ganzen Organismus hat und auf die absolut entgegengesetzte Weise in ihm ist' ('Jenenser Realphilosophie' I p. 163), and advances in haemadynamics, which since the days of Stephen Hales (1677–1761) had been few and far between, soon showed that he was justified in doing so.

In 1808 Thomas Young (1773–1829) delivered the Croonian lecture, 'On the Functions of the Heart and Arteries' ('Miscellaneous Works' ed. Peacock, 2 vols. London, 1855), and showed (i) that the blood pressure gradually diminishes from the heart to the periphery; (ii) that the velocity of the blood becomes less as it passes from the greater to the smaller vessels; (iii) that the resistance is chiefly in the smaller vessels, and that the elasticity of the coats of the great arteries comes into play in overcoming this resistance in the interval between systoles; and (iv) that the contractile coats do not act as propulsive agents, but assist in regulating the distribution of the blood.

Michelet inserted the inverted commas here, they do not occur in the original ('Jenenser Realphilosophie' II p. 151).

122, 33

‚der springende Punkt' i.e. the punctum saliens. See Aristotle 'Historia Animalium' (tr. D. W. Thompson, Oxford, 1910) VI iii 'τοῦτο δε το σημεῖον πηδὰ και κινεῖται'. William Harvey (1578–1658) popularized the phrase through his 'Exercitationes de generatione animalium' (London, 1651) ex. 17. R. Willis, in his English translation of this work, 'The Works of William Harvey' (London, 1847) p. 235, translates Harvey's Latin with a phrase closely resembling Hegel's, . . . 'a leaping point, of the colour of blood . . . such at the outset is animal life'.

123, 18

Hegel wrote, ‚die Muskeln werden weiß' (white) ‚durch diese äußre Ruhe', but he must have meant ‚weich' (flabby).

Until the end of the eighteenth century it was thought that synovia originated in the blood-vessels and medullary matter discharged from the Haversian canals (cf. Clopton Havers (d. 1702) 'Osteologia Nova' London, 1691). Bichat ('Traité des membranes', Paris, 1800) showed that this is not the case, and that the synovial system is part of the serous system, the synovia being produced by the synovial membranes.

Sir Humphry Davy analysed the synovia of oxen and found that it consisted mainly of albumen and water. Cf. Alexander Monro (1733–1817) 'Outlines of the Anatomy of the human body' (Edinburgh, 1813) I pp. 79–82; Sir Benjamin Brodie (1783–1862) 'Pathological researches respecting the diseases of joints' ('London Med. Chir. Trans.' vols. IV and V 1813, 1814).

123, 25

'Panaricium', but more correctly 'paronychium' (Greek Παρωνυχια, from παρα, about, and ὄνυχ- the nail): a purulent swelling on the finger, usually giving rise to a painful inflammation of the tendon sheath and periosteum. It occurs in three varieties, for it is either situated (i) between the epidermis and the skin, (ii) in the sub-cutaneous cellular tissue, or (iii) underneath the sheath of the flexor tendons of the fingers. Hegel is evidently referring to the second variety.

Guiseppe Flajani (1741–1806) gave an account of the whitlows and ways in which to cure them in his 'Osservazioni pratiche sopra l'amputazione' (Rome, 1791, German tr. by C. G. Kühn, Nuremberg, 1799). Cf. J. L. A. Focke 'Tractatio de panaritio' (Göttingen, 1786); P. Sue 'Praktische Bemerkungen ... zur Heilung des Fingergeschwürs' ('Schregers und Harless Annalen' vol. I sect. iii, no. 5).

Hegel's spelling of the word was unusual, 'panaritium' being more common at that time. There were various German equivalents for it i.e. Aaf, Fingerwurm, Nagelgeschwür, Nietnagel, Taal etc.

123, 30

'gelbliches Blutwasser'. Hegel wrote 'geblichtes', but this must be a mistake. Hoffmeister ('Jenenser Realphilosophie' II p. 153 n. 1) suggests 'gebleichtes' (bleached) as a possible alternative reading, but retains Michelet's version in his text. The blood-serum is certainly a greenish yellow.

123, 31

Samuel Thomas von Sömmerring (1755–1830) was the son of a well-known doctor. After a brilliant university career at Göttingen, where he studied under E. G. Baldinger (1738–1804) and H. A. Wrisberg (1739–1808), he spent a year travelling in Holland and Great Britain. He spent the winter of 1778–9 in Edinburgh, and met his countryman George Forster (1754–1794) in London.

In 1779 he was appointed lecturer in anatomy and chirurgy at Cassel, and in 1784 professor of anatomy and physiology at Mainz. His work in Mainz was disturbed by the French occupation of 1792–1793, and in 1794 he left the city and paid a second visit to Great Britain. On his return to Germany he gave up university teaching and settled in Frankfurt-on-Main as a medical practitioner. He was very successful in his practical work, and was one of the first German doctors to practise vaccination.

In 1805 he moved to Munich. He was a member of the Bavarian privy council and academy of sciences; he broadened his scientific interests, and in July 1809 constructed the first electric telegraph. He never felt at home in south Germany however, and when he retired in 1820, he returned to Frankfurt.

He is known mainly on account of his 'Vom Baue des menschlichen Körpers' (Frankfurt-on-Main, 5 vols. 1791–1796), which became the standard work on human anatomy, and was re-issued as such by various editors until well on into the nineteenth century (e.g. the eight volume Leipzig edition of 1839–1845).

Hegel is here referring to part IV p. 83 of this work (Frankfurt-on-Main, 1792), ‚Eine andere Art der Endigung der Arterien ist, daß sie in feinere, kein rothes Blut mehr führende, Zweigchen fortgesetzt werden, welche anfangs in eine gleiche Vene, endlich aber in rothes Blut führende Venchen übergehen. Dies scheint am Auge der Fall zu seyn, wo wegen der Durchsichtigkeit bloß feinere Flüßigkeiten hingelangen. Doch werden diese Gefäßchen bisweilen so sehr erweitert, daß sie rothes Blut durchlassen, z.B. bey der Entzündung'.

In the margin at this point Hegel notes that no circulation takes place in insects, citing J. H. Autenrieth's 'Handbuch der empirischen menschlichen Physiologie' § 346 (Tübingen, 1801–1802) as his authority for this.

126, 32

Bichat 'Recherches physiologiques sur la Vie et la Mort' (4th edition, ed. F. Magendie, Paris, 1822) ch. I pp. 7–8. 'Les fonctions de l'animal forment deux classes très-distinctes. Les unes se composent d'une succession habituelle d'assimilation et d'excrétion; par elles ils transforme sans cesse en sa propre substance les molécules des corps voisins, et rejette ensuite ces molécules, lorsqu' elles lui sont devenues hétérogènes. Il ne vit qu'en lui, par cette classe de fonctions; par l'autre, il existe hors de lui, il est l'habitant du monde, et non, comme le végétal, du lieu qui le vit naître. Il sent et apperçoit ce qui l'entoure, réfléchit ses sensations, se meut volontairement d'après leur influence, et le plus souvent peut communiquer par la voix, ses désirs et ses craintes, ses plaisirs ou ses peines.

J'appelle *vie organique* l'ensemble des fonctions de la première classe, parce que tous les êtres organisés, végétaux ou animaux, en jouissant à un degré plus ou moins marqué, et que la texture organique est la seule condition nécessaire à son exercise. Les fonctions réunies de la seconde classe forment *la vie animale*, ainsi nommée parce qu'elle est l'attribut exclusif du règne animal'.

Michelet prints a corrupt version of the French text.

127, 8

‚den Krystall der Lebendigkeit'; in that the head, the chest etc., are merely juxtaposed, like the laminae of a crystal. Cf. the note on III. 215.

127, 30

‚wo also das Seelenhafte die Hauptsache ausmacht'. ‚Seelenhaft' is an unusual word, generally synonymous with ‚seelenvoll' (animated, soulful, large-minded). Hegel is evidently using it here in its literal sense. The suffix ‚haft' was originally an independent adjective and meant 'connected with'.

129, 24

François Magendie (1783–1855), who edited Bichat (op. cit. 4th ed., Paris, 1822) has the following note on symmetry (p. 15 § 1 'Symétrie des formes extérieurs dans la vie animale'). 'C'est plutôt aux formes extérieurs que le symétrie paraît avoir été primitivement attachée, et c'est en quelque sorte accidentellement, et parce que la nature de leurs fonctions exigeait en général qu'ils fussent placés à l'extérieur, que les organes de relation se sont trouvés modifiés en vertu de cette loi'.

129, 31

Hegel is here translating Bichat (op. cit. p. 22), 'C'est une remarque qui n'a pu échapper à celui dont les dissections ont été un peu multipliées, que les fréquentes variations de formes, de grandeur, de position, de direction des organes internes, comme la rate, le foie, l'estomac, les reins, les organes salivaires, etc. Telles sont ces variétés dans le système vasculaire, qu'à peine deux sujets offrent-ils exactement la même disposition au scalpel de l'anatomiste.'

129, 33

Bichat (loc. cit. p. 15), 'Deux globes parfaitement semblables reçoivent l'impression de la lumière. Le son et les odeurs ont chacun aussi leur organe double analogue. Une membrane unique est affectée aux saveurs, mais la ligne médiane y est manifeste; chaque segment indiqué par elle est semblable à celui du côté opposé'.

130, 3

Albrecht Haller (1708–1777) 'Elementa physiologiae corporis humani' (8 vols. Lausanne, 1757–1766). Volume three of this work is devoted to the respiratory system and the voice.

Aristotle had been of this opinion that in the production of the voice, the larynx functioned in the manner of an ordinary flute or wind instrument. Antoine Ferrein (1693–1769), in his 'De la formation de la voix de l'homme' ('Mém. de l'acad. de sc. de Paris' 1741 p. 409) suggested that the voice might be caused by vibrations. Haller, with some reservations, accepted Ferrein's hypothesis, and by thinking of the larynx as functioning in the same way as a stringed instrument, was led to emphasize the importance of its symmetry in the production of harmonious sounds.

These different hypotheses gave rise to a great deal of research on the nature of the voice in the second half of the eighteenth century; see J. M. Busch 'De mechanismo organi vocis hujusque functione' (Groningen, 1770); W. de Kempelen (1734–1804) 'Le mécanisme de la parole' (Vienna, 1791), James Beattie (1735–1803) 'The Theory of Language' (London, 1788, German tr. Göttingen, 1790). The standard work on the subject in Hegel's day was by K. F. S. Liscovius (1780–1844) 'Theorie der Stimme' (Leipzig, 1814).

130, 5

Hegel is here translating Bichat (op. cit. p. 41) 'La plupart des physiologistes, Haller en particulier, ont indiqué, comme cause de son (la voix) défaut d'harmonie, la discordance des deux moitiés symétriques du larynx, l'inégalité de force dans les nerfs qui vont de chaque côté à cet organe, de réflexion des sons dans 'une et l'autre narines, dans les sinus droits et gauches.'

130, 13

Bichat (op. cit. p. 17), 'Le grand sympathique, partout destiné à la vie intérieure, présente dans la plupart de ses branches une distribution irrégulière: les plexus soléaire, mésenterique, hypogastrique, splénique, stomachique, etc. en sont un exemple.'

131, 4

Bichat (loc. cit. p. 40), 'Cela est si vrai, que l'ensemble des mouvements exécutés avec tous nos membres est d'autant plus précis qu'il y a moins de différence dans l'agilité des muscles gauches et droits. Pourquoi certains animaux franchissent-ils avec tant d'adresse des rochers où la moindre déviation les entrainerait dans l'abîme, courent-ils avec une admirable précision sur des plans à peine égaux en largeur a l'extrémité de leurs membres? Pourquoi la marche de ceux qui sont les plus lourds n'est-elle jamais accompagnée de ces faux pas si communs dans la progression de l'homme? C'est que chez eux la différence étant presque nulle entre les organes locomoteurs de l'un et de l'autre côté, ces organes sont en harmonie constante d'action'.

Cf. F. H. Loschge (1755–1840) 'De sceleto hominis symmetrico' (Erlangen, 1795); F. M. Heiland 'Darstellung des Verhältnisses zwischen der rechten und linken Hälfte des menschlichen Körpers' (Nuremberg, 1807); F. L. H. Ardieu 'Considérations anatomiques et physiologiques sur la ligne médiane qui divise le corps humain en deux moitiés symétriques' (Strassburg, 1812).

131, 9

There seems to be little justification for this view, and Hegel's entertaining it may well be due to the suspicion with which physical culture was regarded by the Berlin establishment in the decade following the downfall of Napoleon.

Between 1810 and 1820 gymnastics came to play an important part in German politics as the result of the work of Friedrich Ludwig Jahn (1778–1852).

Jahn had witnessed the defeat of the Prussian army at Jena in October 1806, and the subsequent French occupation of Berlin stimulated his patriotism. In his 'Deutsches Volksthum' (Lübeck, 1810), he attempted to show the importance of physical fitness to the survival and self-respect of his country, and in 1811, as part of his plan for national regeneration, he founded the first German gymnastic club at Hasenheide near Berlin. One of his most outstanding pupils was Ernst Eiselen (1793–1846), who helped him write his main work on Gymnastics 'Die Deutsche Turnkunst' (Berlin, 1816), and published several books on fencing.

When the war of liberation began in 1813, Jahn and all his able-bodied gymnasts enlisted in Blücher's army. After Waterloo therefore, popular enthusiasm for his ideas spread rapidly, and gymnastic clubs were founded all over Germany. In Hegel's youth, the standard work on physical culture had been the 'Versuch einer Encyclopädie der Leibesübungen' (2 pts. Berlin, 1794–1795) by G. U. A. Vieth (1763–1836), but in this post-war period a great change took place in the general attitude towards the subject. This radical re-orientation is clearly apparent in the later writings of Johann Christoph Friedrich Guths-Muths (1759–1839), who in the 1790's had published several perfectly sober books on physical culture, e.g. 'Gymnastik für die Jugend' (Schnepfenthal, 1796, Eng. tr. J. Johnson, London, 1800). Two decades later this man was swept into writing a 'Turnbuch für die Söhne des Vaterlandes' (Frankfurt-on-Main, 1817), and even a 'Katechismus der Turnkunst' (Frankfurt-on-Main, 1818).

This enthusiasm soon came into conflict with the authorities cultivating the Holy Alliance. At the great Wartburg meeting of October 1817, the German student associations and gymnastic clubs showed themselves to be strongly opposed to the post-war political reaction, and in favour of a unified and liberalized Germany. On March 23, 1819 a student by the name of Karl Ludwig Sand, who had mixed with members of the gymnastic clubs and student associations, murdered the writer August von Kotzebue (b. 1761) for his 'reactionary' views. Metternich used the incident as the occasion for the Carlsbad conference of August 1819. The Carlsbad decrees, which were the outcome of this meeting, had as their main object the suppression of 'demagogical stratagems': a strict censorship was introduced, 'curators' such as C. F. L. Schultz (1781–1834) at Berlin were appointed to keep watch on the universities, and all gymnastic clubs and student associations were banned.

Jahn was arrested, imprisoned until 1825, and kept under observation until 1840. His gymnastic club at Hasenheide was closed, but his work was carried on by Eiselen, who founded a private club at Berlin in 1825, and trained many of the most outstanding German physical instructors of the nineteenth century. See C. M. Bungardt 'Friedrich Ludwig Jahn als Begründer einer völkisch-politischen Erziehung' (Würzburg, 1938); M. Hobohn 'Johann Christoph Guths-Muths' (Quedlinburg, 1939).

Cf. Robert Burton (1577–1640) 'The Anatomy of Melancholy' pt. 2, sect. 2, mem. 4; James Johnson (1777–1845) 'The influence of civic life, sedentary habits and intellectual refinement on human health' (London, 1818, Germ. tr. H. Breslau, Weimar, 1820); August Hornbostel 'Dissertatio de peregrinationis usu in valetudine servanda vel recuperanda' (Vienna, 1816); P. H. Clias 'Anfangsgründe der Gymnastik oder Turnkunst' (Berne, 1816).

132, 30

,ber anbern Seite sich in die Ruhe des Knochens zurücknimmt'. Hegel wrote that this side gathers (collects, concentrates) itself (,sich zusammennimmt'). ('Jenenser Realphilosophie' II p. 156).

133, 3

Michele Troja (1747–1827), in his, 'De novorum ossium' (Paris, 1775, Germ tr. Leipzig, 1780), had suggested that new bone is formed by ossification of the periosteum. Richerand, in his 'Nouveaux élémens de Physiologie' (Paris, 1801, 11th ed. Brussels, 1833) challenged this view. Hegel is quoting from the following passage (p. 284), 'Les fibres celluleuses et vasculaires qui traversent la substance de l'os établissent un commerce sympathique très-étroit entre son périoste et la membrane très-mince qui tapisse ses cavités intérieures, sécrète la moelle, et a reçu le nom *périoste interne*. La membrane médullaire, étant détruite par l'introduction d'un stylet dans le canal intérieur, les couches extérieurs de l'os se gonflent, se separent des couches intérieurs, et forment comme un nouvel os autour du séquestre'.

Cf. Sir Everard Home (1756–1832) 'Experiments and observations on the growth of bones' ('Transactions for the improvement of medical and chirurgical knowledge' vol. II p. 23).

133, 15

Johannes Alois Blumauer (1755–1798), the Austrian satirist. He was educated by the Jesuits and at one time thought of taking Holy Orders, but when the Society was expelled from the Austrian dominions in 1774, he left his native town of Steyer and found a new vocation in Vienna as a librarian. In 1781 he became a freemason, and soon afterwards was made a censor, a post which he held until 1793. He opened a book-shop in Vienna in 1787, but the concern went bankrupt.

He was an energetic and eloquent opponent of ultramontanism, and advocated the separation of church and state. Much of his writing reminds one of Butler's 'Hudibras'. His main butts are the Pope, monkery, the Jesuits, religion in general. His sense of humour is somewhat homely and often dwells upon culinary and degustatory matters.

His 'Virgils Aeneis travestiert' (Frankfurt-on-Main, 1783) is his best known work, and contains a magnificent description of the land of Cockaigne. Hegel is *perhaps* referring to the following passage in book VI ('Aloys Blumauer's sämmtliche Werke' vol. I p. 137, Königsberg, 1827)

,Und litt sie dann von Zeit zu Zeit
(Weil sie nichts pflegt zu käuen)
An einer Unverdaulichkeit,
So fing sie an zu speyen.' etc.

Paul Scarron (1610–1660) seems to have written the first travesty of Virgil, 'Le Virgile travesty en vers burlesques' (Paris, 1648); cf. Charles Cotton (1630–1687) 'Scarronides, or Virgile travestie' (London, 1670).

133, 32

Treviranus mentions two accounts of this phenomenon, one by C. F. Daniel (1714–1771), 'Sammlung medicinischer Gutachten und Zeugnisse . . ., sammt einer Abhandlung über eine besondere Missgeburt ohne Herz und Lungen' (Leipzig, 1776), and the article by Sir Benjamin Brodie (1783–1862) in the 'Philosophical Transactions of the Royal Society' (1809, pt. I pp. 161–168), 'Account of the Dissection of a Human Foetus, in which the Circulation of the Blood was carried on without a Heart.'

In the case investigated by Brodie, the Woman had given birth to twins after a seventh month pregnancy. 'An opportunity lately occurred to me of examining a human foetus, in which the heart was wanting, and the circulation of the blood was carried on by the action of the vessels only . . . It is to be understood, that the circulation in the foetus receives no propelling power from the action of the heart and arteries of the mother. This, although perfectly known to anatomists, it is proper to mention, as it may not be equally known to all the members of this Society . . . But the most interesting circumstance, which we learn from this examination is, that the circulation not only can be carried on without a heart, but that a child so circumstanced can be maintained in its growth, so as to attain the same size as a foetus which is possessed of that organ . . . It may be observed, that all these cases, in which the heart was wanting, the liver was wanting also. It is probable, that the action of the vessels only, without the assistance of the heart, would have been insufficient to propel the blood through the circulation of the liver, which is so extensive in the natural foetus.'

See also V. Malacarne (1744–1816) 'De' monstri umani' (Padua, 1801): J. C. Zimmer 'Physiologische Untersuchungen über Missgeburten' (Rudolstadt, 1806).

134, 9

Haller deals with this subject in 'Elementa physiologiae corporis humani' vols. I and II (Lausanne, 1757–1758). Treviranus is probably referring to two of his earlier works however, which were translated into French, 'Deux mémoires sur le mouvement du sang' (Lausanne, 1756), and republished in a fuller form in his 'Opera minoris argumenti anatomici' (3 vols. Lausanne, 1762–1768). H. Haeser (1811–1885) in his 'Lehrbuch der Geschichte der Medicin' (3 vols. Jena, 1875–1882) vol. II p. 566, mentions an English translation of these memoirs (London, 1757), but there is no trace of it in British catalogues.

134, 16

Julien Jean César Legallois (1770–1814) was born at Cherrueix near Dol in Brittany, and studied at Caen until 1793, when he joined the federalist army. After its defeat he went into hiding in Paris.

In 1801 he graduated at the École de santé in Paris, and in 1813 was appointed doctor at Bicêtre. He died in the February of 1814. He was a member of the Galvanist Society, and his writings show him to have been one of the ablest of the early experimental physiologists. Hegel mentions the 'Moniteur universal' (1811, no. 312) as the source of his information concerning his experiments. Legallois' main work was however 'Expériences sur le principe de la vie, notamment sur celui des mouvemens du coeur, et sur le siège de ce principe' (Paris, 1812). His son published 'Oeuvres de J. J. C. Legallois . . . précédées d'une notice sur l'auteur' (2 vols., Paris, 1828), and there is an account of his work in F. H. Garrison's 'An Introduction to the History of Medicine' (4th ed., London, 1929) pp. 466–467.

The most important result of his somewhat crude and cruel experiments was, as Hegel notes, that they enabled him to indicate the importance of the spinal marrow and the brain in the functioning of the heart, the circulation of the blood, and the respiratory organs.

His conclusions were questioned by A. P. W. Philip (1770–1850) in papers published by the Royal Society (1815 and 1817) and in his 'Experimental inquiry into the laws of the vital functions' (London, 1818). According to Philip, the heart and the vascular system are able to function quite independently of the spinal marrow and the brain. C. F. Nasse (1778–1851), in his, 'Ueber das Verhältnis des Gehirns und Rückenmarks zur Belebung des übrigen Körpers' (Halle, 1818), tried to mediate between these different views by pointing out that the relationship between the heart and the spinal marrow is closer in more highly developed organisms than it is in the lower animals.

135, 1

See 'Le Moniteur Universel' no. 312, Friday, November 8, 1811 (pp. 1189–1190). The gazette carries a lengthy extract from the report of a meeting held on September 9, 1811, at which J. N. Hallé (1754–1822), F. H. A. von Humboldt (1769–1859) and P. F. Percy (1754–1825) investigated Legallois' thesis that the principle of the powers of the heart resides in the *spinal cord*, and not, as had been asserted prior to Haller, in the brain, or, as had been claimed since, simply in 'irritability' or galvanic activity.

Various experiments, involving decapitation and the partial destruction of the spinal cord, are described. Hegel evidently has in mind the following passage, 'Il s'assura d'abord que la destruction de chacune des deux portions dorsale et cervicale de la moelle était mortelle pour les lapins de vingt jours, de même que celle de la portion lombaire, et même dans un tems plus court d'environ deux minutes. Il reconnut ensuite que les mêmes expériences répétées sur des lapins de différens âges, ne donnaient pas les mêmes résultats. En général, la destruction de la moëlle lombaire n'est pas subitement mortelle pour ces animaux avant l'âge de dix jours; plusieurs y survivent même encore à celui de quinze jours. Au-delà de vingt jours l'effet en est le même qu'à vingt jours. Les très-jeunes lapins peuvent de même continuer de vivre après la destruction soit de la moëlle dorsale et dans un plus petit nombre de cas après la destruction de celle-ci qu'après celle de la dorsale. Aucun ne peut survivre ni à l'une ni a l'autre passé l'âge de quinze jours.'

The members of the commission concluded that Legallois' work was, 'un des plus beaux, et certainement le plus important qui ait été fait en physiologie depuis les savantes expériences de Haller'.

135, 9
See the note III. 314.

135, 29
The origin of this information is a communication made to the Bath Philosophical Society in 1816. This Society first met at the Kingston Lecture Rooms, York Street, Bath on Monday January 8, 1816. It was founded by Dr. Wilkinson, who received an account of these lizards from a Suffolk clergyman. Unfortunately, the manuscripts and records relating to this society have been lost. The rector of Elveden at that time was the Rev. Thomas Bull, but the church records contain no evidence of his having had geological interests. See the 'Bath Herald' for January 6, 1816, in which the formation of the society is announced. Dr. Wilkinson sent an account of the matter to Alexander Tilloch (1759–1825), who published it in his 'Philosophical Magazine and Journal' (vol. 48 p. 469, December 1816). Hegel is evidently quoting Treviranus, who had read Tilloch's version.

'A pit having been opened in the summer of 1814, at Elden, Suffolk, for the purpose of raising chalk, I deemed it a favourable opportunity for procuring fossils . . . In this search I . . . had the good fortune to be present at the discovery of two lizards imbedded in the solid chalk, fifty feet below the surface . . . So completely devoid of life did the lizards appear on their first exposure to the air, that I actually considered them in a fossil state . . . I . . . placed them in the sun, the heat of which soon restored them to animation . . . I . . . immersed one in water, keeping the other in a dry place. You may perhaps consider it worthy your observation, that the mouths of the lizards were closed up with a glutinous substance ... The newt which had been immersed in the water ... was at length enabled to open its mouth ... The other lizard ... was unable to open its mouth ... It died in the course of the night ... The remaining lizard continued alive in water for several weeks, during which it appeared to increase in size. It disliked confinement; and ... to my great mortification, effected its escape, nor could I ever after find it.'

Hegel may have misspelt the name of the village on account of his having had in mind John Scott, first Earl of *Eldon* (1751–1838). It is now known as Elveden, and is situated about 3½ miles S.W. of Thetford; in his day it was known as Elden, Elevedon or Elvidon. In this part of Suffolk, the chalk lies beneath a bed of sand, and the opening of the pit in which these creatures were found may have had something to do with the activities of the owner of Elveden Hall, the Earl of Albemarle, 'a very active and experimental farmer, who by improving and planting, has changed the face of the desert which surrounded him.' See James Dugdale's 'The New British Traveller' (London, 1819) vol. iv p. 305.

Cf. 'The Edinburgh Philosophical Journal' nr. xvi p. 403; J. S. T. Gehler 'Physikalisches Wörterbuch' vol. 4 pp. 1300–1301, where many examples of discoveries of this kind are given, and the writer concludes his account of them by assuring us that we may be certain that they are not pre-Adamitic.

135, 35
Haller, in his 'Elementa Physiologiae Corporis Humani' vol. VI pp. 169–170 (Lausanne, 1777) gives many examples of animals able to go without food for months and years. Treviranus (loc. cit. V p. 272) says that he has seen a vineyard-snail (Helix pomotia) live six months without food, and that O. F. Müller (1730–1784), in his 'Vermium terrestrium et fluviatilium historia' vol. II pp. xii–xxxiv (Copenhagen, 1773) mentions headless wood-snails (Helix nemorosa) and slugs having lived without food for more than a year; cf. Alexander Hunter (1729–1809), 'On the Reproduction of the Head of the Garden Snail' in 'Georgical Essays' vol. 5 (York, 1803).

The 'New Pneumatical experiments about Respiration' by Robert Boyle (1627–1691), which was published in the 'Philosophical Transactions of the Royal Society' (1670, pp. 2011–2057) is evidently the authority for Hegel's statement that some animals can do without atmospheric air for lengthy periods. Boyle noticed this characteristic particularly in slow-worms, leeches, shell-fish and crayfish.

The 'Travels to Discover the Source of the Nile in the Years 1768–1773' (1790, 7 vols. Edinburgh, 1804, German tr. by Volkmann 5 vols. Leipzig, 1790–1791) by James Bruce (1730–1794), was his source for the statement that animals can live in very hot water. 'At Feriana ... I found nothing remarkable but the baths of very warm water without the town; in these there was a number of fish, above four inches in length, not unlike gudgeons. Upon trying the heat by the thermometer, I remember to have been much surprised that they could have existed, or even not been boiled, by continuing long in the heat of this medium' (Eng. ed. vol. I pp. 39–40, German tr. vol. I p. 32). The rotifers resuscitated after four years are mentioned by L. Spallanzani (1729-1799) in his 'Opusculi di fisica animale e vegetabile' (2 vols. Modena, 1776) vol. I p. 309.

140, 2

Christoph Friedrich Ludwig Schultz (1781-1834): see the note II. 338. This article has as its title, 'Ueber physiologe Gesichts und Farben Erscheinungen'. It is to be found in J. S. C. Schweigger's 'Journal für Chemie und Physik' vol. XVI pp. 121-157 (Nuremberg, 1816). Hegel shows that he had inside information on its authorship, for it was published anonymously.

Schultz's general theory of vision, as expounded at the beginning of this article, closely resembles Goethe's, and later in the article Goethe is mentioned. Reference is also made to *Kepler's* investigation of double vision, *Lucas Din,* 'De visione, quae oculo fit gemino' (Jena, 1714), C. N. *Le Cat* (1700-1768), 'Traité des sens' (Rouen, 1739), and Joseph *Priestley,* 'History of Discoveries relating to Vision' (London, 1772, Germ. tr. Klügel, 2 pts. Leipzig, 1776).

Hegel is evidently referring to the following sections of Schultz's exposition:

*§ 26 Zum normalen Sehen mit beiden Augen gehört das gleiche Normiren der Dimensionen in beiden Augen,

§ 27 also auch das Durchschneiden der beiden Augen-Achsen in einem und demselben Puncte.

§ 28 Jeder Punct, welcher nicht dieser Durchschnitts- oder Vereinigungs-Punct der beiden Augen-Achsen selbst ist, liegt also vor oder hinter demselben.

§ 29 Er muß also, in so fern er mit beiden Augen gesehen wird, doppelt erscheinen; alles abnorme Sehen mit beiden Augen ist also ein Doppelsehen.'

Cf. Everard Home's article in 'Phil. Trans. Roy. Soc.' vol. 87 p. 8.

140, 22

The first attempts to define coenaesthesis (Gemeingefühl) as the sixth sense were made in the middle of the eighteenth century: see 'Beweis, dass der Mensch nur einen einzigen Hauptsinn, nämlich das Gefühl besitze' (anon. Sorau, 1758): F. J. W. Schröder (1733-1778) 'Von der physicalischen Theorie der Empfindungen' (Quedlinburg, 1764); F. G. de la Roche (1743-1813) 'Analyse des fonctions du système nerveux' (2 vols. Paris 1778, German tr. J. F. A. Merzdorf, Halle, 1794-1795, pt. II pp. 225-303).

I. P. V. Troxler (1780-1866), in his 'Versuche in der organischen Physik' (Jena, 1804) nr. 1 accepted this definition, and distinguished between the three 'spatial' senses touch, feeling, and sight, and the three 'temporal' senses smell, taste and hearing. J. G. Steinbuch (1770-1818) 'Beitrag zur Physiologie der Sinne' (Nuremberg, 1811) p. 307 attempted to define the faculty of speech as the sixth sense. At this time the most outspoken defence of sensory sextuplicity appeared in D. Walther's 'Ueber die Natur und Nothwendigkeit der Sechszahl der Sinne' (Amberg, 1809).

The means by which blind Cheiroptera avoid collision with objects when in flight was unknown at this time, and so provided another reason for postulating a sixth sense: see Spallanzani's article in L. G. Brugnatelli's 'Giornale fisico med.' (1792) vol. I p. 197, and 'Reil's Archiv für die Physiologie' vol. I p. 58. On knowledge without observation, cf. G. E. M. Anscombe 'Intention' (Blackwell, 1963): R. Galambos 'The Avoidance of Obstacles by Flying Bats: Spallanzani's Ideas (1794) and later theories' ('Isis' 1942–1943 pp. 132–140): S. Dijkgraaf 'Spallanzani's unpublished experiments on the sensory basis of object perception in bats' ('Isis' 1960 pp. 9–20).

140, 30

,ber Geruch gehört bem innern Organismus als Luftigkeit an'. Hoffmeister ('Jenenser Realphilosophie' II p. 161) suggests the following version, ,(Der) Geruch (entspricht) bem innern Organismus, Luftigkeit', but Michelet's reading is more readily comprehensible.

140, 39

We have records of four attempts by Hegel to display the rationality of the senses. In the Jena lectures of 1803–1804 ('Jenenser Realphilosophie' I pp. 168–171) he simply took the brain and the nerves to be the focus and organization of the senses, and then related each sense to its inorganic equivalent, i.e. *sensation* in general to gravity, shape and heat, *hearing* and *sight* to sound and colour, *smell* to air, and *taste* to water.

In the Jena lectures of 1804–1805 ('Jenenser Realphilosophie' II pp. 158–162) he took the *ego* to be the focus, and the *feeling* of the skin to be basic to the senses, which he then ranged in accordance with their approximation to the *inwardness* of consciousness, paying little attention to their inorganic equivalents. *Hearing* was taken to be the culminating sense because of its intimate connection with *vocal faculty*, through which the individual is able to give its fullest expression to consciousness.

In the Heidelberg Encyclopaedia of 1817 (ed. Glockner, 1956 pp. 208–209) Hegel worked out the progression from gravity to light, air, water and sound with greater precision, and then attempted to reproduce this progression in assessing the senses. In this new treatment of the subject he managed to combine the essentials of both his previous expositions.

The distinctive feature of his mature views on this subject is the emphasis he lays upon the *triadicity* of his assessment.

Cf. John Elliot (1747–1787) 'Philosophical observations on senses' (London, 1780, German tr. Leipzig, 1785): C. N. Le Cat (1700–1768) 'Traité des sens' (Rouen, 1740): F. J. Schelver (1778–1832) 'Versuch einer Naturgeschichte der Sinneswerkzeuge' (Göttingen, 1798). This last work is probably the source of

Hegel's statement that some of the lower animals may not possess all five senses. See also the addition to § 316.

142, 14

‚Erregungstheorie'. This theory was developed by the followers of John Brown (1735–1788), whose 'The Elements of Medicine' (2 vols. London, 1788) had a great effect upon German medicine about the turn of the century, cf. the note III. 378. According to Brown, animate bodies are distinct from inanimate bodies merely on account of their being susceptible to stimulation. He tended to regard this 'excitability' as an imponderable, and defined it merely as the essential principle of neural and muscular activity.

J. A. Röschlaub (1768–1835) formulated the stimulation theory. He attempted to give philosophic form to the Brunonian system, and improved upon Brown's basic theory by putting forward the idea that this 'excitability' is the result of a reciprocal relationship between a *vital principle* and external stimulation. Brown had regarded disease as nothing but abnormal excitability resulting from an excess or deficiency in *stimulation*. Röschlaub added to this, that before a disease can set in, the excess or deficiency in stimulation must be accompanied by a requisite reaction or lack of reaction in the *body* concerned. In his later writings he attempted to explain health and disease in terms of oxidation and disoxidation. See his, 'Von dem Einflusse der Brownischen Theorie' (Würzburg, 1798): 'Untersuchungen über Pathogenie' (3 vols. Frankfurt-on-Main, 1798–1801): 'Magazin für . . . praktische Heilkunde' (10 vols. Frankfurt-on-Main, 1790–1803): 'Lehrbuch der besonderen Nosologie' (Frankfurt-on-Main, 1807).

The 'Erläuterung der Erregungstheorie' (Heilbronn, 1803), by J. F. Frank (1771–1842) provides an excellent exposition of the theory. It is based on one of Frank's earlier works, 'Erläuterungen der Brownischen Arzneilehre' (Heilbronn, 1797), which gives a very good picture (pp. 193–238) of a doctor putting the theories of Brown to the test in his practical work. As Hegel points out however, these theories were soon abandoned by practising doctors, and taken up by would-be philosophers. He probably has in mind L. A. Liffmann's 'Ideen zu einer neuen Darstellung des Brownschen Systems' (2 vols. Göttingen, 1800–1802), C. G. Kilian's 'Differenz der echten und unechten Erregungstheorie' (Jena, 1803), and W. Liebsch's 'Babel in der neuen Heilkunde' (Göttingen, 1805).

142, 20

Schelling's treatment of this subject is a good example of the empty formalism into which 'philosophic' interpretations of the Brunonian system tended to fall. Hegel is evidently referring to the following passage, ‚Da aber die Funktion des Reizes überhaupt nur in dem Hervorbringen seines Entgegengesetzten liegt, so erhellt, daß der Reiz selbst entgegengesetzter Art, d.h. positiv oder negativ seyn kann, je nachdem er die Thätigkeit erhöht ober herabſtimmt. Aber poſitiv kann ein Reiz nur wirken bei einem gewiſſen Grab ber Receptivität. (z.B. ein geringer Grab Wärme nur bei einem Norb- länber), negativ nur bei einem gewiſſen Grab ber Thätigkeit, (z.b. Kälte- negativ Reiz nur auf einen Süblänber), weil er in jenem Fall die Receptivität, in dieſem die Thätigkeit herabſtimmen ſoll. Bei einem hohen Grab ber Capacität für einen negativen Reiz kann burch dieſen die Thätigkeit nicht verminbert, ſo wie bei einem hohen Grab von Thätigkeit burch poſitiven Reiz nicht vermehrt werben. (Daher allein das Phänomen ber Abstumpfung gegen ben Reiz burch Gewohnheit)'. 'Erster Entwurf eines Systems der Naturphilosophie' (Jena, 1799) p. 83. ('Schellings Werke' ed. Schröter, Munich 1958) II p. 88.

143, 2

Although Hegel never shows anything but the greatest respect for Spinoza, he rarely mentions him without criticizing him. He deals with him at length in his 'Lectures on the History of Philosophy' (tr. Haldane, 3 vols. London, 1963) III pp. 252–290, and assesses many of his ideas in the first two parts of his 'Science of Logic' (tr. Johnston and Struthers, 2 vols. London, 1961).

143, 3

See the note III. 315.

143, 13

John Brown (1735–1788), in his 'Elementa medicinae' (Edinburgh, 1780, Eng. tr. London, 1788, German tr. Copenhagen, 1796) classified diseases as either *sthenic*, i.e. inflammatory, or *asthenic*, i.e. debilitating. See the note III. 379.

143, 26

'Caput mortuum'. In Hegel's day this was already an archaic term. In general usage it was taken to mean any worthless residue, in this case the chemical constituents of organic matter. In German it also had a more specific meaning however, and was used as a term for rotten-stone (Tripel), a decomposed siliceous limestone mainly used in metal-polishing, and colcothar (Eiſenroth), a brownish-red peroxide of iron. Cf. F. A. C. Gren (1760–1798) 'Handbuch der Chemie' (Halle, 1787) vol. I § 143, note; J. F. Pierer (1767–1832) 'Medizinisches Realwörterbuch' (Altenburg, 1829) vol. 8 p. 343; J. C. A. Heyse (1764–1855) 'Fremdwörterbuch' (14th ed. Hanover, 1870).

144, 1

Medical writers such as the later Brunonians, Röschlaub and the followers of Schelling made various attempts to explain disease in chemical terms, cf. B. Hirschel 'Geschichte des Brown'schen Systems und der Erregungstheorie'

(Leipzig, 1846). In assuming this to be a fruitful line of research, they were in substantial agreement with chemists such as A. F. Fourcroy (1755–1809), L. N. Vauquelin (1763–1829) and J. J. Berzelius (1779–1848), who were busily engaged in making chemical analyses of the most various organic products. Hegel was ready to admit that work of this kind had its value (§ 365), but he objected to its being interpreted as providing a full explanation of organic phenomena. He based this objection on his definition of the Notion of living being (§ 337), according to which the *unity* of the organism is *compatible* with the positing of distinct and transitory (e.g. chemical) moments within it.

By the sixties of the last century the founding of microbiology by Pasteur, the discoveries made by Lister and I. Semmelweis (1818–1865) in the field of antiseptic surgery, and the advances made in medical entomology by R. Leuckart (1822–1898) etc. had fully substantiated Hegel's position in so far as he had objected on principle to chemical interpretations of nervous fevers. However, although this subsequent research showed *why* this objection was justified, it did not bear out his reasons for making it, in so far as these reasons were based upon empirical data (cf. § 371).

Outbreaks of 'nervous fever' ravaged the armies of Europe on many occasions throughout the Napoleonic period. There is a fascinatingly detailed account of these epidemics and of the related German, French and English medical literature of the time in H. Haeser (1811–1885) 'Lehrbuch der Geschichte der Medicin' (Jena, 1882) vol. III pp. 571–602. The worth of this literature in light of present knowledge may be judged by the fact that it was not until 1836 that two American doctors, W. Gerhard (1809–1872) and C. W. Pennock (1799–1867) distinguished between typhus and typhoid. See 'On the Typhus-Fever which occurred at Philadelphia in 1836, showing the distinctions between it and dothienenteritis' ('American Journal of Medical Science' February and August 1837).

144, 27

Hegel took evil to be 'nothing but the inadequacy of that which *is* to that which *should* be' ('Encyclopaedia' § 472, cf. §§ 23, 35). He also touches upon the subject in his 'Philosophy of Religion' (tr. Speirs and Sanderson, London, 1962) vol. III pp. 71–72, 'The world in its positive subsistence and the destruction and contradiction within it, occur in distinct contrast to God as the reconciled unity of being-in-self and being-for-self, and this gives rise to those questions concerning the way in which evil is compatible with the absolute unity of God, the original source of wickedness etc., questions which pertain to all religions in which there is a more or less developed consciousness. In the first instance this negative appears as the evil of the world; but it also draws itself back into self-identity, in which it constitutes the self-conscious being-for-self of finite spirit.'

Hegel discusses Voltaire's, Kant's and Fichte's views on evil in 'Glauben und Wissen' (1802, Glockner's ed. Stuttgart, 1958) pp. 419–424, and Leibnitz's views on the subject in 'The History of Philosophy' (tr. Haldane and Simson, London, 1963) vol. III pp. 340–342.

144, 35

Ignaz Paul Vitalis Troxler (1780–1866) was born in the Beromünster district of the canton of Lucerne, and attended the grammar school at Solothurn. He left Switzerland for the first time when the French revolutionary troops invaded the country, and in 1800 began to study philosophy and medicine at Jena, where he fell under the influence of Schelling. He took his doctorate in medicine at Göttingen, visited Vienna, and then returned to his home canton where he practised as a medical doctor until 1807.

It was in these early years that he produced the works to which Hegel is evidently referring, i.e. 'Ideen der Grundlage zur Nosologie und Therapie' (Jena, 1803), 'Versuche in der organischen Physik' (Jena, 1804), and 'Grundriss der Theorie der Medicin' (Vienna, 1805), all of which show the influence of Schelling and elicited his approbation. Typical of his writing at this time is his definition of secretion as ,eine nach innen gerichtete Excretion' and of life as, 'individual productivity, in which the producer and the product devour themselves within the form of self-determination and determinability.'

In 1807 he lost his job in Lucerne because of his outspoken criticism of sanitary conditions in the canton. He then travelled in the Low Countries, France and Italy, and on his return to Beromünster began to play an active part in local politics. His attitude towards Schelling changed, and he began to develop his own views on the importance of anthropology, see 'Blicke in das Wesen des Menschen' (Aarau, 1811). In 1815 he attended the Congress of Vienna on behalf of Switzerland.

In 1820 he was appointed professor of history and philosophy at the Lucerne Lyceum, but when his 'Fürst und Volk nach Buchanan's und Milton's Lehre' (Aarau, 1821) appeared, the Jesuit party on the staff forced him to resign his post and he again began to practise as a medical doctor. In 1823 he was appointed member of the Aarau education committee, in 1830 professor of philosophy at Basel and in 1834 professor at the new university of Bern, a post which he retained until his retirement in 1850.

In these later years F. H. Jacobi (1743–1819) replaced Schelling as the main influence upon his intellectual development. His work as a doctor, politician, teacher and philosopher had given him *breadth* of experience and knowledge, which he tried to deepen and *synthesize* by means of a philosophic anthropology or 'anthroposophy' as he called it. His mature works are very different from his early attempts at a philosophy of medicine. His 'Naturlehre des menschlichen Erkennens oder Metaphysik' (Aarau, 1828) has recently been republished (W. A. Aeppli, Bern, 1944), and his 'Logik. Die Wissenschaft des Denkens und Kritik aller Erkenntniss' (3 parts, Stuttgart and Tübingen, 1829–1830) is of interest on account of its comprehensive and sensitive treatment of the subject. The book contains a short appreciation of Hegel's logic (pt. III).

145, 29
See the note III. 214.

145, 33
‚Der Inſtinct iſt die auf bewußtloſe Weiſe wirkende Zweckthätigkeit'. The word 'instinct' (Latin instinctus, from stinguere, to prick or sting) became common currency among the scholastics through the writings of St. Thomas Aquinas. It was not introduced into English until the sixteenth century however, and the first German writer to use the word in his mother tongue was Johann Jakob Bodmer (1698–1783), in his poem 'Noah' (1752) line 256.

In Hegel's day it was a new word therefore, and there was some discussion as to its exact meaning. It was generally used as a substitute for 'blinder Trieb' or 'blind impulse', and taken to be innate, determined only by the *animality* of a sentient being. It was therefore distinguished from 'Naturtrieb' or 'natural impulse', which was a more comprehensive term, covering the higher spiritual impulses towards justice, honour, truth etc. See J. F. Blumenbach (1752–1840) 'Handbuch der Naturgeschichte' (Göttingen, 1779) sect. III § 33: Erasmus Darwin (1731–1802) 'Zoonomia' (2 vols. London, 1796, German tr. 3 vols. Hanover, 1799) sect. XVI.

146, 6
'The Physics' (tr. Wicksteed and Cornford, 2 vols. Loeb, 1929) Bk. II ch. i, 'For nature is the principle and cause of motion and rest to those things, and those things only, in which she inheres primarily, as distinct from incidentally . . . And all such things have a substantive existence; for each of them is a substratum or "Subject" presupposed by any other category, and it is only in such substrata that nature ever has her seat.

Further, not only nature itself and all things that "have a nature", but also the behaviour of these things in virtue of their inherent characteristics is spoken of as "natural".'

146, 28
Different stages of sleep were recognized at this time and distinctions were drawn between sleepiness (somnolentia), slumber (sopor) and deep sleep (somnus profundus). Individuality, age and climate were generally recognized as playing an important part in sleeping habits. Whether sleep was to be regarded as a condition affecting the whole organism and related directly to its environment, or whether it was to be most clearly understood as a state determined mainly

by 'the highest functions of the nervous system' was a matter of debate however, and it was evidently this debate which determined Hegel's assessment of the subject. Cf. Stephen Dickson 'Dissertatio de somno' (Edinburgh, 1783); Robert Cleghorn 'Dissertatio de somno' (Edinburgh, 1783); Erasmus Darwin (1731–1802) 'Zoonomia' (2 vols. London, 1796, German tr. 3 vols. Hanover, 1799) sect. XVIII; J. E. M. Guiaud (1790–1844) 'Essai physiologique et pathologique sur le sommeil' (Paris, 1816); H. von Buchholz 'Ueber den Schlaf und die verschiedenen Zustände desselben' (Berlin, 1821); F. A. von Ammon (1799–1861) 'Commentatio . . . in qua somni . . . exponuntur et dijudicantur' (Göttingen, 1820).

146, 33

Hegel is here expressing the traditional view that these parasites originate in putrescible phlegm by a kind of spontaneous generation; see Geronimo Gabuccini 'De lumbricis alvum occupantibus' (Venice, 1547): J. R. Sultzberger 'De vermibus in homine' (Leipzig, 1628); cf. William Ramsay (1626–c. 1676) 'Some Physical Considerations of the Matter, Origination and Several Species of Wormes' (London, 1668). This view was accepted because these parasites were known to be incapable of surviving outside their hosts, and because it was thought unlikely that their eggs could develop at any temperature other than that of the body in which they were engendered. The question was still an open one in Hegel's day, and it was not until J. J. Steenstrup (1813–1897) published his famous monograph in 1842 (tr. 'On the Alternation of Generations' Royal Society, 1845), and the work of T. S. Cobbold (1828–1886) 'Entozoa' (London, 1864) and R. Leuckart (1822–1898) 'Die Parasiten des Menschen' (2 vols. Leipzig, 1863–1876, English tr. 1886) had been published, that helminthology took on its modern form.

Linnaeus traced the descent of the liver fluke of sheep from a free-living stage, and P. S. Pallas (1741–1811), in his doctoral dissertation (1760), pointed out that experiments were needed before any reliable statements could be made on the origin of parasitic 'worms'. In 1781 ('Neue nordische Beiträge' vol. I p. 43), Pallas even attempted to prove that the eggs of these insects must have been taken into the hosts from without. However, when the Danish Society of Sciences offered a prize for the best work on this subject in 1780, both the winning essays called Pallas's thesis in question: See J. A. E. Goeze (1731–1793) 'Versuch einer Naturgeschichte der Eingeweidewürmer thierischer Körper' (Leipzig, 1782, ed. J. G. H. Zeder, Leipzig, 1800); M. E. Bloch (1723–1799) 'Abhandlung von der Erzeugung der Eingeweidewürmer' (Berlin, 1782). As late as 1820, G. A. Goldfuss (1782–1848) cited these works as standard authorities: 'Handbuch der Zoologie' (Nuremberg, 1820) pt. I pp. 126–127.

In Hegel's day the classification put forward by C. A. Rudolphi (1771–1832) in 'Entozoorum, sive vermium intestinalium historia naturalis' (2 vols. Amsterdam, 1808–1810) was in general use among German helminthologists.

147, 3

G. S. Poli (1746–1825) 'Memoria sul tremuoto di 26 Luglio 1805' (Naples, 1805) p. 48 et seq., gives a fine description of the general restlessness of the animals in the area just prior to the Neapolitan earthquake of July 26, 1805. Cf. Friedrich Hoffmann (1797–1836) 'Geschichte der Geognosie' (Berlin, 1838) pp. 380–383: II. 51, 25.

147, 22

The Lily Thrips (Liothrips vaneeckei) breeds and feeds and completes its entire life-cycle among the scale leaves of the bulbs of Lilies. Hegel may also have had in mind the Lily Beetle (Crioceris lilii), the grubs of which feed on the leaves of Lilies during the summer, and later pupate in an earthen cell beneath these plants.

Few trees are more liable to the attacks of insect pests than Willows. An account of Willow pests is given in the Ministry of Agriculture's Bulletin no. 29. Hegel may have had in mind Willow Aphides such as Melanoxantherum saliis and Pterochlorus saligna, Willow Leaf Beetles such as Phyllodecta vulgatissima and Galerucella lineola, or the Willow Weevil, Cryptorrhynchus lapathi, which does considerable damage to the cricket-bat Willow, Salix coerulea.

In mentioning the insects peculiar to Fig trees he probably has in mind the caprification mentioned in § 348, III. 99–100.

148, 28

Cf. G. A. Gaultier 'Recherches sur l'organisation de la peau de l'homme, et sur es causes de sa coloration' (Paris, 1810).

148, 34

‚Sie sind alle vielmehr gemischte, durch organische Kochung bezwungene Farben', Cf. the note III. 376.

149, 2

Johann Reinhold Forster (1729–1798) came of a West Prussian family which had emigrated from Scotland about 1642. He studied theology at Halle and worked as a priest at Danzig for some years before discovering that this was not his vocation. In 1765 he left for St. Petersburg with his son Johann Georg Adam Forster (1754–1794), and in the following year they came to England. The father taught French, German and Natural Science at Warrington Academy until 1770, when he moved to London. His miscellaneous scientific and translation work soon made him known in London circles, and he was elected fellow of the Royal Society for his, 'Characteres Generum Plantarum quas in Itinere ad Insulas Maris Australis collegerunt' (London, 1775).

In 1772, when Captain Cook was about to set forth on his second great voyage, Sir Joseph Banks (1743–1820), who should have accompanied him, suddenly fell ill. Lord Sandwich recommended Forster as a replacement, so that father and son sailed with the expedition as naturalists. On their return in 1775, Forster became involved in an undignified squabble with Cook and the Admiralty over the publication of his account of the voyage. On being forbidden to write, he gave his note-books to his son, whose vivid account was published a few weeks before Cook's. This gave rise to more bad feeling, and he was obliged to leave the country in 1779. He spent the last years of his life teaching at Halle. After these turbulent events his son was successively professor of natural history at Wilna and librarian at Mainz.

J. G. A. Forster's 'A Voyage round the World in His Britannic Majesty's Sloop, Resolution, commanded by Capt. James Cook during the years 1772, 1773, 1774 and 1775' (London, 1777) was translated into German (3 vols. Berlin, 1784). Goethe appears to be referring to the following passage in J. R. Forster's 'Observations made during a voyage round the World' (London, 1778) pp. 184–185, 'We cannot help being in raptures, when we tread the paths of O-Taheitean groves, which at each step strike us with the most simple, and at the same time the most beautiful prospects of rural life; presenting scenes and happiness and affluence to our eyes, among a people, which, from our narrow prejudices we are too readily accustomed to call savage . . . On the sea shore, the natives are employed in dragging the net, and taking a variety of beautiful fish, whose dying colours change every moment: or they pick some shells from the reefs . . .'

149, 22

The 'vegetable' nature of hairs and feathers is not an invention of Hegel's. J. L. Choulant (1791–1861) mentions it in his article 'Haare' in Pierer's 'Medizinisches Realwörterbuch' vol. III p. 790 (Leipzig, 1819), ‚Es scheinen daher wirklich die Haare etwas von der Pflanzennatur an sich zu tragen, gleichsam parasitisch auf dem Thierkörper zu wurzeln, und zugleich eine Art von Vermittlung zwischen der äußern Oberfläche des Thierkörpers und der äußern ihn umgebenden Natur darzustellen. Aus dieser Ansicht ergibt sich am natürlichsten, warum gerade an den Lichtseiten der Thiere der Haarwuchs am ausgebildetsten hervortritt . . . Endlich ergibt es sich auch daraus, daß den Haaren des Thierkörpers eine den Pflanzen analoge Function, Einsaugung und Aushauchung, wahrscheinlich auch die Absonderung irgend eines Saftes zukommen müsse.'

Cf. J. K. Pfaff 'De pilorum varietatibus naturalibus et praeternaturalibus' (Halle, 1799); C. A. Rudolphi (1771–1832) 'Dissertatio de pilorum structura' (Greifswald, 1806); A. Rowlandson 'Historical, philosophical and practical essay on the human hair' (London, 1818); Aristotle 'Historia Animalium' (tr. D. W. Thompson, Oxford, 1910) 517b–519a.

150, 5

Treviranus cites certain *beetles* as examples of this: *Dyticidae*, which keep a supply of air under their elytra, and *Hydrophilidae*, which hold air in the pubescence extending on either side beneath their abdomens.

The *Argyroneta* or European fresh-water spider provides the most striking example of an aquatic insect with a capacity for carrying air by means of this pubescence. It is known as the 'silver swimmer' because of its silvery appearance as it swims about under water enveloped in the air which it retains on its sternum and abdomen by means of these hairs.

150, 20

Although Hegel rejects the hypothesis that the living blood is atomistic (cf. the note III. 314), by regarding arterial blood as 'satiated' with oxygen, he anticipates the discovery that the haemoglobin content of red corpuscles enables it to act as an oxygen carrier.

For contemporary views on this subject see D. Ellis 'An inquiry into the changes induced on atmospheric air by ... the respiration of animals' (London, 1807 and 1811): K. J. Zimmermann 'Abhandlung über den Respirationsprocess der Thiere' (Bamberg, 1817): J. Bourdon (1796–1861) 'Récherches sur le mechanisme de la réspiration, et sur la circulation du sang' (Paris, 1820).

151, 3

The functioning of the glands was very imperfectly understood at this time, and nothing was known of the exact nature or function of the thyroid hormone, or of the control of its production by the thyrotrophic hormone produced by the pituitary gland. ‚Der Nutzen der Drüsen ist verschieden, nach den verschiedenen Arten derselben; im allgemeinen bezieht er sich auf die Mischungsveränderung des Blutes durch Ausscheidung eines Stoffes, oder vielleicht auch nur bei einigen durch einen innern thierisch-chemischen Proceß' (Pierer's 'Anatomisch- physiologisches Realwörterbuch' vol. II p. 398, Leipzig, 1818). It was known that changes took place in their texture, and exudation was thought to be the main cause of their becoming harder; see J. F. Meckel (1781–1833) 'Handbuch der menschlichen Anatomie' (Halle, 1815) vol. I pp. 651–652.

Autenrieth and Hegel were only vaguely aware of the nature of the blood and the way in which it supplies the ductless glands and helps to convey their secretions and remove their waste products. It was not until Thomas Wilkinson King (1809–1847) had published his paper on the structure and functions of the thyroid gland in 1836, and E. C. Baber (1843–1890) had published the results of his researches on its minute structure ('Phil. Trans. Roy. Soc.' 1876 p. 557; 1878 p. 56: 1881 p. 577), and shown that its lymphatic vessels contain the same colloid material as its alveoli, that any clear idea of the structure and functioning of the gland became possible.

For early nineteenth century views on the gland see J. A. Schmidtmüller

(1776–1809) 'Ueber die Ausführungsgänge der Schilddrüse' (Landshut, 1804):
A. Maas 'Dissertatio de glandula thyreoidea' (Würzburg, 1810): J. F. Ackermann (1765–1815) 'Dissertatio de corporis thyreoidei vera functione' (Heidelberg, 1811).

151, 23

J. J. Berzelius (1779–1848) analyzed saliva, and discovered that it contains,
'99·29% water, ·29% salivous matter, ·14% mucus, ·17% muriatic alkalis,
·009% lactic natron and osmazone, and ·002% pure natron'. ('Ueberblick über
die Zusammensetzung der thierischen Flüssigkeiten' Nuremberg, 1814).

Hegel probably had this book in mind when he wrote this paragraph. F.
Tiedemann (1781–1856) and L. Gmelin (1788–1853) produced a similar work
'Die Verdauung nach Versuchen' (2 vols. Heidelberg, 1826–1827, French tr.
1827).

153, 3

For contemporary English views on the bile see: J. Maclury 'Experiments
upon the human bile and reflexions on the biliary secretion' (London, 1772):
Richard Powell (1767–1834) 'Observations on the bilis and its diseases' (London,
1800): George Rees (1776–1846) 'Practical observations on disorders of the
stomach with remarks on the use of the bile' (London, 1810). In Hegel's day
the standard German work on the physiology of the bile was by S. Goldwitz
(b. 1758) 'Neue Versuche zu einer wahren Physiologie der Galle' (Bamberg,
1785).

A. F. Fourcroy (1755–1809) suggested that it originates in the blood ('Journal
de physique' vol. I pt. i p. 372). T. G. A. Roose (1771–1803) questioned this
theory in his 'Physiologische Untersuchungen' (Braunschweig, 1796) pt. 5, and
A. A. Parmentier (1737–1813) and N. Deyeux (1753–1837) showed by a series
of experiments that Fourcroy's theory could not be substantiated ('Reil's
Archiv' vol. I art. ii p. 104).

154, 6

Lazzaro Spallanzani (1729–1799) 'Dissertazioni di fisica animale e vegetabile'
(2 vols. Modena, 1780). The first volume of this work deals with digestion, the
second with the genesis of animals and plants. Hegel evidently used the French
translation of it by Jean Senebier (1742–1809) 'Expériences sur la Digestion de
l'homme et de différentes espèces d'animaux' (Geneva, 1783), although C. F.
Michaelis (1754–1814) had translated it into German (Leipzig, 1786).

Hegel gives an account of his experiments in the addition to this paragraph.
They were carried out in order to decide whether digestion operates by means
of trituration, dissolvant juices, fermentation or putrefaction, or whether, as
Hermann Boerhaave (1668–1738) had suggested, it involves all these factors.
Antorio Vallisneri (1662–1730) had suggested that the stomach of the ostrich

worked solely by means of trituration ('Opere fisico mediche' Venice, 1733, vol. I). Francesco Redi (1626–1698), in his 'Esperienze intorne a diverse cose naturali' (Florence, 1671) had made apparent advances in the understanding of digestion, but his conclusions had been questioned by Guiseppe Pozzi (1697–1752).

The method used by Spallanzani was suggested by R. A. F. Réaumur (1683–1757) in an article published by the Académie des Sciences de Paris in 1752.

154, 19

G. E. Stahl (1660–1734), in his 'Zymotechnia universalis' c. 19 (Halle, 1697) attempted to show that the differences between various kinds of fermentation were merely a matter of degree, but Hermann Boerhaave (1668–1738), in his 'Elementa Chemiae' (Lugduni, 1732, English tr. 1735) vol. II p. 166, distinguished between vinous, acidic and putrefactive fermentations, and this classification was still accepted in Hegel's day. A. F. Fourcroy (1755–1809) attempted to show that sugar fermentation and the 'chromatic' fermentation which takes place in leaves are also distinct forms, but his views did not gain general acceptance.

Sugar was taken to be the organic basis of vinous fermentation, and there was a general readiness to accept chemical explanations of acidic fermentation, and of the putrefactive fermentation occurring in humus and decaying animal bodies etc.

L. J. Thénard (1774–1857) was the first to suggest that fermentation is animal and not chemical in nature ('Annal. de Chimie' XLVI, 1803 pp. 224–320), but it was not until 1835 that C. C. Delatour (1777–1859) showed that it is caused by minute organisms ('L'Institut', III, 1835, pp. 133–134).

154, 24

Hegel is evidently referring here to Fourcroy's 'Système de connaissances chimiques' (6 vols. Paris, 1801). In vol. IV (p. 401) of the German translation of this work (Braunschweig, 1801–1803) Fourcroy states that he has been unable to find any difference between saliva and pancreatic juice. Cf. John Thomson's (1765–1846) notes to the English translation of this work. 'The Elements of Chemistry' (5th edition, 3 vols. Edinburgh, 1798).

G. Fordyce (1736–1802) analyzed the pancreatic juice of animals and merely discovered that it contained a certain amount of cooking salt: 'A treatise on the digestion of food' (London, 1791, German tr. Leipzig, 1793 p. 53).

155, 20

‚feinem Zorne gegen das Object'. By using the word ‚Zorn' (wrath, choler), Hegel is evidently indicating the part played by the bile in the formation of the chyle. He evidently has in mind the Hippocratic doctrine of the four juices of the human body, and Galen's parallel doctrine of the four temperaments.

According to these doctrines the bile is the predominant factor in the development of choler or wrath.

156, 16

‚welche wenig ober gar keinen Stickstoff enthalten'. Autenrieth wrote ‚besitzen' (to be endowed with, hold, *possess*), not ‚enthalten' (hold, include, *contain*).

156, 38

‚Die Chemie kriegt aus Beiden zwar etwas Aehnliches heraus'. Hegel wrote ('Jenenser Realphilosophie' II p. 118), ‚Die Chemie zeigt in Beiden etwas Aehnliches' i.e. 'Chemistry indicates something similar in both'.

157, 29

‚Wenn das Organische durch die einzelnen Momente hindurch das Unorganische allmählig zur Identität mit sich bringt'. Hegel's version of this is significantly different ('Jenenser Realphilosophie' II pp. 119–120), ‚Wenn das Organische durch die einzelnen Momente hindurch als zweckmäßig das Unorganische allmählich zur Identität mit sich bringt'. i.e. 'If organic being, as *purpose*, does gradually bring inorganic being into identity with itself'.

157, 33

Michelet introduced the emphasis here.

158, 5

On the Hydra viridis (Armpolyp) see A. J. Rösel (1705–1759) 'Insectenbelustigungen' (Nuremberg, 1755) pt. III sect. ii. G. A. Goldfuss (1782–1844) 'Handbuch der Zoologie' pt. I p. 79 (Nuremberg, 1820).

158, 19

Treviranus cites the Pyrosoma atlanticum as an example of this, and mentions, as his source, the account of this creature given by F. Péron (1775–1810) in 'Annales du Museum d'Histoire Naturelle' vol. IV pp. 437–446 (1804). He does not mention that Péron's description of its 'mode of nutrition' was merely a matter of conjecture however (loc. cit. p. 445).

158, 25

Aphrodites constitute a genus of marine worms with bristles of iridescent hues. In English they are also called Sea-mice, and in German 'Seeraupen' (Sea-caterpillars).

158, 27

Holothuria constitute the typical genus of the Echinoderms. They have an elongated form, a tough leathery integument, and a ring of tentacles around the mouth. See F. Tiedemann (1781–1860) 'Anatomie der Röhrenholothurie, des pomeranzenfarbigen Seesterns und des Stein-Seeigels' (Landshut, 1816).

158, 28

Asteriae constitute a genus of Echinoderms, containing the common Five-rayed Star-fish, with allied species. See Tiedemann (op. cit. pp. 5–9), J. B. Spix (1781–1826) 'Mémoire pour servir à l'histoire de l'astérie rouge' etc. ('Annales du Muséum d'Histoire Naturelle' vol. 13 pp. 438–459, 1809).

158, 29

This point is made by Carl August Ramdohr in his 'Ueber die Verdauungs-werkzeuge der Insecten' (Halle, 1811). Cf. R. A. F. Réaumur (1683–1757) 'Mémoires pour servir à l'Histoire des Insectes' (Paris, 1734) vol. I pt. 2 p. 204.

159, 1

John Latham (1740–1837), in his 'A General Synopsis of Birds' (3 vols. London, 1781–1785) mentions that the flesh of the Missel Thrush (Turdus viscivorus) 'is pretty good eating, though not so much esteemed as the lesser species', and that that of the Fieldfare (Turdus pilaris), 'is tolerably good, though apt to be bitter' (vol. II pp. 17, 24, 25). In England therefore, these birds do not seem to have been popular fare.

In Germany however they were consumed in immense numbers. Johann Andreas Naumann (1747–1826), in his delightful 'Naturgeschichte der Vögel Deutschlands' (ed. J. F. Naumann, 4 vols. Leipzig, 1822–1824), although he discusses the snaring and marketing of these birds, makes no mention of the professional knowledge which Hegel considers to be an open secret. Naumann informs us (vol. II p. 275) that the flesh of the Song thrush (Turdus musicus) has a very fine taste, and that these birds were consumed by the thousand in the autumn, when they were fat. The most highly-prized of the Thrushes, as a table-bird, was the Redwing (Turdus iliacus), and in a season, Naumann estimates (vol. II pp. 287–8), 300,000 brace of these birds were caught on the coasts of East Prussia alone.

The Fieldfare (Turdus pilaris) was caught all the year round and prized on account of the faintly bitter flavour of its flesh, which is due to its diet of juniper berries. Naumann informs us (vol. II p. 309) that they were always on sale in large quantities in the markets of the big towns, and that in the Danzig area 60,000 brace of them were consumed annually. In part of Thuringia, many fowlers took between 600 and 1,200 brace of them a year.

159, 9

See William Bligh (1754–1817) 'A Voyage to the South Sea, . . . including an account of . . . the subsequent voyage . . . in the ship's boat, from Tofoa . . . to Timor' (1790, 2nd ed. London, 1792) pp. 191, 238, 'With respect to the preservation of our health, during a course of sixteen days of heavy and almost continued rain. I would recommend to every one in a similar situation, the method we practised, which is, to dip their clothes in salt-water, and wring them out, as often as they become filled with rain: it was the only resource we had and I believe was of the greatest service to us, for it felt more like a change of dry clothes than could well be imagined. We had occasion to do this so often, that at length all our clothes were wrung to pieces: for, except the few days we passed on the coast of New Holland, we were continually wet either with rain or sea . . . Extreme hunger was . . . too evident, but no one suffered from thirst, nor had we much inclination to drink, that desire, perhaps, being satisfied through the skin.' Cf. Byron's 'The Island' canto I ix (1823): John Barrow 'The Mutiny and Piratical Seizure of H.M.S. Bounty' (London, 1831).

It soon became well known in medical circles that Bligh's men had alleviated their thirst in this way: see Thomas Thomson's 'System der Chemie' (5 vols. tr. F. Wolff, Berlin, 1805–1811) vol. iv p. 681, and Bligh's account awoke a *general* interest in the problem of whether or not the skin is able to absorb moisture. Opinions were sharply divided over this matter of 'cutaneous absorption' as it was called. James Keill (1673–1719) seems to have initiated research in this field: see his 'Account of Animal Secretion' (London,1708). The subject was taken up and dealt with at some length by Georg Heuermann (1722–1768) in his widely read 'Physiologie' (4 pts. Copenhagen and Leipzig, 1751–1755) pt. II ch. 22, but the most influential writer to deal with it was *Haller*: see his 'Elementa physiologiae corporis humani' (8 vols. Lausanne, 1757–1766) vol. IV bk. 12 p. 2 § 20, who came to the conclusion that the skin *was* able to absorb moisture. This view was questioned by Claude Pouteau (1725–1775) in his 'Mémoire contre l'extension donnée à l'action des pores absorbans de la peau' ('Oeuvres posthumes' 3 vols. Paris, 1783) vol. I p. 185, and this difference of opinion gave rise to some very detailed research by William Cruikshank (1745–1800), see his 'The Anatomy of the absorbing vessels of the human body' (London, 1786), 'Experiments on the insensible perspiration of the human body' (London, 1795. German tr. Leipzig, 1798), and by John Abernethy (1764–1831) 'Surgical and Physiological Essays' (2 pts. London, 1793. German tr. Leipzig, 1795).

This work was not primarily concerned with the *skin* however, and did not decide the matter. John Baptiste Clement Rousseau, a native of St. Domingo, graduated at the University of Pennsylvania in 1800 with a dissertation 'On absorption' (Philadelphia, 1800). He was convinced that the liquid was taken in by the *lungs*, and to prove this he fitted a mask which brought him air from an adjoining room. An assistant then applied spirit of turpentine, by means of a sponge, to the whole of his naked body, during the space of an hour. Turpentine, if absorbed by the body, will make the urine smell of violets, but in this case, although he evacuated urine on three occasions, there was no trace of a violet smell. See J. G. Stock 'Account of Dr. Rousseau's Experiments on

Cutaneous Absorption' ('The Edinburgh Medical and Surgical Journal' vol. II pp. 10–14, 1806): J. B. C. Rousseau 'A few words more against cutaneous absorption' ('Philadelphia medical Lyceum' vol. iv no. 4 pp. 201–216. 1808). This experiment inspired Dr. Josephus Bradner Stuart of Albany to counter with 'Experiments and Observations in defence of the doctrine of cutaneous absorption' ('New York Medical Repository' hexade 3, vol. 3 no. 2 art. 6 pp. 137–142, 1812) cf. Leroux's 'Journal de Médecine' vol. 26 pp. 315–319, 1813. After urinating, Dr. Stuart got into a bath of madder at 4.30 p.m. and stayed there for two and a half hours. The temperature of the bath varied between 82°F and 90°F, and that of the air was 34°F. Three hours after he had got out of the bath his urine was dark red, and he continued to pass water of this colour for a further twenty three hours. Similar experiments with a bath of rhubarb juice and with garlic plasters under the armpits showed beyond doubt the cutaneous absorption *does* take place. His conclusions were confirmed by Thomas Sewall (1787–1845): see 'Experiments and observations on cutaneous absorption' published in Thomas Bradley's 'Medical and Physical Journal' 1814, vol. 31 p. 80.

These experiments were well known in Germany, see J. F. Meckel's 'Deutsches Archiv für die Physiologie' vol. I pt. i pp. 151–154: vol. II pp. 146–147 (Halle and Berlin, 1815, 1816): J. F. Pierer 'Anatomisch–physiologisches Realwörterbuch' vol. IV pp. 217–222 (Leipzig, 1821), and evidently formed the basis of Hegel's judgement here.

159, 16

Guillaume Le Pois of Leyden gave the first account of the medicinal properties of ipecacuanha in his 'De medicina Brasiliensi' (Amsterdam, 1648). The French doctor Le Gras was the first to bring the root to Europe (1672), and J. H. Helvetius (1661–1727) popularized it as a cure for dysentry: see his 'Remède contre le cours de ventre' (Paris, 1688): G. W. Leibniz 'De antidysenterico novo' (Hanover, 1696). In 1688 Louis XIV bought the secret of this cure for one thousand louis d'or, and made it public.

In Hegel's day there were various kinds of ipecacuanha on the market: see A. Richard 'Histoire naturelle et médicale des différentes espèces d'ipécacuanha en commerce' (Paris, 1820). It was usually powdered and taken as a tincture in wine (vinum ipecacuanha), and during the eighteenth century was prescribed for *fevers*, see Abraham Vater (1684–1751) 'De Ypecacoanhe' (Wittenberg, 1732), and *cramp*, see J. J. Plenck 'Ueber die krampfstillende Eigenschaft der Ipekakuanha' ('Abhandlungen der Joseph. Akademie' I nr. 15), as well as dysentries.

The root contains an alkaloid 'emetine' which acts as an irritant when brought into contact with the interior of the stomach and produces vomiting. This effect is also brought about after its absorption into the blood by its action on the vomiting centre of the brain. In Hegel's day however, very little was known about the way in which it worked: see 'The Edinburgh Medical and Physical Dictionary' (Edinburgh, 1807).

159, 16

In Hegel's day opium was administered *externally* in order to diminish pain and remove spasmodic affections. It was usually *taken* in the form of a pill, bolus, or electuary however, and was also dissolved in diluted alcohol, white wine, or water.

It was prescribed as a cure for inflammations, fevers, syphilis and cramps, and was used to deaden the pain during births and amputations: see an extensive bibliography in K. F. Burdach's 'Die Literatur der Heilwissenschaft' (3 vols. Gotha, 1810–1821): Thomas Kirkland (1722–1798) 'Thoughts on Amputation' (London, 1780): Samuel Crumpe (1766–1796) 'An inquiry into the nature and properties of opium' (London, 1793, German tr. Leipzig, 1796).

Very little was known about its alkaloid contents, so that it was impossible to administer it with any degree of precision. It was not until 1802 that C. Derosne (1780–1846) isolated a crystalline compound which he called 'opium salt' ('Annales de Chimie' XLV 1802 pp. 257–285). In 1805 F. W. Sertürner (1783–1841) independently obtained the same alkaloid and also isolated mesonic acid ('Trommsdorffs Journ. d. Pharm.' XIV pp. 47–93, 1806); see also a second paper by Sertürner in which he gave this alkaloid the name of morphium ('Trommsdorffs Journ. d. Pharm' XX pp. 99–103, 1811). P. J. Robiquet (1780–1840) identified a new base, narcotine, in 1817 ('Annales de Chimie' V pp. 275–288, 1817).

159, 38

Pierce Smith (1774–1796) published 'Observations of the Structure of the Eyes of Birds' at the age of twenty one ('Phil. Trans. Roy. Soc.' 1795 pt. II pp. 263–269). This paper was communicated to the Royal Society by George Pearson (1751–1828) who had at that time just published his translation of Lavoisier's 'Nomenclature Chimique' (London, 1794). Smith describes himself in this paper as a 'student of physic', and indicates that he has also shown his work to John Thomson (1765–1846) of Edinburgh.

Treviranus took his account of Smith's later work from 'Nordisches Archiv für Naturkunde, Arzneywissenschaft und Chirurgie' vol. III pt. ii pp. 130–136 (Copenhagen, 1803). This publication was edited by Christoph Heinrich Pfaff (1773–1852), Poul Scheel (1773–1811) and C. A. Rudolphi (1771–1832). Scheel had visited Italy in 1797, and while he was in Florence, had obtained an account of Smith's experiments from G. V. M. Fabroni (1752–1822), who had at that time already published a tribute to his dead friend, 'Tributo d'amicizia a Pierce Smith ossia lettere sopra alcune novita fisiologiche, e specialmente sugli usi ed efficacia del sugo gastrico' (Naples, 1796).

In Naples, Smith experimented with the effects of certain drugs on various animals, i.e. of sal-ammoniac on frogs, of opium on frogs, kittens and ravens, and of tobacco on lizards, but when he dissected them after their death, he found that he was unable to draw any definite conclusions from his work.

Treviranus is evidently referring to the following passage in Scheel's article, ‚Dr. Smith fand ferner, daß jeder Theil des thierischen Körpers ein Vermögen besitzt, einen dem Succus gastricus analogen Saft zu ergießen, um abgestorbene Theile zu verzehren oder fremde Körper zu verdauen und einsaugbar zu machen. Er beobachtete dies bei Versuchen, die er anstellte, um noch lebende Ova von Mäusen in dem verwachsen zu machen, bei welchen dieselben völlig verdaut wurden, und verschwanden. Stücken Fleisch, zarte Knochen u. dergl. hatten dasselbe Schicksal, wenn er sie unter das Fell oder in andre Theile eines lebenden Thieres brachte.

Dieser sich in Wunden absondernde Saft und die damit verbundenen auf= gelösten, abgestorbenen thierischen Theile oder coagulirte Lymphe, bilden nach Smith den Eiter, dessen auflösende Kraft man selbst an den Bandagen nicht selten gewahr werde.'

Cf. Robert Watt (1774–1819) 'Bibliotheca Britannica' (4 vols. Edinburgh, 1824) pt. i vol. ii col. 864g.

160, 32

Hegel is here translating from Jean Senebier's version of Spallanzani's 'Dissertazioni di fisica animale e vegetabile' (see the note III. 337) pp. 26, 20, 27, 'Enfin, . . . je fis avaler à tous quelque chose, aux uns des petits tubes de fer-blanc, aux autres des petites boules de verre, à d'autres des balles de plomb hérissées d'aiguilles et de lancettes . . . Il est vrai qu'il n'y eut aucun de ces estomacs qui ne contint quelqu'une de ces petites pièrres, mais leur nombre etoit fort diminué . . . Malgré . . . le froissement des tubes de ferblanc, . . . (et que) les pointes des unes et des autres qui restoient implantées dans la balle de plomb étoient fort émoussées . . . les estomacs eux-mêmes n'avoient pas plus souffert du séjour.'

161, 3

For the effect of asparagus on the urine see, Stuart, 'Asperges: remarques sur l'odeur particulière qu'elles communiquent aux urines' ('Journal de Méde-cine' ed. Corvisart, Léroux and Boyer XXVI pp. 425–426, 1813).

161, 7

Treviranus is referring here to experiments performed on dogs and asses by Sir Everard Home (1763–1832). Home published accounts of them in the Phil. Trans. of the Royal Society (1808, pt. I 45–54, and pp. 133–142). In the first article (p. 50) he describes an experiment performed on a dog on November 8, 1807. Twelve ounces of 'a strong decoction of madder' were injected into the animal after its pylorus had been secured. 'In this experiment, without making allowance for any liquid in the stomach, prior to the decoction of madder being injected, one-fourth part of the quantity thrown in had escaped.'

Home drew the following conclusions from his experiments (pp. 141–142), 'That the liquids received into the stomach beyond what are employed for digestion, are not wholly carried out of it by the common absorbants of the stomach, or the canal of the intestines, but are partly conveyed through the medium of the spleen into the circulation of the liver.

The vessels which communicate between the stomach and the spleen have not been discovered; but . . . there appears to be no other mode in which it can arrive there, but by means of such vessels; and the two different states of the spleen, which correspond with the quantities of liquids that pass from the stomach, are strongly in favour of the existence of such a channel.'

Home retracted these views a few years later ('Phil. Trans. Roy. Soc.' 1811). The arguments of the time for and against the existence of a 'viae urinariae clandestinae' are summarized by J. F. Meckel (1781–1833) 'Handbuch der menschlichen Anatomie' (Halle and Berlin, 1820) vol. IV pp. 479–485; cf. Treviranus (op. cit.) vol. IV pp. 513–521; J. H. Thilow (1761–1837) 'Anatomisch-pathologische Abhandlung' (Erfurt, 1794).

161, 32

Human chyme had not been chemically analyzed at this time (Pierer op. cit. II p. 145, 1818) and analyses of animal chyme had proved inconclusive. Spallanzani (op. cit.) discovered acidity in the stomachs of grain-eating animals, but not in those of carnivorous animals. B. Carminati (1750–1830), in his 'Ricerche sulla natura . . . del succo gastrico' (Milan, 1785, German tr. Vienna, 1785) discovered that the gastric juice of carnivorous animals *is* acidic and that it also counteracts putrefaction.

See: L. Brugnatelli (1761–1814) 'Versuch einer chemischen Zergliederung der Magensäfte' (Crell's 'Beiträge zu den chemischen Annalen' vol. I art, iv p. 69). G. T. Kelch, 'De liquore gastrico, ciborum menstruo' (Regiom., 1797), gives a summary of numerous chemical researches into the nature of gastric juice.

162, 16

See the note III. 338.

162, 20

S. T. Sömmering (1775–1800) suggested that blushing and turning pale were probably the result of a constriction brought about by the nerves, and so affecting the blood-vessels of the face, that in the first instance the blood is prevented from leaving the vessels, while in the second it is prevented from reaching them: 'Vom Baue des menschlichen Körpers' (Frankfurt-on-Main, 1791–1796) 'Hirn- und Nervenlehre' §§ 241, 257.

162, 29

There was some doubt at this time as to whether the spleen performs glandular functions or is merely a mass of vascular tissue, and there always had been doubt as to its general relatedness. Some physiologists such as Aristotle, Galen, Home, Meckel, Autenrieth etc. thought that it functions primarily in relation to the stomach. Others, such as William Hewson (1739–1774) and F. Tiedemann in his 'Versuche . . . über die Verrichtung der Milz' (Heidelberg, 1820) tended to regard it as related primarily to the circulation of the blood. Hegel evidently accepts the third main proposition current at the time, i.e. that it is mainly related to the liver, and has the function of disoxidizing the blood which is subsequently secreted as bile. In holding this view he was in agreement with Sömmering, Richerand, Bichat, P. F. von Walther (1781–1849) etc.

Certain very curious ideas were put forward regarding this gland. Ignaz Döllinger (1770–1841) even suggested that it was merely a second liver, formed by the tendency towards symmetry in vertebrates, and denied full development through the presence of the stomach. ('Grundriss der Naturlehre des menschlichen Organismus' Bamberg and Würzburg, 1805 p. 127).

Cf. G. Stuckeley 'The spleen, its description, uses and diseases' (London, 1723).

163, 24

Cf. S. T. Lucae 'Einige Sätze aus der physiologischen Lehre von den secernirten Säften des menschlichen Organismus'. (Frankfurt-on-Main, 1815).

164, 9

,ber Bilbungstrieb'. See the note III. 350.

165, 1

Treviranus is referring to Berzelius's 'Untersuchung der Zusammensetzung des Menschenkoths', an article published in A. F. Gehlen's 'Neues allgemeines Journal der Chemie' vol. VI pp. 509–541 (1806), and evidently inspired by the work of A. Thaer (1752–1828) and H. Einhof (d. 1808), who had published an account of their researches on cow-dung in the same journal (vol. III p. 276).

In this article Berzelius shows how he attempted to reach an understanding of the chemical changes involved in the process of chylification by isolating the various constituents of human faeces. He broke them down into 73·3% water, ·9% bile, ·9% albumen, 1·2% salts (carbonate, muriate and sulphate of soda, phosphates of magnesia and lime), 14% indissoluble animal matter, and bilin ('Gallenstoff', not 'Gallenharz' or choloidic acid as in Treviranus's account).

The 'peculiar substance which looks like glue', Berzelius refers to it as ,einen eigenthümlichen Stoff', accounted for 7% of the whole, and had also been discovered by Thaer and Einhof in cow-dung. Berzelius describes it as resembling nasal mucus in that it was slimy, grey-green in colour, and difficult to lixiviate with water. He thought that it was probably formed by the combination of bilin with a constituent of the chyme.

The second 'peculiar substance' accounted for 2·7% of the whole, and Berzelius gave the following account for it, ‚Er ist sowohl im Wasser als in Alkohol auflöslich, hat eine rothbraune Farbe, welche durch Säuren hochroth gemacht wird . . . Diese eigenthümliche Materia hat keine Verwantschaft zu den Neutralsalzen . . . Zu den Metalloxyden hat sie eine große Affinität und wird von salzsaurem Zinn, salpetersaurem Silber und essigsaurem Blei beinahe vollständig aus ihrer Auflösung in Wasser niedergeschlagen . . . Sie erst durch Einwirkung der Luft durch eine Veränderung des Gallenstoffs, und vielleicht auch des Eiweißstoffs, gebildet werde.‘

165, 9

On the chemical contents of urine Treviranus is evidently quoting P. H. Nysten (1771–1818) 'Recherches de physiologie et chimie pathologiques' (Paris, 1811) p. 240, and Berzelius, 'Ueberblick über die Zusammensetzungen der thierischen Flüssigkeiten' (Nuremberg, 1814).

As these researches showed, urine contains phosphorus. A. F. Fourcroy showed by chemical analysis that bones contain a high percentage of phosphorus, see J. F. John (1782–1847) 'Tabellen des Thierreichs' (Berlin, 1814) p. 134, and it was probably this element that Treviranus had in mind when making this remark.

165, 11

See L. N. Vauquelin (1763–1829) 'Analyse de la matière cérébrale' (Paris, 1811).

165, 22

Antoine-Francois Fourcroy (1755–1809) was born in Paris and educated at the Collège d'Harcourt. He was encouraged to study medicine by his father's friend Felix Vicq-d'Azyr (1748–1798), the well-known anatomist.

After finishing his university studies in 1780 he did research on zoological and anatomical subjects, but his interest soon shifted to 'animal chemistry', and in 1784 he was appointed to the chair of chemistry at the Jardin du roi.

He played no part in politics during the revolutionary period. In 1801 Napoleon appointed him director general of public education, but he was unable to fulfil his duties satisfactorily and soon fell from favour.

He is remembered mainly as one of the founders of organic chemistry, although the crudity of his methods of analysis merely enabled him to distinguish the chemical constituents of organisms. His 'Philosophie chimique' (Paris, 1792) was translated into many of the European languages, and his 'Médicine éclairée par les sciences physiques' (4 vols. Paris, 1791) and 'Système des connaissances chimiques' (8 vols. Paris, 1801) were widely read. Many of his chemical analyses of organic matters were first presented to the public in periodicals.

Louis-Nicolas Vauquelin (1763–1829) was born in Normandy, and at the age of thirteen was apprenticed to an apothecary in Rouen. When he first arrived in Paris Fourcroy employed him as his servant, but he soon became his pupil, and before long he was his co-operator and friend.

In 1791 he was elected member of the Paris Academy, and during the 1790's held various civil offices, until in 1802 he was appointed professor of chemistry at the Collège de France. He retired in 1812, but continued for several years, to do research and publish articles.

Much of his work was done in conjunction with Fourcroy, although he took a greater interest in inorganic chemistry than did his master. In 1798 for example, he discovered chrome and glucina, and in 1805 isolated kinic acid. He applied the principles of analytical chemistry with great accuracy, and gave accounts of most of his findings in separate articles, which were published in various periodicals.

Treviranus is evidently referring to Vauquelin's articles in 'Annales de Chimie' (1799) vol. 29 pp. 1–26, 'Expèriences sur les excrémens des poules, comparés à la nourriture qu'elles prennent', and to the article 'Sur le guano' by Fourcroy and Vauquelin, which also appeared in 'Tilloch's Philosophical Journal' (1806, pp. 112–115). Cf. Vauquelin's article 'Analyse du chyle de cheval' ('Thomson's Annals of Philosophy' II, 1813 pp. 223–225).

See W. A. Smeaton 'Fourcroy, chemist and revolutionary' (Cambridge, 1962).

165, 30
Treviranus is evidently basing this statement on Vauquelin's article in 'Annales de Chimie' (May, 1812). Many analyses of animal urine were made at this time, the main discovery being that herbivorous animals pass benzoic acid, but little or no uric and phosphoric acid, and that carnivorous animals pass urine containing pure ammonium. For a detailed account of these researches see J. F. Pierer (1767–1832) 'Anatomisch-physiologisches Realwörterbuch' vol. III pp. 882–891 (Leipzig, 1819).

166, 9
Johann Friedrich Blumenbach (1752–1840) was born at Gotha, where his father was a schoolmaster. In 1769 he began to study medicine at Jena, but he soon moved to Göttingen, where it was evidently Professor C. W. Büttner (1716–1801) who awoke his interest in anthropology. In 1775 he took his doctorate at Göttingen, and in the following year he was appointed professor of medicine at the university. Apart from visits to Holland and England in

1791-2, and to Paris in 1806, he stayed at Göttingen for the rest of his life. He lectured there on mineralogy and botany as well as zoology, but his main interests were zoological, and it was in the fields of comparative anatomy, anthropology, and theoretical zoology that he made his most original contributions to science. In 1784 he was elected member of the Göttingen Society of Sciences. See K. H. Marx 'Zum Andenken an Blumenbach' (Göttingen, 1840).

He gave his first lectures on comparative anatomy in 1777, and by 1785 was dealing comprehensively with the subject, although it was not until twenty years later that he published his, 'Handbuch der vergleichenden Anatomie' (Göttingen, 1805, English tr. London, 1807).

He is probably best known as the founder of scientific anthropology. His doctoral dissertation on this subject 'De generis humani varietate nativa' (Göttingen, 1775) was re-issued and translated many times. In it he distinguishes between the five great races of mankind, the white or Caucasian, the yellow or Mongolian, the brown or Malayan, the red or American, and the black or Ethiopian. As part of his anthropological investigations he worked for many years on descriptions of sixty human crania, 'Collectionis suae craniorum diversarum gentium' (8 parts, Göttingen, 1790-1828).

His immensely popular 'Handbuch der Naturgeschichte' (Göttingen, 1779) is largely based on Linnaeus, and is primarily factual and descriptive. It is not therefore typical of his work, the main feature of which consists in its providing *interpretations* of data. In his own day Blumenbach was known principally as the originator of the vitalist theory of the nisus formativus mentioned here by Hegel.

The vitalists held the view that the origin and phenomena of life are due to or produced by a *vital principle*, as distinct from purely chemical or physical force. The early purveyors of the doctrine postulated a 'spiritus animalis' or 'spiritus vitalis' as the principle of living being; see for example J. Actuarius (c. 1490–c. 1560) 'De actionibus et adfectibus spiritus animalis' (Paris, 1557. ed. Fischer, Leipzig, 1774): Caspar Hofmann (1572–1648) 'Dissertatio de spiritibus' (Altdorf, 1616): August Quirinus Rivinus (1652–1732) 'De spiritu hominis vitali' (Leipzig, 1681). By the middle of the eighteenth century however, so many advances had been made in the exact study of human physiology, that vitalism in its traditional form was no longer a defensible doctrine, and radical reinterpretations of it began to be formulated. Haller's work is typical of the vitalist thinking of that time. His general physiological investigations, and especially those concerned with neurology, led him to postulate a 'spiritus nervorum' as the principle of living being: see 'Elementa physiologiae corporis humani' (Lausanne, 1757-1766) vol. IV bk. 10 ch. 8 §§ 16-22. Towards the end of the century Johann Christian Reil (1759-1813) gave classical form to the theory of a life-force (vis vitae) in his 'Von der Lebenskraft' (1796, ed. Sudhoff, Leipzig, 1910).

Blumenbach's 'Ueber den Bildungstrieb und das Zeugungsgeschäft' (Göttingen, 1781, 3rd. ed. 1791) was the most important work in this general reassessment of vitalist principles. His belief in the fixity of the species seems to have been an important factor in his formulation of the nisus formativus, which he defines as follows, 'It is a force effective mainly in a merely mechanical manner, and giving rise in the inorganic sphere to crystallizations and similar formations. It is distinguished by the fact that it is able, in accordance with the infinitely varied and diverse determination of the organized body and its parts, to form the various organizable generative materials into determinate shapes in an equally various but purposefully modified manner. It is therefore within this drive, by the combination of the mechanical principle with that of purposive modifiability, that it is effectuated, in the first instance by motivation into gradual transformation, but then also by the life-long maintenance of these organic formations through nutrition, so that even if the formations happen to have suffered injury, it re-establishes them, so far as possible, by means of reproduction.' Cf. Goethe 'Die Schriften zur Naturwissenschaft' sect. I vol. 9 (ed. D. Kuhn, Weimar, 1954) pp. 99–100.

166, 10

‚Der Kunsttrieb'. The distinction Hegel draws here, between ‚Bildungstrieb' and ‚Kunsttrieb' is not original. The creative impulse (schöpferische Bildungstrieb) was also taken to be a distinct form of the nisus formativus. For an excellent exposition of contemporary views on the subject, see the article ‚Bildungstrieb' by J. F. Pierer (1767–1832), in his 'Medizinisches Realwörterbuch' (Leipzig, 1816) vol. I pp. 757–770.

167, 14

Cuvier 'Le Règne Animal distribué d'après son organisation' (4 vols. Paris, 1817); see vol. I pp. 47–55 'Exposé rapide des fonctions intellectuelles des animaux'. 'L'instinct a été accordé aux animaux comme supplément de l'intelligence, et pour concourir avec elle, et avec la force et le fécondité, au juste degré de conservation de chaque espèce.' Cuvier makes particular mention of the building abilities of bees and wasps.

For the history of the idea of instinct see E. C. Wilm 'The Theories of Instinct' (New Haven, 1925) and W. M. Wheeler 'Instinct: Essays in Philosophical Biology' (Harvard Univ. Press, 1939).

Part three of W. H. Thorpe's 'Learning and Instinct in Animals' (London, 1958) provides an excellent commentary on Cuvier's observation.

168, 8

‚blinde Anhänge'. Treviranus notes that they were called 'Vasa varicosa' by Marcello Malpighi (1628–1694); see 'Opera Omnia' (2 vols. London, 1686); G. Blasius (c. 1625–1692) 'Anatome animalium' (Amsterdam, 1681), and 'les intestines grêles' by Pieter Lyonet (1707–1789); see 'Traité anatomique de la Chenille' (Le Haye, 1762).

168, 17

‚bei den Raupen und Afterraupen'. An ‚Afterraupe' is a caterpillar with more than eighteen feet: see N. I. Lucas 'A Dictionary of the . . . German and English Languages' (2 pts. Bremen, 1863–1868) pt. I p. 71. Strictly speaking a caterpillar is the larva of a butterfly or moth. The word is occasionally used to describe the larvae of other insects however: Treviranus probably has in mind that of the Saw-fly.

168,18

‚Gabelschwanz-Raupe' i.e. Phalaena vinula.

168, 24

‚der mit dem Nebenhoben der Säugthiere übereinstimmt'. Treviranus wrote, ‚der mit dem Nebenhoben der Säugthiere übereinkömmt' (agrees). Hegel's version would appear to be an improvement on the original.

169, 12

Treviranus quotes the 'Traité anatomique de la chenille' (La Haye, 1762) by Pieter Lyonet (1707–1789) as the source of much of this information.

169, 27

For contemporary views on the vocal faculties of animals see: L. Wolff 'Dissertatio de organo vocis mammalium' (Berlin, 1812): Cuvier 'Über den untern Larynx der Vögel' (Reil's Archiv vol. V sect. I no. 2). Cf. the note on the senses III. 327.

E. A. Armstrong, in 'A study of Bird Song' (O.U.P., 1963) has an interesting chapter on bird song as art and play, in which he points out (p. 244) 'that underlying every effort to show that birds have aesthetic taste is the difficulty of proving that any characteristic of bird song is non-utilitarian.'

Cf. J. M. Bechstein (1757–1822) 'Gemeinnützige Naturgeschichte Deutschlands' (4 vols. Leipzig, 1801–1807) vol. ii pp. 77–85.

170, 6

Michelet's version of this sentence begins as follows, ‚Die befriedigte Begierde ist daher . . . '. Hegel wrote ('Jenenser Realphilosophie' II p. 163), ‚Die bestimmte Begierde ist daher . . . '.

170, 8

Michelet inserted these brackets. Cf. 'Jenenscr Realphilosophie' II p. 163.

173, 3

‚burd) biefe Vermittlung bie Gattung mit ſich zuſammenzuſchließen unb zur Exiſtenz zu bringen'.

174, 23

This quotation is taken from part I p. 185 of G. H. von Schubert's 'Ahndungen einer allgemeinen Geschichte des Lebens' (3 vols. Leipzig, 1806, 1807, 1821). In reproducing it Hegel failed to notice a typographical error listed in the errata. He should have deleted 'ganz' from ‚Auch bei bem Männchen ber Breme ſinb bie Hoben nicht nur in ihrem Umriß ganz ebenſo geſtaltet . . .'.

At that time the best illustration of the anatomy of the Gryllus verriccivorus was to be found among the exquisite engravings published by August Johann Rösel (1705–1759) in 'Der Monatlichherausgegebene Insecten-belustigungen' (4 parts Nuremberg, 1746, 1749, 1755, 1761) pt. II B tab. 9. J. F. Blumenbach, in his 'Handbuch der vergleichende Anatomie' Göttingen, 1805) also notes the insect's large testicles, ‚Bey bieſer ſehen nämlich zumahl bie mächtig großen Teſtikel mit ihren bündelweis zuſammengefalteten Gefäßen, ben eben ſo großen Eyerſtöcken mit ben auch gleichſam bündelweis barin vertheilten Eyern, auffalenb ähnlich'.

The ‚Breme' or ‚Bremſe' is evidently the genus 'Tabanus' mentioned in the 'Handbuch der Zoologie' (2 vols. Nuremberg, 1820) which G. A. Goldfuss prepared for Schubert's lectures on natural history (vol. I pp. 428–429). Cf. C. N. Colyer and C. O. Hammond 'Flies of the British Isles' (London, 1951) ch. VI (Tabanidae). In England the fly is sometimes known as a 'brimse': see 'The Historie of Serpents' (London, 1608) p. 769, a curious book by Edward Topsell (d. 1638), 'Those great horse-flies or ox-flies and brimsees that in summer season vex cattle'.

174, 27

Gotthilf Heinrich von Schubert (1780–1860) was one of the most gifted of Schelling's followers. He was born at Hohenstein in the Saxon Erzgebirge, the son of an impecunious clergyman, and was educated at the grammar schools of Greiz and Weimar. In the latter town he came under the influence of Herder, who gave him private tuition. In accordance with the wishes of his father he began to study theology at Leipzig in 1799, but when he moved to Jena in 1800 Schelling's lectures inspired him to take up medicine, and he qualified in this discipline in 1803.

He thought of emigrating to South Africa, but married instead, and practised as a doctor at Altenburg for a couple of years. As he often took no payment for his services to the poor however, he was soon in the direst economic straits, so that the publication of a novel, and the editing of Pierer's 'Medicinische Annalen' were necessary in order to supplement his income as a general practitioner. He sold up everything in 1805, and went to hear Werner lecture at Freiberg. From then on he devoted himself to natural science. In 1809 he was appointed director of a new school (Realschule) in Nuremberg. In 1816 he became tutor to the children of the hereditary archduke of Mecklenburg-Schwerin, and in 1817 professor of natural history at Erlangen. He finished his teaching career as professor of natural history at Munich (1827–1853).

As an attempt to synthesize the findings of the natural sciences the 'Ahndungen einer allgemeinen Geschichte des Lebens' (3 vols. Leipzig, 1806, 1807, 1821) lacks form, order and precision. Schubert's taste for mystical speculation found fruitful expression in his later works on psychology 'Ansichten von der Nachtseite der Naturwissenschaft' (Dresden, 1808), 'Symbolik des Traumes' (Bamberg, 1814), 'Altes und neues aus dem Gebiete der innern Seelenkunde' (Leipzig, 1816), 'Die Geschichte der Seele' (Stuttgart, 1833), which he considered to be his main work, and 'Die Krankheiten und Störungen der menschlichen Seele' (Stuttgart, 1845). His ability to work in a precise, methodical and empirical manner found expression in his comprehensive 'Handbuch der Naturgeschichte' (Nuremberg, 1816–1823).

He enjoyed hiking, and published a delightfully humorous 'Wanderbüchlein eines reisenden Gelehrten' (1823, 3rd. ed. Erlangen 1848). In 1836–7 he visited Palestine with his wife, and wrote an account of the journey, 'Reise in das Morgenland' (Erlangen, 1838). The best of his purely literary productions is his autobiography (3 vols. Erlangen, 1854–1855), which he dedicated to Schelling, ‚Denn was der alte Schüler auf Erden hat und geworden ist, das verdankt er nächst Gott diesem Lehrer‘.

F. R. Merkel 'Der Naturphilosoph Gotthilf Heinrich Schubert und die deutsche Romantik.' (Munich, 1913).

174, 31

Jakob Fidelis Ackermann (1765–1815) was born at Rüdesheim and educated at the grammar school in Cologne. In 1784 he began to study medicine at Würzburg, and later moved to Mainz, where he took his doctorate in 1787. Before returning to Mainz as a don in 1789, he travelled in Germany, Italy and Austria, and spent some time at Pavia, where he attended lectures by Johann Peter Frank (1745–1821), Antonio Scarpa (1747–1832), and Alessandro Volta (1745–1827). In 1792 he was appointed professor of botany and in 1796 professor of Anatomy at Mainz, and when the French changed the organization of the university in 1798, Ackermann gained further promotion. In 1804 he was appointed professor of anatomy and chirurgy at Jena, and in 1805 professor of anatomy and physiology at Heidelberg.

He is best known for his opposition to F. J. Gall's phrenology (see the note II. 430), which he expressed in his 'Die Gall'sche Hirn-, Schädel-, und Organ-Lehre vom Gesichtspunkt der Erfahrung aus beurtheilt und widerlegt' (Heidelberg, 1806), but apart from the work mentioned here by Hegel, he produced several interesting and original books. He was one of the first doctors to make a scientific investigation of cretinism: see 'Ueber die Kretinen, eine besondere Menschenart in den Alpen' (Gotha, 1790), and his contributions to vitalist theory in 'Versuch einer physischen Darstellung der Lebenskraft organischer Körper' (2nd. ed. Jena, 1805) were widely recognized. In his 'De combustionis lentae phaenomenis, quae vitam constituunt' (Jena, 1804) he attempted to explain organic phenomena, by means of the laws of physics and chemistry, as a process of gradual combustion.

Ackermann's first work on sexual differentiation was, 'De discrimine sexuum praeter genitalia' (Mainz, 1788, German tr. by J. Wenzel, Mainz, 1788). Hegel is here referring to his 'Infantis androgyni historia et ichnographia. Accedunt de sexu et generatione disquisitiones physiologicae' (Jena, 1805), which must have been published while Hegel was delivering the lectures at Jena in the winter of 1805–6.

Cf. 'A Mechanical and Critical Enquiry into the Nature of Hermaphrodites' (London, 1741), by James Parsons (1705–1770): I P. V. Troxler 'Versuche in der organischen Physik' (Jena, 1806) no. 6: J. H. Autenrieth 'Ueber die Verschiedenheit beyder Geschlechter und ihrer Zeugungsorgane' (Reil's Archiv. vol. VII sect. i no. 1): F. Jacoby 'Dissertatio de mammalibus hermaphrodites, alterno latere in sexum contrarium vergentibus' (Berlin, 1818).

174, 35

Hoffmeister '(Jenenser Realphilosophie' II p. 165) indicates that this sentence is a translation from a French source, perhaps J. F. Lobstein (1777–1835), 'Recherches et observations sur la position des testicules' (Paris, 1801), and that Hegel gives the original in the margin, 'Les conduits éjaculateurs traversent la prostate et s'ouvrent separement dans l'urètre au fond d'une lacune appelée veramontanum (?)'.

Hegel has mistranslated 'Veru montanum'. The 'Crista galli' is the osseous protuberance running down the middle of the spongy lamina of the ethmoid. It was given this name by earlier anatomists because of the resemblance it bears to a Cock's comb: see Andreas Vesalius (1514–1565) 'De corporis humani fabrica' (Basel, 1546) bk. I ch. 6. Hegel is referring to the elongated, cutaneous eminence on the inner surface of the urethra, which occurs where the bulbous part of this tube passes through the prostate. This feature was referred to as the 'Crista galli gallinacei' by Philipp Verheijen (1648–1710), in his 'Anatomia corporis humani' (Louvain, 1683, German tr. Leipzig, 1704) tab. x, but it was generally known to the German anatomists of Hegel's day as ‚ber Schnepfenkopf', or ‚ber Hahnenkopf der männlichen Harnröhre'. In English writings of the time it is referred to as the *caput gallinaginis*, or *verumontanum*.

175, 8

‚bas aufschwellende Herz'. This phrase appears to be peculiar to Hegel. It was probably suggested to him by the fact that erection is partly the result of the distension of the venous plexuses with *blood*.

175, 13

The parallel development of the male and female sexual organs in the embryo and foetus, and their basic similarity, was generally known and recognized in Hegel's day. See J. F. Pierer's 'Medizinisches Realwörterbuch' vol. III p. 513 (Leipzig, 1819).

Hegel does not touch upon the *comparative anatomy* of these organs, although the placing of this discussion in the dialectical progression indicates that these remarks are meant to apply to the whole field of zoology treated in § 370. J. F. Blumenbach gives the subject a much fuller treatment in his 'Handbuch der vergleichenden Anatomie' (Göttingen, 1805) pp. 429–484.

175, 16

Embryology did not take on its modern form until the research organized by professor Ignaz Döllinger (1770–1841) at Würzburg bore fruit in K. E. von Baer's 'Ueber Entwickelungsgeschichte der Thiere' (2 vols. Königsberg, 1828, 1837): see the note III. 229. The best survey of the state of this science at the close of the eighteenth century is to be found in 'Grundriss der Zergliederungskunst des ungeborenen Kindes in den verschiedenen Zeiten der Schwangerschaft' (2 vols. Frankfurt and Leipzig, 1792, 1795) by G. F. Danz. Cf. K. F Burdach (1776–1847) 'Dissertation de primis momentis formationis foetus' (Regiom., 1814).

Hegel inserted a note in the margin at this juncture ('Jenenser Realphilosophie' II p. 165) which shows that he considered two further theories, ,Feuer, Waſſer, einfache Vorſtellung und ſo die organiſche Natur nicht analyſiert in ihre abſtrakten Momente; Zerlegen ins Chemiſche — unſägliche Kleinigkeiten; ſondern ihre Kraft eben allgemein; nicht Säure, Kali, ohne ſich abzuſtumpfen.'

175, 24

A fuller knowledge of the ovum, the spermatozoon, cell division, and the three layers would have enabled Hegel to write more lucidly at this juncture. A marginal note in the original manuscript ('Jenenser Realphilisophie' II p. 166) shows that his main conception of the subject matter was sound enough, and that his primary concern was to avoid the purely chemical approach to embryology championed by L. N. Vauquelin (1763–1829) in 'Annales de chemie' vol. IX p. 64, and J. F. John (1782–1847) 'Tabellen des Thierreichs' (Berlin, 1814) tab. I A.

Hegel writes, ,Teil iſt Mittel, weſentlich die Vermittlung. Jedes Organ bient, aber zugleich wird baſſelbe auf einfache Weiſe zuſtanbe gebracht (Embryonen leben). Nottwendigkeit irgenbeiner Funktion wird wiberlegt burch ben Fall, wo biefe Funktion nicht ftatt hat. Der Unterfchieb ber Teile ift, baß biefe Anftalten gar nicht einfacher (fein können) — Mafchinen können vereinfacht werben unb finb um fo vollkomner; nicht fo ber Organismus. Wirklichkeit ift, biefe Momente fo entwickelt zu haben.

Das Refultat ift bas bloße unorganifche Leben — wie Glauben an ein Nichts zu haben — Beweis hilft nichts.'

Cf. F. J. Cole 'Early Theories of Sexual Generation' (Oxford, 1930).

175, 32
Michelet quotes this in the original Greek. See 'The Metaphysics' (tr. H. Tredennick, London, 1947) I p. 417 (1044^a 34–36).

176, 5
,Die Gattung erhält fich nur burch ben Untergang ber Inbibibuen bie im Proceße ber Begattung ihre Beftimmung erfüllen'. Nicolin und Pöggeler, in their edition of the 'Enzyklopädie' (Hamburg, 1959) p. 306 make ,erfüllen' singular. This is clearly a mistake.

178, 13
See the note III. 361.

178, 19
'Recherches sur les Ossemens Fossiles de Quadrupèdes' (Paris, 1812) vol. I p. 58 'Heureusement l'anatomie comparée possédoit un principe qui, bien dévelopé, étoit capable de faire évanouir tous les embarrass: c'étoit celui de la corrélation des formes dans les êtres organisés, au moyen duquel chaque sorte d'être pourrait, à le rigeur, être reconnue par chaque fragment de chacune de ses parties.'

180, 36
This remark almost certainly owes something to Lessing's 'Laokoon, oder über die Grenzen der Malerei und Poesie' (1766): see the English translation of this work by E. C. Beasley and H. Zimmern (Bohn's Standard Library, 1879). Lessing sets out to define by analysis the limitations of poetry and the plastic arts, and enunciates the fruitful principle that each art is subject to definite conditions, and that it can accomplish great results only by limiting itself to its special function.

182, 30
In the following paragraphs Hegel makes his own translation of the original French. The English version is a translation of the *German* text.

Cuvier (op. cit. p. 58 et seq), 'Tout être organisé forme un ensemble, un système unique et clos, dont toutes les parties se correspondent mutuellement, et concourent à la même action définitive par une réaction réciproque. Aucune de ces parties ne peut changer sans que les autres changent aussi ; et par conséquent chacune d'elles, prise séparément, indique et donne toutes les autres.

Ainsi, comme je l'ai dit ailleurs, si les intestins d'un animal sont organisés de manière à ne digérer que de la chair recente, il faut aussi que ses mâchoires soient construites pour devorer une proie ; ses griffes pour la saisir et la déchirer ; ses dents pour en découper et en diviser la chair ; le système entier de ses organes du mouvement pour la poursuivre et pour l'atteindre ; ses organes de sens pour l'apercevoir de loin ; il faut même que la nature ait placé dans son cerveau l'instinct nécessaire pour savoir se cacher et tendre des piéges à ses victimes. Telles seront les conditions générales du régime carnivore ; tout animal disposé pour ce régime les réunit infailliblement, car son espèce n'auroit pu subsister sans elles ; mais sous ces conditions générales il en existe de particulières, relatives à la grandeur, à l'espèce, au séjour de la proie, pour laquelle l'animal est disposé ; et de chacune de ces conditions particulières résultent de ces circonstances de détail, dans les formes qui résultent des conditions générales ; ainsi, non seulement la classe, mais l'ordre, mais le genre, et jusqu'à l'espèce, se trouvent exprimés dans la forme de chaque partie.

En effet, pour que la mâchoire puisse saisir, il lui faut une certaine forme de condyle ; une certain rapport entre la position de la résistance et celle de la puissance avec le point d'appui ; un certain volume dans les muscles temporaux qui exige une certaine grandeur dans la fosse qui les reçoit, et une certaine convexité de l'arcade zygomatique sous laquelle ils passent ; cette arcade zygomatique doit aussi avoir une certaine force pour donner appui au muscle masséter.

Pour que l'animal puisse emporter sa proie, il lui faut une certaine force dans les muscles qui soulèvent sa tête, d'où résulte une forme déterminée dans les vertèbres où les muscles ont leurs attaches, et dans l'occiput ou ils s'insèrent.

Pour que les dents puissent couper la chair, il faut qu'elles soient tranchantes, et qu'elles le soient plus ou moins, selon qu'elles auront plus ou moins exclusivement de la chair à couper. Leur base devon être d'autant plus solide, qu'elles auront plus d'os, et plus gros os à briser. Toutes ces circonstances influeront aussi sur le développement de toutes les parties qui servent à mouvoir la mâchoire.

Pour que les griffes puissent saisir cette proie, il faudra une certaine . . . force dans les ongles . . . etc.'.

183, 29

The following paragraph is translated from Cuvier op. cit. pp. 61–62, 'Nous voyons bien, par exemple, que les animaux à sabots doivent tous être herbivores, puisqu'ils n'ont aucun moyen de saisir une proie ; nous voyons bien encore que, n'ayant d'autre usage à faire de leurs pieds de devant que de soutenir leur corps, ils n'ont pas besoin épaule aussi vigoureusement organisée . . . leur régime herbivore exigera des dents à couronne plate pour broyer les semences et les herbages; . . . cette sorte de couronne nécessitant des mouvemens horizontaux pour la trituration le condyle de la mâchoire ne pourra être un gond aussi serré que dans les carnassiers'.

184, 12

Cuvier op. cit. pp. 62–64, 'On conçoit bien encore en gros la nécessité d'un système digestif plus compliqué dans les espèces où le système dentaire est plus imparfait . . . Mais je doute qu'on eût deviné, si l'observation ne l'avoit appris, que les ruminans auroient tous le pied fourchu . . . Par exemple, le système dentaire des animaux à sabots, non ruminans, est en général plus parfait que celui des animaux à pied fourchu ou ruminans . . .'

The subsequent sentence seems to have been added by Hegel as a general summary of Cuvier's subsequent observations.

184, 16

Volcher Coiter (1534–1576) was born in Groningen. In 1555 the town granted him a scholarship for the study of medicine, and as his main interest was anatomy, he left for Italy, the 'De corporis humani fabrica' (Basel, 1543) and the teaching of Andreas Vesalius (1514–1565) having at that time made the schools of anatomy at Padua, Bologna and Pisa the most famous in Europe.

At Pisa he worked under Gabriele Falloppio (1523–1562), who was at that time preparing his 'Observationes anatomicae' (Venice, 1561) and from whom he gained his interest in osteology and learnt the value of exact observation and precise description. At the Sapienza in Rome he met Bartolommeo Eustacchi (d. 1574) who had already conceived the idea of improving on Vesalius's work ('Tabulae anatomicae' ed. J. M. Lancisi, Rome, 1714), and who introduced him to the study of comparative anatomy. He finally settled down in Bologna, where he did research on comparative anatomy under Ulisse Aldrovandi (1522–1605), and on embryology under Giulio Aranzio (1530–1589). He took his doctorate at Bologna and taught anatomy and chirurgy there until he was imprisoned by the Inquisition in 1566.

On his release from prison he left Italy, and in 1568 gained the post of physician in ordinary to Louis duke of Bavaria. In the following year he was appointed town doctor in Nuremberg. He died suddenly on June 2, 1576, when he was about to take up an appointment as military doctor in the army of the Elector Palatine.

Coiter did important work on the development of the bones in the human foetus: see his 'Tractatus anatomicus de ossibus foetus abortivi et infantis dimidium anni nati' ed. H. Eyssonius (1620–1690) (Groningen 1659). His 'Tabulae externarum et internarum humani corporis partium' (Nuremberg, 1572) contains excellent descriptions of the bones and muscles of the auditory organs, the optic nerve, the ganglia of the spinal nerves, and the processes which come into play when the eye is injured.

Treviranus is referring to the work which Coiter appended to Falloppio's 'Lectiones de partibus similaribus corporis humani' (Nuremberg, 1575), in which he provided descriptions and illustrations of the skeletons of various animals. Coiter's writings are most easily accessible in 'A choice selection of medical and biological treatises taken from the works of Volcher Coiter', by B. W. Nuyens and A. Schierbeek, published as vol. 18 of 'Opuscula Selecta Neerlandicorum de Arte Medica' (Amsterdam, 1955). 'De quadrupedum sceletia' appears in an English translation, on pp. 173–218 of this work.

Treviranus evidently has in mind the following passage on the goat (p. 179), 'It is necessary that the poplites should bend inward, for use in walking; the fore limbs have to serve as feet. They consist of three large bones, articulating with each other in order. The first of these corresponds to our humerus. The second upper one corresponds to the ulna, to which, however, the radius is firmly attached . . . Between this bone and the third there are three small bones, well suited for the articulations of the second with the third bone, which the other quadrupeds lack.*'

*Note by the editors. 'This bone is formed by syntose of two metatarsalia, the so-called cannonbone. Coiter did not quite understand this.'

184, 17

Pieter Camper (1722–1789) was born in Leyden, studied there, and took his doctorate there in philosophy and medicine in 1746. He then travelled to England, and to Paris where he met the chirurgeon Antoine Louis (1723–1792) and the obstetrician André Levret (1703–1780). On his return to the Netherlands he was appointed professor of anatomy and chirurgy at Franeker (1749) where he found four undergraduates in the medical faculty. In 1755 he took up a similar appointment at Amsterdam, and in 1763 became professor of medical theory, anatomy, chirurgy and botany at Groningen. On his being appointed rector magnificus of Groningen University in 1766 he delivered an oration 'De pulchro physico'.

In 1773 he retired from university teaching to his country estate. In 1775 he entered politics in support of the house of Orange. His bluff forthright manner proved to be highly successful, and by 1784 he was a member of the Council of State. As a personality he is mainly remarkable for his manysidedness, 'He wanted to be everything', says his biographer (A. Louis 'Éloges' Paris, 1859), 'and he was'. In the history of medicine he is mainly remembered for the excellence of his work in the fields of comparative and pathological anatomy. He made an important contribution to chirurgy through his discovery of the use of elastic bandages, and his 'Ueber die beste Form der Schuhe' (Vienna, 1782) was twice published in English (tr. J. Dowie, London, 1861, 1871). Cf. 'The Works of the late Professor Camper' (tr. T. Cogan, London, 1794). He enjoyed a great reputation in his own day, and it was to him and Blumenbach that Goethe first communicated his discovery of the intermaxillary bone.

J. C. Fabricius (1745–1808), after investigating various skulls, had suggested that the negro might well have originated from a cross between the white man and apes. Camper opposed this theory in his 'Naturgeschichte des Orang-Utang und einiger andern Affenarten des Africanischen Nashorns und des Rennthiers' (Amsterdam 1782 tr. Herbell, Düsseldorf, 1791). Treviranus is evidently referring to the following passage in this work (p. 103), ‚Beym Rennthiere sind gar keine Wadenbeine in den Schenkeln, so wie auch keine in den wiederkauenden Thieren von ganz Europa, auch nicht im Kameel, in der Giraffe und den Hirschen aus Asien gefunden werden. Im Jahre 1774 war ich zu voreilig mit meiner Freude über die Entdeckung, daß diese Nebenröhren allen wiederkauenden Thieren mangeln; denn ich fand nachher, daß schon Coiter ('De Quadruped Sceletis' Hauptst. 2) hieran gedacht hatte. Unterdessen hielt ich diese für eine allgemeine Wahrheit, bis ich den 12 Oktober 1778 das Gerippe des kleinen asiatischen Rehchens erhielt, und bald fand, daß es nicht allein diese Nebenröhren hatte, sondern daß sie auch in Rücksicht des Thiers sehr groß waren.'

184, 23

Cuvier (op. cit. p. 64), 'Il est impossible de donner des raisons de ces rapports; mais, ce qui prouve qu'ils ne soit point l'effet du hasard, c'est que toutes les fois qu'un pied fourchu montre dans l'arrangement de ses dents quelque tendance à se rapprocher des animaux dont nous parlons, il en montre aussi une dans l'arrangement de ses pieds. Ainsi les chameaux qui ont des canines, et même deux ou quatre incisives à la mâchoire supérieure, ont os de plus au tarse, parce que leur scaphoïde n'est pas soudé ou cuboïde.'

184, 29

Cuvier (op. cit. p. 65), 'La moindre facette d'os, la moindre apophyse a un caractère déterminé, relatif à la classe, à l'ordre, au genre, et à l'espèce auxquels elle appartient, au point que toutes les fois que l'on a seulement une extrémité d'os bien conservée, on peut avec de l'application, et en s'aidant avec un peu d'adresse de l'analogie et de la comparison effective, déterminer toutes ces choses aussi surement que si l'on possédoit l'animal entier. J'ai fait bien des fois l'expérience de cette methode sur des portions d'animaux connus, avant d'y mettre entièrement ma confiance pour les fossiles, mais elle a toujours eu des succès si infaillibles, que je n'ai plus aucun doute sur la certitude des résultats qu'elle m'a donnés.'

184, 35

'Ex ungue leonem'. 'Ἐκ τῶ ὀνυχων τὸν λέντα γιγνῶακειν.' 'The lion is known by his claws.' Plutarch ascribed this saying to the Greek poet Alkaios (seventh century B.C.). Lucian said that it derived from the sculptor

Phidias. See Thomas Cooper (1517?–1594) 'Bibliotheca Eliotae' (1559), 'To esteeme the lion by his talons: A prouerbe signifying, to perceiue by a little what the whole matter meaneth'. Ben Jonson (1573?–1637) 'Cynthia's Revels' Act v (Everyman ed. p. 227), 'Ex ungue; you know the old adage, as these, so are the remainder'.

185, 16

See the note III. 336. J. A. Schmidtmüller, in his 'Ueber die Ausführungs-gänge der Schilddrüse' (Landshut, 1804) attempted to re-establish the traditional view that this organ functions as a gland. J. F. Meckel (1781–1833), in his 'Handbuch der menschlichen Anatomie' (4 vols. Halle, 1815–1820) vol. 4 § 2328 had called it in question, and Hegel is evidently basing these statements on his authority. See J. F. Pierer 'Anatomisch-physiologisches Realwörterbuch' vol. 8 pp. 317–319 (Altenburg, 1829).

'*Thyroidaea Glandula*, a large gland . . . Anatomists are uncertain whether it be conglobate or conglomerate; nor has its excretory duct yet been detected. Its use is consequently unknown.' R. Morris and J. Kendrick 'The Edinburgh Medical and Physical Dictionary' (Edinburgh, 1807).

185, 32

Aristotle did not propound a classification of animals in a definite and tabular form, but from a study of his 'Historia animalium', 'De generatione animalium', and 'De partibus animalium', the following classification may be arrived at:

    A. Blood-holding animals, i.e. Vertebrata
        (*i*) viviparous Enaema, i.e. Mammals
        (*ii*) Birds
        (*iii*) four footed or legless Enaema which lay eggs, i.e. Reptiles and
            Amphibia
        (*iv*) Fishes
    B. Bloodless animals, i.e. Invertebrata
        (*i*) soft-bodied Anaema, i.e. Cephalopoda
        (*ii*) soft-shelled Anaema, i.e. Crustacea
        (*iii*) Insects
        (*iv*) shell-bearing Anaema, i.e. Echini, Gastropoda and Lamelli-
            branchia.

Michelet, in a footnote, refers here to the 'Historia Animalium'; see D. W. Thompson's translation (Oxford, 1910).

186, 3

See the note III. 366.

186, 6

See the note III. 275.

186, 10

Jean-Baptiste Antoine Pierre de Monnet, Chevalier de Lamarck (1744–1829), the great French naturalist. In 1793 he was given the job of reclassifying the collection of lower animals in the Paris Museum of Natural History. It was probably while engaged in this work that he first felt impelled to abandon his belief in the immutability of the species. He found that it is often very difficult to draw a clear line between two closely related species, and concluded from this that species in general are the result of gradual improvements in organization rather than acts of special creation. He expressed his views on this subject in his 'Philosophie zoologique, ou Exposition des Considérations relatives à l'histoire naturelle des Animaux' (2 vols. Paris, 1809). There is an English translation of this work by Hugh Elliot 'Zoological Philosophy' (London, 1914).

Hegel evidently has in mind the following passage in this work (p. 117), 'Pour éviter toute equivoque, ou l'emploi d'aucune considération hypothetique . . . je divisai la totalité des animaux connus en deux coupes parfaitement distinctes, savoir:

> Les Animaux à vertèbres,
> Les Animaux sans vertèbres'.

186, 12

See Cuvier's 'Le Regne Animal distribué d'après son Organisation' (4 vols. Paris, 1817) vol. I pp. 55–61. Cuvier distinguishes between 'Animalia vertebrata', 'Animalia mollusca', 'Animalia articulata' such as insects and worms etc., and 'Animalia radiata' or zoophytes.

He gives the following account of the principle he employed in making these divisions, 'D'après ce que nous avons dit sur les méthodes en général, il s'agit de savoir quels sont dans les animaux les caractères les plus influens dont il faudra faire les bases de leurs premières divisions. Il est clair que ce doivent être ceux qui se tirent des fonctions animales; c'est-à-dire, des sensations et du mouvement, car non-seulement ils font de l'être un animal, mais ils établissent en quelque sorte le degré de son animalité.'

186, 14

‚die Rüdenwirbelfäule'. 'The phylum Chordata (or the chordate animals) includes all those animals which at some time or another during their life-history possess a notochord. A *notochord* is an axial stiffening rod extending along the length of the animal and lying immediately above the alimentary canal and below the central nervous system. It may persist throughout life (as in the lancelet, lamprey, and certain fishes) or be replaced, either wholly or partially, in the adult animal by a backbone or vertebral column. If this happens the animals are called *vertebrates*.' Grove, Newell and Carthy 'Animal Biology' (Univ. Tutorial Press, 1962) pp. 298–299.

186, 25

See the note III. 317.

186, 36

Lamarck (op. cit. pp. 138, 161–162), 'On sait que la colonne vertébrale est la base essentielle du squelette, qu'il ne peut pas exister sans elle . . . D'ailleurs, aucun des *animaux sans vertèbres* ne respire par des poumons cellulaires; aucun d'eux n'a de voix, ni conséquemment d'organe pour cette faculté; enfin, ils paroissent, la plupart, dépourvus de véritable sang, c'est-à-dire, de ce fluide essentiellement rouge dans les vertébrés, qui ne doit sa couleur qu' à l'intensité de son animalisation, et surtout qui éprouve une véritable circulation . . .

Outre la *colonne vertébrale*, ici se perd encore *l'iris* qui caractérise les yeux des animaux les plus parfaits . . . *Les reins* de même, ne se trouvent que dans les animaux vertebrés . . . Dorénavant, plus de moelle épinière, plus de grand nerf sympathique.'

187, 11

Lamarck (op. cit. p. 214), 'Mais c'est dans la division des *animaux sans vertèbres* qu'on voit s'anéantir le coeur, le cerveau, les branchies, les glandes conglomérées, les vaisseaux propres à la circulation, l'organe de l'ouïe, celui de la vue, ceux de la génération sexuelle, ceux même du sentiment, ainsi que ceux du mouvement'.

187, 36

‚an verſchiedene Inbibiduen vertheilt'. Treviranus wrote ‚in verſchiedene Inbibiduen vertheilt'.

188, 4

Lamarck (op. cit p. 165), 'Ils respirent par des branchies . . . Ils ont tous un cerveau; des nerfs non noueux, c'est-à-dire, qui ne présentent pas une rangée de ganglions le long d'une moelle longitudinale; des artères et des veines; et un ou plusieurs coeurs uniloculaires. Ce sont les seuls animaux connus qui, possédant un système nerveux, n'ont ni moelle épinière, ni moelle longitudinale noueuse'.

188, 27

Lamarck (op. cit. p. 128) enumerates fourteen divisions *in all*, four of Vertebrata and *ten* of Invertebrata. 'On aura, pour la classification de tous les animaux connus, les quatorze classes suivantes, que je vais encore présenter dans un ordre contraire à celui de la nature.

      1. Les Mammifières.
      2. Les Oiseaux.
      3. Les Reptiles.
      4. Les Poissons.

             Animaux vertébrés.

5. Les Mollusques.
6. Les Cirrhipèdes.
7. Les Annelides.
8. Les Crustacés.
9. Les Arachnides.
10. Les Insectes.   Animaux invertébrés.
11. Les Vers.
12. Les Radiaires.
13. Les Polypes.
14. Les Infusoires.

189, 21

Snakes either have no limbs or merely the claw-like vestiges of the hinder pair. In regarding them as related to fish, Hegel is evidently following Aristotle; see 'Historia Animalium' (tr. D. W. Thompson, Oxford, 1910) 505b etc. They may be regarded as *degenerate* on account of their loss of limbs, and it is now thought probable that their bodily form arose in correlation with a habitat among dense vegetation, in which limbs do not appear to be such efficient organs for motion as lateral undulations.

In Hegel's day their 'rudimentary feet' were a matter of discussion largely on account of the recent edition of the 'Historia mirabilium', attributed to Apollonius Dyscolos (fl. c. 140 A.D.), in which mention is made of a snake with these features. This work had been edited and translated by W. H. Xylander (1532–1576) in his 'Historiae Commentitiae' (Basel, 1568), and was re-issued by L. H. Teucher (Leipzig, 1792). The best edition of it is to be found in 'Physici et medici Graeci minores' (Berlin, 1841) vol. 1 by J. L. Ideler (1809–1842).

Aristotle, in his 'Historia Animalium', (op. cit. 508a 8 . . . 11) says quite clearly that, 'the serpent genus . . . is devoid of legs', but in this later work the Stagyrite is quoted as saying that on Paphos there was a two-legged snake which resembled a crocodile.

189, 23

The Duck-billed platypus (Ornithorhynchus) was described by François Péron (1775–1810) and Charles Lesueur (1778–1846) in their 'Voyage de Decouvertes aux terres australes, 1800–1804' (2 vols. Paris, 1807) vol. I p. 34, and this work was almost certainly the ultimate source of Hegel's information.

It is now taken to be an established fact that both mammals and birds have evolved from reptilian ancestors, but along evolutionary lines which have been distinct from the beginning. The eggs of the three main groups of mammals—Prototheria, Metatheria, and Eutheria—can be arranged, according to the amount of yolk present, to form a graded series. Those of the Prototherians are the largest, and those of the Eutherians the smallest. The eggs of the Duck-billed platypus, although much smaller than those of any reptile, are really quite large, for they measure from 4 to 6 mm in diameter.

189, 24

The Ostrich was sometimes known as the Camel-bird. Thomas Scott (1747–1821) in his notes on the book of Job observes that, 'The Ostrich is called by the Persians the Camel-Bird'—'The Holy Bible . . . with original notes' (London, 1788–1792). G. A. Goldfuss (1782–1844) in his 'Handbuch der Zoologie' (2 vols. Nuremberg, 1820) II p. 234 notices that its urinary bladder and the muscular ring ('Harnblasegipfel') of this organ are large, and collect the urine, so that the bird is able to urinate in the same way as mammals. Cf. Fourcroy and Vauquelin 'Analyse de l'urine de l'austriche' ('Ann. Mus. Hist. Nat.' XVII pp. 310–319, 1811).

190, 4

Lamarck (op. cit. pp. 155–158). This characterization of Fish is Hegel's own, but, as he indicates, it is based on certain observations made by Lamarck viz.: 'Les Poissons. Animaux respirant par des branchies, ayant la peau lisse ou chargée d'écailles, et le corps muni de nageoires . . . On ne retrouve plus en eux l'organe respiratiore des animaux les plus parfaits . . . Ces animaux, ainsi que ceux des rangs postérieurs, n'ont ni trachée-artère, ni larynx, ni voix véritable . . . Ainsi, les poissons offrant, dans leur organisation . . . le sens du tact incapable de faire connoître la form des corps; et se trouvant vraisemblablement sans *odorat*, car les odeurs ne sont transmisses que par l'air.'

190, 16

Lamarck (op. cit. pp. 155–158), 'Leur *foetus*, enfermé dans une enveloppe inorganique (la coque de l'oeuf) qui bientôt ne communique plus avec la mère, peut s'y développer sans se nourrir de sa substance.'

190, 31

Lamarck (op. cit. pp. 150–151), 'Cependant, si l'on considère que les oiseaux aquatiques (comme les palmipèdes), que les échassiers et que les gallinacés ont cet avantage sur tous les autres oiseaux, que leurs petits, en sortant de l'oeuf, peuvent marcher et se nourrir; . . . on reconnoitra qu' (ils) . . . doivent constituer les trois premiers ordres des oiseaux, et que les colombins, les passereaux, les rapaces et les grimpeurs, doivent former les quatres derniers ordres de la classe . . . (parceque) leurs petits, en sortant de l'oeuf ne peuvent marcher, ni se nourrir eux-mêmes.'

190, 36

See John Hunter (1728–1793) 'On certain Receptacles of Air in Birds, which communicate with the Lungs, and are lodged both among the Fleshy Parts and in the Hollow Bones of those Animals' ('Phil. Trans. Roy. Soc.' vol. 64 p. 205, 1774).

191, 8

Cf. E. A. Armstrong 'A Study of Bird Song' (Oxford Univ. Press, 1963), and the note III. 351.

191, 34

For a survey of contemporary views on hair see J. F. Pierer 'Medizinisches Realwörterbuch' vol. III pp. 777–791 (Leipzig, 1819). Cf. J. H. Kneiphof 'Abhandlung von den Haaren' (1754, German tr. Rotenburg, 1777): J. K. Pfaff 'De varietatibus pilorum' (Halle, 1799): C. A. Rudolphi 'Dissertatio de pilorum structura' (Greifswald, 1806).

192, 40

Lamarck (op. cit. pp. 142–143), 'Les mammifières onguiculés; ils ont quatre membres, des ongles aplatis ou pointus à l'extremité de leurs doigts, et que ne les enveloppent point. Ces membres sont en général, propres à saisir les objets, ou au moins à s'y accrocher. C'est parmi eux que se trouvent les animaux les plus parfaits en organisation.

Les mammifières ongulés; ils ont quatre membres, et leurs doigts sont enveloppés entièrement à leur extrémité par une corne arrondie, qu'on nomme sabot. Leur pieds ne servent à aucun autre usage qu'à marcher ou courir sur la terre, et ne sauroient être employés, soit à grimper sur les arbres, soit à saisir aucun objet ou aucune proie, soit à attaquer et déchirer les autres animaux. Ils ne se nourrissent que de matières végétales.

Les mammifières exongulés; ils n'ont que deux membres, et ces membres sont très-courts, aplatis et conformés en nageoires. Leurs doigts, enveloppés par la peau, n'ont ni ongles, ni corne. Ce sont de tous les mammifières ceux dont l'organisation est la moins perfectionnée. Ils n'ont ni bassin, ni pieds de derrière; ils avalent sans mastication préalable; enfin, ils vivent habituellement dans les eaux; mais ils viennent respirer l'air à leur surface. On leur a donné le nom de cétacés.'

193, 6

This 'consequently' ('ἱϙ') evidently assumes the characterization of the continents given in the Addition to § 339.

193, 7

It is clear from this paragraph that Hegel was aware of the *main* developments in zoological classification taking place in the first decades of the last century. The standard classification of the late eighteenth century was of course the avowedly *artificial* system of Linnaeus ('Systema naturae 12th ed. 1766), in which animals were divided into six classes, Mammals, Birds, Amphibia, Fishes, Insects and Worms. The amount of research inspired by this system may be judged from the fact that Lamarck, in his 'Philosophie zoologique' (2 vols. Paris, 1809), recognized ten times as many animal genera as his Swedish predecessor. New affinities came into evidence as data accumulated, and by the turn of the century attempts were being made to establish *natural* systems of classification in all branches of zoology.

Johann Hermann (1738-1800), in his 'Affinitatum Animalium Tabulam' (Argentorati, 1777) was the first to show how the form of one part of an animal's body determines or influences the form of the other parts, but this book attracted little attention. Karl Heinrich Kielmeyer (1765-1844), who was in charge of the scientific collections at Stuttgart after 1816, attempted to base zoology on comparative anatomy and physiology. It was evidently his work which inspired *Cuvier* and as Hegel points out, it was Cuvier's law of the correlation of the parts of an animal's body which opened up the possibility of a comprehensive natural system of classification. Cuvier classified the animal kingdom by dividing it into four branches, characterized by different types of anatomical structure:–

i. Animalia Vertebrata: Mammalia, Birds, Reptiles, Fishes.

ii. Animalia Mollusca: Cephalopoda, Pteropoda, Gastropoda etc.

iii. Animalia Articulata: Annelides, Crustacea, Insects etc.

iv. Animalia Radiata: Intestinal Worms, Polypii, Infusoria etc.

While Hegel appreciated the value of this system, he found it difficult to reject the rival classification put forward by *Lamarck*, whose grading of animals in accordance with their capacity for feeling, sensibility and intelligence, offered him precisely the teleological interpretation he was looking for. Lamarck's zoological 'scala naturae' was as follows:–

A. Apathetic Animals: i. Infusoria ii. Polypii iii. Radiaria iv. Tunicata
                     v. Vermes.

B. Sensitive Animals: vi. Insecta vii. Arachnida viii. Crustacea
                     ix. Annelida x. Cirripedia xi. Conchifera
                     xii. Mollusca.

C. Intelligent Animals: xiii. Fishes xiv. Reptiles xv. Birds xvi. Mammals.

Hegel accepted this 'development from the simplest organization to the most perfect, in which nature is the instrument of spirit', and interpreted it as best he could in the light of Cuvier's comparative anatomy, by emphasizing the part played by 'the various circumstances and conditions of elemental nature' in animal formation. He failed to follow developments in embryology and histology however (note III. 229), the importance of K. F. Heusinger's 'System der Histologie' (2 pts. Eisenach, 1822), and of K. E. von Baer's Beobachtungen und Reflexionen über die Entwickelungsgeschichte der Thiere' (Königsberg, 1829) was evidently unknown to him, and his interpretation of the significance of animal physiology in zoological classification is therefore somewhat crude. Only eight years after his death Theodor Schwann (1810-1882), in his 'Mikroskopische Untersuchungen' (Berlin, 1839, Engl. tr. London 1847), was able to indicate the *cellular* structure of animals and plants, and state, ‚baß es ein gemeinfames Entwidelungsprincip für bie verfchiebenften Elementartheile ber Organismen gibt, unb baß bie Zellenbilbung biefes Entwidelungsprincip ift'. Hegel's exposition, based as it was upon Cuvier, Lamarck and Bichat, gives no indication that such a break-through was imminent.

The immediate origins of the divisions of the animal kingdom diagnosed by Hegel are as follows:-

(a) *Worms* (Vermes) formed the sixth class of the Linnaean system. Linnaeus seems to have used the class for all those animals he was unable to identify with any certainty, and it included what are now known as Mollusca, Coelentera, Protozoa, Tunicata and Echinodermata. O. F. Müller (1730-1784), in his 'Von Würmern des süssen und salzigen Wassers' (Copenhagen, 1771) tried to classify these animals with more precision. In Lamarck's system they constituted the fifth class, and were divided into four orders, Molles (Tape-Worms and Flukes), Rigiduli (Nematoids), Hispiduli (Nais etc.) and Epizoariae (Lernaens etc.).

Shell-fish were placed in the third order of the class Vermes in the Linnaean classification of 1748 and named 'Testacea', whilst naked Mollusca were placed in the second order under the heading 'Zoophyta', together with Echinoderms, Hydroids and Annelids. Ten years later Linnaeus replaced the name 'Zoophyta' by 'Mollusca', which was thus in the first instance applied, not to the Mollusca at present so termed, but to a group consisting chiefly of other organisms. Gradually, however, the term *Mollusca* was used to include those Mollusca formerly placed among the 'Testacea', as well as naked Mollusca. G. S. Poli (1746-1825), in his 'Testacea utriusque Siciliae, eorumque historia et anatome' (3 vols. Parma, 1791-1795 and 1826-1827) divided Mollusca according to their means of motion. Cuvier's 'Mémoires pour servir à l'historie et à l'anatomie des mollusques' (Paris, 1816) was the standard work on them in Hegel's day. Cuvier divided them into Cephalopoda (Cuttles), Gastropoda (Snails, Whelks, Slugs), Pteropoda (Sea-butterflies), Acephala (Clams, Mussels, Oysters), Brachiopoda (Lamp-shells), Nuda (Sea-squirts, Tunicata) Cirrhopoda (Sea-acorns). The last three classes were removed from the 'branch' during the nineteenth century, but the rest of his classification remained intact.

(b) *Insects* were classified by Linnaeus in accordance with the nature of their *wings*, as Coleoptera, Hemiptera, Lepidoptera etc. J. C. Fabricius (1745-1808) took their *masticatory organs* as the basis of his classification, see his 'Systema Entmologiae' (Flensburg and Leipzig, 1775), and J. K. W Illiger (1775-1815), in his edition of J. G. Kugelmann's 'Verzeichniss der Käfer Preussens' (Halle, 1798) attempted with some success to combine the principles of Linnaeus and Fabricius. M. J. C. L. Savigny (1778-1851), in his 'Mémoires sur les Animaux sans Vertèbres' (Paris, 1816), established the homology of the *jaws* of all insects. Cf. J. O. Westwood (1805-1893) 'Modern Classification of Insects' (2 vols. London, 1839-1840).

(c) *Fishes* were so carefully classified on the basis of their external and internal parts by Peter Artedi (1705-1734), see his 'Ichthyologia' (ed. Linneaus, Lugd. Bat. 1738), that it was not until Cuvier and Valenciennes began to publish their 'Histoire naturelle des Poissons' (22 vols. Paris, 1828-1840), in which classification was based upon the skeleton, the form of the gills, the form of the upper jaw and the fins, that any great advances were made. Cuvier's classification was based to some extent on the work of Alexander Monro (1733-1817), see his 'The Structure and Physiology of Fishes Explained' (Edinburgh, 1785, Germ. tr. ed. Camper, Leipzig, 1787). Mark Eliezer Bloch (1723-1799), in his 'Systema Ichthyologiae' (ed. Schneider, Berlin, 1801) put forward a classification based on the number of fins, but this led to many unnatural combinations and distinctions.

Reptiles were known as 'oviparous quadrupeds' until Linnaeus drew attention to their living partly in water and partly on land, and renamed them *Amphibia*. M. J. Brisson (1723-1806), in his 'Règne animal divisé en neuf classes' (Paris, 1756) emphasized the importance of their creeping, and gave them the name *Reptiles* (Latin refere, to creep). J. N. Laurenti, in his 'Specimen medicum exhibens Synopsin Reptilium emendatum' (Vienna, 1768) classified them in accordance with their ways of moving, as Salientia (leaping), Gradientia (walking) and Serpentia (creeping). The first natural system of classification was that propounded by Michael Oppel (1782-1820) in his 'Ordnungen, Familien, und Gattungen der Reptilien' (Munich, 1811). Cuvier's classification into Chelonia, Sauria, Ophidia, Batrachia, was based on osteological considerations. Blasius Merrem (1761-1824), in his 'Versuch eines Systems der Amphibien' (Marburg, 1820) distinguished three orders, Testudinata, Loricata, and Squamata, and diagnosed the sub-divisions in accordance with modifications of the limbs. L. J. Fitzinger, in his 'Neue Classification der Reptilien' (Vienna, 1826) drew up a 'tabula affinitatum generum' in order to demonstrate 'the progress of nature', but in fact had no clear idea of genetic affinity, and merely based his groupings on morphological resemblances.

Birds formed the second of Linnaeus' classes, and were divided by him into six orders, Accipitres, Picae, Anseres, Grallae, Gallinae, Passeres. M. J. Brisson (1723-1806), in his 'Ornithologia' (4 vols. Paris, 1760) diagnosed twenty six orders, and his generic divisions were far more natural than those of Linnaeus, but his work was done without any reference to anatomical structure. In Cuvier's classification, which was standard in the 1820's, Birds formed the second class of Animalia Vertebrata, and were divided into six orders: Accipitres, Passeres, Scansores, Gallinae, Grallae, Palmipedes. There is little evidence of Cuvier's ever having *dissected* Birds however.

The first tentative attempts at working out a natural classification of Birds were made by C. L. Nitsch (1782-1837) in his 'Osteographische Beyträge zur

Naturgeschichte der Vögel' (Leipzig, 1811). In 1820 Nitsch proposed a classification based upon the *nasal glands* (Meckel's 'Deutsches Archiv für die Physiologie' vi pp. 251-269), and in his 'Observationes de avium arteria carotide communi' (Halle, 1829), he drew attention to the classificatory potential of the *vascular system*. In two papers published in the 'Abhandlungen der Berlinischen Akademie: Physischer Klasse' (1813 pp. 237-259, 1817 pp. 178-198), Blasius Merrem (1761-1824) outlined the most satisfactory ornithological classification available to Hegel. He divided Birds according to the presence or absence of the crista on their sternum, and formulated the following classification:-

A. Aves Carinatae: i. Aves aereae   ii. Aves terrestres
iii. Aves aquaticae iv. Aves palustres

B. Aves Ratitae

In his second paper, he supplemented this classification by reference to the nature of the feathers, the position of the furcula and coracoids, the number of lumbar vertebrae and corpals, and the direction of the iliac bones.

Mammals were divided into seven orders by Linnaeus, Primates, Bruta, Ferae, Glires, Pecora, Belluae, Ceta. Cuvier divided them into Bimana, Quadrumana, Carnivora, Marsupialia, Rodentia, Edentata, Pachydermata, Ruminantia and Cetacea. Hegel's classification evidently owes something to the work of Thomas Pennant (1726-1798), 'History of Quadrupeds' (London, 1781, Germ. tr. Bechstein, Weimar, 1799) and J. C. P. Erxleben (1744-1777), 'Systema regni animalis' (Leipzig, 1777), who emphasized the importance of the *feet* and the *teeth* in classification. G. C. C. Storr (1749-1821), in his 'Prodromus methodi mammalium' (Tübingen, 1780) distinguished three orders of Mammals, based on the nature of their hands, feet and fins.

In Hegel's day therefore, zoology was in a state of radical transition, the old artificial systems of classification were being discarded, and various attempts were being made to work out natural systems. By 1850 the advances made in palaeontologyy, embryology, histology, osteology and cytology had prepared the ground for the Darwinian synthesis, but in 1830 theories of evolution such as that put forward by Lamarck in the introduction to his 'Histoire naturelle des animaux sans vertèbres' (Paris, 1815) were still a matter of speculation. Hegel should certainly have followed the developments initiated by Bichat and Cuvier more carefully than he did, but in rejecting evolution (note III. 229), he was making a perfectly competent assessment of the empirical zoology of the 1820's. Cf. F. W. Assmann 'Quellenkunde der vergleichenden Anatcmi:' (Braunschweig, 1847) for a detailed survey of the literature of this period; D. G. Ritchie 'Darwin and Hegel' (London, 1893).

195, 12

Michelet's source for this passage is to be found in Hoffmeister's 'Jenenser Realphilosophie' II pp. 167-169. Much of the original has been omitted.

195, 30

See the note III. 253.

195, 33

Hans Adolf Goeden (1785-1826) was a doctor of medicine, and practised in this capacity at Bunzlau, at Gumbinnen in Lithuania, at Lowenberg in Silesia, and at Friedland in Mecklenburg-Strelitz, where he died on November 14, 1826. From his practical work he gained experience in the curing of inflammations, typhus, arthritis, nervous fever, delirium, scarlet fever etc. and published accounts of his findings in various books and articles.

His development is interesting, because it is in many ways typical of the period through which he lived, and historians of medicine have undoubtedly failed to give his writings the attention they deserve. In his early works he was clearly influenced by the theorizing of Schelling and the Brunonians: see 'Andeutung der Idee des Lebens' (Berlin, 1808), 'Ein Fragment zum System der Krankheiten des Menschen' (Berlin, 1806), and 'Theorie der Entzündung' (Berlin, 1811).

Through the influence of professor Ernst Horn (1772-1848) of Berlin, he then began to publish theoretical works of more practical application: see 'Ueber die Natur und Behandlung der Typhus. Ein Versuch in wissenschaftlich-erfahrenem Sinne', with a preface by Horn (Berlin, 1811): 'Bemerkungen über die Natur und Behandlung der Gicht' and 'Über Febris nervosa epigastrica' in Horn's 'Archiv für medicinische Erfahrung' (Berlin, 1811 and 1812). At this period he also published 'Von dem Wesen der Medizin, eine Einladungschrift zu seinen Vorlesungen' (Berlin, 1812), and it was evidently this which helped to form Hegel's main conception of his work.

In the last decade of his life, he devoted himself to detailed analyses of specific diseases and cures: see 'Von der Arzneykraft der Phosphorsäure gegen den ansteckenden Typhus' (Berlin, 1815), 'Die Geschichte des ansteckenden Typhus' (Breslau, 1816), 'Von dem Wesen und der Heilmethode des Scharlach-Fiebers' (Berlin, 1822), and 'Von dem Delirium Tremens' (Berlin, 1825). These works show a steady development of the idea that the main worth of medical theory lies in the effectiveness of its application. His last work was 'Thomas Sydenham, über seine Bedeutung in der Heilkunst' (Berlin, 1827), in which he evaluated the use Sydenham made of the Baconian method: cf. Sir G. Newman 'Thomas Sydenham, reformer of English medicine' (London, 1924).

Hegel refers to him as 'ein Herr Dr. Göde', evidently on purpose. Goeden had criticised Hegel's treatment of disease and healing in the Heidelberg edition of the 'Encyclopaedia', in an article published in Oken's 'Isis oder Encyclopädische Zeitung' (Jena, 1819) pp. 1127-1138, entitled 'Critische Bemerkungen ueber Hegel's Begriff vom Wesen der Krankheit und der Heilung'. Very few of the natural scientists of Hegel's day paid any attention whatever to his 'Encyclopaedia' or to his lectures, and the outcome of Goeden's bothering to do so was by no means encouraging.

In dealing with Goeden's criticism, Hegel concentrates upon his *theory* of medicine. By the 1820's it was becoming evident that the generalizations made by the Brunonians and their followers, and the systematization of diseases attempted in works such as Cullen's 'Synopsis nosologiae methodicae' (Edinburgh, 1769), were no longer to be defended. Goeden himself was in the process of abondoning many of his early tenets. Hegel was therefore justified in attacking his argument to the extent that it was based on outdated suppositions. He was not justified in ignoring the main points of Goeden's criticism however, which were *(i)* that he had attempted to explain disease in terms of sensibility, irritability and reproduction, and *(ii)* that he had ascribed the organism's being in a diseased state to its being in conflict with its 'inorganic potency'.

The application of cytological discoveries of the 1830's and 1840's to pathology: see Rudolf Virchow (1821-1902) 'Die Cellularpathologie' (Berlin, 1850), Sir Richard Owen's discovery (1835) of *Trichina spiralis*, a parasitic nematode which becomes encysted in the muscles of man and the pig, Agostino Bassi's discovery that silkworm rot is caused by a parasitic cryptogamic fungus ('Del mal del sengo calcinaccio o muscardino' 2 vols. Lodi, 1835-1836), and Pasteur's breakthrough in the field of microbiology etc. were soon to prove the pertinence of Goeden's criticism.

196, 3

,Was im Leben Eins und verschmolzen ist, und innerlich verborgen.' Goeden wrote ,Was im Leben Eins und verschmolzen ist, und innerlich verbunden'. ,Verborgen' has the meaning of 'concealed', 'latent', 'occult', ,verbunden' of 'connected', 'bound', 'joined'.

196, 35

,Die Schädlichkeit.'

197, 12

For a lucid and exhaustive survey of the history of epidemic diseases see Heinrich Haeser (1811-1885) 'Lehrbuch der Geschichte der Medicin und der epidemischen Krankheiten' vol. III (Jena, 1882).

197, 19

The erroneous idea that syphilis was brought from America was given wide currency through the popularity of 'De morbis venereis' (Paris, 1736, English tr. London, 1737, German tr. Leipzig, 1784) by Jean Astruc (1684-1766). Cf. Philipp Gabriel Hensler (1733-1805) 'Geschichte der Lustseuche die zu Ende des fünfzehnten Jahrhunderts ausbrach' (Altona, 1783): Christoph Girtanner (1760-1800) 'Abhandlung über die venerischen Krankheiten' (Göttingen, 1793).

In 1494 Charles VIII of France invaded Italy in order to take the throne of Naples, and entered the city on February 12, 1495 without having encountered the slightest opposition. The ease of this campaign gave his army plenty of time for indulgence, the effects of which became most apparent after the battle of Fornova. When Charles' army was disbanded, his Swiss and German mercenaries spread syphilis north of the Alps.

A detailed account of the early history of syphilis is to be found in H. Haeser (op. cit. III pp. 213-325) and 'Historisch-pathologische Untersuchungen' (Greifswald, 1857) vol. I p. 183. William Beckett (1684-1738) questioned the American origin of syphilis in 'An attempt to prove the antiquity of the venereal disease long before the discovery of the West Indies' ('Phil. Trans. Roy. Soc.' vol. 30 p. 844 et seq. London, 1720). In Germany the disease was first mentioned in 1472, when a chorister was expelled from St. Victor's at Mainz because he was suffering from 'the French disease', 'Supplicans, ut a choro sequestratus in domo sua se continere possit, propter fetulentum morbum qui dicitur Mala Franzos'.

Petrus Anglerius (1457-1526), in a letter written on April 5, 1488 ('Epistolae', Amsterdam, 1670), mentions that in Spain syphilis was known as 'bubas', in Italy as 'morbus gallicus'.

197, 20
This may be a reference to the Scythian invasion of Media under Madyas (Herodotus bk. I chapters 103-105). After plundering the temple of Aphrodite Urania at Ascolon in Syria, the Scythians were stricken, 'with a disease which made them women instead of men'.

197, 27
See J. R. L. Kerckhove 'Histoire des maladies observées à la grande armée française pendant les campagnes de Russie en 1812 et d'Allemangne en 1813' (Utrecht, 1823): C. J. von Scherer (1785-1829) 'Historia morborum, qui in expeditione contra Russiam facta legiones Wuerttembergicas invaserunt' (Tübingen, 1820, German tr. Weber, Tübingen, 1829): M. J. Lemazurier 'Medicinische Geschichte des russischen Feldzugs von 1812' (Jena, 1823).

197, 28
Hegel is evidently referring to the typhus epidemic among the Russian prisoners who were moved through Bavaria to Strassburg after the battle of Austerlitz (December 2, 1805). An account of this outbreak is to be found in Joseph Pichler's 'Darstellungsversuch der im Markgrafthum Mähren gegen Mitte December 1805 ausgebrochenen und bis halben Juni 1806 gewährten Epidemie' (Brünn, 1807).

197, 31
In 1805, Johann Fabricius discovered *Stegomyia fasciata*, a mosquito which is now known as *Aedes aegypti*, and which M. Audouard (1821), Beaupertheuy

(1853) and in 1881 the Cuban physician Carlos Juan Finlay (1833-1915) suggested, but did not prove, was the agent in the transmission of yellow fever. It was not until the first decade of the twentieth century that this suggestion was confirmed by experiment.

In Hegel's day research on yellow fever still included detailed accounts of its geographic distribution: see C. C. Mathäi 'Untersuchung über das gelbe Fieber. Mit einer Uebersichtskarte der Verbreitung des gelben Fiebers' (Hanover, 1827), R. C. B. Avé-Lallement 'Das gelbe Fieber, nach dessen geographischer Verbreitung' (Breslau, 1857).

On the outbreaks in America see: B. Rush 'Account of the bilious remittent yellow fever in Philadelphia 1793' (Philadelphia, 1794, German tr. Tübingen, 1796): J. Hardie 'An account of the malignant fever lately prevalent in the city of New York' (New York, 1799): B. Washington 'Observations on yellow-fever of the district of Columbia' (New York, 1824). On the outbreaks in the Spanish maritime districts see: R. Jackson 'Remarks on the epidemic yellow-fever, which has appeared at intervals on the south coasts of Spain since the year 1800' (London, 1821): Cadet de Metz 'De l'air insalubre et de la fièvre d'Espagne' (Paris, 1822).

For contemporary views on the nature and cure of this disease see: E. Doughty 'Observations and inquiries into the nature and treatment of the yellow-fever' (London, 1816): C. Powell 'A treatise on the nature, causes and cure of the endemic or yellow fever' (London, 1814).

198, 26

Hegel's basic interpretation of disease appears to be very similar to that promulgated by George Fordyce (1736-1802), in his 'Elements of the Practice of Physic' (2 vols. London, 1768-1770): 'A disease is such an alteration of the chemical properties of the fluids or solids, or of their organisation, or of the action of the moving power, as produces an inability or difficulty of performing the functions of the whole, or any part of the system, or pain, or preternatural evacuation.' Soon after Hegel's death however, advances in cytology, bacteriology, parasitology etc. were to bring about a radical change in the general view of this subject.

In this triadic assessment of the forms of disease Hegel makes use of three medical theories prevalent in the second half of the eighteenth century. In § 359 he has made it quite clear why he is unable to accept purely *chemical* explanations of disease. In his treatment of 'noxiousness' however he comes very close to doing so, although his exposition does not rule out the possibility of accounting for epidemics and plagues by means of micro-organisms. The discovery of oxygen by Priestley in 1774 encouraged the development of chemical nosology: see A. F. Fourcroy (1755-1809) 'La médecine éclairée par les sciences physiques' (4 vols. Paris, 1791); John Rollo (d. 1809) 'An account of two causes of diabetes mellitus' (2 vols. London, 1797); J. B. T. Baumès (1756-1828) 'Traité élémentaire de nosologie' (Paris, 1801); G. C. F. Kapp (1780-1806) 'Systematische Darstellung der durch die neuere Chemie in der Heilkunde bewirkten Veränderungen und Verbesserungen' (Erlangen, 1805).

The distinction between *acute* and *chronic* diseases was a commonplace at that time, although there were suggestions that the division would be better if the distinction were between febrile and non-febrile diseases.

Several attempts were made to *arrange* diseases in classes, genera, species etc: see F. B. de Sauvages (1706-1767) 'Traité des classes des maladies' (Paris, 1731); 'Nosologia methodica' (5 vols. Amsterdam, 1763); K. Linnaeus 'Genera morborum' (Upsala, 1763); J. B. M. Sagar (1702-1781) 'Systema morborum symptomaticum' (Vienna, 1771); R. A. Vogel (1724-1774) 'Academicae praelectiones de cognoscendis et curandis praecipuis corporis humani adfectibus' (Göttingen, 1772). The most famous system of nosology was that propounded by William Cullen (1712-1790) however; see 'Synopsis nosologiae methodicae in usum studiosorum' (Edinburgh, 1769: Eng. tr. Edin. 1800, Germ. tr. Leipzig, 1786). Eighteenth century 'nosology' corresponded to the artificial systems of botanical and zoological classification put forward at that time by Linnaeus etc., but whereas in other fields natural systems tended to develop out of these classifications, the study of diseases changed so completely in the first half of the nineteenth century, that very little of these earlier nosological theories survived. The extremely general nature of Hegel's classification seems to indicate that he realized that a radical re-assessment of this subject was about to be undertaken.

198, 29

The beginnings of modern psychiatry are to be found in the work of G. E. Stahl (1660-1734) and J. G. Langermann (1768-1832): see Stahl's 'Theoria medica vera' (Halle, 1708, Germ. tr. Halle, 1802), Langermann's 'Diss. de methodo cognoscendi curandique animi morbos stabilienda' (Jena, 1797), and K. W. Ideler 'Langermann und Stahl als Begründer der Seelenheilkunde dargestellt' (Berlin, 1835). *Vitalists* such as J. A. Unzer (1727-1799) 'Gedanken vom Einfluss der Seele in ihrem Körper' (Halle, 1746) and R. Whytt (1714-1766) 'An essay on the vital and other involuntary motions of animals' (London, 1751), developed Stahl's teaching, and laid the foundations of the varied and specialized investigations of this subject made during Hegel's lifetime.

English psychiatrists were at that time the most advanced in Europe, (see D. H. Tuke 'Chapters in the History of the Insane in the British Isles' 2 vols. London, 1892), and many of their works were translated; see Thomas Arnold (d. 1816) of Leicester, 'Observations on the nature, kinds, causes and prevention of insanity, lunacy or madness' (Leicester, 1782, Germ. tr. Leipzig, 1784); William Perfect (b. 1740) of West Malling, 'Select cases in the different species of insanity, lunacy or madness' (London, 1787, Germ. tr. Leipzig, 1789); and William Pargeter (1760-1810) of Reading, 'Observations on maniacal disorders' (Reading, 1792, Germ. tr. Leipzig, 1793). Pargeter even discusses the healing powers of bathing, massage and music (St. Bartholomew's Hospital Journal vol. 60 pp. 52-60, 1956). In France the outstanding psychiatrist of this period was J. E. D. Esquirol (1772-1840), 'Des maladies mentales' (2 vols. Paris, 1838, Germ. tr. Berlin, 1838).

J. C. Reil (1759-1813) dealt with psychiatry in his 'Rhapsodien über die Anwendung der psychischen Kurmethode auf Geisteszerrüttungen' (Halle, 1803), in which he distinguished between purely *mental* disorders, and disorders of the mind having their roots in physical causes. It may well have been Reil's work which encouraged Hegel to formulate this third form of disease.

J. C. Hoffbauer (1766-1827), in his 'Untersuchung über die Krankheiten der Seele und die verwandten Zustände (3 vols. Halle, 1803, 1807) treated mental disorders from a more purely psychological point of view, and consequently emphasized the importance of moral treatment. J. C. A. Heinroth (1773-1843), in his 'Lehrbuch der Seelengesundheitskunde' (2 vols. Leipzig, 1823, 1824) took sin to be the origin of all disorders of the soul, and defended his standpoint with great ability: cf. the fantastic mysticism of C. J. H. Windischmann's 'Ueber Etwas, was der Heilkunst Noth thut' (Leipzig, 1824), ‚Die Krankheit hat ihren eigentlichen und innersten Sitz in der durch Lust und Begierde zunächst entzündeten und wild gewordenen Seele, und der Arzt, der das Wesen und die Kräfte des Exorcismus nicht kennt, entbehrt das wichtigste Heilmittel. Daher bedarf es einer christlichen Heilkunde.'

In Napoleon's penal code the insane were still classed with animals, 'Ceux qui laisseront divaguer des insensés ou furieux ou animaux malfaisans ou féroces' etc. (Code pénal, 1804, art. 574). This may throw light on the point of Hegel's observation that diseases of the soul are 'rooted in the universal subject, and especially in man.'

For a good modern survey of this subject see R. Hunter and I. Macalpine 'Three Hundred Years of Psychiatry 1535-1860' (Oxford, 1964).

200, 7

R. Morris and J. Kendrick ('The Edinburgh Medical and Physical Dictionary' Edin., 1807) have the following note on coction: '*Coction,* concoction or digestion. The ancients distinguished concoction into several stages, but without any good reason. With them the term coction also signified that alteration, whatever it might be, or however occasioned, which is made in the supposed crude matter of a disease, by which it was either rendered more fit to be discharged, or no longer hurtful to the body. Their reasoning on this subject is now unintelligible.'

The three stages in digestion were chylification ($\chi\eta\lambda\omega\sigma\iota\varsigma$), haematosis ($\alpha\iota\mu\acute{\alpha}\tau\omega\sigma\iota\varsigma$), and homonosis ($\acute{o}\mu o\iota\omega\sigma\iota\varsigma$): see M. Hofmann (1621-1698) 'Dissertatio de alimentorum coctione prima, s. fermentatione, chylosi dicta salva et laesa' (Altdorf, 1662): H. Conring (1606-1681) 'Dissertationes de sanguinis generatione et motu' (Helmstädt, 1641): Galen 'On the natural faculties' bk. 3 ch. i (tr. A. J. Brock, London, 1916).

The fullest treatment of 'coction' as a product of disease is to be found in 'Apologia apologiae pro Germanis contra Galenum' (Amsberg, 1626) p. 313, by Caspar Hofmann (1572-1648), professor of medicine at Altdorf.

200, 32

For late eighteenth century views on the nature of fever see C. Kramp 'Fieberlehre nach mechanischen Grundsätzen' (Heidelberg, 1794), R. Robertson 'An essay on fevers' (London, 1790, Germ. tr. Leipzig, 1796), A. P. Wilson 'A treatise on febrile diseases' (London, 1799, Germ. tr. Leipzig, 1804), J. C. F. Harless 'Neue Untersuchungen über das Fieber überhaupt' (Leipzig, 1803). Cf. Erasmus Darwin (1731-1802), 'Zoonomia; or, the laws of organic life' (2 vols. London, 1796; Germ. tr. 3 vols. Hanover, 1799) vol. II pp. 537-625.

200, 35

Michelet's version of this line is as follows: ‚Zugleich als diese Succeſſion der Functionen iſt das Fieber die Fluibiſation derſelben', Hegel wrote ('Jenenser Realphilosophie' II p. 172, ‚Zugleich als dieſer Fluß der Funktionen iſt es die Bewegung, die Fluibiſation derſelben'. 'In constituting this flux of functions, fever is at the same time its *motion* or fluidification.'

201, 14

‚Das Fieber iſt zuerſt Froſt, Schwere in Kopfe, Kopfweh, Ziehen im Rückgrate, Hautkrampf und Schauder', Hegel's arrangement of this paragraph is somewhat different ('Jenenser Realphilosophie' II p. 172), and he speaks of ‚Fieberfroſt'.

On the symptoms of fever see P. G. Schroeder 'Dissertatio de frequentionibus febrium prodromis' (Göttingen, 1765).

201, 36

See Anton de Haën (1704-1776) 'De sudoribus im morbis acutis' ('Ratio medendi' 15 vols. Vindob. 1758-1773) pt. viii ch. i.

Hegel may have had in mind Aristotle's remarks on 'Sweat in Parts of Animals' III v. (tr. E. S. Forster, Loeb. London, 1937) pp. 252-255. 'In some cases, the sweat consists of a blood-like residue: this is due to a bad general condition in which the body has become loose and flabby, and the blood watery owing to insufficient concoction, which in its turn is due to the weakness and scantiness of the heat in the small blood vessels.'

For Hippocrates' observations on the nature of sweat, see W. H. S. Jones' translation of his works (Loeb, London, 1923-1931) vol. ii p. 14, vol. iv p. 144. Cf. Lucretius 'De Rerum Natura' ed. C. Bailey (3 vols. Oxford, 1947) pp. 562-563, 1696.

203, 25

‚Geiſtig'. See J. Elliot (1747-1787) 'Observations on the affinities of substances in spirit of wine' ('Phil. Trans. Roy. Soc.' 1786 p. 155), and the note III. 226.

204, 4

John Brown (1735-1788), the formulator of this 'system', was born at Buncle in Berwickshire, where his father worked as a casual labourer. After attending a parish school for a few years, he helped his father at weaving, and at the age of thirteen went back to school as a pupil teacher. As a boy, he was cheerful, boisterous and high-spirited, an excellent boxer and wrestler, and remarkable for his memory and the ease with which he learnt Latin.

At the age of eighteen he went up to Edinburgh, and attended lectures on philosophy and divinity. Five years later he returned to his old school as usher, but finding the work uncongenial he returned to Edinburgh, and was allowed to attend lectures given in the medical faculty, free of charge. He soon mastered the principles of medicine as they were then taught, and became immensely popular among the undergraduates on account of his private tutoring and love of good company. He married in 1765, and supplemented his income by running a boarding house, but he was rarely out of debt. His influence upon university life should have opened the way to promotion, but he had an unfortunate knack of unwittingly putting his colleagues irretrievably in the wrong, and the university refused to appoint him.

In 1778 he delivered a course of lectures exposing the errors of William Cullen (1712-1790) and the other professors of medicine. In 1779 he took his doctorate at St. Andrew's, and in the following year published his epochmaking 'Elementa medicinae' (Edinburgh, 1780). He struggled on in Edinburgh for a further six years, but was rarely solvent, and in 1786 he left for London.

At one time Frederick the Great considered inviting him to Berlin. He lived a happy family life and his cheerfulness rarely forsook him, but he was always hard-pressed for money, and at one period he was even imprisoned for his debts. In 1787 he published two critical works, 'Observations on the present spasm, as taught in the university of Edinburgh', and 'Observations on the principles of the old System of Physic' (Italian tr. Pavia. 1792). In 1788 he translated his 'Elementa medicanae' into English in only three weeks: see 'The elements of medicine' (2 vols. London, 1788). Thomas Beddoes' edition of this work contains a good account of Brown and his writings (2 vols. London, 1795); the best German edition of it is by C. H. Pfaff (1773-1852) 'John Brown's System der Heilkunde' (3rd ed. Copenhagen, 1804).

Brown died suddenly of an apoplexy on October 7, 1788, leaving a wife and eight children. The most influential English writer to adopt his system was Erasmus Darwin (1731-1802): see, 'Zoonomia, or the laws of organic life' (London, 1794, Germ. tr. Hanover, 1795). The fullest account of the system in

English is to be found in John Thomson's 'An Account of the life, lectures, and writings of William Cullen' (2 vols. Edinburgh, 1832-1859) vol. ii pp. 222-487. The best account of Brown's influence, which was very extensive in Germany and Italy, is given by B. Hirschel in his 'Geschichte des Brown'schen Systems und der Erregungstheorie' (Dresden and Leipzig, 1846). The system certainly stimulated academic passions; in Göttingen in 1802 for example, a troop of Hanoverian horse had to be used to put down the rioting which broke out between the Brunonians and their opponents.

204, 24

Brown based his system on three main concepts, which he defined in pt. i ch. 2 of 'The Elements of Medicine':

(i) Excitability (Erregbarkeit), he regarded as the state of organization prevalent in the solids and fluids constituting the organism's predisposition to excitement. Some of Brown's followers thought that excitability depended solely upon the state of the muscular fibres, and took it to be the same as *irritability* (see the note III. 302), but this view was not generally accepted.

(ii) Excitement (Erregung), he regarded as the degree of action, the vigour of the system, or the energy of the vital principle present in the organism at any given time. William Cullen (1712-1790) had made the term familiar, but Brown seems to have adopted it because at that time its use did not imply the acceptance of any particular hypothesis.

(iii) Stimuli (Reize), he took to be all those internal and external powers such as passions, heat, food, medicines, contagions, pains etc. which produce *excitement* by acting upon *excitability*.

He considered the organism's excitement to be in a state of perpetual variation brought about by the various stimuli. What he called the *direct debility* of the organism was the result of its lack of stimulus, of food or of heat etc. *Indirect debility* was the exhaustion it experienced after the taking of wine or opium etc., or after strenuous activity. *Asthenic diseases,* which were the result of an exhaustion of excitability, were therefore subdivided into direct and indirect asthenia.

According to Brown, the *health* of an organism depends upon its maintaining a due balance or proportion between its stimuli and its excitability; just as debilitation gives rise to asthenic diseases, so invigoration gives rise to *sthenic diseases*, in which there is a morbid accumulation of excitability. Consequently, the Brunonians regarded health and disease as states exhibiting a *quantitative* difference in degrees of excitability, but as being devoid of any *qualitative* difference. They regarded an excessive accumulation of excitability in a state of fever for example, as being as likely a cause of death as the excessive exhaustion of starvation. According to this theory, successful diagnosis merely requires that a doctor should be able to determine the *amount* of increased or decreased stimulation necessary in order to restore the *balance* between stimuli and excitability which constitutes health.

For an account of the chemical theories of medicine prevalent at the time see the note III. 374.

205, 9

At this juncture ('Jenenser Realphilosophie' II p. 173) Hegel inserted a note in the margin indicating certain exceptions to this theory of medicine.

'*Chronic* illness (constitutes) determinatenesses not susceptible to fever. This course cannot predominate in the case of *lingering fever*.

Simply a general *shake-up* is often as effective as the antidote. As an example of a pre-Brunonian medicament, mention the use of moxa (Span.) as a cure for gout. *Hoven* admitted this.'

'Moxa' is not a Spanish, but a Japanese word (mogusa). The material resembles cotton-wool, and is prepared from the leaf-down of a species of Wormwood (Artemisia Moxa). It was used for curing many disorders by being burnt on the skin, but in the case of gout there was little evidence of its having proved a radical cure.

Friedrich Wilhelm David von Hoven (1759-1838) was doctor at the Würtemberg court and then professor at Würzburg. Hegel is evidently referring to his 'Versuch über das Wechselfieber und seine Heilung, besonders durch die Chinarinde' (2 pts. Winterthur, 1789, 1790).

205, 11

Homoeopathy (ὅμοιος, like; πάθος, disease) is a system of medicine based originally upon the theory that diseases are curable by those drugs which produce effects on the body similar to symptoms caused by the disease (similia similibus curantur). It was worked out by Samuel Friedrich Christian Hahnemann (1755-1843), whose varied scientific interests, unsettled existence and eccentric second marriage led his colleagues to suspect the reliability of his medical knowledge and the validity of his theorizing: see Karsch 'Die Wunder der Homöopathie' (Sondershausen, 1862). For a sympathetic portrait of him see 'F. C. S. Hahnemann. Ein biographisches Denkmal' (anon. Leipzig, 1851).

The main principles of his teaching are to be found in his 'Organon der rationellen Heilkunde' (Dresden, 1810, French tr. Dresden, 1822); see also 'Reine Arzneimittellehre' (6 pts. Dresden, 1811-1820), 'Die chronischen Krankheiten' (2 pts. Dresden, 1828). The lack of precise knowledge of the *ways* in which medicaments bring about their results, and the acceptance of a 'life-force' as the fundamental principle of living being, were the main factors in the formulation of Hahnemann's theories. The principles of his teaching were heavily criticized in F. G. Gmelin's 'Kritik der Principien der Homöopathie' (Tübingen, 1835) and J. Stieglitz's 'Ueber die Homöopathie' (Hanover, 1835).

For a history of the theory see Aug. Rapon 'Histoire de la doctrine médicale homoeopathique' (Lyons, 1847).

206, 24

For a fairly exhaustive bibliography of works relating to emetics published between 1613 and 1765 see George Rudolph Boehmer 'Bibliotheca scriptorum Historiae Naturalis' (Leipzig, 1785-1789) pt. i vol. ii pp. 234-240. Cf. Robert Burton (1577-1640) 'The Anatomy of Melancholy' pt. 2, sect. 4, memb. 2, subsections 1-3.

Nicholas Culpeper (1616-1654), in his translation of 'The London Dispensatory' (London, 1649) has a whole section 'Parts of living animals and excrements', devoted to disgusting animal remedies. English pharmacopoeias only ceased to prescribe excrements in 1721: see A. C. Wootton 'Chronicles of Pharmacy' (2 vols. London, 1910) vol. ii pp. 1-31. Samuel Frederick Gray (fl. 1780-1836) in 'A Supplement to the Pharmacopoeias' (London, 1818, 6th ed. 1836) enumerates no less than eighty two different animal substances: see James Grier 'A History of Pharmacy' (London, 1937) pt. iv ch. xiii.

207, 2

'The Elements of Medicine' (ed. Beddoes, 2 vols. London, 1795) pt. I ch. iii (sect. XIX-XX), 'As there is always some excitability, however small, while life remains, and as the action of the exciting powers always takes place in some degree, I conclude that they have all more or less of stimulant effect, and that this must be either excessive, in due proportion, or too small . . . The same conclusion applies to all other exciting powers, though poisons, contagions, and a few other powers, may to some seem exceptions. But poisons either do not produce the universal diseases, which are our present subject: or, if they do, by producing the same effect as the ordinary exciting powers, their mode of operation must also be allowed to be the same.'

Cf. pt. II ch.I (sect. 146 z), 'To poisons, if they act as general stimulants, all the reasoning that has been employed with respect to the other noxious powers, will apply.'

207, 34

Hegel refers to mesmerism as ‚Magnetismus'. In Great Britain it was generally known as 'animal magnetism', and was little understood. R. Morris and J. Kendrick, in 'The Edinburgh Medical and Physical Dictionary' (Edinburgh, 1807) describe it as follows, 'A sympathy lately supposed by some persons, to exist between the magnet and the human body; by means of which the former became capable of curing many diseases in an unknown way, somewhat resembling the performances of the old magicians. The fanciful system, to call it by no worse name, of animal magnetism, appears to have originated in 1774, from a German philosopher, named Father Hehl, who greatly recommended the use of the magnet in medicine.' Although in the past, mesmerism has been frowned upon in this way by orthodox medicine, largely because of its prostitution by charlatans, it is now recognized to be a most useful method of therapy.

Friedrich Anton Mesmer (1734-1815) began his academic career with a dissertation on the influence of planetary and telluric forces on the human body, see, 'De planetarum influxu in corpus humanum' (Vienna, 1766). This led him on to study the therapeutic powers of natural and artificial magnets, see 'Mémoire sur la découverte du magnetisme animal' (Paris, 1779). He had some difficulty in getting his discoveries recognized. C. d'Eslon's 'Observations sur le magnetisme animal' came out as early as 1780, but in Germany it was not until about 1787, when G. Bicker and Arnold Wienholdt (1749-1804) began to publish their 'Magnetischen Magazin für Niederdeutschland' (8 vols. Bremen, 1787-1789), that mesmerism began to attract much interest. By 1812 the Prussian government thought it worthwhile to set up a commission under C. C. Wolfart (d. 1832) to visit Mesmer at Frauenfeld and investigate the matter. The main result of this move was the publication of Wolfart's 'Mesmerismus oder System der Wechselwirkungen' (Berlin, 1814), 'Erläuterungen zum Mesmerismus' (Berlin, 1815), and 'Jahrbücher des Lebensmagnetismus' (5 vols. Leipzig, 1818-1823).

Mesmerism also attracted the attention of the philosophers of nature of course, who began to speak of a 'recapitulation at a higher level of the lower forces of nature', 'organic polarities', 'spiritual coition', 'ghostly generation' etc.: see Eschenmayer, Kieser and Nasse, 'Archiv für den thierischen Magnetismus' (12 vols. Leipzig and Halle, 1817-1824). Many doctors of the time tended to regard mesmerism as a bogus phenomenon: see J. Stieglitz (1767-1840) 'Ueber den thierischen Magnetismus' (Hanover, 1814), C. H. Pfaff, (1773-1852) 'Ueber und gegen den thierischen Magnetismus' (Hamburg, 1817).

For contemporary English views on the subject, see 'A letter to a Physician in the country on animal magnetism' (London, 1786): J. Martin 'Animal magnetism examined' (London, 1791).

209, 4

‚Der Tod des Individuums aus sich selbst'. See Jacques Choron 'Der Tod im abendländischen Denken' (tr. Birkenhauer, Stuttgart, 1967). H. G. Boehm 'Das Todesproblem bei Hegel und Hölderlin' (Hamburg, 1932).

210, 28

‚Interesse (das Zwischenseyn)'. Hegel is here giving the literal meaning of 'interest'.

211, 16

‚Ueber diesem Tode der Natur, aus dieser todten Hülle, geht eine schönere Natur, geht der Geist hervor.'

212, 24

The significance of the Phoenix as a *religious* symbol is discussed in Hegel's 'Lectures on the Philosophy of Religion' (tr. Speirs and Sanderson, 3 vols. London, 1962), vol. II pp. 83-84. See also 'The Philosophy of History' (tr. Sibree, Dover Publications, 1956) pp. 72-73, 'But the next consideration which allies itself with that of change, is, that change while it imports dissolution, involves at the same time the rise of a *new life*—that while death is the issue of life, life is also the issue of death. This is a grand conception . . . the *Phoenix* as a type of the Life of Nature; eternally preparing for itself its funeral pile, and consuming itself upon it; but so that from its ashes is produced the new, renovated, fresh life'.

213, 26

‚ein Bild der Natur'.

213, 29

'And thus much concerning God; to discourse of whom from the appearances of things, does certainly belong to Natural Philosophy.' Newton added this sentence to the general scholium which concludes the 'Principia Mathematica' as the second edition of the work was being printed (1713): J. Edelston 'Correspondence of Sir Isaac Newton' (London, 1850) p. 155.

INDEX TO NOTES VOL. 3

Made in the USA
Middletown, DE
21 October 2024

62999625R00235